W9-DGI-353

The Politics of Post-Industrial Welfare States

This is the first political science book to focus on new social risks and their implication for politics and policy-making. The welfare states that exist today in most industrial countries were conceived and developed during the post-war years, with the objective of protecting the income of wage-earners against risks such as sickness, unemployment, invalidity or old age. These social risks are still present in today's societies, but they have been supplemented by new social risks, especially in the labour market and family sphere, such as lone parenthood, difficulties in reconciling work and family life, low pay, or long-term unemployment. In general, however, the welfare states that we have inherited from the post-war years provide only limited coverage against these new risks.

This book concentrates on the process of adapting welfare states to changing structures of social risk. First, it looks at how those who are most exposed to the new risks (women, the young, low-skilled workers) mobilise in the political arena and at their demands, then moves on to analyse specific instances of welfare state adaptation in the fields of care policy, pensions and labour market policies. This is a coherent collection of comparative chapters which cover either all, or a sample of, advanced industrial democracies. Together, they show how difficult the adaptation process is, and in particular because of the existence of strong competing claims for public resources by those political actors who fight for the preservation of the traditional welfare state programmes.

Written by high-calibre contributors, including world-class US researchers, this volume will be of great interest to political scientists working on the EU or OECD countries, focusing on social policy and welfare.

Klaus Armingeon is Professor of Political Science, and director, at the Institute of Political Science, University of Berne, Switzerland. He co-edited *Nation and National Identity: The European experience in perspective*; and *The OECD and European Welfare States*. **Giuliano Bonoli** is Professor of Social Policy at the Swiss graduate school for public administration (IDHEAP), Lausanne. He previously worked at the Universities of Fribourg and Bern in Switzerland, and at the University of Bath in the UK. He has edited a number of books, including *European Welfare Futures: Towards a theory of retrenchment*; *The Politics of Pension Reform: Institutions and policy change in Europe*; *Social Democratic Party Policies in Contemporary Europe* (also published by Routledge); *Aging and Pension Reform around the World*; and *Labour Market and Social Protection Reforms in International Perspective*.

Routledge/EUI studies in the political economy of welfare
Series editors: Martin Rhodes and Maurizio Ferrera
The European University Institute, Florence, Italy

This series presents leading-edge research on the recasting of European welfare states. The series is interdisciplinary, featuring contributions from experts in economics, political science and social policy. The books provide a comparative analysis of topical issues, including:

- reforms of the major social programmes – pensions, health, social security
- the changing political cleavages in welfare politics
- policy convergence and social policy innovation
- the impact of globalisation

The Politics of Post-Industrial Welfare States

Adapting post-war social policies to new social risks

Edited by
Klaus Armingeon and Giuliano Bonoli

Routledge
Taylor & Francis Group

LONDON AND NEW YORK

Property of WLU
Social Work Library
DISCARD

First published 2006
by Routledge
2 Park Square, Milton Park, Abingdon, Oxon OX14 4RN

Simultaneously published in the USA and Canada
by Routledge
270 Madison Ave, New York, NY 10016

*Routledge is an imprint of the Taylor & Francis Group,
an informa business*

© 2006 Selection and editorial matter, Klaus Armingeon and
Giuliano Bonoli; individual chapters, the contributors

Typeset in Times by Wearset Ltd, Boldon, Tyne and Wear
Printed and bound in Great Britain by TJ Digital, Padstow, Cornwall

All rights reserved. No part of this book may be reprinted or
reproduced or utilised in any form or by any electronic, mechanical,
or other means, now known or hereafter invented, including
photocopying and recording, or in any information storage or
retrieval system, without permission in writing from the publishers.

British Library Cataloguing in Publication Data
A catalogue record for this book is available from the British Library

Library of Congress Cataloging in Publication Data
A catalog record for this book has been requested

ISBN10: 0-415-38072-3 (hbk)
ISBN10: 0-203-09952-4 (ebk)

ISBN13: 978-0-415-38072-0 (hbk)
ISBN13: 978-0-203-09952-0 (ebk)

Contents

Figures

Tables

Contributors

Karen M. Anderson is Associate Professor in the Department of Political Science at the University of Nijmegen. She received her Ph.D. in political science from the University of Washington. Her research focuses on the comparative political economy of the welfare state, particularly the role of unions and social democratic parties in welfare state restructuring processes. Her work has appeared in *Comparative Political Studies*, *Zeitschrift für Sozialreform*, the *Canadian Journal of Sociology* and the *Journal of Public Policy*.

Klaus Armingeon is Professor of Political Science and director at the Institute of Political Science, University of Berne, Switzerland. Previously he taught, and carried out research, at the Universities of Tüebingen, Konstanz, Mannheim, Heidelberg (Germany), Innsbruck (Austria) and at Duke University (USA). His research has focused on comparative politics, in particular industrial relations, trade unionism, political participation, consociationalism, corporatism and federalism, economic and social policies. Among his recent publications are edited books on Japan and Switzerland compared, and the role of the OECD in national welfare state reforms (2004). Recent articles dealt with changes of corporate government and reforms in the fields of industrial relations and the welfare state (*Kölner Zeitschrift für Soziologie und Sozialpsychologie*, 2005), with institutional changes in OECD democracies (*Comparative European Politics*, 2004) or the effects of negotiation democracy (*European Journal of Political Research*, 2002).

Giuliano Bonoli is Professor of Social Policy at the Swiss graduate school for public administration (IDHEAP), Lausanne, Switzerland. He received his Ph.D. at the University of Kent at Canterbury, England, for a study on pension reform in Europe. He has been involved in several international research projects on the process of welfare state transformation, in particular on pension reform. He has published extensively on these issues, including 'Social policy through labour markets: understanding national differences in the provision of economic security to wage-earners', *Comparative Political Studies*, vol. 36, no. 9, November 2003; 'Two Worlds of Pension Reform in Western Europe', *Comparative Politics*, vol. 35, no. 4, July 2003; and *The Politics of Pension Reform: Institutions and Policy Change in Western Europe*, Cambridge University Press, 2000.

Jochen Clasen is Professor of Comparative Social Research at the University of Stirling, Scotland. His major interests are comparative analyses, welfare state research, social security, employment and unemployment policies.

Daniel Clegg is a Marie Curie research fellow at the Centre de Recherches Politiques de Sciences Po (CEVIPOF) in Paris. His research interests include labour market policies and the comparative politics of welfare state reform, particularly with reference to the 'Bismarckian' welfare states of Continental Europe.

Anne Daguerre is a Research Fellow at Middlesex University, London. Her research interests focus on employment, family and social assistance policies in a comparative perspective (especially between Europe and the United States). Her publications include a book on child protection policies in France and England (*La Protection de l'enfance en France et en Angleterre 1980–1989*) published by l'Harmattan (1999), as well as several articles in the *Journal of European Public Policy*, *la Revue Française de Droit Sanitaire et Social*, *Social Policy and Administration* and the *Journal of European Social Policy*.

Bernhard Ebbinghaus is Professor of Macrosociology at the University of Mannheim and leads a research department at the Mannheim Centre for European Social Research. His research covers comparative social policy and industrial relations in Europe, Japan and the United States. He is author of *Reforming Early Retirement in Europe, Japan and the USA* (Oxford University Press, 2006).

Gerda Falkner is Head of the Department of Political Science at the Institute for Advanced Studies (IHS) in Vienna, Austria. From 1999 to 2003 she directed a research group at the Max Planck Institute for the Study of Societies in Cologne, Germany. Since 1998 she has been Associate Professor for Political Science at the University of Vienna (she is currently on leave). Her book publications include *Complying with Europe?* (Cambridge University Press, 2005; co-authored) and *EU Social Policy in the 1990s: Towards a corporatist policy community* (Routledge, 1998). Her journal publications include articles in the *European Journal of Industrial Relations*, the *European Journal of Social Policy*, the *Journal of European Public Policy*, the *Journal of Common Market Studies* and *West European Politics*. Gerda Falkner is also Vice-President of the Austrian European Union Studies

Association and co-editor of the European Integration Online Papers.

Evelyne Huber (formerly Evelyne Huber Stephens; Morehead Alumni Distinguished Professor of Political Science, University of North Carolina at Chapel Hill) is co-author of *Capitalist Development and Democracy* (University of Chicago Press, 1992) and *Development and Crisis of the Welfare State* (University of Chicago Press, 2001), and editor of *Models of Capitalism: Lessons for Latin America* (Pennsylvania State University Press, 2002). She is investigating the impact of transitions to open economies and/or to democracy on systems of social protection in Latin America and the Caribbean.

Johannes Kananen is currently a Ph.D. student at the Centre for Nordic Studies, University of Helsinki. He has previously worked as a research assistant under Peter Taylor-Gooby at the University of Kent, England. His Ph.D. deals with the relationship between EU and Nordic employment policy.

Hans Keman holds the chair in Comparative Political Science at the Vrije Unversiteit Amsterdam. He is editor of *Acta Politica: International Journal of Political Science* and has been editor of the *European Journal of Political Research*. He has published widely on democracy, European party systems, party governance, coalition theory, institutionalism, and on the welfare state. He has held positions at Leiden, the European University Institute, the Australian University and the State University of New York (at Binghamton).

Herbert Kitschelt is the George V. Allen Professor of International Relations at Duke University. He has been working on patterns of party competition in Western Europe, post-communist Eastern Europe and Latin America as well as on selected questions of comparative political economy and democratic representation. His most recent publication is a forthcoming edited volume (with Steven Wilkinson) entitled *Patrons or Policies?* (Cambridge University Press, 2006).

Trine P. Larsen is a Research Assistant at the Centre for Health Care Studies at the University of Kent, England. Recent publications include a report to the European Commission: *Multi-career Families, Work and Care in Finland, France, Portugal, Italy and the UK*; a chapter entitled 'New Risks at the EU Level' in P. Taylor-Gooby (ed.) *New Risks, New Welfare*; and an article: 'Work and Care Strategies of European Families', *Social Policy and Administration*, vol. 38, 2004.

Traute Meyer is a Senior Lecturer in Social Policy at the University of Southampton; before that, she taught at the Free University of Berlin.

Her research focuses on current changes in European welfare states; she is a member of 'Private Pensions and Social Inclusion' and of 'Formal and Informal Work', two six-country comparative projects funded by the European Union.

Nathalie Morel is a Ph.D. candidate and Assistant Lecturer in Sociology at the University Paris I, Panthéon-Sorbonne, France. She has also been a guest researcher for a year at the Swedish Institute for Social Research in Stockholm. Her Ph.D. dissertation deals with the development and transformation of elderly and childcare policies in France and Sweden since the 1930s. She is also interested more generally in welfare state transformation and comparative social policy, especially from a gender perspective.

Philipp Rehm is a Ph.D. candidate in Duke University's Political Science Department and research fellow at the Wissenschaftszentrum in Berlin. He specialises in political economy.

John D. Stephens (Gerhard E. Lenski, Jr. Professor, Political Science Department, University of North Carolina, Chapel Hill). His main interests are comparative social policy and political economy, with area foci on Europe, the Antipodes, Latin America and the Caribbean. He is the author or co-author of four books, including *Capitalist Development and Democracy* and *Development and Crisis of the Welfare State*, and numerous journal articles.

Peter Taylor-Gooby is Professor of Social Policy at the University of Kent, England. He currently directs the ESRC Social Contexts and Responses to Risk and the EU Welfare Reform and the Management of Societal Change programmes, and directed the ESRC Economic Beliefs and Behavior programme and a large number of other projects. His main interest lies in how people think about social risks and what can be done to help vulnerable groups.

Oliver Treib is Assistant Professor in the Department of Political Science, Institute for Advanced Studies, Vienna. He received his Master's degree and Ph.D. from the University of Cologne. His research topics include EU social policy, implementation of EU directives, new modes of governance, and political cleavage structures in EU politics.

Kees van Kersbergen is Professor of Political Science at the Department of Political Science and director of the research programme of the Centre for Comparative Social Studies of the Faculty of Social Sciences, both at the Vrije Universiteit Amsterdam. His research interests lie in the field of comparative politics and broadly concern issues of change in politics and governance: the changing power of the national state; the changing power and position of political parties in advanced democracies; the development of welfare states and social policy in OECD countries; and European integration and Europeanisation.

Barbara Vis studied economics and political science and works as a Ph.D. student and lecturer at the Department of Political Science of the Vrije Universiteit Amsterdam. Her research interests concern comparative political economy and welfare state development. She is currently working on a dissertation on the politics of the changing work–welfare mix in advanced welfare states.

Acknowledgements

Like all collective efforts, this book has benefited greatly from the support and the advice of several institutions and people. First, we are much indebted to the Swiss national science foundation and to the Swiss Academy of the Human Sciences, which sponsored the initial workshop in Lugano, Switzerland, in September 2003. The workshop provided us with a much-appreciated opportunity to debate and clarify the concept of new social risks and its usefulness in the analysis of social policy. Our thanks should also go to the workshop participants who are not included in the present volume: Maurizio Ferrera, Silja Hausermann, Daniel Kuebler, Stefano Sacchi and Jan Zutavern. The 2004 Conference of Europeanists in Chicago gave us the chance to further discuss our work and to present draft chapters to a wider audience. We are grateful to conference participants who commented on the papers, in particular Lane Kenworthy, Jane Lewis and Richard Menz.

Back in Berne, we were lucky enough to be able to count on the administrative support of Trix Leisibach first and Daniela Heiniger later, in the preparation of the manuscript. Last but not least, we should thank the series editors, Maurizio Ferrera and Martin Rhodes, and Heidi Bagtazo at Routledge, for providing that last bit of encouragement needed to turn a book project into a book.

Part I

The politics of new social risk

1 New social risks and the politics of post-industrial social policies

Giuliano Bonoli

Introduction

The bulk of current research on the transformation of modern welfare states has focused on the issue of retrenchment and, in particular, on how cash-strapped governments have managed, or failed, to reduce the generosity of social programmes introduced during the post-war years. While this may be the most significant development going on in social policy, it is by no means the only one. Socio-economic change, usually described in terms of a shift from industrial to post-industrial economies and societies, has resulted in the emergence of new risk groups that clearly do not belong to the traditional clientele of the post-war welfare state and yet are experiencing major welfare losses. Over the past two decades or so, together with efforts aimed at containing the growth in social expenditure we have also seen the emergence of new policies catering for these social groups.

Risk structures have changed quite dramatically since the early post-war years. Trends in earnings inequality and labour market instability mean that today employment income alone is sometimes not sufficient to ensure a poverty-free existence, especially for families with children. Family instability, which is also on the increase, is on the other hand associated with a higher incidence of poverty, especially among lone parents. The risk of poverty is lower among the increasingly numerous two-earner couples, who are nonetheless facing entirely new problems and dilemmas in terms of reconciling work and family life. All these contingencies can be labelled 'new social risks' (NSRs) and refer to situations that are typical of the post-industrial labour market and family structures in which we live today. They have little in common except the fact that they are generally not well covered by the welfare states that we have inherited from the post-war years, and that they tend to affect the same social groups, especially younger people, women and those with low skills.

Today, new social risks are ubiquitous in Western countries. The social transformations that have brought NSR into existence are progressing at different speeds in different countries, but overall, partly because of economic and cultural globalisation, they are having a massive impact in most places. The welfare states that we have inherited from the post-war years are gradually being adapted to the new emerging risk structures. However, the pace of adaptation and the degree of success vary across countries. Broadly speaking, the Nordic countries seem to have gone furthest in this process, by providing structures that facilitate the reconciliation of work and family life, by developing an arsenal of active labour market policies and a wage-setting system that protect the incomes of low-skilled workers, and by operating inclusive pension systems and comprehensive care service provision for elderly people.

Other welfare states have, generally speaking, been less successful in this restructuring process. Even though awareness of the societal consequences of inadequate NSR coverage is mounting in conservative welfare states such as Italy or Germany, these have taken only moderate steps, if any steps at all, in the direction of better protection of NSR groups. However, even within this world of welfare provision one can find some substantial differences. France, for instance, stands out as a country where reconciling work and family life is significantly facilitated by a large policy effort in the fields of childcare, parental leave, and so forth. Working mothers get generous pension bonuses that compensate for likely career interruptions. The long-term unemployed, if numerous, can rely on several active labour market programmes. Finally, Liberal welfare states have long ignored the emergence of NSR, and as a result are covered mostly by market instruments, with big inequalities in terms of access and quality of services. Risks related to the labour market have been dealt with by a strategy of strengthening work incentives, relying on both income supplements for low-paid workers (such as the American Earned Income Tax Credit) and workfare programmes.

But cross-national variation is not the only puzzle one encounters when studying the emergence of policies that provide coverage against new social risks. What is also striking is the apparent incongruence between the political weakness of those who are hit by these contingencies and the fact that policies meant to improve their living conditions are adopted. The expansion of post-war welfare states was very much the result of the mobilisation of the would-be beneficiaries of the social programmes adopted: the working class. Whether through Social Democratic or Christian Democratic parties and unions, wage-earners were able to impose a welfare model in which economic and social security for them was paramount (Esping-Andersen 1985; Huber and Stephens 2001a; Korpi 1983).

Things are obviously different for the groups who are currently hit by NSR. First, unlike those of industrial workers, their material interests have little in common, and this is arguably a major obstacle to successful mobilisation. Middle-class parents who find it difficult to reconcile work and family life are unlikely to join forces with low-skilled unemployed youth. The fact that their problems were not being taken care of by post-war welfare states is hardly a sufficient motive for doing so. Second, NSRs tend to be concentrated among the young, women and those with low skills – all features that are associated with reduced political influence, whether in terms of political participation (Norris 2002) or of presence in representative outfits such as parliaments, cabinets (Siaroff 2000b) and in labour movements (Ebbinghaus, Chapter 6). The power resources of those who are hit by NSR do not seem in any way comparable to those of the working class during the heydays of the post-war welfare state. Policies that provide coverage against NSR, to the extent that they are being developed, are unlikely to be the result of pressure by NSR groups. The most NSR groups can hope for, under current circumstances, is to be targeted by vote-seeking politicians looking for opportunities to claim credit for improvements.

The power resources of NSR groups alone cannot explain the development of post-industrial social policies. However, if this factor is considered together with other variables identified as determinants of social policy-making by previous research, the predictive power of the model increases dramatically. The main claim made in this chapter is that post-industrial social policies can be explained using the same independent variables that are known to have influenced the development of post-war welfare states: socio-economic developments, political mobilisation and institutional effects. There are nonetheless some important differences in the way in which these independent variables interact. Of crucial importance, for instance, seems to be the timing of the various relevant socio-economic, political and institutional trajectories followed by countries. Depending on this, national configurations of independent variables may be more or less favourable to the development of new social policies. As will be shown in the following, configurations of independent variables in relation to NSR policies have differed across welfare regimes, with the result that countries belonging to different 'worlds' of welfare capitalism have followed different trajectories. Before considering this explanation, however, the chapter presents a definition of NSRs and an attempt to map cross-national variation in the extent to which they are covered.

Defining new social risks

The concept of new social risks is being used with increasing frequency in the literature on the welfare state (see, for example, Esping-Andersen 1999; Hemerijck 2002). However, a precise definition of what is considered under this label is often missing. In this book, NSRs are seen as situations in which individuals experience welfare losses and which have arisen as a result of the socio-economic transformations that have taken place over the past three to four decades and are generally subsumed under the heading of post-industrialisation. Above all, deindustrialisation and the tertiarisation of employment, as well as the massive entry of women into the labour force, have increased the instability of family structures and the destandardisation of employment. New social risks, as they are understood here, include the following.

Reconciling work and family life

The massive entry of women into the labour market has meant that the standard division of labour within families that was typical of the *trente glorieuses* has collapsed. The domestic and childcare work that used to be performed on an unpaid basis by housewives now needs to be externalised. It can be either obtained from the state or bought on the market. The difficulties faced by families in this respect (but most significantly by women) are a major source of frustration and can result in important losses of welfare, for example if a parent reduces working hours because of the unavailability of adequate childcare facilities. To the extent that dual-earner couples with children are considerably less likely to be in poverty than families that follow the 'male breadwinner model' (Esping-Andersen 2002: 58), inability to reconcile work and family life can, especially for low-income parents, be associated with a poverty risk.

Single parenthood

Change in family structures and behaviour have resulted in increased rates of single parenthood across OECD countries, which presents a distinctive set of social policy problems (access to an adequate income, childcare, relationship between parenthood and work when children are very young). What is more, the incidence of poverty is particularly high for lone parents, especially if they are not in work (Esping-Andersen 2002: 37). For them, ability to reconcile work and family life may be crucial if poverty is to be avoided.

Having a frail relative

As in the case of children, during the *trente glorieuses* care for frail elderly or disabled people was mostly provided by non-employed women on an unpaid, informal basis. Again, with the change in women's patterns of labour market participation, this task needs to be externalised too. The inability to do so (because of lack of services) may also result in important welfare losses.

Possessing low or obsolete skills

Low-skilled individuals have, obviously, always existed. However, during the post-war years, low-skilled workers were predominantly employed in manufacturing industry. They were able to benefit from productivity increases due to technological advances, so that their wages rose together with those of the rest of the population. The strong mobilising capacity of the trade unions among industrial workers further sustained their wages, which came to constitute the guarantee of a poverty-free existence. Today, low-skilled individuals are mostly employed in the low-value added service sector or unemployed. Low-value added services such as retail sale, cleaning, catering, and so forth are known for providing very little scope for productivity increases (Pierson 1998). In countries where wage determination is essentially based on market mechanisms, this means that low-skilled individuals are seriously exposed to the risk of being paid a poverty wage (the United States, United Kingdom, Switzerland). The situation is different in countries where wage determination, especially at the lower end of the distribution, is controlled by governments (through generous minimum wage legislation) or by the social partners (through encompassing collective agreements). Under these circumstances the wages of low-skilled workers are protected, but job creation in these sectors is limited, so that many low-skilled individuals are in fact unemployed (Iversen and Wren 1998). Overall, the fact of possessing low or obsolete skills today entails a major risk of welfare loss, considerably higher than in the post-war years.

Insufficient social security coverage

The shift to a post-industrial employment structure has resulted in the presence in modern labour markets of career profiles that are very different from that of the standard male worker of the *trente glorieuses*, characterised by full-time continuous employment from an early age and with a steadily rising salary. Yet the social security schemes (most notably pensions) that we have inherited from the post-war years are still clearly based on these traditional assumptions regarding labour market participation. Pension coverage, in most West European countries, is optimal for workers who spend their entire working life in full-time employment. Part-time work usually results in reduced pension entitlements, as do career interruptions due to childbearing. The result of the presence of these new career profiles in the labour market may be, if pension systems are not adapted, the translation of the labour market and working poor problems of today into a poverty problem for older people in thirty or forty years' time. From an individual point of view, the fact of following an 'atypical' career pattern represents a risk of insufficient social security coverage, and hence a loss of welfare.

New social risks in post-industrial societies

These situations are caused by different factors, but have a number of things in common. First, they are all 'new', in the sense that they are typical of the post-industrial societies in which we live today. During the *trente glorieuses*, the period of male full employment and sustained economic growth that characterised the post-war years, these risks were extremely marginal, if they existed at all.

Second, different NSR tend to be concentrated on the same groups of individuals, usually younger people, families with small children, or working women. While it is difficult to set clear borders around the section of the population that is most exposed to new social risks, it is clear that the categories mentioned here are to some extent overlapping. This partially overlapping character of NSR results in the existence of a section of the population, varying in size in different countries, that is hit by various contingencies. Low-skilled single parents, low-income working mothers or low-skilled young unemployed people are likely to experience additional difficulties because of the accumulation of disadvantage that affects their position. These situations are also those that most often result in social exclusion (Room 1999).

Third, NSR groups have a further thing in common. They are generally not well served by the post-war welfare states. These tended to focus their efforts on core workers with stable employment and uninterrupted careers. In an ideal-typical post-war welfare state concerned above all with the preservation of the income of the male breadwinner, the groups identified here as mostly exposed to NSR do not benefit from social policies.

NSR groups can be regarded as a social category whose members, as a result of the socio-economic transformations associated with the shift to a post-industrial society, are having a particularly hard time. It would not be correct to label them the 'losers' of post-industrial societies. For some of them, especially women, the new social structures represent tremendous opportunities in terms of emancipation, but they also generate powerful dilemmas. This combination of opportunities and difficulties is also what characterised industrial workers during industrialisation. Work in the factories and life in the cities were hard, but they brought new opportunities in terms of access to cash income, technology capable of enhancing quality of life, and so forth.

Mapping diversity in post-industrial social policy

To measure the degree of development and the effectiveness of post-industrial social policies is far from being a straightforward task. To some extent this exercise reflects the difficulties encountered by students of the post-war welfare state when trying to measure the 'welfare effort' made by different countries. Comparative social policy turned first to easily available indicators, such as spending as a proportion of GDP on the relevant programmes (Wilensky 1975), and later to more sophisticated ones that paid attention to the outcomes of social policies in terms of redistribution or decommodification (Esping-Andersen 1990; Huber and Stephens

2001a). My attempt to map cross-national variation in the provision of NSR coverage follows a similar approach. It starts by looking at spending figures and then tries to develop indicators based on social outcomes.

Figure 1.1 provides expenditure data on two key dimensions of provision against NSR, family services and active labour market policies. Together, these two areas of policy address many of the risks mentioned earlier, including single parenthood, reconciling work and family life, and possessing low skills. The clustering of countries along these two key dimensions of post-industrial social policy is reminiscent of Esping-Andersen's classification of welfare regimes, possibly with a distinction between Continental and Southern European countries, as in Ferrera (1998). The Nordic countries are the biggest spenders in both policy areas, second strongest are the conservative welfare states of Continental Europe, and third those of Southern Europe together with Liberal welfare states. Interestingly, the two dimensions seem to be related to each other, suggesting that the same factors impact on policy efforts in each of the two areas.

The use of expenditure data to gauge the size of the effort made in a given policy area has been criticised on number of grounds, including the fact that the denominator (GDP) may be more important than the numerator in determining the value of the indicator; that expenditure data are very sensitive to the number of beneficiaries; and that the same amount of money can be spent in different ways with different social outcomes (Esping-Andersen 1990). For this reason, next I provide an alternative measure of the extent to which NSR are covered by Western welfare

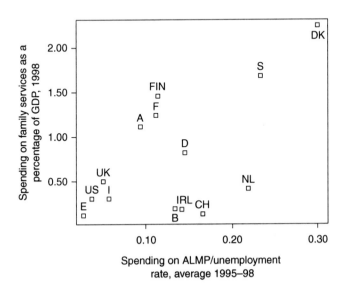

Figure 1.1 Expenditure on family services and on active labour market policies (ALMP) 1998 (source: OECD 2001b, 2002a).

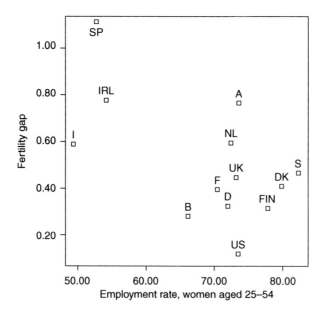

Figure 1.2 Fertility gap and female employment rate, age group 25–54, 2001 (source: Fertility gap: own calculations on Eurobarometer 56.2 Mikrocensus Familie, Switzerland; Bélanger and Ouellet 2001. Female employment: OECD 2002a).

states, a measure that relies on welfare outcomes instead of expenditures. Two distinct analyses are performed, in relation to family and labour market-related risks respectively.

Figure 1.2 aims at assessing the extent to which women are able to reconcile work and family life in different welfare states. The problem of reconciling work and family life is understood in terms of the possible inability to simultaneously fulfil labour market and fertility aspirations. Figure 1.2 uses two indicators: the fertility gap, i.e. the difference between the number of children women aged 15–45 would like to have and the number they are actually likely to have (the fertility rate); and the employment rate of women aged 25–54, the age group for whom the possible trade-off between work and motherhood is likely to be bigger.

From Figure 1.2 a familiar picture again emerges. The risk of being unable to reconcile work and family life seems to be weakest in the Nordic countries, which combine high female employment rates with low fertility gaps. It is average in Continental European countries and in the United Kingdom, and highest in Spain, Italy and Ireland. The last-mentioned three countries combine some of the highest fertility gaps with the lowest employment rates. The fact that these are all countries with a strong Catholic tradition suggests that religion may be an important explanatory factor here. The United States stands out for having a very low fertility gap. The standard explanation found in the literature for this apparent puzzle is that in the United States, low wages for (mostly low-skilled) care workers make the provision of childcare affordable to many (Esping-Andersen 1999). However, an additional factor may help explain why American women seem to be better able to simultaneously fulfil their employment and fertility aspirations than their European counterparts. Gender equality in the labour market has progressed faster than in other countries in recent years, also thanks to strictly enforced anti-discrimination legislation. Because women are less penalised in the labour market, they can more easily afford to have children (Castles 2002). This observation suggests that protection against NSR may not necessarily require redistributive programmes, but can also result from appropriate labour market regulation.

Two indicators are also needed to assess the extent to which labour market-related risks are covered. Post-industrialisation can be associated with big wage inequalities and the emergence of a working poor problem (e.g. in the United States) or with a high incidence of low-skill unemployment in countries where high minimum wages and employment protection laws inhibit job creation in the low-skill sector (Esping-Andersen 2000). These two problems, wage inequality and low-skill unemployment, can be considered to be two manifestations of the same underlying development. Protection against the consequences of possessing low or obsolete skills can take different forms, such as upskilling (e.g. through active labour market policies) or measures designed to improve the living conditions of low-skilled workers, such as minimum wages or tax credits.

Figure 1.3 provides empirical evidence on these two aspects of labour market-related NSR by looking at wage inequality and the level of low-skill unemployment. Wage inequality is measured by the ratio between the upper limits of the fifth and first deciles of the earnings distribution. This indicator allows us to capture wage inequality between the middle classes, earning around the median wage, and those who are on low-paid jobs. The level of low-skill unemployment is the unemployment rate of people with less than upper secondary education.

The picture emerging from Figure 1.3 is less consistent with the regime typology. Among the Nordic countries, Sweden and Denmark are faring comparatively well on both inequality and low-skill unemployment, Finland less so on the second dimension (but in a context of overall higher unemployment). Continental European countries do not seem to cluster in relation to these two dimensions. From a theoretical point of view, one would have expected these countries to show up in the bottom right-hand part of the graph. In fact, only Germany falls clearly in this category. France, Belgium and Italy are not far away, though. Interestingly, the Netherlands is closer to the Nordic model here. Finally, we would have expected Liberal welfare states to be in the top left-hand quadrant (high

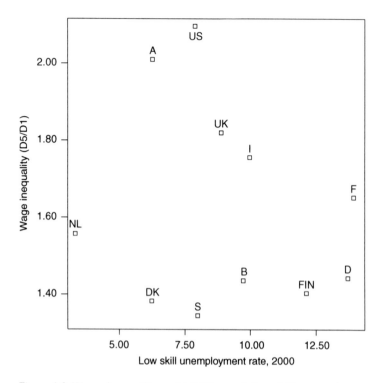

Figure 1.3 Wage inequality, mid-1990s, and low-skill unemployment rate, 2000 (source: OECD 1996, 2002a).

wage inequality and a low level of low-skill unemployment), but in reality they tend to lie in the second dimension.

This brief review of expenditure and outcome provides a fairly comprehensive picture of how selected NSR are covered in different welfare states. The main result is that it is clearly the Nordic countries that have gone furthest in providing good-quality coverage, in relation to both dimensions (family and labour market). Family-related risks are covered by an arsenal of instruments that include highly subsidised childcare, generous parental leave provision and a highly developed system of social services for frail elderly people. Risks originating from labour market change, on the other hand, are well covered by active labour market policies, and the wages of low-skilled workers are propped up by encompassing collective agreements. In Continental welfare states we also find good coverage against the risk of being paid poverty wages, thanks to relatively high minimum wages (set either by legislation or by collective agreements); but then, especially in Germany, there is a high risk of unemployment for low-skilled individuals. Coverage against family-related risks, by contrast, is generally less developed than in Nordic welfare states, although there is a clear difference between the conservative welfare states of Europe and those of Southern Europe. In the latter, in fact, the absence of a tradition in family policy (Ferrera 1996) makes it more difficult to develop policies that help cover family-related social risks. Finally, Liberal welfare states, consistently with their historical orientation, have relied on market mechanisms to meet the social demands associated with the emergence of NSRs. In the case of reconciling work and family life this approach has produced results in the United States that are comparable to those achieved in the Nordic countries. There are, however, fundamental differences in distributional terms, which manifest themselves in big educational inequalities beginning with childcare services of very different levels of quality (Esping-Andersen 2002: 50). With regard to labour market-based NSRs, the main thrust of policy has been towards reinforcing the problem-solving capacity of market mechanisms by strengthening work incentives through workfare and tax credit programmes.

If we were to produce a tentative rank ordering of countries in relation to how successful they have been in adapting to the changed nature of social risk over the past two decades, we would without doubt put the Nordic countries in first place. They would be followed by the Conservative welfare states of Continental Europe, where post-war welfare institutions turned out to be at least of some use to groups exposed to NSR. Finally, the new policies are underdeveloped, in fact practically non-existent, in Southern European countries. The reliance on market mechanisms in Liberal welfare states means that in this 'world', protection against NSRs will vary significantly across social divisions.

This rank ordering of welfare states contrasts with that of post-war welfare states. The traditional social risks of old age, invalidity, cyclical unemployment and sickness were best covered in the Nordic countries and in Conservative welfare states such as Germany and Italy. If we focus on the protection of the male breadwinner's income, the backbone of post-war welfare states, then Conservative countries are the most generous. In the field of pensions, for example, for the career profile of a standard male industrial worker, provision is vastly more generous in Italy or Germany than in Sweden or Denmark. The difference is not so much in replacement rates but in the age of retirement: the effective age of retirement for Swedish men is around 65, whereas Italians retire on average six years earlier (Scherer 2001). In relation to unemployment, Southern European welfare states apparently stand out for their lack of decent provision. However, here too replacement rates tell only part of the story. Strict employment protection laws resulted in a sort of pre-emptive coverage of the risk of unemployment: workers could not be laid off, so that the absence of generous unemployment benefits was less of a problem. In fact, the status-preserving character of conservative welfare states turned out to be an excellent quality of social policies designed to cover against social risks experienced by core industrial workers. It was for them, after all, that Bismarck initiated social insurance.

The evidence reviewed in this section raises a number of questions. Why did the political forces behind the post-war welfare state in the Nordic countries mobilise for its modernisation and the inclusion of NSR policies as early as the 1970s? Why did the same political forces in Continental and Southern Europe fight, and obtain additional improvements in traditional social policies? And why are Continental European welfare states slowly turning now to NSR? These are all puzzles that demand explanation.

Accounting for divergent trajectories of adaptation

While this book may seem to overuse the word 'new', its main claim is that in order to explain post-industrial social policies we need to turn to 'old' theories. The key independent variables that account for the development of policies that provide coverage against NSR are found among those that were identified as responsible for the development of post-war welfare states: problem pressure, political mobilisation of the would-be beneficiaries of the new policies, and institutional effects such as policy feedbacks. But the development of post-industrial social policies is not simply a rerun of the construction of post-war welfare states with a different casting. What has changed is the configuration of the relevant independent variables. This configuration of independent variables is different in different regimes.

Of crucial importance in this account is the issue of the *timing* of the processes that characterise the different independent variables (see also Fargion 2000). Does the emergence of problem pressure coincide with advances in the mobilising capacity of the would-be beneficiaries of the new policies? Does it occur in a context of budgetary problems due to the financial requirements of the post-war social programmes? These questions seem crucial in determining the likelihood of seeing NSR policies develop. The next three sections explore the empirical dimension of these questions. They focus mostly on four countries, selected so as to represent the four varieties of welfare regimes: Sweden, Germany, Italy and the United Kingdom.

Problem pressure

Political scientists know that problems alone do not create policies, but the emergence of a new problem experienced by large sections of the electorate will, in a well-functioning democracy, awake the appetite of vote-hungry political entrepreneurs and result in the new problem being brought into the political arena. This mechanism, however, in the current context of austerity, may have lost some attractiveness for policy-makers, who tend to be more concerned with avoiding blame for unpopular decisions than with claiming credit for popular ones (Pierson 1994; Weaver 1986). Nonetheless, several authors have, in recent years, pointed out the possible existence of an impact of new needs on social policy-making. Scarbrough, for instance, argues that the resilience of welfare states in the 1980s and 1990s can be explained with reference to the emergence of new social problems such as 'divorce, single parenthood . . . rising part time and temporary employment . . . [and] the growing number of outsiders' (2000: 230–1). Econometric studies of recent changes in social expenditure have confirmed the importance of social problems such as unemployment as independent variables (Huber and Stephens 2001a; Siegel 2000).

The social transformations that are behind the emergence of NSRs have progressed at a different pace in different countries, with the result that different countries have been exposed to some of the new problems at different moments in time. With regard to deindustrialisation, or the replacement of industrial jobs by service employment, the Nordic countries have been front runners. In Sweden, as early as 1970 less than 40 per cent of the workforce was employed in industry, a level that Germany was to reach only in the early 1990s. Data for Britain are available only since 1979, but deindustrialisation appears to have occurred rather fast there too. Industrial employment represented less than 40 per cent of total employment in 1979, and declined throughout the 1980s to stabilise at around 30 per cent in the 1990s. Italy had a relatively low proportion of industrial employment at the beginning of the 1970s, but the decline was less steep than in Sweden or Britain (OECD 2004a).

The second important transformation behind the emergence of NSRs is women's changing role in society: their massive entry into the labour market, and their corresponding gradual abandonment of the role of full-time carers. Here too we see clear differences in timing among the different welfare regimes. Interestingly, however, in the early 1960s differences were not particularly big. In 1963, Germany, Sweden and the United Kingdom all had female employment rates in the region of 50 per cent. Things, however, changed dramatically in the following years. In Sweden, women's employment increased fast, and exceeded 60 per cent in 1973, a level that Britain would arrive at only in 1989, and which Germany has not reached yet. In Italy, women's employment remained stable at a very low level throughout the past four decades, and it is only in the late 1980s and in the late 1990s that we see clear upswings to reach the 40 per cent level. Here too, if all countries have seen an increase in women's employment, the timing and the extent of the process display big cross-national differences.

Let us turn to the family field. Instability here is a major new source of social risk, divorce and lone parenthood being associated with welfare losses and higher poverty rates. Over the past three decades, divorce rates have increased in all OECD countries, but at a very different pace. In 1970, in Sweden and Denmark there were 30 and 26 divorces respectively for every hundred marriages, a level that the United Kingdom reached in the late 1970s, France and Germany in the early 1980s, and Italy and Spain have not reached yet (Eurostat 1999).

If post-industrialisation is a general development, it is quite clear that not all countries are progressing at the same pace towards it. The socio-economic trends associated with it that can result in new needs and demands have clearly progressed faster in Sweden, somewhat less fast in the United Kingdom, and relatively slowly in Germany and Italy. Sweden in the early 1970s already displayed many of the features typical of a post-industrial labour market: low and declining levels of industrial employment, expansion of service employment, and high female employment rates. In contrast, by the 1970s the United Kingdom, Germany and Italy had not greatly changed since the immediate post-war years. For these countries, the watershed that signals the entry into the post-industrial age is the 1980s (the United Kingdom) or even the 1990s (Germany and Italy).

This difference in timing reflects the different degrees of development of post-industrial social policies observed in the previous section, which lends support to the view that problem pressure is responsible for the adoption of new policies. The implication of this view on the emergence of post-industrial social policies is that these are likely to develop everywhere, the main difference being one of timing. Countries such as Italy and Germany are laggards simply because problem pressure appeared later there. Can one as a result expect countries to converge on similar levels of coverage against NSR eventually? So far, there is little evidence that this is the case. Countries like the Netherlands and Switzerland, and to a lesser extent Germany, saw a substantial expansion in female employment in the 1980s and in the 1990s, but no, or only minor, increases in spending on family services. In addition, divergence in spending on active labour market programmes (ALMP) has persisted throughout the past two decades, in spite of a dramatic increase in the unemployment rate in low-spending countries (OECD 2001b). Problem pressure certainly does matter, but as in so many other policy fields, we seem to be very far from a linear and positive relationship between needs and demands on the one hand and policy responses on the other. For a more plausible explanation, we need to take into account other variables as well.

Power resources of the would-be beneficiaries

The social groups who are most likely to experience the contingencies I have labelled NSRs are not among the most politically influential in our societies. As we have seen, those who are most hit by NSRs tend to be women, younger persons and individuals with low skills – three social characteristics that tend to be associated with a lack of political influence.

As a result, it seems difficult to draw a parallel between the current phase of expansion of post-industrial social policies with the period of welfare state development, especially after World War II. The constituency behind the post-war welfare state, wage-earners, were able to impose their priorities in the political arena and obtain the adoption of welfare states that provided coverage against the most serious social risks of the time.

NSR policies, to start with, make reference to different potential constituencies with different policy preferences. Childcare is likely to appeal to younger women, regardless of class. Active labour market policies are beneficial for low-skilled people, especially younger ones for whom they can constitute a stepping stone into employment. More generally, low-skilled people are likely to be well served by tax credits, wage floors and measures that improve the quality of employment. As a result, theoretically we would not expect NSR groups to mobilise in any cohesive way, by forming parties or associations. People who are hit by several NSR simultaneously, e.g. younger low-skilled women, could be expected to mobilise coherently, but then they would hardly be numerous enough to carry any significant political weight.

The empirical analysis of the policy preferences of NSR groups contained in this book confirms this view of weak cohesion. Kitschelt and Rehm (Chapter 3) show that the socio-demographic features associated with high exposure to NSR – being a woman, being young and being low skilled – are associated with distinctive preferences in social policy. The problem, in so far as the cohesion of NSR groups is concerned, is that their effects tend to be in different directions. For example, the young and women support more spending on education, but not the low skilled. In the end, a composite variable that combines the socio-demographic features of NSR-exposed individuals turns out to be statistically non-significant as a predictor of policy preferences. Using different data and running separate analyses for different countries, Kananen *et al.* reach similar conclusions (Chapter 4), suggesting that variations in regime type are of little importance in forging a cohesive NSR victims' group.

The ability of NSR groups to influence policy is further limited by their lower political participation. Two social traits associated with high exposure to NSR also happen to be powerful predictors of lower voting turnout across Western democracies. Age is a particularly strong predictor of political participation. Using survey data for 17 countries, Norris finds that age is by far the best predictor of voting turnout at the individual level. On average, turnout for the under-25s is just 55 per cent, whereas it reaches 88 per cent for late middle-aged voters (Norris 2002: ch. 5). After age (and together with income), education is the second-best predictor of voting turnout, though its impact varies across countries.

In addition to lower participation, NSR groups are also less likely to be represented in key decision-making and representative institutions. Parliaments, cabinets and the membership of political parties and trade unions tend to be dominated by middle-aged men, while women and younger people are often under-represented. Only in the Nordic countries does women's presence in parliaments and government approach 50 per cent. In all other Western democracies, female members of Parliament constitute a minority, a minority that in some cases barely exceeds 10 per cent of seats, as in Italy and in France in the early 2000s (Bonoli 2005; Siaroff 2000b). In the Nordic countries women saw their presence in parliaments increase earlier. In Sweden, for instance, the proportion of female members of Parliament doubled in the 1970s (from 14 per cent in 1971 to 28 per cent in 1980), whereas other countries, such as Germany or the United Kingdom, have seen increases much more recently, reaching the 15 per cent threshold in 1987 and 1997 respectively. With regard to age, the average age of members of Parliament varies between the late forties and the late fifties. The youngest parliaments are found in the Nordic countries: in 2002 the average age was 47 in Denmark and Finland, and 49 in Sweden. The oldest are in France and in Germany, whose members of Parliament in the same year had an average age of 57 and 54 respectively (Bonoli 2005).

The situation is rather similar in relation to labour movements, key political actors in shaping employment and social policy in most West European countries. Ebbinghaus's calculations show that in most countries, trade union memberships tend to be made up mostly of middle-aged and older men. But here too there are important international variations. The Nordic countries have both the most feminised and the youngest labour movements, followed by the United Kingdom. The image of the unions being an older men's club is in fact accurate only for Continental European countries. According to Ebbinghaus (Chapter 6), the greater tendency of women and younger workers to be trade union members in the Nordic countries can be explained with reference to the Ghent system of unemployment compensation in force in those counters. Under this system, access to unemployment insurance benefits requires union membership.

Figures on the presence of NSR groups in key decision-making bodies show a clear tendency towards under-representation in Continental European countries, and, to a somewhat lesser extent, in the United Kingdom. In contrast, in the Nordic countries, NSR groups do not seem to be systematically less present in these bodies than other social groups. These figures, however, do not tell us much regarding the extent to which NSR groups' interests are effectively represented in the political arena. Female or younger members of Parliament do not have a clear mandate to represent people with similar socio-demographic characteristics, nor are they generally accountable to this particular group of voters. Nevertheless, they may be comparatively more successful in attracting the support of voters with similar gender and age profiles, and as a result face incentives to shape their policy positions to the advantage of these groups. Whether presence matters for interest representation or not is a question that probably cannot be answered on the basis of theoretical reasoning, and needs to be settled empirically.

Feminist political science has long been concerned with the issue of whether women's presence in decision-making bodies, especially parliaments, does make a difference with regard to the policies that are adopted. Overall, the message that one gets from this literature is that the presence of women in parliaments matters for decisions on issues that are of particular concern to women, such as childcare policy, or equal opportunities (Norris and Lovenduski 1989, 2003; Sawer 2000; Tramblay 1998).

On balance, the power resources of NSR groups seem rather limited in the current context. There are, however, some important cross-national differences, NSR groups being more likely to be present in representative bodies in the Nordic countries. It is possible that in these countries the power resources of NSR groups, particularly of women, have played a role in the creation of highly developed post-industrial welfare states. In other countries, especially in Continental and Southern Europe, the power resources of NSR groups are probably insufficient to influence policy. But from a theoretical point of view it is difficult to say more than this in relation to the possible impact of the political mobilisation of the would-be beneficiaries on the adoption of new policies. The question, as a result, needs to be settled empirically. Two chapters of this book shed light on this issue.

First, Huber and Stephens (Chapter 7), in their analysis of the determinants of various measurements of welfare effort and of social policy outcomes in so far as NSR are concerned, find a key predictor in the political mobilisation of women, measured in terms of women's presence in non-religious associations. Women's political mobilisation turns out to be powerfully associated with spending on social services, more so than the strength of the left.

An important role of the political mobilisation of women is also found in Daguerre's study of the development of childcare policies in four countries (Chapter 10). The evidence that the feminist movement and the presence of women in key political organisations played a crucial role is strong only in the Swedish case. In that country, women within the trade unions and the Social Democratic party were instrumental in putting childcare, and more general policies to help parents reconcile work and family life, high on the political agenda, whereas the feminist movement put pressure from outside the established political system. This important role of women's mobilisation, however, is not found in the three other case studies she analyses. In the United Kingdom, France and Switzerland she finds a long-standing commitment to campaigning for childcare policies by these organisations, but little evidence that they are able to influence policy on their own. When policy change happens, it is generally as a result of an alliance struck between actors representing, on the one hand, women's interests and, on the other, employers concerned with the problem of labour shortage.

These two studies confirm the view outlined in the theoretical discussion above. The power resources of the would-be beneficiaries of post-industrial social policies have mattered in the Nordic countries and in so far as women's exposure to NSRs is concerned. This independent variable seems considerably less useful in accounting for policy developments in Continental and Southern Europe, and in relation to policies targeted on other NSR groups, though. It seems difficult to explain why childcare and policies to help parents reconcile work and family life are relatively well developed in France, a country where women's presence in politics has been traditionally limited. At the same time, women's political influence has increased quite dramatically in Germany over the past decade, as the proportion of female members of Parliament trebled between 1986 and 2001 (from 10 per cent to 31 per cent). This, however, has not resulted in a radical reorientation of the German welfare state along Swedish lines. Finally, the power resources of the would-be beneficiaries seem a rather unhelpful variable in accounting for the development of policies that provide coverage to NSR groups not defined by gender, such as the working poor or the low-skilled unemployed, essentially because their power resources are insignificant.

Institutions: policy feedbacks and the role of old policies

Since the emergence of neo-institutionalism as a strand of political science in the 1980s, students of the welfare state have uncovered a number of different institutional effects in social policy-making. In general they refer to the impact of previous decisions and policies on current change (see, for example, Pierson 1993, 1994). Such effects are likely to be present also in the process of building a post-industrial welfare state. More precisely, we can expect at least two different effects to be in play. First, the welfare states built during the post-war years have been shaping the political landscape in a way that can be more or less favourable to the development of new social policies (policy feedback). Second, the policies adopted during the *trente glorieuses* can be adapted more or less easily to the changed context of societal demands and needs.

Policy feedbacks

The institutions of the post-war welfare state shape the politics of the policies that are being introduced in response to the emergence of NSR. This effect is likely to be particularly strong given the current climate of public budget constraints and, as Paul Pierson aptly put it, 'permanent austerity' (1998). In such a context, political decisions must be made on how to share the limited available resources, and we can expect competing interests to fight to obtain a larger share of them. These competing interests are to a large extent defined by welfare state structures inherited from the post-war years.

Pensioners, as well as those who are approaching retirement age, are likely to mobilise for the maintenance of the generous post-war pension arrangements, by claiming additional resources (such as extra VAT points, eco taxes, contribution increases) for these schemes. The effectiveness of their mobilisation will depend, all other things being equal, on their numbers, but also on the extent to which they are dependent on public pension schemes for their retirement income. Countries with a high proportion of the population already retired or nearing retirement age and where pensioners rely almost exclusively on state pension provision are likely to see the strongest opposition to pension cuts, and, as a result, a tendency to assign the limited extra resources generated by economic growth to public pension schemes. A similar argument can be made also in relation to healthcare, where expenditure is also strongly related to age. In these countries, competition for scarce resources is unlikely to result in a significant expansion of NSR policies.

In contrast, funds for developing a post-industrial welfare state are more likely to be available in countries with a comparatively smaller proportion of retired people and/or where pensioners rely on a mix of public and private provision for their retirement income. In these countries the constituency that defends the preservation of the post-war welfare state is likely to be weaker, and extra resources may be used for developing a post-industrial welfare state.

In order to measure the size and the mobilising capacity of the post-war welfare state constituency, we need an indicator that reflects both the number of beneficiaries and the degree to which they depend on post-war arrangement. Public pensions being the cornerstone of the post-war welfare state, it has been decided to use expenditure on this programme as a proportion of GDP. This indicator, in addition, fulfils the twofold requirement outlined above: spending increases in line with the number of beneficiaries and depends on the generosity of pensions.

Throughout the period covered (1980–98), spending on public pensions is considerably higher in the two Continental European countries (Germany and Italy) than in the two Nordic countries selected (Sweden and Denmark, see Figure 1.4).[1] But on the basis of the argument put forward in this chapter, pension expenditure figures should not be compared in the same year. What matters is the amount spent on pensions when societal developments produce demands for new social policies. Above we have seen that trends such as deindustrialisation, family change or the entry of women into the labour force have occurred at different times in different West European countries.

As a result, for the purpose of this chapter the most meaningful comparison of pension expenditure trajectories is not between different

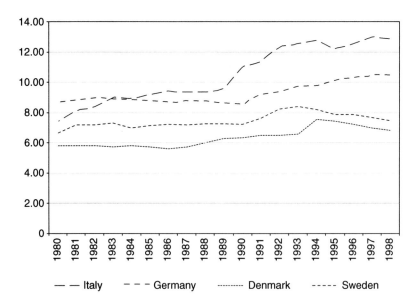

Figure 1.4 Pension expenditure as a proportion of GDP (source: OECD 2001b).

countries in the same year, but at similar stages in the shift from an industrial to a post-industrial society and economy. Broadly speaking, most trends that go under this rubric reached a critical level in the Nordic countries in the 1970s, in the United Kingdom in the 1980s, in Germany in the mid-1990s and in Italy in the late 1990s to early 2000s. The extent to which the new demands generated by these trends can result in the adoption of new policy measures is of course limited by the strength of competing claims. These are obviously stronger in 2000s Italy than they were in 1970s Sweden.

In a context of competing claims and scarce resources, politicians need to be cautious in deciding which policies they want to favour. This issue is likely to constitute a dilemma especially for Social Democratic and, to a lesser extent, Christian Democratic parties. For Social Democratic parties, the natural inclination to favour new policy measures that provide protection against NSR may conflict with the electoral interest they clearly have in defending post-war arrangements, particularly pensions. Today, in Continental European countries, population ageing, welfare state maturation (especially in Bismarckian welfare states) and the higher electoral turnout of older people are all powerful incentives for political parties to prioritise the protection of the post-war welfare state over the development of a post-industrial one (Keman *et al.*, Chapter 2).

Christian Democratic parties are likely to face a similar dilemma, with the difference that they may be less inclined to provide protection against family-related risks resulting from choices that are not consistent with Catholic social thinking. Possibly as a way out of this dilemma, their involvement in NSR policies has tended to focus on policies that concern older people. In this respect the example of long-term care in France and in Germany is instructive. In both countries, centre-right politicians looking for credit-claiming opportunities in the 1980s and 1990s did turn to welfare expansion, and decided to strengthen policies for older people by setting up new schemes for financing long-term care. Both the German Christian Democrats and the French Gaullists made long-term care a key theme in important elections (Morel, Chapter 11).

Social Democratic parties in the Nordic countries, by setting out on the development of a new welfare state earlier, were able to avoid, to some extent at least, this confrontation between competing claims. Moreover, the early expansion of public social services today constitutes an additional factor favouring the development of policies that provide NSR coverage. In fact, as shown by Armingeon (Chapter 5) on the basis of public opinion data, support for these policies does not come only, and probably not even predominantly, from those who are likely to benefit from them. Instead, it is often those who work in the organisations that provide the services who support welfare expansion in NSR policies. Here, the comparatively large size of the public sector in the Nordic countries makes the adoption of new NSR policies or the improvement of existing ones a politically attractive option, even in comparison to more spending on pensions.

The interaction between two processes, welfare state maturation and the emergence of new social risks and demands, has played a crucial role in determining the different degree of success in developing post-industrial welfare states across different regimes.

Old institutions matter

By the end of the *trente glorieuses*, more or less all West European countries had developed comprehensive systems of social protection and labour market regulation providing coverage against the main traditional social risks. The instruments chosen to that end, however, were very different. Some countries limited state intervention to redistribution (the United Kingdom), while others intervened in the functioning of labour markets with clear social policy objectives, either through legislation (France, Italy) or through collectively negotiated agreements (Germany, the Nordic countries) (Bonoli 2003b; Whiteside and Salais 1998).

These different instruments have turned out to vary in their suitability to respond to the new social demands and needs resulting from the transition to a post-industrial society. In the Nordic countries, some of the social transformations associated with the surfacing of NSRs have not resulted in the emergence of widespread social problems. In fact, the risks associated with service employment (low wages, insecurity) and with family change (reconciling work and family life) were, in some circumstances, already well covered by programmes developed in the context of the post-war welfare states, often for a different purpose. This is above all the case in Sweden (and to an extent in the other Nordic countries), which in the 1950s developed an employment regime based on egalitarian collective wage bargaining and on active labour market policies, the so-called Rehn–Meidner model (Benner and Vad 2000). These two instruments turned out to be particularly useful in dealing with the side effects of post-industrialisation: inegalitarian wage pressures and the possible emergence of a working poor problem, and the risk of skill obsolescence.

Old institutions matter also because they can be more or less amenable to adaptation. Clasen and Clegg (Chapter 9) show that the inclusion of activation elements in unemployment compensation schemes has been politically more feasible in countries where the government has more or less direct control over these policies, such as Denmark and the United Kingdom. In contrast, in Germany and in France, where unemployment insurance is managed by the social partners, the inclusion of activation elements has been considerably more difficult. The French pre-school system (*école maternelle*) constitutes a second, often-quoted example of a long-standing institution that can be adapted to new demands. Pre-schools were first introduced at the end of the nineteenth century in the context of an ongoing struggle between Republicans and the Catholics for the control of the education system. Today, thanks also to various adjustments, for example in opening times, the *école maternelle* represents a highly valued and widely used form of childcare for children aged three to six (Morgan 2001).

The choices made by the architects of the post-war welfare state clearly have consequences in relation to the extent to which NSR are covered. In some contexts, for example in the Nordic countries, employment-related NSR may not even be perceived as such because their emergence is *de facto* pre-empted by existing policies. Such instances, however, are rather rare. In most cases, successful coverage against NSR requires the adoption of new policies or the radical reorientation of existing ones.

Conclusion: three roads towards a post-industrial welfare state

As highlighted in the previous section, the courses followed by different countries in relation to the key independent variables of social policy-making have differed somewhat over the past three decades or so, in a way that is roughly consistent with Esping-Andersen's regime typology. As a result, we can expect trajectories towards a post-industrial welfare state to differ across 'worlds' of welfare capitalism.

In Liberal countries (the United States and the United Kingdom), the transition towards a post-industrial society has been regulated essentially by market mechanisms. Changes in demand for particular skills have resulted in downward adjustments of relative wages for low-skilled workers. Demands for family services have been met by the private sector. There are nonetheless differences between the two countries. In the United Kingdom, welfare markets seem to work less well than in the United States, so that childcare remains a problem in that country, but the state is now intervening somewhat more, especially since Labour's accession to government in 1997. In the late 1990s and early 2000s some high-profile actions were taken in the field of active labour market policies and childcare. As Clasen and Clegg (Chapter 9) and Daguerre (Chapter 10) show, in both cases adaptation seemed to be targeted towards a constituency larger than the would-be beneficiaries only. Active labour market policies were framed in a way that emphasised compulsion and as a result were likely to be supported by scrounger-fearing middle-class voters, whereas childcare responded to employers' expectations. In Switzerland, a welfare state that possesses many Liberal features, a similar development took place. In so far as these policies respond to economic requirement and middle-class concerns, they do not contradict the Liberal preference in social policy for self-reliance and market solutions.

In the Nordic countries, parallel developments in relation to the various independent variables combined in a way that was extremely favourable to the development of a large post-industrial welfare state. To start with, various elements of the post-war settlement turned out to be particularly useful for groups exposed to NSR: above all, active labour market policies and encompassing collective agreements. As a result, the development of a post-industrial labour market did not generate big social problems, as in the conservative and liberal welfare states. Second, family change and the widespread entry of women into the labour market started in the 1970s, much earlier than in other countries, and coincided with a peak in women's political activism. In addition, at that time the increase in the financial requirements of the post-war welfare state due to population ageing and scheme maturation had not taken place yet. As a result, new demands for family services could be accommodated more easily.

The transition towards a post-industrial welfare state seems to be more difficult in conservative welfare states. Here, the post-war settlement contained measures that turned out to protect NSR groups, but also measures that contributed to excluding them from access to employment, such as strong employment protection laws. In addition, the social trends associated with post-industrialisation emerged later than in the Nordic countries, with a delay of 20–30 years. By the time these trends were generating new demands for policies (the 1990s), the financial requirements of the extremely generous post-war welfare states found in these countries had increased substantially. As a result, demands for new policies are in direct competition with the expectation that the post-war welfare state will be kept in place. Population ageing and low political participation of NSR groups result in an unbalanced relationship between groups with competing demands on the welfare state, which is unlikely to result in the generalised expansion of a post-war welfare state.

As a result, adaptation in conservative welfare states is taking place through minor adjustments, often in association with other policy object-ives. The adaptation of pension systems to women's career profiles, more often punctuated by interruptions and part-time employment than those of men, is instructive in this respect. Sweden and Germany both adopted major pension reforms in the 1990s. In both countries, cost containment-oriented reforms were going to penalise workers who had taken career breaks. Particularly affected were those women who had withdrawn from the labour market in order to care for their children. In order to make the reform more acceptable, one element of the reforms was the introduction of contribution credits for careers. In Germany the reform package went as far as establishing a minimum pension guarantee, which did not exist in the previous system and constitutes a last-resort safety net for those who will not be able to obtain a decent pension through their contributions. These measures certainly represent an improvement of pension coverage for NSR groups, but were clearly not the main motive behind the reform (Anderson and Meyer, Chapter 8).

The Southern variant of conservative welfare states seems to be facing even bigger difficulties in developing a post-industrial welfare state. The extreme generosity of the post-war welfare state, the rapid process of population ageing and the weak political influence of NSR groups makes it extremely unlikely that available resources will be assigned to the develop-ment of new social policies rather than keeping the post-war welfare state. In addition, the absence of a tradition of anti-poverty policies and family policy makes it difficult in these countries to adapt through 'institutional recycling', or the reorientation of old policies to suit new needs, which as we have seen happened in France with its pre-school system. The corner-stones of the post-war settlement of these countries, such as employment protection legislation, are not only of little use to NSR groups, but seem to be actually detrimental to them (Esping-Andersen 2000). EU policies that encourage the development of NSR coverage are likely to encounter the stiffest resistance in these countries (Treib and Falkner, Chapter 12).

Note

1 Unfortunately, it has not been possible to include the United Kingdom, as the OECD changed its accounting method for that country in 1989, and now pro-vides total spending figures for public and private compulsory pensions.

2 Political parties and new social risks

The double backlash against Social Democracy and Christian Democracy

Hans Keman, Kees van Kersbergen and Barbara Vis

Introduction

After the Second World War, state intervention under party government was increasingly seen as crucial for the reconstruction and development of society. The regulation of work and welfare became a legitimate political goal and a precondition for domestic peace. The established post-war consensus – enabling coalescent behaviour in government across Western Europe – predominantly manifested itself in two political groupings, Social Democracy and Christian Democracy. It was parties belonging to these two 'families' that became the main architects of the welfare state. During the first period after the war, the contours of the Scandinavian (Social Democratic) and the Continental (Conservative) model of the welfare state emerged and expanded. Both types of welfare state contributed to the reconstruction of the national economy, each in its own way 'planning' the economy, rearranging industrial relations, creating and regulating labour markets, implementing income policies, and dealing with social risks, particularly developing (state) pensions for the elderly and organising education for young people and healthcare for all in need (Flora 1986; Briggs 2000/1969).

In this chapter we examine how and to what extent political parties have coped with the profound change of the social and economic context that has taken place since the mid-1980s (Esping-Andersen 1999; Kitschelt *et al.* 1999). We contend that these changes have affected the original architecture of the welfare state across Europe, including the social and political support structures upon which it rests. We argue that Social Democracy and Christian Democracy are facing difficult policy choices as they attempt to adjust existing welfare state arrangements in view of changing patterns of work and income. In particular, if and when in government, these parties find it hard to deal with the new social risks that have emerged since the late 1980s. New social risks concern those situations in which individuals experience welfare losses that have arisen as a result of the transformation towards post-industrial society, in particular shifts in employment, the growing entry of women into the labour force and the sharp increase in the elderly segment of the population. Such risks are generally not well served by the extant welfare states (see Chapter 1).

The difficult policy choices are, in fact, dilemmas that tend to upset the existing allegiance and legitimacy of party government and state intervention. In particular, the 'politics of mediation' is affected – that is to say, the ideologically (and in the case of Christian Democracy also religiously) inspired, institutionally rooted and politically practised conviction that conflicts of social interests can and must be reconciled politically in order to foster solidarity (Social Democracy) or to restore the natural and organic harmony of society (Christian Democracy) (van Kersbergen 1995, 1999; Huber and Stephens 2001a; Keman and Pennings 2004). This politics of mediation has been the principal modus operandi of public policy-making in many countries of (mainly) Social Democratic and Christian Democratic rule. Under conditions of economic growth and prosperity, the parties could initiate social, cultural and economic policies that facilitated such a politics of mediation. In other words, the politics of mediation concerns the configuration of socio-cultural and economic interest intermediation and Social Democratic and Christian Democratic governance. The typical yet variable patterns of institutionalised interaction that were the result have been an important source of legitimacy of the developing welfare state and of the allegiance of large segments of the electorate.

However – and this is the crux of this chapter's argument – the support of these segments for Social Democracy and Christian Democracy has been based on an electoral constituency that was mainly employed in the secondary sector and sufficiently covered by traditional welfare schemes such as (state-directed) pensions, and unemployment or accident insurance. As European society changed from industrial to post-industrial – a change supported and boosted by Social Democratic and Christian Democratic policies – employees in the new employment (mainly third and fourth) sector developed different values, different organisational affiliations (or none at all) and different security needs compared to the classical worker or lower-level white-collar employee of the industrial age. We argue, therefore, that these new groups in society are less inclined to adhere to the traditional organisations that are part of the politics of mediation, and arguably also show a smaller likelihood to vote for Social Democracy and Christian Democracy or to adhere to the respective intermediary organisations. Hence, when in government these parties cannot afford to cut severely the coverage of the security needs of the diminishing share of industrial-sector employees, but likewise they are unable to cater for the security needs of the new and highly fragmented groups of employees in the service sector. In that sense, we put forward in this chapter the thesis that Social Democracy and Christian Democracy are caught in a vicious circle in which they are producing a self-defeating political strategy. More specifically, we argue that the emergence of new social risks for certain new groups and the way parties are coping with them is jeopardising the power resources of Social Democracy and Christian Democracy. Owing to the changing pattern of welfare statism and labour market regulation, Social Democracy and Christian Democracy have been caught out by the present predicament, which – ironically – was partly created by themselves. This 'dialectical' movement contributes to the gradual erosion of their electoral power base and decreases the influence they exert through the politics of mediation. This complex argument, implying a 'loop' process, will be outlined in more detail before we delve into the empirical analysis.

The argument

The practice of the politics of mediation required first and foremost the creation and legitimisation of 'interfaces' between the political centre and organised interests in society. These linkages were seen as crucial for the functioning and organisation of the welfare state, be it the provision of social security or the regulation of industrial relations (Armingeon 1983; Katzenstein 1985). This type of societal interest intermediation was one of the central features of politics in Scandinavia as controlled by Social Democracy (Castles 1978; Stephens *et al.* 1999), and on the European continent as co-organised by Christian Democracy (Wilensky 1981; van Kersbergen 1995). Although the politics of mediation is frequently narrowed down to 'corporatism', we stress that the role and position of political parties in government are crucial for making this institutional arrangement work (Lijphart and Crépaz 1991; Keman and Pennings 1995; Woldendorp 1997). The politics of mediation is essential for understanding not only how the post-war welfare state in Europe came about, but also the emergence of new social risks, the policy responses to them and their political repercussions.

The post-war development of the welfare state is by and large a result of the parties in government, which acted not only as mediators but also as 'ideologues' that translated their general ideas into domestic policy-making (Scharpf 1992; van Kersbergen 1995). These ideas established the origins of path-dependent trajectories that still shape present policy responses in an era of increasing social, economic and demographic challenges to the welfare state and of (neo-)liberal ideologies that contest the post-war consensus on what the state can and should do about the emerging new social risks (Bonoli *et al.* 2000; Taylor-Gooby 2002). These risks are considered 'new' because they appear particularly to affect different groups in society from those affected hitherto (Esping-Andersen 1999; Goodin *et al.* 1999). The 'new' social risks during the life cycle produce welfare losses for an individual-cum-citizen who, to a large extent, depends on market forces. They concern *different* groups in society (e.g. women, youth, elderly people and other 'minorities'; Schmidt 1993; Daly 2000b) and *larger* groups than before (e.g. the retiring and ageing population; Ebbinghaus 2000). These groups tend to become 'outsiders' (Dalton and Wattenberg 2000; Kitschelt 2001; Rueda 2005). Moreover, structural developments like deindustrialisation, internationalisation of markets, variations in acquired skills and the emergence of a Europe-wide political union have changed the political-economic context in which governments have to operate and select policy responses. This implies that the original structuration of welfare in general, and labour market policy-making in particular, had to change as well (e.g. Kuhnle 2000; Scharpf and Schmidt 2000).

We contend not only that certain groups are more vulnerable in their particular situation, but also that these groups' risks do not concur with and are not primarily catered for by Social Democracy and Christian Democracy. This implies a decline in the politics of mediation and may well affect the power resources of the traditional parties in government (Allan and Scruggs 2004; Keman and Pennings 2004). In other words, although Social Democracy and Christian Democracy are seemingly well represented in government, they are at the same time more dependent than before on different partners in coalition government and more often confronted with new challengers within their respective party systems (Mair 2002). This situation, which has come to the fore since the late 1980s, has brought about a series of policy issues that appear as intricate political problems of choice for party governments in Europe.

In a nutshell, during recent decades the socio-economic context has changed, ideas on the role of the state have changed, and the groups in need of welfare have changed. Parties and party governments find it increasingly difficult to reflect societal interests and individual needs through systems of interest intermediation and elections, and this negatively affects their power resources (Schmidt 1996; Golden *et al.* 1999; Mair 2002).

The problems of policy choice for the parties in government are so intricate as they involve what Iversen and Wren (1998) have identified as the *trilemma* of equality, employment and budgetary restraint that has replaced the more familiar *dilemma* of equality (or solidarity) and employment. And it is precisely the main architects of the post-war welfare state – Social Democracy and Christian Democracy – that face this situation. Whereas they were once capable of devising policies aimed at overcoming the trade-off between equality (solidarity) and employment, in the new context the (partly self-imposed) necessity of fiscal austerity has aggravated the trade-off and precludes the possibility of reconciling equality (solidarity) and employment. They find it difficult to reconcile conflicting goals under conditions of changing views on the welfare state, state intervention and contesting ideologies (Huber *et al.* 1993; Pierson 1996; Scharpf 2000; Iversen 2001; Schwartz 2001; Allan and Scruggs, 2004). In view of a de-aligning electorate, their capacity to maintain legitimacy by means of mediation decreases (Mair 2002), resulting in a decreasing share of the vote for Christian Democratic parties almost everywhere in Europe and a much more volatile pattern of voting for Social Democratic parties (albeit less so in the Mediterranean area). Given the budget constraints, they find it difficult to translate governing power into viable policy responses that give a politically convincing solution to the dilemma of equality (solidarity) and employment.

In other words, Social Democracy and Christian Democracy as democratic parties have severe problems with directing state and society, trying to avert or at least reduce social risks across society as a whole and to flourish electorally at the same time. Since it is difficult to uphold the welfare state as it is, welfare state reform efforts tend to affront the traditional political support of the parties. At the same time, there are groups *other* than the traditional core constituencies of the parties that now suffer most 'welfare losses' and that are therefore disinclined to support either of the main original architects of the welfare state. This double backlash is a major factor for understanding the shaky electoral support for Social Democracy and Christian Democracy, as well as their apparent reduced policy-making capacities since the 1980s.

Structure of the chapter

We examine this *problématique* by comparing the behaviour patterns of Social Democratic and Christian Democratic parties in 16 European welfare states.[1] We focus on the policy-making intentions and activities of these parties in the field of active and passive labour market policies and social security expenditure (focusing on transfer payments to households) for the period 1985–2000. These variables then allow us to investigate patterned changes of welfare statism in the face of new social risks and to study how such changes are associated with the decreasing relevance of the politics of mediation and the eroding power of political parties in contemporary European democracies. In addition, we consider the necessity to balance budgets to be a major constraint on the policy-making capacities of party governments.

We will first examine the waning powers of Social Democracy and Christian Democracy and the change in their ideology and policy ideas. This clarifies their political position in Western Europe and the extent to which they are (still) willing to make, and capable of making, policy (van Kersbergen 1997). We then investigate social risks and political constituencies by looking at patterns of policy mixes in West European countries, particularly active and passive labour market policies. Next we look at the relationship between Social Democracy and Christian Democracy and the new mix of work and welfare. Specifically, we study the patterned variation of policy choices between work and welfare, trying to identify the occurrence of new social risks and the power resources of both Social Democracy and Christian Democracy. We conclude by arguing that our analysis indicates that there is a double backlash against Social Democracy and Christian Democracy.

Waning powers and ideological change

Waning powers

Although the parties representing the Social Democratic and Christian Democratic party families are still among the largest across Europe, they are no longer the powers 'that be' (Mair 2002; Powell 2004). According to some observers, the changing characteristics of party systems, which are in part influenced by the waning of traditional cleavages and a tendency towards individualisation (Van Deth and Scarbrough 1995; Dalton and Wattenberg 2000), have caused traditional party differences to matter less. As a consequence, segments of the electorate seem to be less represented by these traditional party families. In the eyes of the voter they are 'powers of the past' (Keman and Pennings 2004). Table 2.1 illustrates these observations. Serious changes in electoral volatility and vote share in Europe can be observed during the 1990s. Electoral volatility increased on average by 5.2 per cent and in some cases has rocketed, such as in France, Italy, the Netherlands and Norway (Mair 2002). Both the Christian Democratic and Social Democratic parties seem to be suffering from this electoral volatility.[2] These parties used to dominate in many West European party systems and frequently participated in (coalition) governments. On average, these parties could still form majority governments together in 1985 (having 51.6 per cent of the vote share), but could no longer do so in 2000 (having suffered a 7.1 per cent vote loss on average).

The decreasing share of the vote and the increasing electoral volatility, however, are not straightforwardly related to these parties' participation in government. As Table 2.1 shows, partisan control of government by Christian Democracy is still considerable, but lower than before. In a number of countries Christian Democracy used to be the genuine pivot party, as no coalition government could be formed without it (e.g. Belgium, Italy, the Netherlands). Only in Germany and Austria do both parties remain 'normal' parties of government. Likewise, the government-forming powers of Social Democracy have become more unstable since the 1980s. Remarkably, this instability is less apparent in the 'new' democracies in Southern Europe. Here, however, Christian Democratic parties are less strong or absent, and one-party governments are more frequent, resulting in complete alternations of party government between the left and the right.[3]

Table 2.1 Electoral volatility and indicators of the power of Social Democracy and Christian Democracy, 1985–2000

Country	EV, 1991–2000	Change in EV, 1980/90– 1991/2000	Level of Soc. Dem. vote share, 2000	Change in Social Dem. vote share, 1985–2000	Level of Christian Dem. vote share, 2000	Change in Chr. Dem. vote share, 1985–2000	SDingov, 1985–2000	CDingov, 1985–2000	Innovation of composition of government, 1985–2000
Austria	10.3	5.7	33.2	−14.4	26.9	−16.3	44.3	45.5	0.19
Belgium	10.8	5.5	19.7	−8.7	20.0	−9.3	52.2	41.4	0.55
Denmark	12.4	2.7	36.0	4.4	2.5	−0.2	54.0	2.8	0.61
Finland	11.0	3.1	22.9	−3.8	4.2	1.2	29.0	3.3	0.77
France	15.4	6.6	25.5	−11.1	0.0	0.0	51.5	10.8	0.72
Germany	9.0	4.0	40.9	2.7	35.1	−13.7	17.0	64.8	0.25
Greece	7.8	−3.5	43.3	−2.5	0.0	0.0	64.0	0.0	0.45
Ireland	11.7	3.6	10.4	1.0	28.0	−11.2	19.5	13.5	0.62
Italy	22.9	13.0	32.0	−13.5	15.7	−17.2	24.0	30.0	0.69
Netherlands	19.1	6.8	29.0	−1.4	20.4	−9.0	39.8	27.8	0.67
Norway	16.1	5.4	35.0	−5.8	13.7	5.4	72.8	5.0	0.50
Portugal	11.3	0.7	44.0	22.6	9.2	−0.8	33.0	12.2	0.50
Spain	9.6	0.8	34.1	−14.3	0.0	0.0	53.4	0.0	0.63
Sweden	13.8	7.5	36.4	8.3	11.8	9.9	74.9	8.1	0.67
Switzerland	8.0	3.6	22.5	−0.4	15.9	−4.5	100.0	100.0	1.00
Gt Britain	9.3	1.0	43.2	15.6	0.0	0.0	30.6	0.0	0.30
Average	12.5	5.2	31.8	−1.3	12.7	−4.8	47.5	22.8	0.60

Sources: Mair (2002); Gallagher et al. (2005: 294); Armingeon et al. (2002); Woldendorp et al. (2000); Inter-Parliamentary Union website.

Explanation: EV = electoral volatility (mean aggregate volatility for 1991–2000, change is difference with the 1981–90 mean); Vote Share: share of total votes cast; SDingov and CDingov = participation in government weighted for total days; Social Democratic and Christian Democratic parties are coded according to Budge et al. (2001: appendix 1). Alternation: Frequency and extent of government composition [1.0 = no change; high value means little change in the overall party composition, low value much, and encompassing change of government] based on Mair.

Although Social Democracy and Christian Democracy together held 44.5 per cent of the vote in 2000, it can be concluded that the parties have experienced a loss of power resources in electoral terms. Electoral decline did not imply a corresponding loss of government power: together both parties were in government for around 70 per cent of the time between 1985 and 2000 (though without Switzerland, the only case without government alternation, the figure would have been 60 per cent). Yet it should be noted that the alternation index of (coalition) government shows that in most cases changes of government happen regularly and frequently involve many parties. All in all, it should be noted that the cross-national variation in power is considerable and that nowhere are Social Democracy or Christian Democracy dominating as they used to do. In our view, this signifies the decline of (the success of) the politics of mediation, the related type of policy performance and its appreciation across Europe.

Ideological convergence?

An explanation for the waning power of Social Democracy and Christian Democracy could be that they are substantially converging programmatically and that, in addition, there has been a concomitant shift in welfare state-related issues, in particular in the 1990s. For if both party families shed their ideological baggage, they would not only lose a part of their 'core' support, but also create room for electoral competition by other parties. The convergent direction of Social Democracy and Christian Democracy would then allow other parties to substitute for these 'old' parties or to occupy the space left open in the left–right dimension of the party system. In addition, other parties would be able to take issue with Social Democracy and Christian Democracy on progressive–conservative issues such as public welfare (Pennings and Keman 2003). The irony would be that both parties' attempt to 'catch all' voters may be conducive to catching each other out and – in the act – estranging themselves from their original electorate (van Kersbergen 1997; Kitschelt 1999; Krouwel 1999).

A converging party system and a declining alignment of voters may deteriorate the power resources of Social Democracy and Christian Democracy. While they were still present in government during the 1990s, the situation is such that – given strict fiscal constraints – a dilemma between equality and solidarity has emerged that presents itself as a choice between providing work or guaranteeing welfare. Either choice is likely to backfire electorally.

The idea of convergence of ideas on policy priorities and coalescing party behaviour is supported if we examine the post-war programmatic changes of Social Democracy and Christian Democracy across Europe. In Table 2.2 we present the developments of both party families at the aggregated level. The focus in Table 2.2 is on three distinct periods: (1) the period of reconstruction immediately after the Second World War

(1945–50); (2) the 1970s (1970–75), when the welfare state reached its completion; and (3) the recent period (after 1990) of adjustment and policy reform. We look at the ideological development of Social Democracy and Christian Democracy by using two general scales that designate the two-dimensional space within a party system (*LvsR* = Left versus Right; *PvsC* = Progressive versus Conservative; see Pennings and Keman 2003 for more details), and three scales that indicate a party's position towards more or less generous welfare state policies (Welfare), its attention towards special groups within the electorate such as labour groups, elderly people and minorities (Special Groups), and towards more or less state intervention in the economy (Planned Economy).

Table 2.2 shows that each of the three temporal cross-sections has a distinctive pattern (also note the high standard deviation, indicating quite some *inter*-party variation across systems). In most countries there is a development from a leftish orientation – at its peak in the 1970s with 12.07 for Social Democratic parties – towards the right in the 1990s (1.52). Conservative issues form a relevant category to denote party differences but tend to become less pronounced, i.e. across most parties but not for Christian Democratic ones (and almost seven points more than Social Democracy). The position of Special Groups in society remains important for most parties through time and is – like Welfare State – more or less a constant at the level of party systems. Both programmatic topics, however, are slowly moving to the level of all parties (under All Parties in Table 2.2), indicating a movement towards the centre. Finally, the issue of a Planned Economy or state interventionism was plainly more salient in the 1970s than before or after this period. The overall post-war pattern shows that the welfare state has remained an important and stable issue throughout time, whereas the role of the state in directing society appears to have faded away in this era of neo-liberalism (Scharpf 1992; King and Wood 1999).

In terms of party differences and issue saliency, the Left versus Right distinction is losing weight, in particular since 1975. The distance between Social Democracy and Christian Democracy has been reduced over time from around ten points to six in the 1990s. In particular, the change within the Social Democratic party family on this central dimension of party competition is remarkable: −10.55. Interestingly enough, the scores on Progressive versus Conservative have developed differently. This distinction did not separate Christian Democracy from Social Democracy immediately after the war, but only became an issue later on. This is an important finding, as it most probably reflects each party family's view of how to change the welfare state and in what direction (e.g. caring for the family or the individual, differences in view on work and social security benefits for different segments of society), but not so much the efforts to maintain a welfare state. In other words, Welfare State remains a policy concern that is equally important for both party families, as does the

Table 2.2 Ideological differences between Social Democracy and Christian Democracy, 1945–98

	1945–50	*1970–75*	*After 1990*
All parties			
Left v. Right	6.17	7.76	−1.65
SD =	(9.81)	(11.19)	(9.32)
Progressive v. Conservative	−6.39	−3.81	−4.59
SD =	(13.89)	(18.65)	(11.29)
Welfare state	11.80	13.59	12.07
SD =	(10.40)	(7.59)	(7.40)
Planned economy	4.92	7.00	2.79
SD =	(4.87)	(7.20)	(2.56)
Special groups	6.28	7.50	6.17
SD =	(6.00)	(7.32)	(7.17)
N =	**144**	**155**	**181**
Social Democracy			
Left v. Right	11.26	12.07	1.52
SD =	(5.77)	(13.17)	(18.25)
Progressive v. Conservative	−6.36	1.07	0.24
SD =	(15.43)	(9.39)	(8.63)
Welfare state	13.75	14.90	15.73
SD =	(12.94)	(7.41)	(8.56)
Planned economy	7.02	8.57	2.86
SD =	(5.03)	(7.16)	(2.44)
Special groups	8.63	9.19	7.17
SD =	(7.62)	(6.69)	(5.51)
N =	**32**	**39**	**43**
Christian Democracy			
Left v. Right	0.56	−0.45	−4.87
SD =	(9.77)	(5.92)	(9.16)
Progressive v. Conservative	−6.30	−7.56	−8.17
SD =	(13.46)	(21.01)	(12.13)
Welfare state	9.75	11.16	10.06
SD =	(5.74)	(6.13)	(7.07)
Planned economy	2.76	3.51	2.26
SD =	(4.20)	(3.76)	(2.06)
Special groups	5.06	6.22	6.94
SD =	(3.75)	(4.60)	(5.21)
N =	**20**	**34**	**35**

Source: Derived from data set in Budge *et al.* (2001).

Explanation: All figures represent proportions of a party programme; *Left v. Right* and *Progressive v. Conservative* are sums of positive and negative scores (respectively Left minus Right and Progressive minus Conservative issues, maximum = +100 and −100; 0 being the median score): a positive score indicates more inclination to the Left and more Progressive of a party (see for operationalisation Pennings and Keman (2003); *Welfare State* and *Planned Economy* are taken directly from Budge *et al.* (2001: 228) and are additive sums (the higher the value the more these issues are emphasised); *Special Groups* is the sum of three variables representing special attention to Labour Groups, Minorities and Underprivileged Groups (Youth, Women and Elderly in society); *N* = number of parties under review; *SD* = Standard Deviation; *Social Democratic* and *Christian Democratic* parties are coded according to Budge *et al.* (2001: appendix 1).

attention paid to Special Groups (although this is a more salient issue for Social Democracy). However, the way this is translated into concrete policy-making may well remain to be different. And precisely this linkage between setting policy priorities by parties and policy formation by party government appears to have become strained in the recent period by such constraints as internationalisation and post-industrialisation. This is weakening an effective working of the politics of mediation (Pierson 1996; van Kersbergen 2000; Green-Pedersen 2002).

Table 2.2 also shows that the two party families have become less distinctive during the 1990s in terms of distances on the various indicators used. The changes we observe over time and within each party family demonstrate a converging pattern. Moreover, this tendency is reinforced by the observation that neither party family is far from the national party system averages. This signifies that they can be considered central parties in most party systems; they are still strong if not dominant. The indicator Planned Economy is a stronger element in Social Democratic programmes, but is not absent within Christian Democratic ones. However, the scores show that the issue's saliency is low (and thus indicating less emphasis on elements typical of the politics of mediation). The conclusion is that – apart from the programmatic attention for Welfare State and Special Groups – all indicators show change, in particular between the 1970s and the 1990s. The overall direction of these changes is from Left towards Right, from Progressive towards Conservative and from more towards less state intervention. The pattern of convergence can be recognised in the fact that the ideological differences between Social Democracy and Christian Democracy are becoming less pronounced, or remain the same and relatively small. If we judge the All Parties category in Table 2.2 and keep in mind that the maximum range is 200, the differences are not above six points in the 1990s for Left versus Right and Welfare State.

Interestingly, in addition to a convergence in the ideas on welfare provision and social justice *per se*, we find convergence in the *overall* view on socio-economic issues (as condensed in the Left versus Right positions of parties) and in the role the state should play. Therefore, programme shifts, as indicated by party differences, show a tendency towards coalescence between many parties, and Social Democracy and Christian Democracy in particular. This shift in party contestation within party systems has allowed for discrete changes in welfare programmes and labour market policies under the aegis of party governments of variable composition. In other words, parties still matter, but – as we shall see later on – they do so differently. This observation may well point to a lesser role for the societal bargaining part of the politics of mediation and a gradual centralisation of policy-making towards the parliamentary level and government.

This contention still holds if one disaggregates and specifies these shifts at the country level: 11 of the 15 Social Democratic parties have de-emphasised their programme's stance on welfare and state intervention, and a similar pattern can be observed in Christian Democratic parties (seven out of 13). Together with the observed movement within most party systems to both the right and conservatism, the central (and dominant) parties apparently have room for manoeuvre to pursue a more restrictive policy combined with a preference for a retreat of the state as an active director of employment and welfare. It goes almost without saying that this has affected the politics of mediation of Social Democracy and Christian Democracy and helps to explain the slow but steady downward trend in their ability to seek and gain office (Korpi and Palme 2003; Keman and Pennings 2004).

In sum, the waning power of Social Democratic and Christian Democratic parties across Europe is associated with a discrete change in overall ideological position within party systems and a distinctive shift in the choices made as regards public policy priorities in the 1990s. The emerging ideological convergence between Social Democracy and Christian Democracy has resulted in the promoting of welfare statism with less state intervention and a more conservative inclination that is embedded in frequently alternating party governance.

If this observation is correct, then it makes sense to expect that social risks are looming for more groups and that these groups will be hurt more than before. This is certainly new in comparison to the golden era of the European worlds of welfare. In the next section we analyse how and to what extent these political changes have affected social policies, including labour market policies. Have social risks indeed become greater (again), and more so for some groups in society, including single parents, young unemployed people, or older people without the proper skills required to participate successfully in the labour market? And, if so, how does this affect the political power of Social Democracy and Christian Democracy?

Social risks and political constituencies

We propose that the electoral downturn must also be understood – at least in part – as the result of the changing format of the welfare state affecting certain groups in society differently from before. When austerity policies are pursued while a party is in office, it can be expected that certain electoral constituencies will vote differently or not vote at all (in particular the younger cohorts of the electorate).

Work and welfare have always been the cornerstones of post-war public policy formation in Western Europe (Scharpf 1992; van Kersbergen and Becker 2002). An important change concerns the distribution of social risks as different people are now affected. Extant welfare programmes and labour market policies often do not cater for new needs. Hence, a dilemma has come to the fore that affects how parties (can and will) translate these crucial issues into public policies.

In spite of the well-known big changes (internationalisation of the economy, growing interdependence, the retreat of the mixed economy and the state as the dominant force shaping society; Rhodes 2001; Schwartz 2001), we hold that *party government* remains the traditional political actor that allows, impedes or at least mediates the transformation of the welfare state (Allan and Scruggs 2004). Moreover, in so far as there has been a change in welfare state-related policies, the existing constituencies of the Christian Democratic and Social Democratic parties have in large part been responsible for the direction of change. Both the electorates and the organised interests must be seen as political determinants (other things being equal) of the degree and direction of change in recalibrating work and welfare (Golden *et al.* 1999; Korpi and Palme 2003). How policies are made to reorganise the welfare state is a matter of political competition not only between parties, but also between segments of the population and their organisations representing vested interests (Esping-Andersen 1999; van Kersbergen 1999). For if the support for Christian Democracy and Social Democracy has changed, this may imply a weakening not only of these parties as such, but also of the effectiveness of the politics of mediation. The debate on the welfare state and related new social risks is part of this *problématique*. This line of thought will be examined in the next subsection, together with other parameters of change.

Patterns of unemployment

During the late 1980s and early 1990s the patterns of unemployment in Europe changed considerably (Esping-Andersen 1996; Clayton and Pontusson 1998). As we expect such changes to have political repercussions, it is perhaps somewhat surprising that little attention has been paid to the social consequences of these changes for segments within the population and for the functioning of the politics of mediation (Kitschelt 1999).

The literature mentions many causal variables, such as fiscal and economic constraints, the impact of Europe on policy-making (Scharpf 1996; Rhodes 2001), the role of institutions and national governance (Visser and Hemerijck 1997; van Kersbergen 2000), changing welfare state regimes (Pierson 1996), and the behaviour of parties (in government) (Schmidt 1996; Kitschelt 2001; Keman 2002). However, most studies tell us little about how these factors have affected the public at large, nor do they inform us of the effects of these developments on the dominant parties. James (1996) and Beattie and McGillivray (1995) rightly point out that retrenchment and recommodification do occur, but that the effects on different population segments vary considerably. The effects are particularly negative for those who are attempting to enter the labour market and for those who (are forced to) leave (Therborn 1986; Schmidt 1993; Daly 2000b). So, the reshaping of the welfare state during the 1990s appears to produce 'collateral damage' to the younger and older population segments. Gough (1996) and Schmidt (1993) have shown that although female participation varies across Europe, it is negatively affected by part-time contracts and the reorganisation of income maintenance programmes (Visser and Hemerijck 1997; Goodin *et al.* 1999). Table 2.3 shows how unemployment has developed between 1985 and 2000.

In 2000 the rate of unemployment in Europe averaged 7.6 per cent, roughly the same level as in 1985 (a − 0.7 per cent change). This apparent stability, however, is the effect of a (strong) rise in Sweden, Finland, Greece and Italy that was balanced by a fall in Ireland, the Netherlands, Portugal, Spain and Great Britain. Looking behind this average, we see that the levels of unemployment for women, men of 55 and over and, in particular, young people are higher and increasing (with 6.6 per cent) than those for adult male workers, which are decreasing. The cross-national variation is also considerable. In Germany, Finland, Sweden and Spain older men are often unemployed, whereas only in Ireland, Great Britain and Denmark are older men getting back to work (again). The youth category, however, is the most dramatic of all: 31.9 per cent of those in this segment are without a job in 2000, and in some countries – France, Greece, Italy and Spain – the proportion is over 50 per cent. In 2000, 40 per cent of all men and women were long-term unemployed. Part-time labour is growing everywhere (except in Greece, Italy, Portugal and Spain), although the social risk involved here depends on the level of job protection, among other things (OECD 1999, 2004a), which varies by country. Still, it is obvious that – except for male workers between 25 and 54 – the chances of being in work are not high.

Although the overall rates of unemployment have diminished, it is still a considerable social problem. Moreover, certain demographic categories are now more severely affected by the risk of unemployment than others. Given the fact that most passive programmes do not cater for these differences and that active labour market measures were – in most countries – developed only in the 1990s, some groups face social risks that are at best only partially covered by the old programmes.

One might expect that this would have an effect on the voting behaviour of those segments within the electorate. For example, the proportion of elderly people is gradually growing and currently amounts to 15.5 per cent of the population across Western Europe (OECD 2002b), and young people are less willing to turn out on election day. On average, voter turnout decreased by 8 per cent between 1985 and 2000. Franklin *et al.* (2004) argue that this in large part is indeed due to the younger segment of the electorates across Europe. How do parties, in particular Social Democratic and Christian Democratic parties, cope with these changes? As we have seen, the priorities set by these parties' programmes have changed over time, and they are tending to converge ideologically. It seems likely that party governments are primarily concerned with types of policy-making that aim to solve the problem of reducing big government to create balanced budgets and at the same

Table 2.3 Patterns of unemployment, 1985–2000

Country	Total 2000	Change total 8500	Male 2000	Change male 8500	Male 55+ 2000	Change male 55+ 8500	Female 2000	Change female 8500	Female 55+ 2000	Change female 55+ 8500	Youth 2000	Change youth 8500
Austria	4.7	−1.2	4.5	−0.6	5.3	0.2	4.6	−0.5	3.4	−0.1	11.9	−1.7
Belgium	8.6	−1.5	6.1	2.1	4.5	1.4	9.0	−1.3	8.1	3.2	45.1	15.8
Denmark	6.6	−2.2	3.7	−3.8	3.2	−2.0	4.9	−3.5	5.6	−1.9	20.0	−2.9
Finland	10.2	4.2	7.9	5.4	10.9	9.1	9.0	7.4	9.4	6.6	43.2	24.5
France	10.7	0.9	9.0	3.1	8.7	2.7	12.6	1.9	8.7	1.1	53.9	14.7
Germany	8.2	0.6	7.3	2.6	12.8	2.9	8.7	1.6	15.5	0.3	16.8	5.5
Greece	11.1	4.5	5.7	2.5	2.9	0.9	13.9	5.3	3.7	2.5	60.7	13.0
Ireland	5.6	−7.2	5.7	−6.1	4.2	−4.3	4.8	−8.7	4.3	−4.0	16.9	−18.1
Italy	11.6	2.8	6.9	3.0	4.6	2.9	13.6	2.3	5.6	3.6	66.9	8.1
Netherlands	2.9	−5.0	2.1	−2.9	2.1	−0.7	4.1	−6.8	3.9	−2.5	14.8	−7.4
Norway	4.0	1.4	2.6	−2.1	1.3	−1.7	2.2	−1.7	0.8	−1.1	19.1	−4.3
Portugal	7.3	−5.0	3.4	1.2	3.9	1.7	4.6	−1.2	2.0	0.2	17.8	−2.1
Spain	12.9	−5.2	9.2	−0.1	9.4	1.0	21.0	0.4	11.2	4.0	59.0	−3.9
Sweden	6.7	4.0	6.5	5.2	7.3	6.0	5.9	3.7	5.9	4.3	28.4	19.3
Switzerland	3.5	2.2	2.2	1.4	2.5	1.1	3.2	0.6	2.8	2.1	11.3	4.9
Gt Britain	6.7	−4.5	5.4	−0.2	6.4	−2.0	4.3	−1.6	3.2	−1.8	24.3	4.2
Average	7.6	−0.7	5.5	0.7	5.6	1.2	7.9	−0.1	5.9	1.0	31.9	4.4

Source: OECD Labour Force Statistics 2002.

Explanation: All figures are percentages of the total labour force and for the categories mentioned; Youth = 16–23 years old; changes are absolute differences. '8500' means 1985–2000.

time investing in new programmes – such as active labour market policies – to cater for new needs.

Since the 1980s both the labour force and the population have become
more vulnerable to income deficiencies, which are in part produced by the
new policies related to the welfare state. The reshaping of the welfare
state is, in fact, creating some of the new social risks. This can be
demonstrated by the fact that in most European countries neither the size
of the public economy nor the transfer payments to households have
increased (see Table 2.6, later in the chapter). In addition, eligibility for
various social security benefits (sickness pay and unemployment) has
become tougher, and benefits are now lower than in the 1980s (Scruggs
2004). In other words, certain groups in society are more hurt by the
change of employment patterns and income supplements than others. And
it is exactly these people who make up political constituencies that are
usually underorganised in trade unions and less well represented within
the mainstream political parties in government (Scruggs and Lange 2001).
This implies a divide in the degree of social risks for those groups (the
'outsiders'), which is reinforced by the growth of the inactive population
(be it 55-plus or elderly people: Beattie and McGillivray 1995) representing an important part of the electorate. We expect not only that these
demographic developments are likely to affect the electoral and policy-
seeking behaviour of both Christian Democracy and Social Democracy,
but also that these are – at least in part – produced by the policy mix of
labour market intervention and income maintenance. How have these
parties fared in active and passive labour market policies since 1985?

New policy mixes? Patterns of active and passive labour market policies

In most countries, social policy (including labour market policy) formed
the backbone of a coalition between employers and employees (Armingeon 1983) that was politically safeguarded by Social Democracy and
Christian Democracy. Both parties had close ties with the trade unions
and, in the case of Christian Democracy in particular, with organised interests representing capital (Wilensky 1981; Woldendorp 1997). The policy
interests of the trinity government–capital–labour were more or less
directly mediated through the two party families. Each of them had an
explicit interest in the pursuit of income maintenance programmes and the
creation of labour market programmes. However, the political and economic context changed. First, the EMU criteria constrained the policy
room for manoeuvre at the national level, particularly curbing overall
levels of public expenditure and restricting public debt. Second, the effects
of deindustrialisation influenced the structure of labour markets, for
example in terms of 'flexicurity' and (early) retirement policies that coincided in the late 1990s (Scharpf and Schmidt 2000; Iversen 2001). Third,

the ideological move towards less state intervention and towards a more right-wing stance at the level of party systems affected the role of party government as policy-maker. These developments and their effects on the development of public policy required a new style of governance. This style, so one could argue, has led to new policy mixes that differ from the traditional arrangements between government, capital and labour and that alter the way welfare state policies relate to social risks and political change (Rhodes 2001).

This becomes clearer when we examine the new policy mixes of active and passive labour market policies. Recent OECD data make it possible to break down public expenditure on labour market policies and to specify variations in active and passive types of policy instruments. Public (and mandatory) expenditure on passive labour market programmes is essentially expenditure on unemployment benefits and early retirement schemes. Public (and mandatory) expenditure on active labour market policies is expenditure on training, (re)schooling, education, subsidised job programmes, incentives for employers to take on the long-term unemployed and/or unskilled and the like (OECD 2001a).

The extent of activation is usually measured by active expenditures as a share of gross domestic product (GDP). This measure, however, captures activation inadequately. A priori, a better measure is active spending per person unemployed relative to GDP per person employed (OECD 2003c). A truly active orientation, however, only arises if, in addition, active spending as a percentage of active and passive spending on labour market programmes combined is relatively high (OECD 2003c). Armingeon (2005), for example, uses both active spending per person unemployed relative to GDP and the share of active labour market programmes (ALMP) spending (as a percentage of GDP) in total labour market spending (as a percentage of GDP) as indicators for ALMP effort. Similarly, we argue that if there is a development towards more active expenditure per person unemployed relative to GDP, this can be considered a trend towards 'work before welfare'. Conversely, more passive expenditure per person unemployed relative to GDP without an explicit policy movement towards active labour market measures implies that decommodification remains a main trend in social welfare. In Table 2.4 we examine the direction of change in active and passive spending per unemployed person, measuring active (passive) spending per unemployed person as expenditures on active (passive) labour market programmes multiplied by 100 and divided by the standardised unemployment rate (cf. Armingeon 2005).

Table 2.4 shows that the largest change in active and passive spending per unemployed took place only recently (1995–2000). Comparison of this period with the period 1985–95 shows that most countries changed direction and thus their policy mix concerning the provision of welfare and work. Sweden, Spain, the Netherlands and Portugal are the only countries that stayed on their original course. Sweden kept lowering both active and

Table 2.4 Mapping of active and passive spending per unemployed person, 1985–2000

	1985–95	1985–2000	1990–2000	1995–2000
Lower active spending per unemployed; Lower passive spending per unemployed	FIN, SWE, UK	FIN, NOR, SWE, SWI, UK	FIN, GRE, SWE, SWI, UK	FRG, GRE, NOR, SWE
Lower active spending per unemployed; Higher passive spending per unemployed	SWI		FRG	
Higher active spending per unemployed; Lower passive spending per unemployed	BEL, DK, FRA, SPA	DK, FRA, GRE, IRE, SPA	BEL, FRA, IRE, NOR, SPA	AUS, FIN, IRE, ITA, SPA, SWI, UK
Higher active spending per unemployed; Higher passive spending per unemployed	AUS, FRG, GRE, IRE, NL, NOR, POR	AUS, BEL, FRG, NL, POR	AUS, DK, NL, POR	BEL, DK, FRA, NL, POR

Sources: Active spending per unemployed: Armingeon (2005) [standardised unemployment rates: *OECD Labour Market Statistics*; active labour market expenditures: OECD *Social Expenditure Database* 2004]; passive spending per unemployed: own calculations, using data set in Armingeon (2005).

Explanation: Active (passive) spending per unemployed person is computed as expenditures on active (passive) labour market programmes × 100 divided by the standardised unemployment rate. Active labour market programmes include spending on public employment services and administration, labour market training, youth measures, measures for the disabled and subsidised employment; passive labour market programmes' expenditures include unemployment compensation and early retirement for labour market reasons (see OECD 2001a).

No data available for Italy before 1995; data for Switzerland and Ireland, 1998 instead of 2000; active expenditures for Italy, 1999 instead of 2000.

passive spending per person unemployed, Spain chose to stimulate work before welfare, and the Netherlands and Portugal raised their spending on welfare as well as on work. Yet the most remarkable observation from Table 2.4 is that there are still three main policy trajectories left: (1) both passive and active spending per unemployed is reduced; (2) active and passive spending per unemployed is increased simultaneously; and (3) the active type remains but the passive part is reduced. As stated, for an activation orientation, i.e. a focus on work, a rise in active spending per unemployed person should be matched by a rise in active spending as a share of total spending on labour market programmes. Similarly, for a deactivation orientation, i.e. a focus on welfare, a lowering of active spending per unemployed person should be matched by a decrease in active spending as a share of total spending on labour market programmes.

Interestingly, this is not what we see in Table 2.5 for a substantial

Table 2.5 Active spending in total spending on labour market programmes, 1985–2000

Country	1985–95	1985–2000	1990–2000	1995–2000
Austria	−*1.06*	10.41	8.45	11.47
Belgium	5.30	9.50	5.85	4.20
Denmark	7.30	11.69	13.86	4.39
Finland	−12.58	−9.08	−14.72	3.50
France	20.38	22.44	13.92	2.06
Germany	4.44	7.51	−9.21	*3.07*
Greece	18.47	16.77	*5.02*	−1.70
Ireland	7.87	31.65	26.90	23.78
Italy	–	–	–	36.65
Netherlands	5.63	20.52	12.29	14.89
Norway	−*0.60*	*7.69*	18.59	*8.29*
Portugal	−*3.25*	−*9.60*	−*22.76*	−*6.35*
Spain	7.25	29.08	13.26	21.83
Sweden	−19.83	−20.81	−15.76	−0.98
Switzerland	−12.66	*4.38*	−15.16	17.04
United Kingdom	*0.84*	*18.78*	*6.44*	17.94
Average	*1.83*	*10.1*	*3.13*	*9.54*

Source: Armingeon (2005).

Explanation: Active spending in total spending on labour market programmes is measured by total spending on active labour market programmes (ALMP) divided by total spending on ALMP and passive labour market programmes (PLMP) combined. ALMP comprise spending on public employment services and administration, labour market training, youth measures, measures for the disabled and subsidised employment. PLMP expenditures include unemployment compensation and early retirement for labour market reasons (see OECD 2001a).

The cases for which there is a mismatch between active spending per unemployed and active spending as share of total spending on labour market programmes, for example active spending per unemployed +; active spending as share of total spending −/−, are indicated in **bold italics**.

Data for Denmark and Portugal, 1986 instead of 1985; data for Italy, 1996 instead of 1995; data for Greece, 1998 instead of 2000; data for Ireland, 2001 instead of 2000.

number of cases (indicated in bold and italics). Between 1985 and 1995, for example, the United Kingdom lowered its active spending per unemployed person but increased its active expenditure as a share of total expenditure. For Austria, Norway and Portugal, active spending per unemployed person rose, while their active expenditures as a share of total expenditures decreased. Nevertheless, in general we observe retrenchment in terms of spending per unemployed in 11 of the 16 countries, which is predominantly a lowering of passive spending. Only four countries (Germany, Greece, Norway and Sweden) lowered their active spending between 1995 and 2000. As we already know, this affects mainly the young segment of the labour force, and women. These segments become increasingly dependent on others – be it the 'breadwinner' or the 'paterfamilias'.

We see, furthermore, that the greatest change in the policy mix of work and welfare came about only recently. This finding concurs with the observation on the programme changes of Social Democratic and Christian Democratic parties, in particular in the 1990s. The converging ideological trend was towards less faith in state interventionism as such, but a continuing appreciation of specific welfare-related policies. Also, conservative ideas became more dominant in both party families. We also see that active labour market incentives in terms of spending per unemployed increased almost everywhere.

These observations lead us to suppose that the politics of mediation has either failed in its representative role or – faced with inevitable choices – has selectively favoured the adult, established and well-protected part of the labour force (as can be derived from the distribution of unemployment categories in Table 2.3). In turn, such a choice (be it conscious or not) may have brought about the volatile patterns in electoral outcomes and concomitant office-seeking powers of those parties that were the architects of the post-war, traditional welfare state. Such parties often represent older generations as well as those who have vested interests in the present distribution of work and welfare.

Concluding this section, we stress that new groups in society become (or remain) excluded from, and have minimal access to, the protective measures against the risks that the contemporary welfare state is covering. We expect that the changing patterns of employment and the changing policy mixes of work and welfare will have an impact on the electoral and office-seeking capacities of Social Democracy and Christian Democracy.

Social Democracy, Christian Democracy and the new mix of work and welfare

Many analysts stress that there has been a watershed in terms of conditions that have altered the policy-making capacities of the existing welfare state. This development is often interpreted as a result of exogenous factors, like globalisation and, more particularly in Western Europe,

European integration (Schwartz 2001). From this stem the policy dilemmas that explain the reduced policy capacity of states. However important this may be, endogenous factors should not be underestimated. As explained, we speak of new and old groups rather than of new social risks *only*, as work and welfare are still the main social concerns for the majority of the population. The electorate expects the state to cater for these wants, and, consequently, income replacement schemes and labour market programmes continue to be at the very heart of public policy formation in West European governments.

In this section we analyse the relationship between the political power resources of these parties and the policy mixes that have been developed between 1985 and 2000. Table 2.6 reports the patterns of programme convergence and observed shift in public expenditures (see also Table 2.1 for governmental participation by Social Democracy and Christian Democracy and Table 2.5 for labour market policy mixes).

The data in Table 2.6 show a change in the Left–Right dimension in most polities. In a number of cases this concerns both party families – as in Austria, Germany and Ireland; in others it concerns Social Democracy in particular (Scandinavia and Great Britain). This can be explained by party system dynamics that are idiosyncratic, by the emergence of right-wing challengers (as in Austria and Italy) and by the emergence of 'Christian' parties (mainly in Scandinavia). As we already noted, the overall trend is towards convergence. On average, the differences between Social Democracy and Christian Democracy are decreasing, the average change being 5.3 and 3.9 points respectively. Note that, on average, the programmatic emphases on the Welfare State dimension remain stable over time and display little change. Although the changes in individual countries are in some cases considerable, overall the Social Democratic and Christian Democratic party families are converging. So, notwithstanding existing party differences, governing by either of these parties (but also together) implies that on welfare-related topics, coalescing behaviour can be expected. As Table 2.1 reported, on average both party families have been in office quite often during our period of investigation, and regularly govern together. More particularly, Social Democracy and Christian Democracy have been responsible for policy-making for 70 per cent of the time (exceptions are France and Great Britain). The patterns of active and passive labour market programme expenditure that is at least partly a product of these developments have already been discussed (see the subsection 'New policy mixes?').

Table 2.6 also reports on the changing policy outputs regarding transfer payments and total social expenditures between 1985 and 2000. The change over time is considerable. What we see is that most countries reduce their total expenditures – only Greece and Switzerland display an increase – and simultaneously cut back their transfers to households, albeit less than Total Expenditures. So, with the exception of a few countries,[4] there is indeed a trend towards retrenchment.

Table 2.6 Patterns of ideological change and policy outputs, 1985–2000

| | Change in party programme | | | | Party differences | | Change 1985–2000 | |
| | Left v. Right | | Welfare State | | L v. R | Welfare | Total expenditures | Transfers households |
	SD	CD	SD	CD				
Austria	-13.4	-44.7	5.0	-6.2	25.9	10.9	-3.7	-1.6
Belgium	6.6	0.6	-8.4	-1.8	14.9	4.4	-14.5	-6.4
Denmark	-12.7	13.1	-12.7	5.9	31.2	3.3	-8.7	0.8
Finland	7.1	3.1	31.4	-15.0	13.2	11.4	0.4	1.8
France	15.4	5.0	4.1	4.7	23.7	8.9	-3.3	-4.1
Germany	-22.7	-45.4	2.0	-9.2	29.3	6.8	-3.7	2.6
Greece	0.5	11.3	3.3	10.6	41.6	10.1	8.6	1.5
Ireland	-22.1	-12.0	-10.5	2.9	16.6	16.8	-15.9	-8.4
Italy	1.4	10.2	9.1	4.9	16.7	6.2	-6.3	-0.4
Netherlands	6.9	0.3	9.2	-0.5	10.4	1.9	-13.0	-14.2
Norway	-12.9	-3.1	2.5	1.5	16.8	2.6	-4.8	-0.9
Portugal	1.0	-7.1	0.0	0.0	14.0	0.0	-0.2	1.3
Spain	-3.5	5.9	-13.5	-8.7	18.4	3.7	-2.8	-3.7
Sweden	-5.0	-6.7	10.5	16.1	3.8	2.2	-11.8	0.1
Switzerland	-9.6	5.9	-6.3	8.2	14.1	5.0	3.1	-1.8
Great Britain	-22.1	0.9	-10.5	-5.1	7.8	4.0	-8.7	-0.6
Average	-5.3	-3.9	0.9	0.5	18.7	6.1	-5.3	-2.1

Source: See Tables 2.2 and 2.4; Armingeon et al. (2002a).

Explanation: *Change in party programme* = differences between emphases in 1985 and 2000; *SD* = Social Democracy; *CD* = Christian Democracy; *Party differences* = position of SD and CD in 2000 on Left v. Right and Welfare (see Table 2.2); *Total expenditures* = percentage change in outlays of general government; *Transfers households* = percentage change in transfer payments to households.

To what extent can this development be considered a (partial) result of Social Democracy and Christian Democracy having been in power? We consider that the so-called partisan theory of policy-making (Schmidt 1996; Keman 1997; Allan and Scruggs 2004) is still relevant. Simplified, this theory's argument is that party differences are relevant to an understanding of policy variations across polities. In addition, the type and complexion of party government affects how these variations in policy change are directed. Therefore, we expect that the differences in programme between Social Democracy and Christian Democracy and their presence in government matter, as regards the observed policy changes.

Using an admittedly simple technique, namely bivariate correlations, we do find some support for this expectation. So, the larger the differences between Christian Democracy and Social Democracy on the Left–Right dimension are, the less total expenditures grow over time ($r = -0.49$). In addition, the more both parties emphasise a generous welfare state, the higher public expenditures on transfer payments tend to be ($r = 0.76$). It turns out that the problem of 'squaring the circle' of reducing 'big' government and spending on social security is politically hazardous. The relation between governmental participation and the volatile (but generally decreasing) electoral support for both parties shows that the longer both parties have been in office after 1985, the bigger is their electoral loss. This effect is strongest when Social Democracy and Christian Democracy govern together ($r = -0.60$ and $r = -0.62$ respectively). In other words, austerity policies that tend to result in retrenchment of social spending appear to have contributed to the loss in power resources. This effect is particularly strong in those countries where the two parties depend on each other to control government. For example, in Austria, Belgium, Ireland and the Netherlands – where both party families have lost electoral support – we observe a reduction in transfer payments, affecting the 'insiders', in combination with a stronger emphasis on activation, affecting the 'outsiders'. A different pattern can be discerned in the Scandinavian countries, which display the most drastic policy changes. In Sweden, for example, both welfare and work are clearly de-emphasised (see Tables 2.4 and 2.5). Although governmental powers are to some extent waning, the effects seem obvious in terms of electoral developments. Voters turn out less (-6.25 per cent) and, as we show in Table 2.1, volatility is comparatively high (about 12 per cent) and – except in Denmark – electoral support is steadily diminishing.

Again, these political developments appear to indicate the emergence of a *problématique* that poses problems for politicians to produce austerity policies without de-aligning their electoral support across the electorate as a whole. The extent to which this fate can be avoided depends on the extent to which the politics of mediation of Social Democracy and Christian Democracy is still functional in maintaining a legitimate level of redistributive justice and employment. This is apparently no longer the case in the face of the post-industrial social risks that affect large segments within society. The same seems to hold for the ideological convergence between the two party families that results in policy patterns for the two groups of parties that make them hard to distinguish for the individual voter (see Goodin *et al.* 1999).

Conclusion: the double backlash against Social Democracy and Christian Democracy

In this chapter we have argued that changing welfare statism has led to a development in which both work and welfare are organised in a different mix as compared with formerly. During the 1990s this led to patterns of unemployment that put some new groups in a more difficult position than others. These new groups were identified as the younger segment of the labour force, adult female workers and older people. Many of them are not organised within trade unions or the traditional parties and are not represented in the systemic politics of mediation.

The political style of Christian Democracy, and also of Social Demo-cracy, used to aim at cross-class coalitions, both electorally and in govern-ment formation. The parties offered their own specific work–welfare mix that was appealing to a broad clientele. Both parties thus sought social and economic stability within society through their policies and by various other means, including the promotion of corporatist interest intermedia-tion. The typical politics of mediation, however, appears to have been eroded. Moreover, policy responses that aim at recalibrating work and welfare do not seem to be very effective in terms of employment for all, and often result in an unequal treatment of the welfare clientele.

We argue that this is the background of a 'double backlash' against Social Democracy and Christian Democracy: neither the traditional adher-ents of the parties nor the new social risk groups are likely to be loyal and steady supporters. It is difficult to build social coalitions, as there seems to be evolving a societal gap between the 'old' established groups (the 'insid-ers') and the 'new' groups that are under-represented socially and politic-ally (the 'outsiders'). The politics of mediation would imply that the new groups should organise themselves and that political parties should strive for a realignment between these groups and the insiders by means of cross-group coalitions and intermediating practices. However, this does not seem to be occurring. In spite of increasing retrenchment, neither a significant growth in the social and political organisations representing the new groups, nor a distinctive increase in social conflict, has occurred. Old policies for old groups are retrenched, new policies for new groups are underdeveloped.

In short, owing to the changing pattern of welfare statism and labour market regulation, Social Democracy and Christian Democracy have been caught out by the present – partly self-created – developments. The fundamental predicament of traditional political parties in Europe, then, is that they cannot cope with the new conditions of policy formation without resorting to unwarranted austerity and welfare retrenchment, while at the same time maintaining the power resources necessary to find a new equilibrium that caters for the majority of the population. The parties have been seeking to square the circle of catering for the wants and needs of an increasingly heterogeneous society in which established linkages between organised segments within the population and parties are disappearing. Social Democracy and Christian Democracy have done this in the face of a double backlash that is causing their power to wane, culminating in the exhaustion of the politics of mediation and electoral decline between 1985 and 2000.

Notes

1 The countries included are Austria, Belgium, Denmark, Finland, France, Germany, Greece, Ireland, Italy, the Netherlands, Norway, Portugal, Spain, Sweden, Switzerland and Great Britain.
2 It is interesting to note that since 2000, electoral volatility has increased dramatically in Austria (21.1 per cent in 2001) and the Netherlands (22.5 per cent in 2002).
3 Italy used to have multi-party governments dominated by the Democrazia Cristiana. However, since the 1990s this has no longer been the case.
4 The German increase in transfers can be understood as a result of the effects of unification after 1989.

3 New social risk and political preferences

Herbert Kitschelt and Philipp Rehm

Introduction

Citizens may try to calculate the magnitude of the expected stream of income they expect to receive in a pure system of voluntary market exchange, when they develop preferences among alternative social and economic policies. That expected stream of income results from the interaction of the magnitude and the certainty of income flows under conditions of market contracting. People whose income flow is small and/or uncertain have lower expected incomes than market participants with expectations of a high and comparatively certain flow. The former will want to employ authoritative redistribution of resources in favor of the less well-off through government policies to improve their own income position. The latter will want to leave market allocation alone as much as possible.

Some of the endowments and experiences that enter people's calculation of expected income flows under market conditions have been relevant for as long as capitalist market societies have existed, such as the vulnerability of those who lack ownership of fixed capital and real estate compared to those who have to rely on the sale of their labor. Other risks of low or uncertain income flows under market arrangements may have become more pronounced in recent decades. Among comparatively wealthy OECD countries situated near the world innovation frontier, high skill levels acquired in formal education, for example, appear to pay off more strongly in market-determined wage income in post-industrial capitalism caught up in the rapid spread of new information and communication technologies than during the post-World War II 'golden age' of reconstruction and rapid industrial growth after the first oil crisis of 1973–74.

Our chapter seeks to assess how attributes that shape citizens' expectations concerning income derived from market exchange also affect their preferences among market-correcting social policies. Indeed, there are a multiplicity of 'old' and 'new' risk conditions that turn out to play a role. These risk conditions, however, are highly heterogeneous and do not cluster around two distinctive groups that could be captured with the labels of 'old' or 'new' risk groups. At least when it comes to 'new' risk groups, there are in fact multiple groups with rather different character-istics and somewhat diverging social policy preference functions. The het-erogeneity of market conditions may make it difficult even for those groups exposed to one or another of the 'new' risks to agree on similar policies. Some new risk groups may favor different redistributive remedies to the deprivations they expect to suffer under conditions of pure market allocation than others. This is what our analysis in this chapter suggests.

But the heterogeneity of new risk groups may subvert their ability to coalesce around joint policy goals in a more fundamental way if the following three conditions hold jointly. First, the attributes that character-ize new risk groups are also systematically associated with other salient non-economic political preferences that concern questions of political or socio-cultural governance, for example modes of political participation, rules safeguarding the personal autonomy of lifestyles, cultural group pluralism, and societal investments in collective goods that affect social consumption patterns beyond income ('superior goods'). Second, new risk groups that vigorously support income redistribution in one or another form disagree sharply in their preferences over those other salient political and socio-cultural preferences. And third, these disagreements are conse-quential for the kinds of political agents (legislative representatives bundled in political parties offering different policy programs) that indi-viduals with new risk attributes are likely to choose in the arena of elect-oral competition.

Elsewhere, we have shown that these three propositions are empirically accurate (Kitschelt and Rehm 2004). Different bearer groups of new social risks opt not only for different political-cultural preferences, but also for rather different parties. In fact, because of the weight of political-cultural interests in respondents' preference schedules, majorities in some new risk groups appear to support political partisan alternatives that manifestly oppose their well-considered social policy interests. People who appear jointly under the label of new social risk bearers, such as single mothers or young males with little education and few skills, may end up voicing parti-san interests that are diametrically opposed to each other.

In this chapter we will rely on ISSP's 'Role of Government III' data-set (1996). However, in our effort to identify the origins of preferences over alternative social policies and relate new risk groups to new social policy remedies, data constraints leave us unable to explore all relevant facets of the phenomenon. Thus, we are unable to cover specifically preferences over policies as well as individual risk conditions that address (1) the expensive and time-consuming care of elderly frail parents, such as long-term care insurance and elderly care services; (2) the increasingly labor- and capital-intensive process of raising children in a society that requires children to acquire a great deal of social and human capital during their upbringing in order to become successful labor market participants as adults, such as childcare facilities and parental leave policies; and (3) the need for retraining due to structural economic change that makes skills and whole industries obsolete over time. What we can do regarding the policy preferences is to treat these risks as exemplars of broader risk classes, some of whose elements we can investigate empirically because we have survey questions on people's preferences over related social policy issues. With respect to risk conditions, we can rely on general traits of respondents that may tap their exposure to new risks, such as their age, gender, involvement in raising children in a single-parent household or their education. Yet having any of the broader traits (identified in terms of age, gender, education...) may make respondents *expect* to cope with new risks at some point in their not too distant future and therefore build such expectations into their policy preference schedules. Indeed, we think it is a promising area of future research to coherently incorporate individual expectations into comparative attitudinal research.

At this point, let us clarify what we do and do not need to assume about the rationality of individual citizens in processing information about their effective risk situation in a capitalist market society. As long as critical minorities in each risk class have a keen understanding of their risk conditions and of the policies that improve their risk exposure, we should find systematic statistical relations between aggregate group characteristics and policy preferences, *even if* the vast majority of citizens have a poor understanding of their interests, which makes them voice policy preferences in a randomized fashion. A minority of 'rational information misers' is all that is needed in order to produce what look like rational relations at the level of population aggregates (cf. Erikson *et al.* 2002). As a consequence, individual-level regressions of respondents' traits on policy preferences yield a modest explained variance not only because of rampant measurement error but also because of the limited share of rational information misers in mass publics. If, however, we cannot find any relationship at all between citizens' market-relevant traits and social policy preferences, this would cast doubt on the validity of our rational information miser thesis.

We begin the chapter by distinguishing a variety of market risk conditions and policies that can address them through the authoritative redistribution of resources. Some of these conditions may be labeled 'new' simply because they have affected quantitatively greater proportions of the population in recent decades. In the second section we detail a variety of personal and social attributes that make citizens more or less vulnerable to such risk conditions. Our hypotheses in each case stipulate that traits that indicate high vulnerability prompt preferences to support policies that reduce such vulnerabilities. After operationalizing our variables in the third section, we test the relationship between citizens' risk conditions and their preferences concerning policies that address such conditions in a set of advanced post-industrial capitalist democracies with data collected by the International Social Science Program (ISSP) in 1996. Following a concluding section, the appendix contains additional tables.

Risk conditions

Let us distinguish different risk conditions, some of which become particularly pronounced in post-industrial societies. Likely risk exposure is spread over different kinds of social constituencies, characterized by specific occupational profiles, exposure to organizational governance structures, patterns of demographic reproduction and socio-cultural consumption. Let us first state what we believe are socio-economic conditions in post-industrial capitalism that generate market risks.

In terms of *occupational profiles*, in such societies there is an increasing demand for labor market participants with very high analytical, social and cultural skills. Individuals acquire and refine such skills in a process of life-long learning to cope with ever-changing intellectual, social and managerial problems in a creative fashion. As long as the absolute and relative demand for such skills is growing, the market rewards that individuals derive from their human capital will be increasing.

In terms of *organizational task and governance structures*, post-industrial societies rely on work organizations and associational networks in which the interactive management of people – customers, clients, co-workers, supervisors and subordinates – occupies an increasing share of people's work time. 'Pedagogical' and symbolic-cultural activities that attempt to affect other people's skills, preferences and even self-conceptions become a vital part of many employees' job experience. The processing of material and intellectual objects is still decisive for many jobs, but becomes less pronounced at the margin, as symbolic-interactive tasks gain ground.

In terms of *demographic reproduction*, post-industrial society requires time-consuming and expensive efforts to treat non-labor market participants, i.e. children and the elderly. The opportunity costs for raising children due to lost market income are becoming greater, both because it is becoming more expensive to raise children and because the wage losses due to childcare activities are becoming greater. The proportion of elderly retirees in the population is rising with increasing life expectancy due to better hygiene, diets, medical care and occupational conditions, and lifestyles characterized by health awareness. Consequently, health and pension expenses associated with their upkeep are sky-rocketing as well.

In terms of *socio-cultural consumption*, after basic needs for food, shelter and social networks have been met, people's aspirations focus on ever more sophisticated goods, and especially on services delivering social and cultural experiences, many of which are often associated with the enjoyment of collective goods (e.g. clean environments and natural attractions, interesting cultural spaces in urban areas). The occupational, organizational and demographic properties of post-industrial societies are directly relevant for people's formation of social policy preferences. Let us characterize four risk classes and associated policies.

General existential risks: inability to work due to illness and old age

Most members of society, regardless of asset endowments or occupational location, are likely to become ill or grow old at some point in time. At least as long as genetic testing is unavailable or not permitted to sort individuals into different risk classes, over one's lifetime everyone faces equivalent actuarial risk profiles. Young people may discount these risks to some degree. Women may have slightly lower discount rates, as they have longer life expectancy. Furthermore, with regard to new social risks, the culturally defined role of women in family reproduction still makes them more likely to shoulder the burden of caring for elderly parents.

The wide dispersal of general existential risks may make it politically easier to devise pension and healthcare policies that are universalistic: risk pooling is in everybody's interest. This contrasts with areas of risk exposure that are clearly differentiated across social groups separated by relatively high degrees of closure, i.e. boundaries that are difficult to overcome through social mobility during one's life course, or even intergenerational mobility.

Group-specific risks I: obsolescence of skills due to structural change

Whether self-employed or wage-earning, people may face higher risks of losing their labor-based income if they have invested in skills that cannot be redeployed easily should demand for their services decline. In a similar vein, people with a lack of skills are facing dim prospects in post-industrial societies with a marginally declining reliance on low-skilled labor.

The high incidence of unemployment or wages near to or below the poverty line is a manifestation of the risks incurred by people with low or obsolescent skills. Social policies to remedy such conditions include generous unemployment benefits, redistributive income taxes or negative income taxes for the poor, means-tested welfare payments, retraining programs and, more generally, educational subsidies for the poor. Policy support can also accrue to companies that are in risk of shedding asset-poor or asset-specific labor. Such measures include subsidies and corporate tax relief, as well as regulatory or external trade measures (tariffs, quotas) to protect firms from cheaper competitors.

Rapid structural economic change that makes existing skills worthless and calls for the rapid acquisition of new skills may contribute to the growth of the welfare state (Iversen and Cusack 2000). More specifically, in democracies that do not restrict the mobilization of special interests, but have opted for free trade in an environment of high external exposure, politicians sooner or later are compelled to compensate particularly risk-exposed categories of citizens with social policy protection (Katzenstein 1985; Adserà and Boix 2002).

Trade exposure is hardly a new social risk, but it hits different economic sectors and occupational skills over time. What is a new social risk, however, is the relatively and even absolutely declining income stream accruing to people in low-skilled jobs, documented by the gradual fall in real wages for unskilled workers and increasing income inequality in most post-industrial societies over the past 20–30 years.

Overall, because of the targeted, specific nature of the labor market groups and industries affected by skill obsolescence, politicians might find it harder to craft general policies around such concerns. Two exceptions to this rule may exist. First, very export-exposed countries distribute the actuarial risks of losing one's employment due to skill obsolescence sufficiently to generate universalistic policies (see earlier). By contrast, where actuarial risks are highly concentrated, politicians may tailor protective measures to the needs of small specific groups *provided* the support of such groups is vital for their electoral survival and *provided* the costs of such policy measures can be contained and widely dispersed across the general public.[1]

Group-specific risks II: the uncertain returns on higher education

On average, higher education yields generous economic returns in terms of lifetime incomes. But the distribution of these returns is widely dispersed, making such education a risky proposition. Of course, the risks of not earning a comfortable living based on one's educational achievements are much higher in some fields (comparative literature, art history, political science...) than others (law, business, mathematics...). Nevertheless, the dispersal of educational rewards is sufficiently high to make social groups whose members and offspring are particularly able and inclined to seek out higher education call for public policies that reduce the cost of such investments and thus increase the expected private benefit of such education. Because of problems of adverse selection and moral hazard, private insurance is not available to protect against the loss of income due to failure to turn the expense of an advanced educational degree into a lifetime stream of higher earnings.

In some ways, the risk structure on education and the policies addressing that risk structure have the opposite distributive implications as compared with social policies addressing the risks of skill obsolescence. Whereas the latter target poor and destitute people and may yield a progressive redistribution of income, public investments in higher education resulting in lower education costs for students *de facto* redistribute income to the affluent, as long as the affluent are most intent and able to have their offspring take advantage of public facilities of higher education.

Group-specific risks III: loss of earnings due to demographic reproduction

The risks of raising children shares with other group-specific risks the characteristic that not all members of society opt into this risk. With general risks, it shares the trait that once people have opted into the risk of having children, very large categories of people face broadly similar cost and risk exposure. Furthermore, with general risks it shares the socio-cultural demographic characteristic that women are particularly exposed, as long as prevailing tacit social norms expect them to deliver most of the labor input to sustain demographic reproduction.

Policies that address demographic redistribution include child subsidies, public funding for childcare facilities, parental leave policies, and parental protection in labor contracts (time off work for childcare). We have no items concerning these issues in the empirical survey data we are employing. But given the risk profile of demographic reproduction, social policy preferences over general life course risk and the specific risk of skill obsolescence should give us a pretty good idea of how policy preferences over ways to cope with demographic risk are distributed.

Risk groups

Political sociology, from Marx, Durkheim and Weber to Erikson and Goldthorpe (1992), has always strived to construct a relationship between people's 'objective' insertion in the social structure ('class in itself') and their political consciousness ('class for itself'), expressed in political preference schedules, partisan choices, and associated cognitive constructs about the relationship between socio-economic position, policy preferences and efficient collective political strategies to realize the latter ('ideologies'). But the class categories of conventional political sociology have insufficiently reflected the variety of risks to which citizens are exposed in markets and the organizational conditions under which citizens process information about risks in markets. In this section we will discuss what we think are the varieties of risks that individuals are exposed to. In doing so, we derive hypotheses that we will test in the following section (see Table 3.1).

The *Marxist* class conception involves a pretty clear risk logic. Those who own the means of production can protect themselves better than can workers from the general risks of life and from the obsolescence of skills. But this theory turned out to be too simplistic to explain the formation of citizens' preference schedules. First Marx himself noted the conservatism of the 'British worker', and subsequently many Marxists and non-Marxists resorted to cultural or 'false consciousness' explanations, for example about the relationship between a religious outlook and the absence of class consciousness. Further ancillary theories focused on the work experience in large factories and the association with labor unions as facilitators of class consciousness.

But these ancillary theories contradicting Marx's original insights moved the locus of political preference formation for the most part away from the economic sphere of markets and work organizations. With the revisionist socialists and Max Weber in the early decades of the twentieth century, and later with the sociology of organization and technocracy from the 1920s to the 1950s, scholars returned to an analysis of political preference formation at the workplace. Max Weber provided at least two important propositions. First, in addition to ownership of the means of production, a variety of asset types, such as education or social networks, are likely to affect people's market income and therefore may account for actors' political preferences and thus ultimately their class consciousness. In other words, 'market classes', as categories of people with similar assets they can convert into income flows in a market, do not necessarily coincide with 'property classes'. Second, the political consciousness of actors may depend on their location in the hierarchy of a work organization. Those in positions of command, whether they do or do not own the means of production, are involved in the execution of a logic of capital accumulation and as such will embrace capitalist preferences.[2] Furthermore, those at the bottom of the hierarchy of command, but tied into the command process on a daily basis, such as the administrative workforce, also tend to assert a logic of capital accumulation, even though in a diluted or muted fashion, rather than a proletarian class consciousness. This idea gave rise to the sociology of white-collar employee politics and the division between manual and intellectual labor that was also anticipated in Marx's sociologically never fully developed division between value-creating, productive manual labor and value-consuming, unproductive non-manual labor. These divisions later influence the *ad hoc* division of societal groups into seven class categories proposed by Goldthorpe and authoritatively developed by Erikson and Goldthorpe (1992), distinguishing between manual and non-manual labor and, within each category, routine, skilled and directive work, plus a category for directive professionals ('service class 1') and small independents. This categorization has dominated most empirical survey instruments since the 1960s.

The most fruitful work in Weber's succession has been carried out by people such as Dahrendorf (1959) and Erik Olin Wright (1985), who in different fashions tried to combine a consideration of citizens' market assets and their location in the organizational command structure as sources of class consciousness, expressed in distinctive political preference schedules. Our own categorization of risk groups builds on, but modifies and extends, these insights with ideas one might place in the genealogy of works by Bourdieu (1977) and Habermas (1982), namely that the concrete practice of social interaction in the workplace leaves an imprint on citizens' political consciousness. Furthermore, it considers the demographic distribution of risks, something none of the classical theories of political preference formation deemed necessary, although until the advent of feminist theory there were always *ad hoc* assertions about the unique consciousness of women.

Let us now review different elements of people's market and organizational situation as contributors to their political preference schedules over the four components of social policy introduced in the previous section. We set aside trade-related hypotheses about the international comparative advantages of factor ownership (capital, labor, land) or sectoral employment (export-exposed versus sheltered sectors, relative competitiveness of the exposed sector). These hypotheses cannot be tested with our data-set (see Mayda and Rodrik 2005, and Rehm 2004 for contradictory results on this).

Property classes

We are going back here to the Marxist notion of class in capitalism as identified by market participants' dependence on or autonomy from earning income by selling their labor. While we have no data on property distribution, empirical studies show a strong correlation between property and income. Property distribution, in fact, is much more concentrated than income. It increases exponentially with income. Income, then, is a tracer of property classes. It is a better tracer of property classes than self-employment, because the mass of the self-employed tend to be marginal small owners without employees.[3] Many members of the latter category may have an almost 'proletarian' market location in terms of asset control and income.

High property ownership predisposes individuals against hedging strategies through authoritative social policy of any kind, whether they involve only risk pooling against general existential risks or income redistribution in favor of specific vulnerable risk groups. High income should correlate with a rejection of social policy claims of any kind.

Market classes

Market classes are distinguished by asset distributions they can bring to bear on their market income. If we control for income, and thus indirectly property, we are here dealing primarily with the residual that captures the *uncertainty and volatility of market-derived income flows*. The greater that uncertainty, the more citizens call for hedging strategies that may involve public policies to protect them from market risks.

There are at least four conditions that affect the (un)certainty of market-derived income flows:

1   *Education:* Higher education implies greater cognitive capacities to cope with new and different work situations. Higher education

reduces market risks due to unemployment and demographic reproduction, as it is easier for highly educated people to arrange flexible
work times. Higher education, however, predisposes respondents to
demand greater hedging towards risks of acquiring higher education,
because respondents themselves and their offspring are much more
likely to seek out such education and to welcome protection against
the uncertainty of pay-offs in higher education.

2   *Sectoral employment, exposure to hard budget constraint:* Individuals
    employed in market-exposed sectors may express marginally less
    demand for protection from general existential risks than people
    employed in non-profit and public sectors.[4] Only the former can go
    bankrupt, when labor costs exceed revenue. Furthermore, non-profit
    and public-sector employment benefits directly, in terms of employ-
    ment, from strong expenditure on protection from general existential
    risks, particularly in the area of healthcare. The same logic may also
    predispose employees in non-market-exposed sectors, such as public
    education and social services dealing with demographic risks (child-
    care, elder care), to call for more public policies of risk pooling and
    risk redistribution, while private-sector respondents are more con-
    cerned with the costs of such policies (see Armingeon 2004). By con-
    trast, it is private-sector employees who may be more apprehensive
    concerning the need for a generous risk-pooling scheme for unem-
    ployment insurance than non-profit sector respondents, who generally
    face much lower risks of losing their jobs. Unfortunately, the data-set
    we are using lacks 'clean' variables on these issues. Therefore, we will
    not be able to test these hypotheses.

3   *Asset-specific skills:* Net of income, general education and non-profit
    employment, market participants with highly specific skills that allow
    them to search for alternative employment only in a vanishingly small
    labor market segment, if they lose their job, should ask for more risk-
    hedging – pooling and redistributing protection from the risks of skill
    obsolescence – than other groups. The exposure to risk 'is inversely
    related to the portability of skills' (Iversen and Soskice 2001: 875). The
    fewer options individuals have to earn a return on their skill invest-
    ments, the more they will be worried about their prospective income
    flows derived purely from voluntary market transactions.

4   *Labor market status: unemployment and non-employment:* Net of
    other conditions, the unemployed, defined as people who seek but
    cannot find employment, will be most concerned about risk-hedging
    strategies toward unemployment and possibly toward means-tested
    income redistribution, but will not substantially differ from everyone
    else on policies addressing general existential, educational and demo-
    graphic risks. Non-employment, finally, is a residual, amorphous cat-
    egory that combines a heterogeneous aggregate of conditions, ranging
    from discouraged workers via homemakers and retirees all the way to

independently wealthy rentiers. Net of discouraged workers and retirees, for whom we partially control with the age variable, the category may primarily encompass people living under sufficiently affluent conditions to predispose them against a variety of public policy measures.

Demographics and market classes

Market conditions affect people both as producers and as consumers. When it comes to demographic risks, there are likely to be different consumer groups, characterized by age and gender, with different demand preferences for risk-pooling and redistributing public policies. For obvious reasons, *older* people will articulate a greater concern about general existential risk-pooling social policy programs such as public pension and healthcare insurance. Insofar as people aged above 40 are in labor markets, they will also be more concerned about hedging against risks of skill obsolescence, which is harder to overcome through retraining at a more advanced age. By contrast, older people will express fewer sympathies for investments in general education – specifically, higher education – and have a mixed profile on policies toward demographic risks: elder care yes, childcare no.

Gender also has distinctive impact on preferences over social policy, as long as we accept the premises that (1) culturally gendered division of labor in the realm of demographic reproduction prevails and allocates most of the family work to women; and (2) women tend to have longer life expectancies than men. Under these conditions it is likely that women will express substantially stronger preferences for social policies that address general existential risks, demographic risks and educational risks (to cover their children) than men. There may be little gender difference, however, with regard to the risks of low skill or skill obsolescence.

Command and (self-)control: organizational practice and preference formation

Political preferences over social policies may finally be influenced by concrete experiences in work organizations that shape employees' exposure to the logic of capital accumulation in markets. Building on Oesch's (forthcoming) unpublished paper, we propose a two-dimensional scheme to distinguish experiences in work organizations. While Oesch's fine categorizations highlight important distinctions, we operate with a rougher trichotomy for the purposes of our chapter. Although we propose to slightly alter this trichotomy when it comes to socio-cultural (as opposed to social policy) preferences, we will not do so in this chapter (see Kitschelt and Rehm 2004).

The *first* dimension distinguishes individuals based on a hierarchy of rank that reaches from the top, where individuals make strategic decisions over the allocation of scarce resources, to the bottom, where they execute them according to specific commands or general rules. This dimension builds on Dahrendorf's and E.O. Wright's insistence that the exercise of authority ('command') shapes social relations, net of property relations, income or education. Those who allocate scarce resources wish to devise incentive systems that limit the dissipation of resources further down the hierarchy and focus effort on organizational goals set by the chief executives, whether they are individuals or collegial boards, as in law and financial firms or even university departments. Market-based incentives systems and constraints help those at the top to discipline their subordinates. Whoever stands at the apex of an organizational ladder is more inclined to abide by the imperatives of efficient resource allocation than are those at the bottom. In social policy terms there will be less sympathy with risk-pooling and egalitarian redistributive policies among those high up in the command structure of a hierarchy than among those at the bottom.

But there is a *second* horizontal division that can relate more to Weber's distinction between formal and substantive rationality, but may also be captured by Bourdieu's (1977) concept of 'habitus' or Habermas's (1982) distinction between instrumental-strategic and symbolic-interactive orientations ('control'). There are distinct task structures or fields of occupational practice that may generate or at least reinforce diverse preference schedules actors adopt when considering social and economic policy-making. On the one hand, there are *administrative-managerial* and *entrepreneurial* activities centered on the formal-rational logic of capital accounting that preoccupy executives as well as their rank-and-file operators in corporate management. On the other hand, there are jobs that emphasize a substantive rationality of producing some object, process or service governed by purely *technical* considerations or by *social criteria of interaction* with clients and customers. Actors working in technical environments, but especially those located in social-interactive environments, may act in accordance with internal professional criteria of performance that ignore or diverge from imperatives of formal capital accounting concerned with the profitability of firms engaged in market competition. In other words, they follow logics of action, together with professional and situative performance standards, that are more or less autonomous from rationales of formal capital accounting, regardless of whether they are in positions of authority or not.

Cross-tabling the positions in the organizational hierarchy ('command') against the task structures of work organization and occupations ('control'), and subdividing further according to the prescripts of Oesch (forthcoming), we obtain Figure 3.1 with a total of 17 cells (see also Table A-3.1).

While we lose information and some explanatory power by aggregating these cells into fewer categories, the virtues of parsimony may recommend some simplification. First, there are positions where both organizational practices of command and control lead us to predict an orientation toward a logic of capital accumulation, resulting in hostility toward risk-pooling and egalitarian redistribution through social policy. The white cells in Figure 3.1 indicate this region of *capital accumulators*. Note that we added top levels of engineers and scientist to this logic as well, as they are typically involved in managerial activities.

At the contrasting opposite pole are participants in the workforce who are at the bottom of organizational hierarchies and also relatively insulated from the formal logic of capital accounting by following substantive domain-specific discretionary practices and routines. Among these *routine operators* in the dark-shaded cells of manufacturing and services we would expect most sympathy for redistributive social policy. In between are light gray fields with positions of rather heterogeneous complexion (*intermediate occupations or mixed service functionaries*). What they have in common is that one of the two dimensions of organizational practice – either the dimension of command hierarchy or the dimension of control of work practices – leads us to predict redistributive social policy orientations, while the other does not. For our empirical analysis of social policy positions, this mixed group of employees in diverse service-sector jobs with intermediate combinations of control and command may serve as the reference category from which to estimate the net effect of organizational experiences on social policy preference schedules.

A glance at Figure 3.1 immediately tells us that there is some correlation between the occupational location in white, light gray or dark gray fields with other class categorizations such as income, education, asset specificity and possibly gender. In fact, in order to calculate the net effect of organizational experiences, as characterized by practices of command and control, on social policy preferences, we need to control for property and market classes, as well as for demographic factors. The crucial issue is whether there is any net effect of organizational practices of occupational experiences, once we have controlled for the more obvious class attributes.

A landscape of risk and preference distributions

Table 3.1 summarizes our predictions over four types of social policies and numerous attributes that characterize citizens' socio-economic situation.

Figure 3.1 Differentiation of vertical hierarchy ('command') and horizontal task structures ('self-control') in the occupational profile of affluent democracies (source: ISSP 1996, occupational coding by Oesch 2003 from ISCO-88 (see appendix, Table A-3.1); here, covers 12 countries: Australia, Britain, Canada, France, Germany (West), Germany (East), Ireland, New Zealand, Norway, Sweden, Switzerland and the United States).

Note
Capital accumulators (white): 3,328 (27.1%); *mixed service functionaries* (light gray): 4,315 (35.2%); *routine operators*: 4,629 (37.8%).

	FORMAL LOGIC OF CAPITAL ACCOUNTING (external control of organizational practices)	TASK STRUCTURES OF WORK ORGANIZATIONS AND OCCUPATIONS ('control')			SUBSTANTIVE TECHNICAL OR CLIENT-INTERACTIVE STANDARDS (internal control of organizational practices)
	Managerial-administrative context	Entrepreneurial logic of self-employment		Technical logic of performance in production and innovation	Symbolic-interactive logic of client services
HIGH COMMAND	Higher-grade managers 9.7% (n=1,192)	Large employer 1.2% (n=155)	Self-employed professionals 0.8% (n=101)	Technical experts 5.5% (n=676)	Socio-cultural professionals 7.5% (n=924)
POSITION IN THE ORGANIZATIONAL HIERARCHY	Associate managers 8.7% (n=892)	Petty bourgeoisie with employees 2.5% (n=312)		Technicians 4.4% (n=545)	Socio-cultural semi-professionals 6.1% (n=754)
	Skilled office workers 9.9% (n=1,223)	Petty bourgeoisie without employees 5.2% (n=643)		Skilled crafts 12.7% (n=1,557)	Skilled service 3.3% (n=407)
LOW COMMAND	Routine office workers (n=226)	Empty category		Routine operatives 6.9% (n=843) / Routine agriculture 2.1% (n=256)	Routine service 12.7% (n=1,566)

Most interesting may be those attributes that yield heterogeneous predictions over the range of risk-pooling and reward-redistributing social policies. Highly educated people may reject redistributive policies save those that address the uncertainties of returns on educational investments. Asset specificity should only affect preferences over policies insuring people against the consequences of weak or obsolete skills, such as unemployment insurance and general income redistribution. The unemployed stand out with regard to unemployment insurance. Older people are partial to policies that boost the size and security of their revenue flows (pensions, healthcare, unemployment and income redistribution, elder care), but not those of others (education, childcare). Women are more positive on just about all policies, except risks due to weak and obsolete skills.

In light of the table, let us also reflect on the homogeneity and heterogeneity of new risk groups. There is obvious diversity, if not conflict, among new risk groups contingent upon age and gender. Let us identify three 'poles' of new risk groups that show rather different risk profiles. Let us take predicted preference schedules of three ideal-typical groups, characterized by attributes that place them in market classes and demographic categories and that highlight 'new' social risks. The first group is constituted by young, less educated males whose income has eroded and who are exposed to high risks of unemployment. The second group are younger, well-educated females who may be most concerned about raising children and caring for elderly parents. Third, there are elderly, less educated men who are mostly concerned about retirement and general existential risks. For heuristic purposes one could add up the expected direction of support for different social policies from each of these groups. Performing this heuristic exercise would demonstrate that group interests vary quite substantially across groups and across policy areas. If we were to confirm this pattern empirically, it would make it unlikely that 'new' social risk groups could ever be more than a statistical category. Disagreements over public policies among different elements of the 'new' social risk constituencies are sufficiently deep to make it all but impossible to expect a pooling of resources in the pursuit of joint collective action to promote agreed-upon policy objectives.

Variable operationalization

We are working with the ISSP's 'Role of Government III' data-set (1996). Critically for our purpose, the survey yields detailed policy preferences questions as well as the occupational ISCO codings, for 12 advanced post-industrial democracies: Australia, Britain, Canada, France, East Germany, West Germany, Ireland, New Zealand, Norway, Sweden, Switzerland and the United States. Insufficient data are available for Austria, Belgium, Denmark, Italy, Japan and the Netherlands, to mention the remaining important wealthy capitalist democracies.

Table 3.1 Risk groups and risk remedies: support of social policy: theoretical predictions

		General existential risks (health, old age)	Group-specific risk i: weak and obsolescent skills	Group-specific risk ii: uncertainty of educational investment	Group-specific risk iii: demographic risks (childcare, elder care)
Property classes	Income	Negative	Negative	Negative	Negative
Market classes	Education	Negative	Negative	Positive	Negative/neutral
	Market exposure	Negative	Positive	Negative	Neutral
	Asset-specific skills	Neutral	Positive	Neutral	Neutral
	Unemployed	Neutral	Positive	Neutral	Neutral
	Non-employed	Neutral/negative	Neutral/negative	Neutral/negative	Neutral/negative
Demographic traits	Age	Positive	Positive/neutral	Negative	Negative/positive
	Gender: female	Positive	Neutral	Positive	Positive
Organizational practices and experiences	Capital accumulators	Negative	Negative	Negative	Negative
	Routine operators	Positive	Positive	Neutral	Positive
	Intermediate occupations	Neutral	Neutral	Neutral	Neutral

For each of three dimensions of social policy, save the coverage of demographic risks, for which there are no items in the questionnaire, we have chosen one representative policy item as the *dependent variable*. Exploratory and confirmatory factor analyses show that these items load highly on underlying dimensions together with other policy issues belonging to the same class of social policy risks.[5] For general existential risks, we take a question on *government spending for healthcare* (v26), while we could have also taken a question on government policy vis-à-vis old age pensions (v30). For specific group risks due to low or obsolescent skills, we have a whole range of issue items that cover redistributive policies toward weak market groups. We have here selected an item concerning *government spending for unemployment benefits* (v31), although we could just as well have chosen another item on unemployment benefits (v41), or items concerning government policy to reduce income inequality (v16 and v42), government policy to create jobs (v24 and v36) and even targeted assistance to the less well off through public housing (v44) and financial help to university students from low-income families (v43).[6]

For group-specific risks II, uncertainties of returns to educational investments, we have a related issue on *government educational expenditure* (v28). Interestingly, response patterns on that item do not co-vary much with the group-specific risk I battery concerning means-tested benefits to the less well off. Instead, respondents' preferences on education co-vary with preferences for environmental protection and preferences for expenditures promoting culture and the arts, suggesting that this variable does not map onto the redistributional dimension of advanced capitalist party systems.

As we have indicated, we do not have questions directly tapping the new risks due to the impending demographic revolution, such as childcare and especially elder care. We can glean likely response patterns only from what we know about other general and group-specific risks.

Table 3.2 provides information about the univariate distribution of responses on the three policy items in the survey. As one might expect, on

Table 3.2 Public preferences concerning social policies

	General existential risks (health, old age)	Group-specific risk i: weak and obsolescent skills	Group-specific risk ii: uncertainty of educational investment
Spend much more	23.5%	7.6%	21.0%
Spend more	44.6%	22.2%	43.6%
Spend the same as now	26.8%	47.5%	31.5%
Spend less	4.5%	17.5%	3.2%
Spend much less	0.7%	5.2%	0.7%
n	19,646	19,338	19,491

general existential risks (i.e. health expenditures) the distribution of responses is more skewed toward greater expenses than on the group-specific risks of unemployment. The pattern on education looks similar to that on healthcare, with almost two-thirds of respondents advocating mild or vigorous expansion of public investment. Nevertheless, even on these two items the response patterns reveal substantial variance that deserves exploration.

Table A-3.2 provides information about the operationalization of all *independent variables*, except the 'command and control' organizational experiences we have already discussed (see Figure 3.1). In order to probe into patterns of unique new social risk exposure, we also created dummy variables for two of the three groups that define the 'poles' of the new social risk groups: young, less educated males and young, highly educated females. We should keep in mind, however, that an insignificant coefficient on any of these dummies only means that there is no synergetic effect of the variable combinations. New risks may still matter in that individual variables (age, gender, education) affect people's responses on risk items.

Initial estimations also included 'single-parent households' as a predictor of social policy preferences and as one common new social risk condition. Including this item results in the loss of over 30 percent of all cases. Furthermore, no single regression we ran with this variable included yielded anything significant. Heads of single-parent households have preferences that are very similar to those of all female respondents.

For the operationalizations of skill specificity, we follow Iversen and Soskice's (2001) seminal analysis; see Table A-3.3 for a detailed discussion.

For each dependent variable, we estimate two specifications. The first contains just our theoretically relevant variables, with predictions as outlined in Table 3.1, plus country dummies for 11 countries, organized by the type of welfare state that prevails in them. Britain is our reference category. We do not have the space here to analyze and discuss the contextual effects that the nature of established welfare states may exercise in shaping national preference distributions over social policies. Nevertheless, we estimate fixed effects; the country dummies are needed to extract national idiosyncrasies in order to highlight the political-economic- and social structure-based patterns of preference formation. Since there are no strong expectations a priori regarding the country effects, and in order to economize on space, we will not discuss results related to the country dummies.

The second equation for each dependent variable also includes two associational practices of respondents. The first concerns their religion, the second labor union membership. The theory behind these controls is that voluntary associations can play a key role in shaping citizens' political preference orientations. If this is the case, church attendance or union membership should produce an independent effect on citizens' preferences over social policy alternatives, net of political-economic and social structural background variables. Furthermore, the associational variables should not substantially reduce the effects of the political-economic and structural variables. If, however, associational variables are explanatory only because they soak up variance otherwise explained by the background variables, or if they are statistically insignificant and insubstantial, then associational practices are irrelevant.

Since our dependent variables are ordinal (five answer categories), we have estimated the multiple regressions of policy preferences on our independent variables with ordered probit regressions.[7] Furthermore, we have run separate regressions for each country. Given the relatively small samples to work with, many of the effects observed in the pooled analysis become statistically insignificant at the country level. We found no single country, however, in which the pattern of coefficients contradicts the aggregate-level findings. Typically, most or all of the coefficients have the same sign as at the aggregate level. The few coefficients that have a different sign are small and insignificant.[8]

Results: how risk groups relate to risk conditions

Table 3.3 provides the results of the multiple regression ordered probit estimations of the determinants of social policy issues we discussed above. With regard to general existential risks, represented by *public healthcare expenditures* (Table 3.3, model 1), our statistics reveal significant effects in the expected direction (low values on the dependent variables stand for approval of higher expenditures). Less well educated, lower-income, older women (but not older men), particularly if they are labor force participants and if they are not in the occupational categories covering 'capital accumulators', are sympathetic to a further expansion of the welfare state. Note that for general existential risks, which in most countries translate into universalistic insurance programs covering the entire population, asset specificity of skills does not matter. This result appears to us to be in the spirit of Iversen and Soskice's (2001) theory, *although* their article tries to establish an empirical link between preferences over social policies that do not directly address skill-based labor market vulnerabilities and the presence of asset-specific skill endowments.

Union membership more than church attendance shows systematic association with preferences over social policies addressing general existential risks (Table 3.3, model 2). They do not measurably subtract from the coefficients obtained in the first equation on the other political-economic and social structural background variables. Organizational association thus has a net preference effect, although we cannot determine whether this is based on self-selection (entry) or intra-organizational socialization.

With regard to the specific risks of low skill and skill obsolescence, resulting in unemployment, the variable set that makes a difference is broader than in the case of general socio-demographic risks and social policies addressing them. To judge by the response pattern on opinions concerning *expenditures for unemployment insurance*, all the usual suspects matter in the expected way (see Table 3.3, models 3 and 4). Having higher income and education, and being young, male and a 'capital accumulator', are all conditions that make people less inclined to endorse higher expenditures. Older respondents, particularly if from the occupational group of manual routine operators, tend to endorse more government expenditure for unemployment insurance. In a similar vein there is a marginally statistically significant relation between respondents' occupational asset specificity, on the one hand, and their support for a generous funding of unemployment insurance. In line with Iversen and Soskice's original setup, we would expect to find this statistical relationship even when occupational asset specificity is not associated with support for public social policies that help people to hedge against general existential risks. However, the relationship is not very robust.

Our third dependent variable, preferences over more *general educational government expenditure*, reveals a rather different response pattern (Table 3.3, models 5 and 6). The findings suggest that more educational expenditure, particularly in higher education, provides a risk-hedging strategy primarily for the more affluent and educated, who are more likely to benefit directly from educational learning opportunities or indirectly by way of their offspring being more likely to take advantage of public funding for institutions of higher learning. As a consequence, the effect of higher income and membership in the group of 'capital accumulators' is only marginally negative for general education policy, once appropriate statistical controls are applied. Furthermore, better-educated people embrace more educational expenditure, especially those in occupational categories whose entry particularly calls for formal certificates in higher education, such as independently employed financial and economic professionals as well as (semi-)professionals in client-interactive and cultural occupations. How the logic of self-interest affects evaluations of educational expenditure shows up also in the predictive power of respondents' demographics, such as age and gender. Older people are substantially less willing to see educational expenditures rise. By contrast, women put greater emphasis on educational expenditures than men, presumably because of their greater involvement in children's upbringing.

Our theoretical argument expects a number of socio-demographic attributes not to matter for people's preferences over general educational expenditures. This applies to the asset specificity of skills, adherence to the occupational category of routine operators, unemployment, and membership in particular new social risk categories. None of these variables actually matters as a predictor of preferences over educational expenditures. This creates an interesting contrast to the support patterns for group-specific risk reduction with regard to low and obsolescent skills.

Table 3.3 Determinants of policy preferences

		Govmnt spend: health (v26)[a]		Govmnt spend: unempl. benefit (v31)[a]		Govmnt spend: education (v28)[a]	
		(1)	(2)	(3)	(4)	(5)	(6)
Property classes	Income (households, in 20 groups)	0.017 (0.002)**	0.022 (0.003)**	0.024 (0.002)**	0.026 (0.003)**	0.003 (0.002)	0.003 (0.003)
Market classes	Education (highest degree)	0.065 (0.010)**	0.101 (0.013)**	0.016 (0.010)	0.052 (0.012)**	−0.047 (0.010)**	−0.038 (0.013)**
	Skill specificity, comp.[b]	0.019 (0.014)	0.005 (0.019)	−0.023 (0.014)	−0.044 (0.018)*	−0.005 (0.014)	−0.012 (0.019)
	Unemployed	−0.004 (0.055)	0.005 (0.078)	−0.407 (0.054)**	−0.64 (0.077)**	0.034 (0.054)	−0.039 (0.077)
	Non-employed	0.119 (0.033)**	0.122 (0.042)**	0.095 (0.033)**	0.03 (0.034)	0.044 (0.033)	−0.001 (0.041)
Demographic traits	Age	0 (0.001)	−0.003 (0.001)	−0.004 (0.001)	−0.004 (0.001)	0.004 (0.001)**	0.005 (0.001)**
	Female	−0.408 (0.076)**	−0.408 (0.096)**	−0.348 (0.075)**	−0.343 (0.095)**	−0.232 (0.076)**	−0.167 (0.096)
	Age * Female	0.005 (0.002)**	0.004 (0.002)	0.004 (0.002)*	0.003 (0.002)	0.003 (0.002)	0 (0.002)
Organizational practices and experiences	Capital accumulators	0.17 (0.027)**	0.166 (0.033)**	0.094 (0.027)**	0.071 (0.033)*	0.113 (0.027)**	0.091 (0.033)**
	Routine operators	−0.071 (0.027)**	−0.054 (0.034)	−0.14 (0.027)**	−0.102 (0.034)**	0.041 (0.027)	0.062 (0.034)
	Mixed service functionaries	reference category	reference category	reference category	reference category	reference category	reference category
New social risk outliers	Young (<30), low-medium educated men	−0.078 (0.063)	0.08 (0.082)	−0.047 (0.062)	0.022 (0.081)	0.017 (0.062)	0.076 (0.030)**
	Young (<30), highly educated women	0.028 (0.048)	0.024 (0.059)	0.091 (0.047)	0.075 (0.058)	0.05 (0.048)	0.082 (0.059)
Control:	Union member	−	−0.133 (0.030)**	−	−0.224 (0.029)**	−	−0.1 (0.030)**
Associational memberships	Church attendance	−	0.051 (0.009)**	−	0.036 (0.008)**	−	0.034 (0.009)**

Country dummies						
Liberal-residual welfare states						
Australia	0.413 (0.060)**	—	0.713 (0.058)**	—	0.346 (0.059)**	—
Canada	1.06 (0.067)**	0.936 (0.080)**	0.39 (0.064)**	0.24 (0.078)**	0.593 (0.066)**	0.535 (0.079)**
New Zealand	0.298 (0.067)**	0.215 (0.070)**	0.922 (0.064)**	0.852 (0.068)**	0.133 (0.066)*	0.084
United States	0.865 (0.058)**	0.709 (0.067)**	0.102 (0.064)**	−0.004	0.293 (0.057)**	0.185 (0.066)**
United Kingdom	reference category					
Continental Conservative welfare states						
France	1.186 (0.059)**	1.146 (0.063)**	0.391 (0.057)**	0.338 (0.060)**	0.618 (0.058)**	0.588 (0.061)**
Germany[c]	1.006 (0.058)**	1.072 (0.067)**	−0.157 (0.056)**	−0.135 (0.065)*	0.735 (0.057)**	0.712 (0.066)**
Switzerland	1.566 (0.058)**	1.497 (0.061)**	0.141 (0.055)*	0.057	0.882 (0.056)**	0.833 (0.059)**
Social Democratic welfare states						
Norway	0.388 (0.060)**	0.374 (0.062)**	0.179 (0.057)**	0.208 (0.060)**	0.928 (0.059)**	0.937 (0.061)**
Sweden	0.538 (0.063)**	0.601 (0.068)**	−0.307 (0.061)**	−0.199 (0.065)**	0.608 (0.062)**	0.653 (0.066)**
Emerging welfare states						
Ireland	0.308 (0.062)**	0.143 (0.069)*	−0.353 (0.059)**	−0.459 (0.066)**	0.454 (0.060)**	0.356 (0.067)**
Spain	0.598 (0.056)**	—	−0.359 (0.054)**	—	0.299 (0.055)**	—
Observations	11,806	7,675	11,664	7,614	11,744	7,651
Explained variance / Pseudo *R*-squared	0.08	0.1	0.07	0.07	0.03	0.03

Notes

a Ordered probit regressions [no weights]; standard errors in parentheses; *significant at 5%; **significant at 1%; low values: in favour of...

b From Iversen and Soskice (2001).

c Results do not change if dummies for East and West Germany are included.

With regard to the country dummies, it is somewhat striking that most of them are almost all the time statistically significant. This finding suggests that in future work a great deal of contextualization is in order, both theoretically and statistically.

Table 3.4 simulates the substantive effects of belonging to certain market and organizational groups on support for various social policies as a way to establish the relative strength of explanatory powers exhibited by different aspects of respondents' class location and asset control (based on Table 3.3). The table demonstrates that the patterns vary substantially across the different social policy types. Each cell entry answers the question of the percentage by which the probability of a respondent's support for the highest increase of public expenditure on each of the social policies changes when that respondent moves from a low to a high value on the focal-independent variable, with all other independent variables held constant.

Table 3.4 shows that in the determination of political preferences over social policies, class notions in the sense of property, market and organizational experience do matter, even though often only marginally. *In each instance, however, the single greatest effect is exercised by the socio-demographic variables (gender or age), followed by education.* Gender drives public opinion over social policies coping with general existential risks more than do any of the attributes of market classes, and much more than does property class membership. The same applies for unemployment insurance, although all probability scores are now much lower. And finally, a similar pattern emerges on educational expenditure, although now age and gender have opposite signs.

This last observation leads us back to the theoretical discussion of the heterogeneity of new social risk groups. Table 3.4 allows us to gauge the heterogeneity of new social risk constituencies empirically, if we identify them with being less educated, older or female. On general existential risks (*health* expenditure), less educated and female voters have similar views, but not the elderly people. On *unemployment* insurance, all new social risk attributes lead to the prediction of more support for such insurance, but the magnitude of the effect is greatest for gender. Finally, on *education* policy, being female has just the opposite effect on public policy preferences as compared with having low education or being elderly! Given these heterogeneities, it is difficult to see how any singular collective political actors could combine in one encompassing social movement or political party all groups particularly exposed to various new social risks associated with age, gender and education (we elaborate on this in Kitschelt and Rehm 2004).

Table 3.4 Substantive effects of market and organizational traits on social policy preferences

	Change in the probability of endorsing maximum public expenditure increase for each of the following social policies:		
	Model (1): govmnt spend: health[a]	*Model (2): govmnt spend: unempl. benefit*[a]	*Model (3): govmnt spend: education*[a]
Income (from 20th to 80th percentile)	−7.7%	−2.6%	−1.3%
Education (from lowest level = 1 to highest level = 7)	−15.2%	−0.8%	+10.3%
Asset specificity (from 20th to 80th percentile)	−0.8%	+2.3%	+1.6%
Unemployed (from employed to unemployed)	0.2%	5.1%	−1.1%
Non-employed (from employed to non-employed)	−4.5%	−0.7%	−1.6%
Organizational experience of different occupations:			
Capital accumulator	−6.4%	−0.8%	−4.1%
Routine operator	+2.7%	+1.4%	−1.4%
Difference between lowest and highest category	9.1%	2.2%	5.5%
Age (lowest = 15 to highest = 96)	0.4%	+2.7%	−11.8%
Being female	+16.1%	+4.1%	+8.8%

Note
a Simulations based on models in Table 3.3. Continuous (dummy) variables are set to their mean (minimum). All simulations were computed with Clarify (Tomz *et al.* 2003).

Conclusion

This chapter explores how attributes that shape citizens' expectations over income derived from market exchange also affect their preferences over market-correcting social policies. We arrive at five major conclusions.

First, a sociological account of the origins of citizens' preferences over social policies to manage various types of market risks cannot rely on any single formulation of class theory, whether in the sense of property classes, market classes or organizational asset classes. Accounts that do so are likely to suffer from omitted variable bias. Our analysis instead shows that all of these theoretical conceptualizations of interest formation matter, and leave their imprint on empirically observed political consciousness. What matters only marginally, however, is the role of asset-specific skills in the mode that Iversen and Soskice (2001) suggested, in an elegant, thought-provoking article.

Second, and related, our analysis has shown that people's organizational experiences with command and control have a distinctive impact on their political consciousness, even once we control for the respondent's property and market class location. Our analysis cannot determine, however, whether this effect of organizational experiences is due to self-selection and occupational recruitment, or due to learning and socialization in the organizational environment.

Third, a comparatively strong force shaping political preferences over social policies has to do with socio-demographics, the economic risks and rewards associated with gender and age in a post-industrial economy. Our analysis suggests that demographic attributes are as important as, if not more important than, property and market conceptions of political preference formation. While we have no intertemporal comparative data, we suspect that the strength of demographics on political opinions is a recent phenomenon typical of the most advanced capitalist post-industrial societies at a time when they have experienced a major influx of women into the labor force without a corresponding reallocation of reproductive responsibilities from women to men and are about to experience a dramatic surge in the proportion of retirees relative to working-age citizens. Were comparable data available for the golden age of capitalism in the 1950s and 1960s, we would anticipate that being female contributed much less, if anything, to support for expansionary public social policies. In a similar vein, we would not expect to find an age cohort-based divide between the young and the old that is as pronounced as it is in the early twenty-first century on matters of general education and of risk-hedging social policies targeted at labor market participants with weak or vulnerable human capital investments. New social risks, we suggest, are to be found in these categories.

Fourth, our analysis of the role of class and demographic locations for citizens' preferences over social policies shows that attributes that signal the likely exposure of respondents to new social risks indeed matter for their political preference formation. Upon closer inspection, however, it turns out that respondents with diverse attributes of new social risk groups also develop rather diverse political orientations. Even if we confine ourselves to the domain of social policy-making and do not take into account the fact that political coalition-building is a process that spans a variety of policy areas and relates them to encompassing programmatic political packages, it is hard to see how the different policy preference profiles of young, less educated males, younger females at all levels of education, but particularly higher education, and elderly retirees can be easily rallied around a single focal political organization. New social risks do indeed exist and do shape policy preferences, but in a cross-cutting way.

Fifth, without providing even an *ad hoc* interpretation of empirical regression coefficients, our analysis suggests that unique national experiences, captured by country dummy variables, do have a substantial effect on central tendencies of political preference formation in national mass publics. Esping-Andersen's (1990) distinction of three types of welfare states helps us to identify different patterns of dummy variable coefficients in our multivariate regressions, but it yields inexplicable surprises when examining the empirical support levels for social policies in a cross-national comparison. It will be the task of future work to translate the explained variance of policy preferences captured by country proper names employed as dummy variables into theoretical concepts and propositions that go beyond Esping-Andersen's work. The cutting edge of the mode of investigation on which our chapter is embarking will shift from individual-level analysis of citizens' political preference schedules to multi-level models that theoretically map and empirically examine the interaction of individual-level conditions and attributes, such as class and socio-demographic characteristics, with contextual conditions that characterize entire polities and economic institutions in order to account for political preference profiles of social policy over time and across space.

Appendix

Table A-3.1 Oesch's coding of ISCO-88 onto 17 categories

Employment status	Self-employed professionals	Technical experts	Higher-grade managers	Socio-cultural professionals
Large employers — SELF and 10 or more employees	SELF and 2000–2470 (and less than 10 employees)	2100–2213	1000–1251, 2410–2419, 2441, 2470	2220–2323, 2350–2351, 2359, 2420–2440, 2442–2443, 2445, 2451, 2460
		Technicians	*Associate managers*	*Socio-cultural semi-professionals*
Petty bourgeoisie with employees — SELF and less than 10 employees (and not 2000–2470)		3100–3213, 3471	1252–1319, 3410–3449, 3452	2330–2340, 2352, 2444, 2446–2450, 2452–2455, 3220, 3222–3224, 3226, 3229–3232, 3240–3400, 3450–3451, 3460–3470, 3472–3480
		Skilled crafts	*Skilled office*	*Skilled service*
Petty bourgeoisie without employees		110, 7120–7142, 7200–7233, 7240–7423, 7430–7520, 8311, 8324, 8333	4000–4112, 4114–4141, 4143, 4190–4210, 4213–4221	3221, 3225, 3227–3228, 5122, 5141, 5143, 5110–5113, 5150–5163, 5200–5210, 8323
		Routine operatives / *Routine agriculture*	*Routine office*	*Routine service*
SELF and no employees (and not 2000–2470)		Routine operatives: 7100–7113, 7129–7130, 7143, 7234, 7424, 8000–8310, 8312, 8334–8400, 9160–9162, 9300–9333 — Routine agriculture: 6000–6210, 8330–8332, 9200–9213	4113, 4142, 4144, 4211–4212, 4222–4223	5120–5121, 5123–5130, 5131–5140, 5142, 5149, 5169, 5220–5230, 8320–8322, 9100–9153

Source: Oesch (forthcoming).

Table A-3.2 Description of variables

Name in Table 3.4	Operationalizations/explanation	Obs.	Mean	St. Dv.	Min.	Max.
Govmnt spend: health (v26)	Please show whether you would like to see more or less government spending [on health]. Remember that if you say 'much more', it might require a tax increase to pay for it.[a]	19,646	2.14	0.85	1	5
Govmnt spend: unempl. benefit (v31)	Please show whether you would like to see more or less government spending [on unemployment benefits]. Remember that if you say 'much more', it might require a tax increase to pay for it.[a]	19,338	2.90	0.95	1	5
Govmnt spend: education (v28)	Please show whether you would like to see more or less government spending [on education]. Remember that if you say 'much more', it might require a tax increase to pay for it.[a]	19,491	2.19	0.83	1	5
Income (households, in 20 groups)	Household income, in percentiles (20) (from low to high)	17,107	9.67	5.79	1	20
Education (highest degree)	Highest educational degree (from low to high)	19,955	4.65	1.41	1	7
Skill specificity, comp.	Skill specificity, as suggested in Iversen and Soskice (2001); composite index. See Table A-3.3	14,199	1.28	0.93	0.38	10.31
Unemployed	Dummy = 1 for respondent unemployed	19,832	0.05	0.23	0	1
Non-employed	Dummy = 1 for respondent not employed	19,832	0.36	0.48	0	1
Age	Respondent's age	20,072	45.72	16.46	16	97
Female	Dummy = 1 for female respondent	20,140	0.51	0.50	0	1
Age * Female	Interaction Age * Female	20,049	23.51	25.95	0	97
Capital accumulators	Derived from Oesch (forthcoming). See Table 3.1	20,222	0.17	0.38	0	1
Routine operators	Derived from Oesch (forthcoming). See Table 3.1	14,665	0.41	0.49	0	1
Intermediate occupations	Derived from Oesch (forthcoming). See Table 3.1	14,665	0.36	0.48	0	1
Young (<30), low-medium educated men	Respondent younger than 30, educational degree at most 4, male	19,796	0.03	0.18	0	1
Young (<30), highly educated women	Respondent younger than 30, educational degree 5 or higher, female	19,815	0.07	0.26	0	1
Union member	Dummy = 1 for respondent union member (Australia and Spain missing)	14,933	0.24	0.43	0	1
Church attendance	Church attendance (from 1: 'never' to 6: 'once a week or more often')	16,805	2.66	1.74	1	6

Note
a 1 Spend much more; 2 spend more; 3 spend the same as now; 4 spend less; 5 spend much less.

Table A-3.3 Operationalization of skill specificity

The skill specificity indicator used in this chapter ('Skill Specificity, comp (TI and DS)') is operationalized as suggested by Torben Iversen and David Soskice in their article 'An Asset Theory of Social Policy Preferences' (Iversen and Soskice 2001). This indicator exploits the skill-based hierarchical structure of the 'International Standard Classifications of Occupations (ISCO-88)'. The latter has two dimensions: skill level, 'which is a function of the range and complexity of the tasks involved, where complexity of tasks has priority over the range'; and skill specialization, 'which reflects type of knowledge applied, tools and equipment used, material worked on, or with, and the nature of the goods and services produced' (ILO 1999: 6). Therefore, the focus of ISCO-88 'is on the skills required to carry out the tasks and duties of an occupation – and not on whether a worker in a particular occupation is more or less skilled than another worker in the same or other occupation' (ILO 1999: 6).

ISCO-88[a] partitions the universe of occupations into ten broad categories at the one-digit level: 0 Armed forces; 1 Legislators, senior officials and managers; 2 Professionals; 3 Technicians and associate professionals; 4 Clerks; 5 Service workers and shop and market sales workers; 6 Skilled agricultural and fishery workers; 7 Craft and related trades workers; 8 Plant and machine operators and assemblers; 9 Elementary occupations.

Each of these categories is subdivided into two to four two-digit groups. For example, 'Professionals' (one-digit group 2) are divided into: 21 Physical, mathematical and engineering science professionals; 22 Life science and health professionals; 23 Teaching professionals; and 24 Other professionals. The logic continues up to the four-digit level, which gives fairly detailed job descriptions (e.g. ISCO-88 code 2443 is for 'Philosophers, historians and political scientists').

For deriving their skill specificity indicators, Iversen and Soskice (2001) compare the share of unit groups in any higher-level class to the share of the workforce in that class:

$$s\_spec\_1 = \frac{s\_num1}{s\_den1} = \frac{(\text{number of 4-digit units within 1-digit major group})/390}{(\text{'number of people in a 1-digit ISCO group'})/(\text{'number of classified people'})}$$

$$s\_spec\_2 = \frac{s\_num2}{s\_den2} = \frac{(\text{number of 4-digit units within 2-digit major group})/390}{(\text{'number of people in a 2-digit ISCO group'})/(\text{'number of classified people'})}$$

Their first skill specificity indicator, s1, then becomes:

$$s1 = \frac{\frac{1}{2}(s\_spec\_1 + s\_spec\_2)}{isco\_skl}$$

where isco_skl are the skill levels attributed to each one-digit ISCO-88 group. In addition, s1 is divided by its standard deviation.

The second skill specificity indicator, s2, is calculated similarly, but instead of dividing by isco_skl it uses 'educational degree' as proxy for skill level.

Finally, the composite index, used in Tables 3.3 and 3.4, is simply the mean of s1 and s2.

What does this index really measure? A few observations can be made. First, the index is a relative measure. By dividing by skill level (s1) or highest educational degree (s2), absolute low skill specificity becomes relative high skill specificity, and vice versa. In other words, we should expect a negative correlation between skill specificity and education. Second, the numerator captures something like 'the specificity of the labor market within one major group'. It is completely determined by the way the ISCO coding is done, i.e. external to the data-set. Since the ISCO groups 3, 7, and 8 are especially fine-grained (i.e. they have many four-digit job descriptions), we should expect those groups to rank relatively high on the skill specificity scale. Third, the denominator captures something like 'the actual size of the labor market'. The skill specificity decreases if the actual labor market gets bigger. Note that the denominator is calculated on all (sample-wide) data, not on the national samples. This implicitly assumes labor mobility between all countries in the sample (an index calculated at the national level correlates with the sample level index at about 0.75; see Rehm 2004). Finally, a comparison of skill specificity with 'classes' identified in Oesch (forthcoming) (see Table 3.1) suggests that 'skilled craft' and 'routine service' have especially skill-specific occupations (composite index), whereas 'skilled service', 'routine service' and 'socio-cultural professionals' have especially low skill-specific occupations – which is somewhat implausible.

Note

a The Role of Government III (ISSP 1996) does not have a single 'clean' ISCO-88 variable. Some countries are coded according to ISCO-68 (e.g. Norway, Spain, the United States), others by country-specific codings (e.g. Australia, Sweden, the United Kingdom). If possible, we translated all other codes into ISCO-88, but for some countries that is not possible (e.g. Italy). Several people provided the public good of correspondence tables: Harry Ganzeboom (www.fss.uu.nl/soc/hg/isco6888.inc); Erik Bihagen (http://www.mdh.se/isb/sociologi/personal/erikbih; www.cf.ac.uk/socsi/CAMSIS/occu-nits/distribution.html); Paul Lambert (www.cf.ac.uk/socsi/CAMSIS/occunits/distribution.html). See also Ganzenboom and Treiman (1994, 1996). We are very grateful for these very helpful tools. Also, Torben Iversen has been unusually helpful in replicating the index.

Notes

A first version of this chapter was presented at the conference 'The Politics of New Social Risks', Lugano, Switzerland, 25–27 September 2003. We would like to thank the participants for their comments.

1 As Rogowski (1987) and Lange and Garrett (1996) have suggested, institutional arrangements – such as the presence of single-member district plurality elections to national legislatures rather than proportional representation in multi-member districts – may facilitate the representation of small particularistic economic interests.

2 This, of course, sets aside the principal–agent problem between owners and managers, of which Weber was fully aware. Nevertheless, it can be said that, faced with the big social and economic policy alternatives, managers are likely to share the owners' perspective even if we take principal–agent relations into account.

3 This is confirmed by the ISSP survey in the countries for which we have data. Among the self-employed in the 12 countries covered by our analysis ($N = 1{,}206$), the majority are 'petty bourgeois' without employees (53.3 percent), followed by small employers (25.9 percent), self-employed professionals (8.4 percent) and large employers (12.4 percent).

4 Note that 'market exposure' in this conceptualization has nothing to do with trade and capital flows across borders, but simply with 'hard budget constraints', namely that work organizations are inside or outside the profit-making economic sector.

5 Factor analyses can be obtained from the authors.

6 In an earlier version of this chapter (Kitschelt and Rehm 2003) and in another paper (Kitschelt and Rehm 2004), we indeed employ the factor scores for this dimension as the dependent variable.

7 We abstained from using weights. Also, we do not impute missing values but perform listwise deletion.

8 In the country-level equations explaining social policy alternatives, the most consistently significant statistical performers are (1) income; (2) gender (primarily in regressions on unemployment); and (3) occupational experience as 'capital accumulator'. With regard to targeted social policy programs, education has an inconsistent effect.

4 Public attitudes and new social risk reform

Johannes Kananen, Peter Taylor-Gooby and Trine P. Larsen

Introduction

Giuliano Bonoli has identified the New Social Risks (NSR) that some citizens of advanced modern societies face, alongside the Old Social Risks (OSR), which were the focus of the policies developed by European welfare states during the post-war period (Chapter 1). NSR concern the pressures from changes in labour markets and family and household structures that are apparent in all welfare states, and also the impacts of welfare state restructuring on vulnerable groups. They contrast with the OSR, which arose in the life-course of typical citizens in industrial society and concerned needs for retirement, widows' and disability pensions, healthcare and child endowment. The significance of NSR is twofold: first, they create demands for new services at a time when much of the debate about the future of the welfare state is about spending constraints, the substitution of private or family services for government provision and the targeting of scarce state resources on the most needy. Second, they offer opportunities to develop state provision, which enables governments to achieve other (and typically economic goals) at a time when much of the analysis sees spending on traditional welfare state services as simply a burden on the productive sector of the economy.

As Chapter 1 points out, NSR create demands for extra state services in three main areas. New needs for childcare and elder care emerge, to meet the demands resulting from the movement of women, and particularly of mothers, into paid employment. Labour market activation policies are developed, whether positive, through training and job support programmes, or negative, through 'make work pay' benefit cuts and constraints, as the supply of jobs for unskilled manual workers diminishes and as employment, particularly for those with lower skill levels, becomes less secure. Targeted help is needed for those who lose out as a result of new policies which shift some of the responsibility for services such as pensions away from the state. As has already been pointed out, these developments can help governments in pursuing other goals, so that, as Levy (1999) puts it, the new direction in policy can create a 'virtuous circle' whereby spending on child and elder care and on activation expands the labour force and enables the economy to present a more competitive face to the world, and targeted support enables cutbacks in state spending on mass services.

These arguments have influenced policy debates at the national level and also at that of the European Union. As Chapter 1 argues, the politics of NSR differs from that of OSR in a number of ways. Most importantly, NSR typically affect minorities (for example, unskilled school leavers) and impact during transitory life-stages (for example, on parents, when children are at the pre-school stage), so that they do not readily command the substantial constituencies of support that OSR policies, such as the expansion of pensions or healthcare, were able to draw on. If the story of the post-war growth of welfare states is one in which working- and middle-class interests were able to press governments to spend the dividend of economic growth on social provision (Baldwin 1990; Huber and Stephens 2001a), an important strand in more recent developments concerns the complexity of the political processes surrounding NSR policy development. In this chapter we trace one aspect of this, by using attitude data from a recent Eurobarometer survey to examine the extent to which the views of those most directly affected by NSR are distinctive. The key question is how far political support for NSR policy is directly related to one's status as an NSR bearer. If it is, support for reforms is likely to be fragmented, so that new policies will involve compromise and political manoeuvring.

In this chapter we focus on NSR in two areas: in relation to labour markets and in relation to pension policy. The reasons for choosing these areas are that they offer a contrast between NSR that affect people at different life-stages (at the entry to and during working life, and after working life is completed), between risks derived from different causes and between what might be seen as primary and secondary risk. Labour market risks affect unskilled manual workers and those with few qualifications most powerfully (see Chapter 1), whereas pension risks affect those with interrupted contribution records or without access to (or the resources to purchase) adequate occupational or private provision. Labour market risks are primary in the sense that they result from the impact of globalisation and new technologies on individual opportunities, whereas the pension risks are created by other policy developments in response to demographic and fiscal pressures, cutting back or privatising provision, or tightening the link between contributions and benefits. Since the risks differ substantially, we can have greater confidence that any pattern in attitudes that emerges across the two areas is associated with NSR as such and not with a particular domestic policy issue.

We have chosen three countries to examine in detail, because they offer contrasting settings, often being used as the leading examples of the three main welfare state regimes in Europe (respectively corporatist, Social Democratic and Liberal), and contain different approaches to NSR.[1] In Germany the response to NSR has developed gradually and relatively recently, and is currently incomplete. The policies so far pursued both in the labour market and in pensions appear to indicate that change away from a corporatist labour market, which limits risks through benefits and a social insurance pension system, is limited. Sweden has the most well-established NSR policies and has developed labour market activation through training, has supported access to employment and encouragement, and has developed pension policies that combine funded and pay-as-you-go schemes within a framework of relatively high state spending. The United Kingdom, by contrast, has tended to pursue 'make-work-pay' strategies, holding down out-of-work benefits and supplementing low wages, with some recent expansion of training schemes. Pension policies have also pursued a Liberal market route, seeking to devise a satisfactory regime under which the bulk of pensions can be privately provided. Thus, a general perspective would see Sweden and the United Kingdom as having moved furthest in response to NSR, but in rather different directions. Swedish policies tend to use state intervention to support positive outcomes and risks, whereas the United Kingdom stresses containment of state spending and places more stress on market forces and incentives.

Research methods

This chapter uses attitude survey material to examine responses to NSR. Chapter 1 develops the theoretical point that the politics of NSR might be expected to differ from that of OSR. One important aspect is that NSR bearers (those most affected by NSR) differ from OSR bearers, and in particular may be expected to have less political influence – there are fewer of them and they tend to occupy lower-status social positions. The question of how far views on NSR policies are divided by status in relation to NSR is therefore of considerable importance, especially in a context where governments are keen to promote NSR policies. We analyse the relationship between NSR status and attitudes to NSR policy reforms through logistic modelling.

For convenience, the argument is organised around two hypotheses: first, one would expect pro-reform attitudes to be strongest across the population (both NSR bearers and others) where NSR reforms (which differ substantially between countries) are furthest advanced. Second, on the basis of the argument in Chapter 1, we suggest that being an NSR bearer is likely to dispose one favourably to pro-NSR policies, whereas other groups will not be favourably disposed.

These hypotheses reflect two analyses of political attitudes and behaviour that are brought together in March and Olsen's seminal *Discovering Institutions*. This work identifies two logics to political decision-making appropriateness and consequentiality. Appropriateness involves 'what the situation is, what role is being fulfilled, and what the obligations of that role in that situation are' (Mark and Olsen 1989: 160). People tend to follow the framework of expectations and assumptions inherent in the institutional framework which they inhabit. Consequentiality refers to 'preferences and expectations about consequences. Behavior is willful, reflecting an attempt to make outcomes fulfill subjective desires, to the extent possible' (ibid.). This approach leads to a rational-actor attempt to meet one's interests, as one understands them. From the appropriateness perspective, an institutional framework well developed in respect of NSR would tend to set the stage for pro-NSR attitudes; from the consequentiality perspective, NSR interests are likely to engender support for NSR policies.

These two hypotheses provide the basis for our discussion. Because a number of other factors, including political party support, age, labour occupational category and income, have been shown to influence attitudes to welfare state policies (see, for example, Svallfors and Taylor-Gooby 1999; Papadakis and Bean 1993), these must also be taken into account in the models.

It is evident that NSR reforms necessarily enjoy some level of support where they have been carried out. Less evident is why support should be stronger in a country where NSR coverage is wider or where reforms are more advanced than in a country where it is less so. Here we might find some support from regime theories. We have already noted that NSR reforms follow the pattern of regime differentiation. Svallfors (1997, 2004) has examined class cleavages and conflict patterns across different countries, chosen to reflect Esping-Andersen's regime categorisation (Esping-Andersen 1999), with regard to attitudes towards the welfare state. While class cleavages are rather similar in different countries, he also finds that welfare regime type determines the level at which these cleavages occur (see also Taylor-Gooby 2001). Attitudes towards government redistribution and egalitarian income distribution are strongest in the Social Democratic regime and weakest in the Liberal regime (Taylor-Gooby 2004: 132). Svallfors argues that 'the weight of exposure to different institutional regimes creates diverging world views even between people in similar structural locations' (1997: 291). As NSR reforms follow to a large extent the regime differentiation, we would also expect in the case of NSR to find that attitudes in favour of NSR policies are strongest in regimes where these policies have gone furthest.

We also suggest that being an NSR bearer is likely to dispose one favourably to pro-NSR policies, whereas other groups will not be favourably disposed. Being in favour of NSR policies is by definition in the self-interest of NSR bearers. This hypothesis does not necessarily, however, contain the assumption that people's opinions are formed only according to their self-interest. Kangas (1997) has examined to what extent people's self-interests (*homo economicus*) and their sense of solidarity (*homo sociologicus*) affect their attitudes towards redistribution and welfare state issues. He finds that attitudes are not formed in an either/or fashion – that is, people cannot simply be divided into egoists and altruists. In accordance, we do not expect 100 per cent support of NSR policies from NSR bearers, but it is reasonable to expect that NSR bearers on aggregate are more likely to support NSR policies than other groups. Kangas also finds that the more specific survey questions are, the more they tend to appeal to people's self-interests rather than their sense of solidarity. Therefore, if asked on a specific level, NSR groups should differ from others in their views about NSR policies.

In the study we used Eurobarometer 56.1, carried out in 2001, as the basis for analysis. The Eurobarometer survey series is carried out across all EU member states, using random sampling with approximately 1,000 interviews in each member country (except Germany, where 2,000 interviews take place to enable separate analysis of East and West; the United Kingdom, where 300 are added to cover Northern Ireland; and Luxembourg, where the sample is 600 – Gallie and Paugam 2002, appendix 2). It is generally regarded as of high quality and forms a suitable basis for analysis of public opinion across Europe.

The survey asks respondents to signify agreement or disagreement with a number of statements relevant to NSR in relation to the labour market and pension provision. We selected the following:

Labour market

Three statements allow us to examine responses to different aspects of NSR policies:

Q1: The government should provide a decent standard of living for the unemployed (state responsibility). The statement corresponds to a more traditional approach to unemployment in which the role of government is to meet needs, and there is less concern with encouraging unemployed people to take paid jobs.

Q2: The unemployed should be forced to take a job quickly, even if it is not as good as their previous job (compulsory work). This represents what might be seen as a negative approach to activation.

Q3: The unemployed should be given the time and opportunity to improve their education and skills (positive activation). This represents a more positive approach, concerned to develop the capacity of the unemployed person to engage in paid work.

The statements cover a more traditional welfare state approach to unemployment and negative and positive activation measures, designed to address NSR. They enable us to examine support for NSR policies and the policy direction of that support.

Pensions

We analysed responses to three statements which contrast a welfare state approach to pensions, where government rather than employers or insurance companies takes main responsibilities, with approaches that reflect the two directions evident in policies to reduce state spending and expand individual responsibility – a targeted assistance-based approach, and a stricter actuarial approach that bases entitlement on contribution record. It is the latter two approaches that have been important in recent pension policies, and which run the risk of creating NSR for those who fail to gain access to assistance or to maintain the required contribution record. The issue of provision might also divide NSR and OSR bearers, as increased private provision leads to a closer link between contributions and earnings.

Q4: People who cannot pay sufficient contributions into a pension scheme (e.g. the unemployed, those on low earnings) should receive some extra help from the state for old age (generous assistance).

Q5: The amount of one's pension should be strictly based on the amount of contributions one has paid into the pension scheme (actuarial logic).

Q6: Pensions should be provided mainly by state or public schemes, mainly by occupational schemes or mainly by private arrangements between individuals, insurance companies, banks etc. (state responsibility – the variable is coded 1 for state and 0 for employer or private).

NSR status

Those most vulnerable to labour market risks are the groups with weak attachment to paid work and those in poverty. The variables used to measure this vulnerability in the survey are based on experience of unemployment and on subjective social exclusion. We identify those with a substantial record of unemployment (more than one year of unemployment during the past five years) and those who are currently unemployed.

NSR in relation to pensions are most important for those who are most likely to be affected by current reforms – particularly those with weak work and therefore poor contribution records, and those on low incomes, who find difficulty in paying high contributions. The unemployment variables mentioned above and also low income are likely to be important.

The impact of people's standing on their support for NSR policy reforms is likely to depend to some extent on their understanding of their social position in relation to risks. For this reason, we also use a variable that reflects subjective social exclusion. This is based on an index made up from five variables which reflect the extent to which someone feels a member of society:

- *I don't feel the value of what I do is recognised by the people I meet.*
- *I feel left out of society.*
- *I don't feel I have a chance to play a useful part in society.*
- *Some people look down on me because of my income or job situation.*
- *The area in which I live has not got a good reputation.*

These variables have elsewhere (Gallie and Paugam 2002: 59) been shown to reflect the same underlying dimension with a Cronbach test score of 0.73. The sense of being excluded is higher for lower-income groups. Individuals who have financial difficulties, as well as the unemployed, are also most likely to be faced with social devaluation. The index is also related to age, so that those between 35 and 44 years old are the ones most affected by social devaluation, whereas younger (15–24) and older (65-plus) groups are significantly less likely to experience a sense of exclusion (Gallie and Paugam 2002: 60–1). These are dimensions that correspond to the way we identify NSR bearers.

Other explanatory variables

A number of other variables have been shown by previous work to influence attitudes to welfare state policies. The most important are: political party support and more broadly, position on a left–right spectrum; age and life-cycle stage; gender; occupational position and social class; and income group (see, for example, Svallfors and Taylor-Gooby 1999; Papadakis and Bean 1993), and we included these in the analysis. The survey did not include information on other variables that have been shown to relate to welfare attitudes (education, access to media and family composition) and we were unable to include these.

Procedure

Our argument has identified two guiding hypotheses, to do with the extent to which new social risk policies are likely to be supported in different countries and the support of different social groups, depending on their NSR status, for such policies. We are now in a position to test the hypothesis about the different levels of support for NSR policies in different countries. Our analysis indicated that NSR reforms have proceeded furthest in both labour market and pensions in Sweden and the United Kingdom, but in different directions.

In Sweden, positive labour market activation policies are well established, and the Swedish system is internationally recognised as a leader in this field. More recently, negative 'make-work-pay' policies have been introduced for some groups. In effect, policies for sickness and disability pensions provide support for substantial numbers who are marginal in the labour force and enable the system to avoid the worst pressures of high structural unemployment in creating income inequalities and damaging social integration. Pension reforms have taken place in such a way as to preserve the inclusive nature of the existing state system, but to introduce regulated private provision alongside it. In the United Kingdom, reforms are relatively recent and the balance of change is towards negative activation, with an important policy emphasis on constructing incentive systems that encourage people into paid work. In the area of pensions, the response to NSR has been an attempt to promote non-state pensions, which are likely to impose pressures and increase the risks faced by the most vulnerable groups with weakest labour market records.

In Germany a number of labour market reforms have been pursued with the general object of enhancing flexibility, but it has proved difficult to carry a restructuring through to conclusion, owing to the capacity of the entrenched social actors to delay or prevent change. Similarly, pension reforms are incomplete. The current reforms seek to reduce the rate of increase of state pension spending and have supported a modest expansion of private provision.

These changes suggest that we should expect NSR reforms to receive the strongest endorsement in Sweden and the United Kingdom, but in the former the endorsement will generally be for positive activation and pension reform that meets social needs, while in the latter it should be more towards compulsion into paid work and a stricter link between contributions and benefits. In Germany, endorsement of change in any direction should be limited. Table 4.1 shows a pattern in Germany of relatively low support for state responsibility (Q1), but equal numbers endorsing compulsory work (Q2) and more positive individualised activation policies (Q3). For pensions, state responsibility is strongly supported (Q6), but there is again a balanced division between generous assistance (Q4) and a strict actuarial logic (Q5) as the alternatives. This fits the interpretation of Germany as facing difficulties in fixing on a specific approach to current pressures. State responsibility in the area of employment policy is more strongly supported in the United Kingdom, and still more so in Sweden. There is marked support for positive activation in Sweden as predicted, but also quite strong support for compulsory work. In the United Kingdom the strongest support is for positive activation, with some support for compulsory work policies.

For pensions, the largest groups support state responsibility in both the United Kingdom and Sweden, and in Sweden there is much stronger support for generous assistance from the state than for a strict contributions-based approach, as predicted. However, the pattern is similar in the United Kingdom, although rather less marked. These data show some support for the view that popular attitudes in a country follow the general direction of public policy in the cases of Germany (indecisive and with a strong work ethic) and Sweden (committed to universal citizenship welfare and also to positive individualised activation), but also indicate a

Table 4.1 Support for NSR policies for unemployment and pensions by country

	Labour market policies		Pension policies			
	State responsibility (Q1)	Compulsory work (Q2)	Positive activation (Q3)	General assistance (Q4)	Actuarial logic (Q5)	State responsibility (Q6)
Germany	15.7	36.1	36.1	24.4	26.3	45.0
UK	24.4	35.3	45.3	36.8	26.0	54.2
Sweden	39.0	43.8	58.8	51.5	24.3	67.4
Mean	23.8	38.7	44.2	34.4	25.7	53.0

substantial group in the population out of tune with government thinking in the United Kingdom.

We now move on to consider the extent to which different social groups support NSR reform.

Findings

We use logistic regression models to examine the relationship between NSR status, demographic and social position, and political support and attitudes to NSR policies. The coefficients in Tables 4.2–4.7 are regression coefficients, so any non-zero value indicates differing opinions compared to the reference group. A negative sign indicates a smaller likelihood of approval of the statement in question, and a positive sign a greater likelihood. Statistical significance of differences is shown in the tables as well, but it should be noted that they only apply in comparison with the reference group. There may well be other significant differences within one variable.

Labour market policies

According to the second hypothesis, we might expect those most exposed to NSR to support pro-NSR policies more than other groups. Those with a weak attachment to the labour market can be seen as most exposed to labour market risks. Thus, we might expect these groups to support state responsibility (Q1) and positive activation (Q3), and relate more negatively to compulsory work (Q2). The following tables show the relationships between our key variables and attitudes towards NSR policies.

In the models, NSR exposure and weak attachment to labour markets were operationalised by current labour market status and employment history. For clarity, the tables show only the variables relevant to the hypothesis, but it should be kept in mind that background variables such as political affiliation, age and gender are controlled for.

In Germany, those currently unemployed support state responsibility and skill opportunity, as might be expected. There are, however, other groups that seem to support these policies as well, for instance the retired. With regard to skill opportunity, manual workers and house persons together with the unemployed and retired express clear support for these policies compared to the reference group (other white-collars).

A high risk of unemployment (more than one year of unemployment during the past five years) is positively related to support for NSR policies, but the difference compared to the reference group is not significant in this sample. According to the hypothesis, we might have expected low income and subjective social exclusion to increase the probability to support state responsibility and skill opportunity. This is not, however, fully supported by these models, as income does not make a very significant impact on

Table 4.2 Support for NSR unemployment policies in Germany: logistic model

Variables/model	State respons.	Compuls. work	Skill opport.
Constant	−1.50	−0.07	−0.02
Occupation			
Self-employed	−0.13	−0.10	0.01
Manual workers	0.35	0.14	0.54**
Other white-collars	Reference		
Managers	−0.03	0.14	0.42
House person	0.31	−0.06	1.09***
Students	−0.27	−0.48	0.20
Unemployed	1.09**	−0.14	0.70*
Retired or unable to work	1.11**	−0.08	0.89***
Income (quartiles)			
Below lower quartile	0.36	0.01	−0.12
Lower quartile to median	Reference		
Mean	−0.06	0.07	0.05
Median to upper quartile	−0.10	−0.19	0.09
Above upper quartile	−0.01	0.04	0.58***
High risk of unemployment			
No	Reference		
Yes	0.24	0.01	0.19
Subjective social exclusion	−0.01	−0.04**	−0.04**
Observations	2,009	2,009	2,009
R-square (Nagelkerke)	0.11	0.05	0.06

Notes
*: $P < 0.05$, **: $P < 0.01$, ***: $P < 0.001$.

opinions. Those who score high on the index of subjective social exclusion tend to be less in favour of compulsory work. They also tend to be less in favour of skill opportunity.

In Sweden, a high risk of unemployment increases the probability of supporting state responsibility with regard to unemployment policy. As expected, those with a weak attachment to the labour market also tend to oppose compulsory work and be in favour of skill opportunity, although the differences are not statistically significant in these two models.

Subjective social exclusion does not show a significant impact on attitudes towards NSR policies in Sweden. This is also the case with regard to pensions, which is interesting because the variable shows more explanatory power in the other countries.

The lowest-income groups tend to be more in favour of state responsibility and skill opportunity, as expected. Those below the lower quartile are significantly more likely to be in favour of state responsibility compared to other income groups. It should be noted that the category of 'mean' represents missing information and thus has no relevant interpretation in the models.

Those currently unemployed tended to be more in favour of state responsibility and skill opportunity than other occupational groups, but

Table 4.3 Support for NSR unemployment policies in Sweden: logistic model

Variables/model	State respons.	Compuls. work	Skill opport.
Constant	0.10	−0.36	0.65**
Occupation			
Self-employed	−0.49	0.23	−0.01
Manual workers	−0.15	0.07	0.33
Other white-collars	Reference		
Managers	−0.25	−0.19	−0.15
House person	0.23	−0.59	0.30
Students	−0.31	0.05	0.75*
Unemployed	0.72	0.02	0.58
Retired or unable to work	0.54	0.38	0.62
Income (quartiles)			
Below lower quartile	0.54**	0.03	0.08
Lower quartile to median	Reference		
Mean	0.60*	−0.09	−0.19
Median to upper quartile	−0.02	−0.28	−0.40*
Above upper quartile	0.22	0.37	−0.05
High risk of unemployment			
No	Reference		
Yes	0.94**	−0.48	0.14
Subjective social exclusion	−0.02	−0.03	−0.03
Observations	1,000	1,000	1,000
R-square (Nagelkerke)	0.14	0.15	0.06

Notes
*: $P < 0.05$, **: $P < 0.01$, ***: $P < 0.001$.

the difference compared to the reference group (other white-collars) was not statistically significant.

Unemployment is the strongest factor contributing to support for NSR policies in the United Kingdom. Being unemployed increases significantly the likelihood supporting state responsibility, compared to the reference group. The self-employed are clearly less in favour of state responsibility than the other groups. This finding is in line with the hypothesis that NSR bearers are in favour of pro-NSR policies. There are, however, other groups in favour of these policies as well, and the relationship is not as clear with regard to compulsory work and skill opportunity.

As in Sweden, a high risk of unemployment is significantly related to attitudes towards NSR policies. In the United Kingdom, those with a weak attachment to the labour market are clearly more in favour of state responsibility and skill opportunity than those with a more established labour market status. Subjective social exclusion also relates positively to state responsibility, while the impact is not as strong with regard to compulsory work and skill opportunity.

Thus, taking the results from all three countries into account, labour market position relates to ideas about labour market strategy in a way that might be expected, and which supports the hypothesis. NSR status shows a

Table 4.4 Support for NSR unemployment policies in the UK: logistic model

Variables/model	State respons.	Compuls. work	Skill opport.
Constant	−2.00***	−0.39	0.32
Occupation			
Self-employed	−0.31**	0.03	0.33
Manual workers	0.37	0.36	−0.06
Other white-collars	*Reference*		
Managers	0.38	−0.27	0.28
House person	0.90**	−0.14	0.09
Students	0.58	0.65	0.51
Unemployed	0.91*	−0.30	0.43
Retired or unable to work	0.48	−0.02	−0.03
Income (quartiles)			
Below lower quartile	0.41	−0.23	0.14
Lower quartile to median	*Reference*		
Mean	−0.19	−0.29	−0.39*
Median to upper quartile	−0.10	−0.03	0.17
Above upper quartile	−0.31	0.03	−0.22
High risk of unemployment			
No	*Reference*		
Yes	0.48*	0.09	0.58*
Subjective social exclusion	0.07***	−0.02	−0.01
Observations	1,003	1,003	1,003
R-square (Nagelkerke)	0.13	0.04	0.04

Notes
*: *P*<0.05, **: *P*<0.01, ***: *P*<0.001.

complex relationship, with those at greatest risk of unemployment tending in general to support more generous policies towards their own group. However, it seems clear that there is no simple division to be drawn between NSR bearers and others in their support for particular strategies, so that the politics of NSR policy-making are not sharply differentiated by NSR status, but are integrated into more general political attitudes.

Pension policies

We identified the most important NSR bearers in the area of pensions as those with weak employment records and those on low income. In the models, these factors are, as in the labour market models, reflected by the variables of occupation and high risk of unemployment. According to the hypothesis, we might expect these groups to relate positively to policies alleviating the consequences of a poor contribution record (Q4: generous assistance) and to prefer pensions provided mainly by the state or public schemes (Q6: state responsibility). We also might expect them to be less in favour of policies stressing individual responsibility in contributory pensions (Q5: actuarial logic).

Table 4.5 Support for NSR pension policies in Germany: logistic model

Variables/model	Generous assist.	Actuarial logic	State respons.
Constant	−0.86***	−0.49*	−0.28
Occupation			
Self-employed	−0.02	0.30	0.08
Manual workers	0.39	0.18	0.38*
Other white-collars	Reference		
Managers	0.20	−0.21	0.04
House person	0.80**	0.60*	−0.08
Students	0.63*	0.04	−0.21
Unemployed	1.57***	−0.00	0.32
Retired or unable to work	0.88**	0.08	0.11
Income (quartiles)			
Below lower quartile	0.17	−0.23	0.02
Lower quartile to median	Reference		
Mean	−0.12	−0.07	−0.32*
Median to upper quartile	0.16	0.23	−0.23
Above upper quartile	0.20	0.18	−0.49**
High risk of unemployment			
No	Reference		
Yes	0.36	0.03	0.40
Subjective social exclusion	−0.01	−0.05***	0.02
Observations	2,009	2,009	2,009
R-square (Nagelkerke)	0.12	0.05	0.06

Notes
*: $P < 0.05$, **: $P < 0.01$, ***: $P < 0.001$.

In relation to Germany, the question about generous assistance (Q4) reveals a division between workers and non-workers, with the latter being clearly more in favour of state involvement. This could indicate an insider–outsider division with regard to the corporatist German pension system. Those outside the regime are less in favour of the logic that it is based on. This finding is, however, not that clearly reflected in attitudes towards an actuarial logic. In fact, house persons are more in favour of generous assistance than the reference group (other white-collars), but also more in favour of the actuarial logic.

Income is most related to opinions about state responsibility. Those belonging to higher-income groups tend to be less in favour of pension systems provided mainly by the state or public schemes. Those who score high on the index of subjective social exclusion are less likely to support the actuarial logic statement. These are findings that are in line with the hypothesis.

In Sweden the difference between occupational groups in attitudes towards pension policies does not seem to be very big. Only one group, the retired and those unable to work, stand out as being more in favour of state responsibility compared to the reference group (other white-collars). Neither does the variable of subjective social exclusion show much of a relationship in any of the three models.

Table 4.6 Support for NSR pension policies in Sweden: logistic model

Variables/model	Generous assist.	Actuarial logic	State respons.
Constant	*0.45*	*−1.10****	*0.73***
Occupation			
Self-employed	−0.45	0.74	−0.23
Manual workers	0.20	0.38	0.29
Other white-collars	*Reference*		
Managers	−0.14	−0.32	−0.27
House person	1.19	−0.05	0.04
Students	−0.01	−0.30	−0.10
Unemployed	0.15	0.70	−0.03
Retired or unable to work	0.44	0.30	0.78*
Income (quartiles)			
Below lower quartile	0.23	0.14	−0.09
Lower quartile to median	*Reference*		
Mean	−0.02	0.34	−0.13
Median to upper quartile	−0.15	−0.58*	−0.01
Above upper quartile	0.13	−0.70*	−0.19
High risk of unemployment			
No	*Reference*		
Yes	0.54*	−0.31	0.35
Subjective social exclusion	−0.02	−0.05	−0.01
Observations	1,000	1,000	1,000
R-square (Nagelkerke)	0.08	0.13	0.07

Notes
*: $P < 0.05$, **: $P < 0.01$, ***: $P < 0.001$.

The contribution principle seems to divide opinions between different income groups. Those with a high income are clearly less likely to support the actuarial statement (that the amount of pensions should strictly be based on contributions). This is a slightly surprising result, as these groups hardly have difficulties in maintaining a decent contribution record. A high risk of unemployment increases the likelihood to support generous assistance, which is an expected finding.

Unemployment shows a pattern in the United Kingdom – with regard to both state responsibility and generous assistance. The unemployed are, in comparison with the reference group, significantly more in favour of state responsibility. Manual workers and house persons are also among those more in favour of state-provided pensions. Those with a high risk of unemployment tend to favour generous assistance. They can be seen as NSR risk-bearers with regards to pensions, so the finding is in line with the hypothesis.

Subjective social exclusion related positively to support of state responsibility. In the other models the relationship did not turn out to be significant, although the direction of the relationship was as expected. Thus, in the area of pensions too, NSR status corresponds, as expected, to

Table 4.7 Support for NSR pension policies in the UK: logistic model

Variables/model	Generous assist.	Actuarial logic	State respons.
Constant	−0.44	−0.091***	−0.36
Occupation			
Self-employed	0.43	−0.008*	0.49
Manual workers	0.21	−0.04	0.72**
Other white-collars	Reference		
Managers	0.08	0.27	−0.10
House person	0.16	−0.15	0.68*
Students	0.36	−0.04	0.49
Unemployed	0.07	0.00	1.37***
Retired or unable to work	0.36	−0.16	0.38
Income (quartiles)			
Below lower quartile	0.17	−0.16	0.39
Lower quartile to median	Reference		
Mean	−0.31	−0.17	−0.16
Median to upper quartile	−0.63**	−0.14	0.07
Above upper quartile	−0.22	−0.24	0.04
High risk of unemployment			
No	Reference		
Yes	0.52**	−0.29	−0.03
Subjective social exclusion	0.01	−0.03	0.05**
Observations	1,303	1,303	1,303
R-square (Nagelkerke)	0.04	0.06	0.09

Notes
*: $P<0.05$, **: $P<0.01$, ***: $P<0.001$.

support for a generous state and for state-targeted activity to benefit the relevant groups, but it is by no means the only variable corresponding to this view – most importantly, political attitudes and broader position in the labour market also link to support for positive policies.

Conclusions

This chapter examines the relationship between being directly affected by NSR (being unemployed or at risk of unemployment, being socially excluded or affected by pension reform) and support for welfare state policies of the various kinds that are currently being developed in different national settings. We identified a range of policies and used the examples of Germany, Sweden and the United Kingdom to make a broad distinction between three policy approaches to NSR. In the German cases the challenges to the labour market and pensions settlement are well recognised, but policy is currently being developed in the face of opposition which has access to a number of veto points, so that reform is at present inconclusive. In Sweden the general direction of reform is to preserve a strong welfare state and to defend equal citizenship, whereas in the United Kingdom the government is willing to accept a degree of social inequality to promote labour market flexibility and support an expanding private sector.

We found a general correspondence between public attitudes and these policy stances in Germany and Sweden, but less so in the United Kingdom, where many citizens dissent from the policy direction (Table 4.1). Logistic regression models showed that the pattern of attitudes is, as one might expect in an area where strong political opinions and the interests of different groups cross-cut each other, complex. Age group relates to policy ideas. This could be interpreted in terms of NSR, but may also relate to the impact of rapid change on different groups. Gender, which figures largely in NSR debates, does not make a strong impact. There is no clear distinction between NSR bearers and all other social groups in the models. The position is not a simple one, but in general, NSR issues are not to be seen as a separate domain in which only those affected are likely to respond to policy initiatives while others – and the majority – are uninterested. Rather, they are part of the normal business of political debate over welfare state reform.

This has two implications. First, the argument that governments are likely to face intractable issues in promoting NSR policies, since the groups directly affected are the only ones to support reform and they are weak and short-lasting, is not supported. Second, however, there is a clear distinction between more and less generous approaches to NSR. It seems that NSR bearers are often (not surprisingly) lined up on the generous side, but that other groups play a stronger role. Thus, the insertion of NSR into welfare state politics may be as much a matter of debates over which kind of approach to follow in relation to NSR as of whether to have NSR policies at all. If NSR are part of 'normal welfare state politics', this does not mean that NSR solutions are necessarily those that meet the needs of NSR bearers effectively and adequately, as equal citizens.

Note

1 This summary rests on the more detailed discussion of policies in relation to new social risks in the three countries covered by Taylor-Gooby (2004). The authors are grateful to participants in the WRAMSOC project (Andreas Aust, Frank Bönker, Anne Daguerre, Olli Kangas, Virpi Timonen and Hellmut Wollmann) for preparing the background papers and documents on which the summary is based.

5 Reconciling competing claims of the welfare state clientele

The politics of old and new social risk coverage in comparative perspective

Klaus Armingeon

Introduction

Social risks such as poverty due to retirement from working life, unemployment or illness are covered by schemes of the traditional welfare state such as pensions, unemployment and health insurances. New social risks emerge due to the transformation of labor markets and of family structures during the past three decades or so. Among these risks are those of reconciling work and family, or of low education in a knowledge-based post-industrial economy (Bonoli 2005).

Why do some countries expand coverage of new social risks while containing expenditures for old risks; why do other nations experience expenditure growth for old risk, while there is little increase in schemes for new risks? And why do some countries contain expenditure growth for both types of risk coverage? This is the guiding question of this chapter. As in the case of old-risk policies, there is strong evidence that it is the political left which promotes coverage of new social risks. When a country is expanding the traditional social policies such as pension systems or healthcare, the major conflict has been between the supporters of the pro-welfare state parties (left-wing parties, and in Continental Europe Christian Democratic parties) and the electorates of the other parties. Expansion of the new social policies and the ensuing resource shifts from old to new schemes (or the relatively lower speed of expansion of expenditures of old risks schemes) may create major distributional conflict within the population and within the electorate of left-wing parties. In particular, it is the older generations and those seeing themselves at the bottom of the social hierarchy who oppose a shift of resources from the coverage of old to the coverage of new risks. Hence, new-risk policies are risky in electoral terms for the left. The risk can be taken if there are large groups in the population and in the electorate of left-wing parties supporting increased funding of new risk schemes. For various reasons, these are in particular the employees of the public sector. Therefore, a large public sector becomes one of the major facilitating conditions for the reform of a welfare state which increasingly emphasizes the coverage of new social risks. In countries with a large public sector, left-wing political parties are in a much better position to expand the coverage of new risks. This is the basic argument of this chapter. My main empirical evidence comes from attitudinal data on education and pension expenditures. Arguably, these two areas are major examples of policies relevant for 'new' and old risks respectively: in the knowledge-based post-industrial economies, a poor education is a key risk factor; and pensions are – together with health insurance – of the utmost importance to prevent poverty resulting from the old risks of industrial society.

A note on terminology is in order: New social risks can be understood as poverty risks which emerge in the course of societal modernization. Poverty of single mothers is a case in point (see Huber and Stephens, Chapter 7). In addition to this narrow usage of the term, new social risk may also denote risks of individual frustration, societal inefficiency or neglect caused by the same processes of modernization. An example is well-qualified female employees who fail to reconcile family needs with career aspirations and decide to care for their children or their frail relatives, owing to the lack of sufficient childcare institutions or caring facilities for the elderly. However, if this well-trained part of the labor force opts for gainful employment and if family care facilities are not sufficiently provided, children and elderly face the risk of neglect (Bonoli Chapter 1, this volume; 2005). In this chapter I will use the term in the second sense for two reasons: (1) Post-tax and transfer poverty is widespread primarily in non-Continental European countries with a Liberal welfare state (such as the United States, Australia or Canada); in the majority of other countries, poverty prevention is no longer the primary concern of the welfare state. (2) The wider definition of new risks concerns a much larger share of the population in the majority of established OECD democracies.

From the examples given, it is clear that new social risks are frequent among females and young people – in and outside the labor market – while old social risks are more frequent among the male employed labor force and pensioners (cf. Esping-Andersen 1999). There is little reason to assume that the different beneficiaries of 'new' policies – from an ill-trained foreign worker in an active labor market program to a female academic re-entering the labor market after having given birth to a child – can combine and mobilize as a coherent and powerful group. Therefore, the expansion of new schemes presupposes that a political actor – a political party, for instance – takes up the issue. In addition, the electoral risks of this strategy can be taken if there is little opposition within the electorate or if this opposition remains weak and can be canceled out by support coming from diverse groups. In this regard, the politics of coverage of new social risks is mainly the art of muting the opposition by the defenders of the old welfare state schemes.

My argument presupposes that variation on the aggregate level – indicators of social policies – can partly be explained by variation on the individual level – that is, attitudinal conflicts over welfare state programs. There is ample evidence that welfare state policies vary by 'worlds of welfare' (Esping-Andersen 1990; Huber and Stephens 2001a; Schmidt 1988). Much less convincing evidence is available for the contention that the individual-level correlations between socio-economic characteristics and attitudes toward the welfare state differ systematically by type of welfare state (Svallfors 1997, 2004; Hult and Svallfors 2002). By implication, if attitudes are relevant for policies, variations between types of welfare states have to be explained by international variations in the size of segments of the population holding group-specific attitudes, either in the total electorate or in the electorate of certain political parties. Hence I have to demonstrate and link plausibly these variations on various levels (country groups, electorates and individuals).

This chapter starts with a description of the research design and the data basis. For the aggregate level, the second section describes the covariation of types of social security expenditures and country groups. A third section then presents the findings of the analyses related to the individual level and the links between social groups, parties and old and new social policies.

Data and research design

Since I argue that differences of the size of social groups with different welfare state attitudes translate into different spending patterns, this study has to rely on both individual-level and aggregate-level data. For the international comparison I select the democratic OECD countries in Europe (the European Union less Cyprus and Malta plus Switzerland and Norway), North America, Japan and Australasia. For some analyses these countries are grouped into four categories. I distinguish between a Continental world of welfare, including the established democracies of the western part of Continental Europe, a Scandinavian world of welfare (to which Finland is added), a Liberal world composed of the Anglo-Saxon nations plus Japan, and, as the most recent type, the emerging welfare states of the new democracies in that part of Central and Eastern Europe that joined the European Union in 2004 (for this classification, see Flora 1993).

For the aggregate level, the dependent variable is expenditures (percentage of GDP) for certain welfare state policies. Expenditures are more clearly related to political decisions than to outcome indicators such as poverty rates. They are superior to data on programs, since the latter are difficult to classify and it is hard to aggregate them into a few consistent variables. On the other hand, expenditure data conceal the effects on recipients, since they do not indicate the share of expenditures clawed back by the state (Adema 2001); they do not display the share of resources spent on administration; they do not give information on whether schemes give little to many, or much to a few; and they do not show the extent to which they are redistributive. If 5 percent of GDP is spent on child allowances, we do not know whether this goes exclusively to the poorest families or helps to secure the consumption patterns of middle-class families once the number of children increases. In addition, they do not tell much about the structure of the scheme for which money is spent. Fortunately, in our case the analysis of expenditure data leads to findings similar to those of the analysis of policy programs and policy outcomes (Esping-Andersen 1990, 1999; Huber and Stephens, Chapter 7).

For expenditure data my main source is the OECD Social Expenditure Database, covering the years 1980–98 (OECD 2003c) and expenditures for public education (OECD 1993, 2003b). I distinguish between three major types of welfare state policies:

1 Those which maintain income in the phase of the life cycle after the regular end of employment (old age cash benefits).
2 Those that are closely work related and maintain income during the normal phase of employment (disability cash benefits, occupational injury and disease benefits; sickness benefits; survivors' pensions; family cash benefits, unemployment compensations; health expenditures; housing benefits; and other policies not classified by OECD).
3 Those that help to reconcile work and family and those that support people entering the labor market or allow for a basic professional reorientation (services for elderly or disabled persons; family services; active labor market policy). These schemes cover new social risks (for a thorough discussion, see Bonoli 2004a). Expenditure for education can be considered to belong to that group of policies too, by avoiding exclusion from or marginalization in the labor market ('welfare to work'). Since I do not have comparable figures for the 1980s, I kept these statistics on educational expenditures separate but will discuss them as policies covering new social risks.

I assume that there are differences across time, countries and country groups, and hence I calculate and compare figures – if possible – for 1980, 1998 and for the separate countries and the country groups.

The data for attitudes towards the welfare state come from the International Social Survey Programme 'Role of Government', conducted around 1996 in 22 countries in the Anglo-Saxon world, Scandinavia, Continental Europe ('old democracies') and Eastern Europe ('new democracies') (Zentralarchiv für Empirische Sozialforschung 2000). Where analyses have been done for all countries or country groups, the data have been pooled and weighted so that each country is given the same weight. Unfortunately, the countries in the two data-sets do not match exactly; however, since main results are presented on a country-by-country basis too, these mismatches are acceptable. The 'Role of Government' surveys include a number of questions about welfare state policies. Since we know that answers vary with the precise framing of the survey questions (Kitschelt 2001: 269; Kangas 1997), only those questions are used which are very specific and leave little room for sweeping statements influenced by social desirability or general ideological outlook.

The support for work-related welfare state policies has been measured using the following question:

> Listed below are various areas of government spending. Please show whether you would like to see more or less government spending in each area. Remember that if you say 'much more', it might require a tax increase to pay for it': Unemployment benefits (1 spend much more, 2 spend more, 3 spend the same as now, 4 spend less, 5 spend much less). Similarly, and also indicating work-related welfare state policies, but not as closely as unemployment benefits: 'More or less government spending for health'.

The support for pension policies was measured by the question 'More or less government spending for old age pensions?' The best question for identifying the support base for policies covering new social risk has been 'More or less government spending for education?' Given this database, information on support for 'old' social risks is much better than for 'new' risks. Only the question about spending for education measures support for the covering of 'new risks' such as the danger of joblessness and income losses due to new challenges of the labor market, which only can be coped with by better general education. However, we do not know whether the support for these schemes co-varies with support for, say, expenditures for active labor market policy, childcare or care for the frail elderly. Hence, much of the following empirical argument is based on the conflicts about old social policies. This makes sense, since there is little reason to assume that the beneficiaries of new social policies are a coherent group able to mobilize in the political system. Rather, the important questions concern the conflicts over 'old' welfare state policies that are relevant for resource shifts towards 'new' policies.

Table 5.1 displays some summary statistics on attitudes toward the welfare state. The larger the figure, the less the support for welfare state policies. The significance of these data is limited, since support may depend on the level of actual expenditure and the need for social security. In general, the welfare state enjoys strong support in each world of welfare, and there is little difference in this regard between the schemes for health, pensions and education. The median citizen favors expenditure growth of all these programs in all but the Continental countries. There the median citizen is in favor of the same amount being spent on pensions as hitherto. In contrast, increased spending for unemployment benefits

Table 5.1 Opposition to government expenditures in four types of welfare states, 1996, means

	Liberal	Cont.	Scand.	Eastern
Govmnt spend: health, 1 much more, 5 much less	2.0	2.3	1.9	1.8
Govmnt spend: education, 1 much more, 5 much less	2.1	2.2	2.4	1.9
Govmnt spend: retirement, 1 much more, 5 much less	2.3	2.4	2.3	2.0
Govmnt spend: unempl benefit, 1 much more, 5 much less	3.0	2.8	2.8	2.7

Source: ISSP *Role of Government*, 1996. The lower the figures, the less opposition, i.e. the more the support.

encounters much less support everywhere, the median position being for no more and no less than at present. Considering the arithmetical means, welfare state expenditure is somewhat more supported in the East, probably due to the much greater need for social security and less actual spending in terms of both share of GDP and absolute figures.

The period under consideration is the middle and late 1990s (1996 for attitudes, 1998 for expenditure data). For most countries, both aggregate and individual data are available: Australia, Canada, the Czech Republic, France, Germany (in the case of attitudinal data, split into West and East Germany, the latter assigned to Eastern Europe), Great Britain, Ireland, Italy, Japan, New Zealand, Norway, Poland, Sweden, Switzerland, the United States.[1] For certain countries there are only aggregate data on expenditures: Austria, Belgium, Denmark, Finland, Greece, Luxembourg, the Netherlands, Portugal, Spain and Slovakia. And for Hungary and Slovenia only individual-level data could be analyzed. The Baltic states (Latvia, Lithuania and Estonia) are missing in both data-sets.

Covering old and new risks: expenditures in international comparison

In the political discourse in most Western countries, welfare state expenditures are assumed to have reached their limit. Apart from normative reasons, such as mistrust of state intervention and strong confidence in market forces and their beneficial effects, there are at least three empirical changes substantiating doubts about further increases of the size of welfare state developments: the reduced fiscal room for maneuver due to liberalization of capital markets (Scharpf and Schmidt 2000), the demographic changes which will – all other things being equal – increase spending on pensions and healthcare, and the substantial abatement of poverty and need thanks to the old welfare state and economic growth. Therefore, the likelihood of strong increases in both old- and new-risk policies is limited. More realistic is the assumption that policy development will resemble a zero-sum game: a precondition for increases in new social risk coverage is a containment of expenditures for old social risks. Even if expenditures for 'old' risk still grow, the rate of growth of 'new' schemes may be larger. All this could cause distributional conflicts within the welfare state's clientele. New-risk schemes will endanger the level of generosity of expenditure on old schemes.

Since new social risks are closely related to societal modernization experienced across all modern societies, we expect similar increases for such schemes over a longer period of time. This is not borne out by the data, as shown in Figure 5.1 and Table A-5.1 (the latter is in the appendix to this chapter).

The expenditure for new social risks (in the narrow sense) is rather limited. Across all the nations under study, it is 1.9 percent of GDP, slightly more than 20 years ago (1.4 percent). Differences between country groups are obvious. In 1980, Scandinavian countries already spent much more on new social risks than Liberal or Continental welfare states did in 1998 – not to speak of Eastern welfare states concentrating expenditures on work-related schemes and old age pensions. The outstanding characteristic of Continental welfare states is the strong increase in old age benefits; by 1998 they even exceeded the spending level of Scandinavian countries in this field. In the Liberal welfare states the strongest increase took place with regard to work-related expenditures, while the increase in old age benefits and in new social risk expenditures has been contained. Scandinavia has a leading role with regard to level and change of spending for

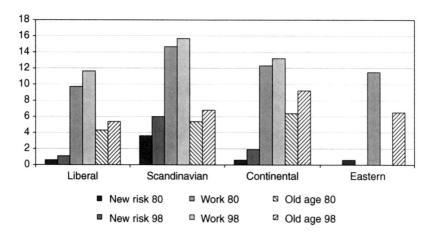

Figure 5.1 Expenditures for welfare schemes, 1980 and 1998 (as a percentage of GDP).

public education; while the Liberal and Continental welfare states stagnate on a similar level and the Eastern countries are clearly below even the Continental level. Expenditures for new social risks (in the narrow sense) and for public education are closely correlated (0.78) – with the Nordic European countries leading in both dimensions.

One could summarize these data by saying that the Scandinavian countries started from an already high level of expenditure for new social risk in the 1980s and experienced the strongest increase while containing expenditures for work-related schemes and old age benefits. In contrast, most spending effort in the Continental countries went into old age pensions, while the Liberal countries have been successful in containing the increase in pension payments but have been less successful in keeping down expenditures for work-related schemes.

There is an obvious answer to the question of why the emerging Eastern European countries focused on 'old risks'. This can be explained in a functionalist perspective, according to which old risks of employment and maintaining income after retirement are served first. However, this functional logic cannot explain why the Liberal and Continental countries are lagging behind Scandinavia and are not much advanced in converging – although societal changes such as increasing female labor force participation are similar across all countries.

Redistributional conflicts among the welfare state clientele

What type of political party is in favor of policies covering new social risks? For the traditional welfare state, comparative research has provided robust findings. In particular, in the post-war years until the end of the so-called golden age (the 1950s to the middle or late 1970s), the welfare state was expanded as a result of the power of left-wing (mainly Social Democratic) and center (mainly Christian Democratic) parties. In Continental Europe it was predominantly the Christian Democratic parties and in the peripheral Nordic countries the Social Democrats that were the main proponents of welfare state expansion in the party system (Castles 1982; Schmidt 1982; van Kersbergen 1995; Huber *et al.* 1993). It is an open question whether during the past 20 years the impact of parties on size and quality of the welfare state has waned (Huber and Stephens 2001a) or remained significant (Korpi and Palme 2003; Castles 2004). The Scandinavian experience, with strong Social Democratic parties and a vanguard role for these countries in the development of new social risks policy, points to a positive correlation. This is plausible, since Social Democratic parties have always been strong supporters of gender equality and decent living conditions for citizens irrespective of their status and family situation. In contrast, being strongly influenced by norms of the Catholic Church, Christian Democratic parties put emphasis on a welfare state centered on the family with the male breadwinner. Hence with regard to center parties we would not expect much support for welfare state policies covering new social risk, which to a large extent are related to the decline of the traditional family and gender equality.

If party stances are deducted from attitudes of party supporters,[2] regressions of attitudes toward welfare state expenditures in the fields of health, education, retirement and unemployment benefits lead to these conclusions: (1) There are only three Continental countries in the sample of the Role of Government surveys for which data on attitudes and party affiliation to left-wing and center parties were available: West Germany, France and Switzerland. In no case were the coefficients for supporters of center parties (the CDU/CSU in Germany, the CVP/CSP in Switzerland, the UDF in France) significant[3] and in the expected direction. (2) Hence, if welfare state policies have a clear partisan basis (measured as attitudes of party supporters), this is made up of left-wing (Social Democratic, Communist, Green) parties. With the exception of both Germanies, Hungary, Poland, Slovakia and Japan, in all countries there is a significant correlation between affiliation to a left-wing party and strong support for unemployment benefits. Of similar magnitude is support for more spending for education (exceptions being Hungary, Ireland, Norway, Slovakia, Poland, Canada and Japan). Less clear is the general significant strong support of those with a left-wing party affiliation for pension (only in Australia, the United Kingdom, the United States, Sweden, New Zealand and France) and health expenditures (only in Australia, the United Kingdom, the United States, Sweden, the Czech Republic, New Zealand and France).

Since the left supports both old and new social risk policies, the politics of expanding the schemes for new risks could be the same as those for traditional policies. However, given the restrictions on general expenditure growth, more coverage of new social risks implies containment of, or even a decrease in, expenditures for old risks – that is, less generous pension schemes or shifts in the standard age of retirement. But even if both types of schemes grow, the different growth rates may pit different segments of the welfare state clientele against each other. Attitudinal data indicate potential redistributive conflict within the welfare state clientele (Roller 1995, 2002; Ullrich 2000; Pettersen 1995; Esping-Andersen 1999: 148; Blekesaune and Quadagno 2003). Those who will lose out – for example, because their pensions are stagnating or declining – will oppose new social policies, while the beneficiaries of the new schemes are likely to support them. In the following I will focus on four potential cleavages in the welfare state clientele: age, gender, public versus private employment, and subjective class.

Age

The largest welfare state schemes are those covering pensions and health-care. There is no reason for a cleavage between older and younger age groups, if one starts from the assumption that eventually we will all become old and that we are all likely to be ill at some time. On the other hand, pensions are paid out of current funds, thereby reducing the resources for other policies and creating a conflict of interest between young and old. The young single mother will be more interested in having childcare right now, whereas her pension arrangements are in the very distant future. The older people are, the more important are pensions, and the less important are schemes focusing on the younger generations.

Gender

In Continental Europe the welfare state has been oriented towards income maintenance of the traditional family with a male breadwinner. Unlike Scandinavian welfare states, the Continental welfare state has not been particularly woman-friendly. Women are increasingly likely to have to cope with new social risks due to the decline of the traditional family model and they are more likely to be employed in the public sector, which delivers coverage against new risks (public childcare facilities, schools, etc.). Therefore, one might assume that women would support new social risks policies particularly strongly. Empirical research by Ronald Inglehart and Pippa Norris (2000) suggests another hypothesis. These authors argue that women have moved systematically to the left of men in advanced post-industrial societies. This change is caused by societal developments, most notably the inclusion of women into the labor market. Also, women are more likely to be recipients of benefits as widows ('old' risks) or as single mothers. There may be differences in values too: women seem to emphasize the equality and need principle, while men emphasize the merit principle (cf. Blekesaune and Quadagno 2003). From these arguments, women are expected to be generally more in favor of welfare state expenditures, particularly expenditures for new social risk coverage.

Class

The welfare state tends to care for those in need, and historically its major aim has been poverty prevention. This applies more to the 'old' than to the 'new' welfare state. Risks of poverty are the more prevalent, the lower the position of a citizen in the social hierarchy. For attitudes toward the welfare state, the perception of one's own situation is arguably more important than objective data such as income or occupational position. On these grounds, support for 'old' schemes is expected to vary with subjective class,[4] while correlations are assumed to be much lower for schemes that do not obviously tackle poverty problems; healthcare and, most notably, education are examples.

Public versus private sector

A fourth line of conflict may run between employees in the public and those in the private sector.[5] For private-sector employees, the welfare state is a two-edged institution: it provides social security but may reduce the competitiveness of the firm and hence may endanger jobs. In contrast, public-sector employees do not have to fear job losses due to the effect of taxes and social security contributions. Frequently, expansion of welfare state expenditures is coterminous with more jobs in the public sector. This applies in particular to those schemes which provide services (care, education, social work), while offering few transfer opportunities. This is notably true for policies covering new social risks. Therefore, we would assume that public-sector employees would support welfare state schemes generally and in particular those with a strong 'service' component (e.g. employees in public education). A similar, more sophisticated argument relates to client-interactive jobs (in the public sector) and various types of jobs in the exposed market sector (Kitschelt and Rehm, Chapter 3). However, the empirical analyses showed that age, class, gender and the public sector turned out to be of primary importance, with the division between the public and private sectors often being of much more importance than the divisions (by income) within the group of employees in the private or public sector.

Family situation may be of great importance for attitudes toward the welfare state, too. Analyses that have been run with a dichotomous variable (households with at least one child versus households with no children) produced weak and often insignificant results, though.

Hence, in this analysis I will restrict myself to these four variables and the regression of support for these four social policy areas (health, pension, education, unemployment benefits) on age, gender, subjective class and employment in the public sector.

In order to easily compare the unstandardized regression coefficients, independent variables have been reduced to the range from 0 to 1. Age has been recoded so that an increase of one unit corresponds to an interval of 50 years of age.

For summary purposes, all national surveys have been pooled into one, giving each nation the same weight. For further illustration, the country-by-country results for a Social Democratic welfare state (Sweden), a Liberal welfare state (the United Kingdom), a large (West Germany) and a small Continental welfare state (Switzerland), and an Eastern welfare state (the Czech Republic) are given in Table 5.2. It should be kept in mind that the support variable is inverted – that is, the variable has lower values the more expansion is favored. A negative sign between – say – age and retirement spending indicates that support increases with age.

The findings can be condensed into four conclusions: The most important variable for explaining attitudes toward the traditional welfare state is

Table 5.2 Attitudes towards the welfare state: age, gender, public sector and subjective class position

	All	Sweden	Germany (W.)	Switzerland	Great Britain	Czech R.
Health						
Constant	1.67*	1.67*	1.83*	2.39*	1.43*	1.68*
Age	−0.08*	−0.07	0.21	0.00	−0.04	0.07
Gender	0.16*	0.22*	0.21*	0.22*	0.02	0.18*
Public sector	−0.12*	−0.09	−0.03	0.10	−0.08	−0.08
Class	0.72*	0.71*	0.62*	0.45	0.74*	0.23
R^2	0.05	0.09	0.03	0.02	0.05	0.01
Education						
Constant	1.94*	2.35	2.53	2.46*	1.54*	2.27
Age	0.10*	0.09	0.06	0.20	0.18*	0.04
Gender	0.08*	0.02	−0.01	0.02	0.07	−0.05
Public sector	−0.18*	−0.06	−0.21*	0.07	−0.07	−0.13
Class	0.20*	−0.29*	−0.16	−0.38	0.37*	−0.14
R^2	0.02	0.01	0.01	0.00	0.02	0.00
Retirement						
Constant	2.16*	2.13*	2.01*	2.43*	2.12*	2.71*
Age	−0.39*	−0.36*	0.21	−0.07	−0.50*	−0.63*
Gender	0.15*	0.25*	0.17*	0.13*	0.05	0.14*
Public sector	−0.06*	−0.03	0.08	−0.12	0.04	−0.05
Class	0.84*	0.90*	0.56*	0.36	0.75*	0.24
R^2	0.08	0.14	0.04	0.01	0.09	0.04
Unemployment						
Constant	2.50*	1.96*	2.42*	2.58*	2.70*	2.93*
Age	−0.03	0.04	−0.04	0.16	−0.28*	0.18
Gender	0.12*	0.25*	0.15	0.14*	0.10	0.12
Public sector	−0.06*	−0.18*	0.00	0.01	−0.11	0.06
Class	0.79*	1.34*	0.91*	0.38	1.09*	0.33
R^2	0.04	0.16	0.05	0.01	0.06	0.00

Notes
For the operationalization of the dependent and independent variables, see text.
*: $p < 0.05$.

subjective class. The lower the subjective class position, the stronger the support for welfare state expenditures, in particular in the fields of health, unemployment benefits and pensions. Class has a less prominent role in the Czech Republic. More importantly, the country-specific coefficients have different signs and are – with the exception of Great Britain, Hungary, Sweden and Canada – not significant. In 11 countries these are negative, and in only six countries are they positive (Australia, Germany (East), Great Britain, Italy, New Zealand, Canada, France). In substantive terms, class position is weakly connected to educational spending – in contrast to the attitudes toward the other three welfare state schemes. As already stated, education is only one aspect of new social risks policies, though. Other new social risk policies that have a clearer aspect of poverty prevention and redistribution in favor of those at the bottom of the social hierarchy may be supported much more strongly by citizens belonging to lower classes. In general, from the findings of these regression analyses, it is plain that the traditional welfare state is very much class based, and that shifts from old to new risk coverage are likely to meet resistance by those who feel themselves to be at the bottom of the social hierarchy.

The second finding concerns the correlation between gender (coded as 1 for men and 0 for women) and support of the welfare state. Across old and new schemes, female citizens support the expansion of the welfare state more strongly than men.

The third result is the outstanding effect of the age variable with regard to one type of scheme at the core of the old welfare state: pensions. There is a clear age cleavage in case of one of the most expansive programs of the old welfare state: it is definitely defended by elderly people, while younger cohorts are much less clear in their support. Hence, if shifts to new social risks policies imply relatively less spending for old risks, those in subjectively low class positions and elderly people will be the clear defenders of the old schemes.

Finally, being employed in the public sector has effects similar to those of being female, as regards support for the welfare state. Employees in the public sector support both 'old' and 'new' welfare state schemes, and the coefficients can be interpreted in the sense that their support is even more pronounced for programs such as health and education than it is for pensions and unemployment benefits. This makes sense in various respects: health schemes and education offer far more jobs than the transfer of pension or unemployment benefits; many public employees already work in the field of health and education; and it is in health and education that the client-interactive jobs (with the assumed effects of political socialization) are particularly frequent.

A major problem with this type of data concerns the impact on actual political behavior. Asking for more welfare state expenditure is very inconsequential in the social situation of a survey. This is different from the situation in an election, when citizens have to choose between parties supporting welfare state expenditures and parties supporting tax reductions. For example, in the Role of Government survey, 28 percent of respondents (pooled sample) were inconsistent and supported more expenditure for pension schemes and yet, some questions later, stated that they prefer tax reduction to social expenditure growth. For these reasons, I compared the answers to the four questions concerning welfare schemes, with regard to preferences. Even if one is in favor of generally more (less) expenditure, on which schemes should more (less) money be spent? I calculated the differences between their respective rank scores (from 1: spend much more, to 5: spend much less), giving an indicator of differences of preferences: spending for education versus spending for pensions; spending for education versus spending for health services; spending versus education versus spending for unemployment benefits; spending for pensions versus spending for health; and so on. This gave six pairs of comparison. A value of −4 – for example, education versus retirement – indicates that a respondent was in favor of spending much more on the first area (education), while supported spending much less on the second area (pensions); +4 indicates the opposite attitude. A value of 0 results from a respondent who supports expenditure change to the same extent in both schemes. These rank differences have been regressed onto the main four independent variables of this study.

Table 5.3 shows the results for the pooled sample. To judge by the explained variance or the amount of the coefficients, the conflict between spending for retirement and spending for education is the strongest, except in the case of the gender variables. Elderly private-sector employees, and people in lower classes, favor pensions over education. Country-by-country analyses confirmed that result. The coefficient for the class variable was in the expected direction in all countries and it was significant in 11 out of 18 societies. The coefficient for the age variable has had the expected direction, except in the case of Germany (West), Italy and Japan (there it was positive, albeit insignificant). It was significant in 13 of the 15 cases, with the expected direction. The public-sector variable produced the expected direction of the coefficient in 15 societies (although in only three cases was the coefficient significant), but not in Hungary, Slovenia or Switzerland.

If we simplify further the results, the support bases of old and new social risk policies can be described as shown in Table 5.4.

From these findings it follows that pushing forward new social risks policies is risky for parties with electorates over-representing those in lower classes, those in the private sector and elderly people. In contrast, new social risks policies may be rewarding in electoral terms for parties with large proportions of public-sector employees, or with younger and middle- or higher-class voters. Large proportions of female voters and supporters are favorable for welfare state expansion in both old and new fields.

If we shift back to the aggregate level, can we then explain the success of the Scandinavian left in expanding new social risks policies in terms of the structure of their constituency? There is little reason to believe that. I did multiple logistic regressions of support for left-wing parties (various types of party affiliation) and of votes for left-wing parties on age, gender, public-sector employment and subjective class position. Left-wing parties still are parties of the lower classes, significantly over-represented among the supporters in Sweden, Norway, Australia, the United Kingdom, Ireland, the Czech Republic and New Zealand. The same result is

Table 5.3 Differences of preferences

Differences of preferences	Pooled samples		Independent variables (entries are unstandardized regression coefficients)			
	R^2	N	Age	Gender	Public sector	Class
Education v. pensions	0.04	10,497	0.49*	-0.07*	-0.12*	-0.64*
Education v. healthcare	0.02	10,620	0.19*	-0.08*	-0.06*	-0.51*
Education v. unemployment benefits	0.02	10,400	0.14*	-0.04	-0.12*	-0.58*
Pensions v. healthcare	0.01	10,550	-0.31*	-0.02*	0.05*	0.12*
Pensions v. unemployment benefits	0.01	10,374	-0.38*	0.03	-0.01	0.05
Healthcare v. unemployment benefits	0.00	10,435	-0.06	0.05*	-0.06*	-0.07

Notes

'Differences of preferences' is calculated as the difference of the values for the first statement (1 spend much more, 2 spend more, 3 spend the same as now, 4 spend less, 5 spend much less for education, pensions, health, unemployment benefits) minus the values for the second statement. For example, if a respondent is in favor of much more expenditure for education and much less for pensions, he or she will have a '−4'.

For the operationalization of the independent variables see text.

*$p < 0.05$.

Table 5.4 The support bases of old and new schemes

	Lower class position	Elderly	Women	Public-sector employees
Attitudes towards 'old' schemes	Very much in favor	Very much in favor, in particular pensions	Very much in favor generally	Much in favor
Attitudes towards 'new' schemes	In favor, if old schemes are not endangered	Mixed; probably not in favor	Very much in favor generally	Very much in favor

obtained for the analyses of voters, with only Ireland being without significant class effects and Canada now having these effects. Public-sector employees are significantly over-represented among supporters of the left only in the United Kingdom, Japan, France and Australia, and nearly the same result is obtained for the electorate. Only the United Kingdom has non-significant coefficients, while Sweden has significant over-representation. Left-wing parties are not particularly parties of female voters, except in Eastern Germany and Norway. And with regard to party affiliation, they do not enjoy significant extra support among women as compared with men in any country under consideration. Finally, there is little reason to assume that left-wing parties are parties of the younger generation. This is only the case in Australia (voters and supporters). If there is any correlation with age, left-wing parties seem rather to be parties of the elderly, in particular in the post-communist countries. Older voters are over-represented among supporters in Hungary, the Czech Republic, Slovenia and Poland and among voters in the Czech Republic, Slovenia, Poland, and Norway and the United Kingdom.

Hence, if we want to explain why the Scandinavian parties of the left succeeded in pushing forward new social risk policies, this hardly can be done in terms of the structure of their constituencies. The Scandinavian left is at least as supportive of the old schemes as the left-leaning voters and supporters in other countries. Therefore, an explanation has to go back to the observation that generally the level of left-wing power and the size of the public sector – both being beneficial to expansion of new social risks policies – are much higher in those countries that expanded the coverage of new social risks particularly strongly. Our measure of the power of the left is the share of left-wing parties in cabinet seats, aggregated for 1980–98 (Armingeon *et al.* 2005) and the size of the public sector is measured as public-sector employees as a percentage of the labor force (OECD: various sources).[6]

The results of the analysis of the increase (1998 versus 1980) and the level of spending for the coverage of new social risks are depicted in Figure 5.2. The conclusion is straightforward:[7] Left-wing parties are the parties most favorable to both new and old social risks policies. They can take the electoral risks of expanding new social risks policies if the support basis of these policies is particularly strong. This is the case if public-sector employment is large. Hence, nations with a strong public sector offer the best preconditions for left-wing parties to build a new welfare state and even shift resources from the old to the new welfare state.

Conclusions

This chapter started from a comparison of level and change of public expenditures for the coverage of old and new social risks in OECD democracies. A clear variation by worlds of welfare can be detected. Post-

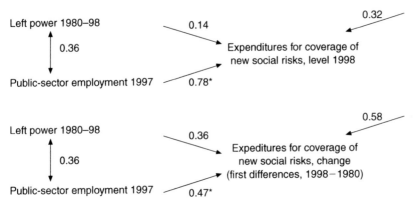

Figure 5.2 Expenditures for coverage of new social risks, left power and public sector.

communist countries are laggards in building up coverage for new social risks. This comes as no surprise, since poverty prevention in the fields of unemployment, pensions and health has priority over the coverage of new risks, which are only partially linked to the goal of poverty prevention. Liberal welfare states continued the strategy of containment of expenditures in all fields of social policy. They shifted the coverage of new risks to the market. In these nations the reconciliation of work and family became feasible – at least for middle-class families – owing to the low taxes and social security contributions from wages. Hence, nannies and care for frail elderly relatives are affordable to many middle-class families (Scharpf 2000). Continental welfare states increased expenditures for all types of social risks, with particular emphasis on the old risks, be they work or pension related. Nordic welfare states were already leaders in spending for the coverage for new social risks in the 1980s, and they have experienced the strongest growth in these types of expenditures compared to all other worlds of welfare.

How can we explain this variation? Are the politics of new social risk coverage nothing but a duplication of the politics of 'old' risk coverage? I argue that this is partly true with regard to the political promoters of welfare state expansion: left-wing parties are particularly in favor of new risk coverage (while in the few cases for which data were available, center parties did not show a strong inclination towards new social policies). However, this is not the case with regard to the social groups supporting the welfare state. The coverage of new risks may have redistributive implications within the welfare clientele. Therefore, expansion of new social policies is dependent on muting the opposition (and electoral risks) coming from the clientele of the old welfare state. The strongest supporters of the old welfare state are the elderly and those at the bottom of the social hierarchy. Most support can be garnered from female citizens – who support old and new schemes equally – and from the employees of the public sector, who support both old and new schemes and even may have a tendency to give priority to the growth of new schemes, if both types of programs cannot be expanded simultaneously. The odds that left-wing (mostly Social Democratic) parties will feel able to take these risks, are not too good compared to their national competitors from the center and the right. Social Democratic parties are still parties with a class basis, they do not attract female voters in particular, they are not parties of the younger part of the electorate, and the share of public-sector employees is not particularly strong among their support bases in nearly all countries. Hence, international variation cannot be explained by the difference in terms of age, gender and employment sector between voters for left and for non-left parties. In particular, given their class basis, Social Democratic parties should have more problems than bourgeois parties in expanding new schemes. The puzzle can be solved if we compare the size of the relevant groups between countries. With regard to age and gender structures, little variation is to be expected. Subjective class position varies between

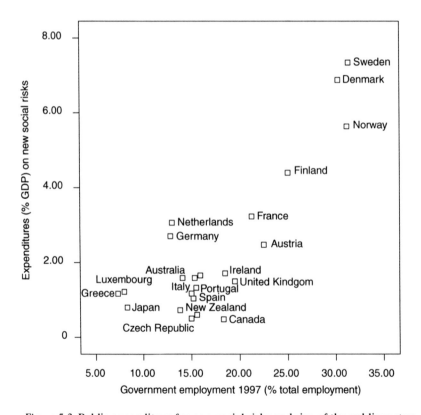

Figure 5.3 Public expenditure for new social risks and size of the public sector.

countries; and there is no evidence that in the Nordic countries the share of those in lower-class strata is smaller than in the other old OECD democracies. Hence, the crucial variable is the size of the public sector. Generally, public-sector employees are in favor of welfare state expansion – probably since many of them work in labor- or service-intensive parts of the welfare state. In fact, there is a strong correlation between size of the public sector and spending for new social risks. There is of course some circularity in the argument – since some of the employees of the public sector work in the fields of new risk coverage – but given the small size of the new social policies, this may be very limited.

With regard to the analyses of attitudes, this chapter has had to concentrate on support for old social risks, while for new schemes only data for educational expenditures have been available. However, if we look at the strong cleavages in the field of pension spending, it becomes clear that the art of new social policy expansion is the art of reconciling and balancing various segments of the welfare state clientele, which is far from homogeneous with regard to support for new policies. The political coherence of the beneficiaries of the new schemes is of limited importance, though. They hardly have a chance to combine and mobilize. Hence, the strength of the political promoters of the new welfare state is the weakness of the unconditional and definitive defenders of the old schemes, in particular pension schemes.

Putting it in simplified and stark terms, and focusing on the most expansive schemes in the policy field of old versus new risks coverage, Social Democratic parties mainly have to deal with the pensions versus schools dilemma. They can minimize their electoral risks of a 'new politics' strategy if public-sector employment is large.

Appendix

Table A-5.1 Public expenditures covering old and new social risks, 1980–98

Country	Total (less educat.) 1980	Total (less educat.) 1989	Public educat. 1991	Public educat. 1999	New risks 1980	New risks 1998	Work related risks 1980	Work related risks 1998	Old age cash benefits 1980s	Old age cash benefits 1998
Japan	10.1	14.7	3.7	3.5	0.3	0.8	6.9	8.2	2.9	5.7
United States	13.1	14.6	5.5	5.2	0.6	0.5	7.5	8.9	5.0	5.2
Ireland	16.9	15.8	5.5	4.3	0.6	1.7	12.3	11.6	4.0	2.5
Australia	11.3	17.8	5.5	5.0	0.2	1.6	8.0	11.9	3.2	4.3
Canada	13.3	18.0	6.7	5.7	0.4	0.5	10.0	12.4	2.8	5.1
United Kingdom	18.2	24.7	5.3	4.7	1.6	1.6	11.5	13.3	5.1	9.8
New Zealand	19.2	21.0	–	6.3	0.7	0.7	11.5	14.8	7.0	5.5
Mean Lib. wfs	**14.6**	**18.1**	**5.4**	**5.0**	**0.6**	**1.1**	**9.7**	**11.6**	**4.3**	**5.4**
SD Lib. wfs	**3.5**	**3.7**	**1.0**	**0.9**	**0.5**	**0.5**	**2.2**	**2.3**	**1.5**	**2.2**
Finland	18.5	26.5	6.1	6.2	2.7	4.4	11.1	15.2	4.7	7.0
Norway	18.6	27.0	6.8	7.4	1.7	5.6	12.3	15.4	4.5	6.0
Denmark	29.1	29.8	6.1	8.1	4.9	6.8	18.4	16.2	5.8	6.8
Sweden	29.0	31.0	6.5	7.7	5.2	7.4	17.2	16.2	6.7	7.5
Mean Scand. wfs	**23.8**	**28.6**	**6.4**	**7.4**	**3.6**	**6.0**	**14.7**	**15.7**	**5.4**	**6.8**
SD Scand. wfs	**6.1**	**2.2**	**0.3**	**0.8**	**1.7**	**1.3**	**3.6**	**0.5**	**1.0**	**0.6**
Spain	15.8	19.7	4.5	4.5	0.3	1.1	10.9	10.5	4.6	8.1
Portugal	11.6	18.2	5.5	5.7	0.1	1.3	8.1	10.6	3.4	6.3
Italy	18.4	25.1	–	4.5	0.3	1.1	10.7	11.1	7.4	12.8
Greece	11.5	22.7	–	3.6	0.0	1.2	6.3	11.3	5.1	10.2
Luxembourg	23.3	22.1	–	–	0.7	1.2	16.1	12.9	6.5	8.0
Germany	20.3	27.3	4.0	4.7	0.7	2.8	10.9	14.0	8.7	10.5
Austria	23.3	26.8	5.4	6.3	1.3	2.5	13.6	14.4	8.5	9.9

Netherlands	27.3	23.9	5.6	4.8	1.7	3.0	19.0	14.7	6.5	6.2
France	21.1	28.8	5.4	6.0	0.9	3.2	12.7	15.0	7.6	10.6
Belgium	24.2	24.5	5.4	5.5	0.3	1.7	17.8	15.5	6.1	7.4
Switzerland	15.2	28.3	5.4	5.5	0.2	1.6	9.3	15.5	5.6	11.2
Mean Cont. wfs	**19.3**	**24.3**	**5.2**	**5.1**	**0.6**	**1.9**	**12.3**	**13.2**	**6.4**	**9.2**
SD Cont. WFS	**5.2**	**3.4**	**0.6**	**0.8**	**0.5**	**0.8**	**4.0**	**2.0**	**1.6**	**2.1**
Slovak R.	–	13.6	–	4.3	–	0.5	–	7.8	–	5.2
Czech Republic	–	19.4	–	4.4	–	0.6	–	12.4	–	6.4
Poland	–	22.8	–	5.2	–	0.7	–	14.2	–	8.0
Mean Eastern wfs		**18.6**		**4.6**		**0.6**		**11.5**		**6.5**
SD Eastern wfs		**4.7**		**0.5**		**0.1**		**3.3**		**1.4**
Mean: all	**18.6**	**22.4**	**5.5**	**5.4**	**1.1**	**2.2**	**11.9**	**12.9**	**5.5**	**7.4**
SD: all	**5.7**	**5.1**	**0.8**	**1.2**	**1.4**	**1.9**	**3.8**	**2.4**	**1.7**	**2.5**

Acknowledgements

Earlier versions of this chapter were presented at the conference 'The Politics of New Social Risks', Lugano, Switzerland, 25–27 September 2003, and at the Conference of Europeanists, Chicago, 11–13 March 2004. I would like to thank the participants of both conferences, and in particular Giuliano Bonoli and Lane Kenworthy, for their comments.

Notes

1 For the United States, one crucial independent variable of the following analyses – employment in the public sector – is missing, and hence this country is excluded from many analyses. The same applies to Italy. There we lack data on party affiliation and voting behaviour.
2 Unfortunately, in the Role of Government surveys, party supporters were measured differently; either as party sympathy, voting intention if there were to be an election the following Sunday, or feelings of closeness to a party.
3 Here and in the following, significance is if $p < 0.05$, two-tailed.
4 'Which social class do you attribute yourself to?' 1 lower class, 2 working class, 3 lower middle class, 4 middle class, 5 upper middle class, 6 upper class. No data on subjective social class are available for Spain.
5 The exact wording of the question varies between countries. The variable 'public sector' is coded 0 if the respondent is self-employed or works in the private sector; it has the value 1 if the respondent works for government, a publicly owned firm or a non-profit organization.
6 Data on left-wing power is available only for the established OECD democracies – that is, the Central and East European countries are excluded from this analysis.

   Political mobilization of women, measured as the difference between male and female membership of political organizations (parties, trade unions, environmental groups), did not turn out to have a significant direct effect on new social risks policies, although a strong correlation exists with both left-wing power and size of the public sector. Source for female political mobilization: World Values Surveys, 1996; and if no data were available for 1996, World Values Survey 1990. Since we measured mobilization of women as the difference between male and female membership, the higher the figure, the less are women politically mobilized. Hence, the variable is labeled 'political mobilization of men relative to women'.

   The correlation between left power (lp), public sector size (ps), political mobilization of men relative to women (mm) and level and change of new risks expenditures (lnsr; chnrs) are for the sample without the post-communist countries:

   mm with ps: -0.57^*; mm with lp: -0.33; mm with lnsr: -0.43; mm with chnsr: -0.39;
   ps with lp: 0.36; ps with lnsr: 0.83^{**}; ps with chnsr: 0.60^{**};
   lp with lnsr: 0.42^*; lp with chnsr: 0.53^*
   lnsr with chnsr: 0.75^{**}

7 It should be added that there may be some circularity between size of public sector and new social risks efforts, since the latter are expressed in a larger number of teachers, social workers, etc. However, this cannot explain all of the very strong correlation of Figure 5.3.

6 Trade union movements in post-industrial welfare states

Opening up to new social interests?

Bernhard Ebbinghaus

Introduction

Although trade unions were founded to fight for better protection against social risks of employees in the industrialising period, they seem in today's post-industrial welfare states less representative of and attuned to groups facing new social risks. During the early post-war decades, trade union movements successfully organised most of the core industrial workforce, mainly blue-collar workers in industry, transport and public services. Unions fought for social rights and a fair family wage for male breadwinners. At the end of the golden age, in the early 1970s, more than half of all union members in Western European unions were still employed in industry and mining, mostly men. In the main union confederations the largest affiliate was still the blue-collar metal workers' union or a general union of unskilled workers. Despite increased labour force participation and efforts to organise new social groups, only a minority of members were then women, white-collar workers or public-sector employees (Ebbinghaus and Visser 2000). Facing increased economic and social challenges, trade unions seek to open up to new social groups, while maintaining their strongholds among blue-collar industrial workers and in the public sector. As unions have made inroads into new groups, their social composition has become more heterogeneous, and the representation of interests is more difficult in both collective bargaining and lobbying. In addition, traditionally close ties of the main union movements with allied (left-wing) political parties have been de-emphasised by both sides, partly in an effort to respond to the changing social and political landscape (Taylor 1989).

Over the long twentieth century, trade unions have advanced the extension of social and industrial citizenship rights (Marshall 1950) for their core membership, the blue-collar industrial workforce. In the collective bargaining arena they secured and advanced the working conditions of dependent workers, raised wages and salaries in line with and beyond inflation, reduced working hours, pushed for secure work places, and bargained for fringe benefits as well as workplace representation rights. Where they were unable to achieve widespread regulation of employment conditions, they lobbied for state intervention, often with the help of allied political parties, particularly when they were in government (van Waarden 1995). Moreover, trade unions were major forces pushing for the extension of social rights (Esping-Andersen 1992). This included social protection against the main social risks of modern industrial societies: accidents, sickness, old age and disability, unemployment, poverty, and family responsibilities. In the golden age of post-war welfare state expansion, public services were also expanded, providing additional job opportunities in union-friendly workplaces with good employment conditions, particularly for women. This century-long struggle for advancing social and employment rights against the 'old social risks' (OSR) – that is, the protection of the male breadwinner – has been the hallmark of the union movement's collective identity formation.

New territories for trade union interest representation, however, are marginalised social groups who bear 'new social risks' (NSR). Giuliano Bonoli (Chapter 1) provides a useful threefold classification of NSR policies:

1   the difficulties of *reconciling* increased *work* participation and traditional *family* or caring responsibilities, particularly for women with children or needy relatives;
2   the unemployment and poverty trap for those with *low skills* in a knowledge society;
3   the insufficient social security *coverage* of those weaker social groups that have interrupted working careers, fall below mandatory insurance retirements or receive no private fringe benefits.

Not all these risks are strictly new: for instance, an unemployment and poverty risk always existed for low-skilled workers. Nevertheless, the claim is that these 'new' social risks are today a more substantial problem (as female labour force participation increases) or that these risks are more severe (as job opportunities for low-skilled workers become squeezed in knowledge societies). Furthermore, they are often the consequence of welfare state retrenchment (as increased privatisation will lead to gaps in coverage) or incomplete adaptation (or recalibration) of social protection to new needs.

The traditional work-based orientation of social protection against old social risks and its relevance for the regulation of employment can be understood using the model of transitional labour markets (Schmid 2002), which is helpful in delineating the old and new social risks (see Figure 6.1). Two important types of social insurance were devised to protect against the old social risks inherent in industrial societies: (1) work incapacity due to disability or old age; and (2) unemployment due to lack of labour demand. While old age and disability pensions were sought to regulate and provide for the exit from the labour market, the unemployment insurance helped to maintain income and skills during the transitional phase of a temporary exit from work. For the labour movement, the advancement of social insurance against old age incapacity and unemployment were in the best interests of their core workforce. The use of early retirement provisions, for instance, helped to alleviate the labour market and provided a sufficient non-work income; in fact, it was seen as a deferred social wage (Ebbinghaus forthcoming). Yet even with respect to these traditional social risks, 'new' problems emerge. Repeated spells of long-term unemployment have become a 'trap' for the low skilled, while low-paid jobs increase the risk of the working poor. The large-scale use of early retirement and the demographic challenges to pension system will lead to reduced pension benefits, more old age unemployment, and increased pressure to work longer.

Traditional social policy instruments are not attuned to the new social risks that arise (1) with the transition from school to work (the entry phase); and (2) the problem of reconciling family responsibility and work (the family–work interface of transitional labour markets). The first problem affects young people. Particularly in Southern Europe, overall youth unemployment is considerably higher than for other age groups, while in Northern countries with an apprenticeship system the lack of training of unskilled workers is a major problem for future employment chances (Detzel and Rubery 2002; Samek Lodovici 2000). Trade unions have often failed to take the interests of the young as seriously as they have the protection of those senior workers with breadwinner responsibilities. Moreover, they favour a high skill–high wage strategy that seems detrimental to job opportunities for low-skilled youth. As to the second problem, the increased participation of women in the labour market

Figure 6.1 Labour market transitions and old versus new social risks.

requires changes in the regulation of part-time work, particularly the adaptation of employment rights and social protection (O'Reilly and Fagan 1998). Trade unions have found it difficult to accept part-time work and to push for better reconciliation of work and family responsibilities: 'Trade unions have often tried to restrict the spread of part-time jobs, fearing that this will undermine full-time standards. Paradoxically, where unions have viewed part-time work negatively it has expanded without protection and has been further marginalised' (Smith *et al.* 1998: 48). In addition, the expansion of care infrastructure for children of working mothers and parental leave provisions are important policies that would make it easier to reconcile work and family responsibilities (Daly 2000a).

The question that I will address in this chapter is the degree to which trade unions remain dominated by the interests of the old social risks or whether they are now opening up to the interests of 'new' social risk-bearers. How do unions balance reactive strategies to retrenchment efforts by defending the acquired social rights and the more proactive policies of seeking solutions to the new social risks? I will review the mobilisation and representation of old versus new social interests, discussing the potential implications for union strategies. In the first part, the main social status and interest groups that could be seen as facing old social risks will be discussed in the context of the ongoing membership crisis. An overview is given of OSR groups: the traditional industrial blue-collar workforce, the well-protected public-sector employees, the privileged but often under-represented white-collar employees in the private sector, and the older workers who favour the status quo. In a second part, some of the social groupings that face the new social risks will be discussed: youth, the unemployed, the low skilled, women, as well as part-time and flexibly employed workers. The purpose of this chapter is to compare the importance of OSR versus NSR interests in trade union movements in Western Europe. It is largely an explorative mapping of the major differences in the openness of trade unions across Europe. My aim is to reveal some of the obstacles in organising both old and new social risk interests.

Trade unions and OSR interests

The challenge of trade unions has to be seen in the context of the problems of membership recruitment. Over the past two decades, trade unions have been facing major difficulties in recruiting members among both old and new social groups. Since the 1980s, union density – the proportion of wage earners who are union members – has declined in all but a few European countries (Ebbinghaus and Visser 2000). Explanations for 'de-unionisation' – the decline in union membership and density – as well as cross-national variations in 'union strength' have been manifold, stressing structural, cyclical and institutional factors (Ebbinghaus and Visser 1999; Wallerstein and Western 2000). Long-term socio-economic changes make collective organisation more difficult: deindustrialisation and the growth of private services; white-collar, atypical and part-time employment; and changes in normative orientation from collectivism towards individualism. These secular changes, however, only partially explain the development over time, and they largely fail to account for cross-national variations (Ebbinghaus and Visser 1999). In contrast to popular ideas about the negative impact of globalisation, increased trade, capital openness or direct investment have not uniformly led to de-unionisation; instead, the 'fate' of unions is contingent on institutional mediating factors (Scruggs and Lange 2002; Traxler *et al.* 2001). Table 6.1 indicates that the Nordic and Belgian union movements still enjoy the highest level of union density, particularly in Sweden, Denmark and Finland, which rank at the top, followed by Belgium and Norway. The success of these union movements has been attributed to the 'selective incentive' of union-run (so-called 'Ghent') unemployment insurance (Rothstein 1992; Western 1997), as well as a combination of centralised and decentralised union activities and better union access to workplaces (Hancké 1993; Kjellberg 1998).

The core workforce: blue-collar workers

Despite the changing labour force, trade unions tend to represent the traditional core workforce; they do indeed lag behind the structural changes. The exceptions are unions in the Nordic countries and Belgium: owing to the high unionisation level, these union movements are more encompassing and represent post-industrial society more closely. Among the other countries, however, blue-collar workers still represent a large share of union members, while they are now in a clear minority position in post-industrial labour forces. For instance, blue-collar workers still make up the majority of German DGB membership; similar patterns are found in Switzerland. Yet in Austria and Belgium the industrial workers' unions face competition from important white-collar and public-sector unions. In the Netherlands, which moved most quickly towards a service economy, the industrial unions could only maintain its leading ranking vis-à-vis the public-sector unions by means of large-scale mergers (Ebbinghaus 2004). Although considerable organisational consolidation within the manufacturing and public service sectors has changed the union landscape in these countries, they are still lagging behind in organising the expanding occupational groups, in particular white-collar and private service-sector workers (Dølvik 2001a).

In Southern Europe the level of unionisation in the private sector is about half (or less) that in the public sector (see Table 6.2). Although blue-collar unions dominated in the past, it is the low or declining union density in the private sector that is contributing most to changing the union landscape. Since the 1980s, British unions have witnessed a substantial decline in the level of membership among men, from over 50 per cent

Table 6.1 Membership share and union density in Western Europe, 1998/2000

	Employed density*	Unemployed density*	Ratio U/E ratio*	Non-actives share**	Men density**	Women density**	Ratio W/M ratio**	Female share**
Denmark	85.7	79.5	0.93	9	87	89	1.02	50
Finland	–	–	–	18	75	83	1.11	54
Norway	64.9	17.7	0.27	24	55	60	1.09	44
Sweden	84.9	71.7	0.84	18	79	85	1.08	46
GB	34.3	15.8	0.46	(15)	30	29	0.97	46
Ireland	42.6	15.4	0.36	?	40	46	1.14	(44)
Austria	41.4	36.0	0.87	17	55	33	0.61	32
Belgium	–	–	–	18	59	49	0.83	(25)
Germany (W.)	25.3	11.1	0.44	19	37	21	0.56	33
Germany (E.)	16.3	8.0	0.49	–	–	–	–	–
Netherlands	32.4	17.4	0.54	18	31	20	0.65	27
Switzerland	34.1	17.7	0.52	15	*38	*29	0.77	*>35
France	18.5	2.0	0.11	(25)	*19	*18	0.91	*>45
Italy	36.3	5.7	0.16	51	*36	*37	1.05	*>40
Portugal	21.3	7.7	0.36	?	*23	*19	0.83	*>45
Spain	18.6	7.9	0.42	?	*21	*13	0.63	*>30

Source: Ebbinghaus (2002a), ISSP (1998), author's calculations.

Notes
*Union density (%) 1998: ISSP (1998); Spain: 1997; non-actives: retired people, self-employed and students; > ISSP (1998) estimate; **union density (%) or membership share (%) 2000 (see Ebbinghaus 2002a).

to below 30 per cent, largely due to dramatic blue-collar de-unionisation. As a consequence, the male blue-collar unions no longer dominate the Trades Union Congress (TUC). A less dramatic decline has been witnessed in Ireland, since the general workers' union (which also organises in the public sector) is the dominant union. The Swedish Trade Union Confederation (LO) is predominantly blue collar (except for few unions in services), and the majority of all Swedish union members still are blue-collar workers. The Danish, Finnish and Norwegian sister organisations, also aligned with the left, remain dominantly blue collar, though again a large proportion of their members work in the public sector. In contrast to Continental Europe, however, these main union confederations have a much less pronounced over-representation of men (around 55 per cent), and the strength of blue-collar unionisation is not a result of weakness in the public sector or the white-collar area.

The public-sector stronghold

The public sector remains among the best-organised sectors, despite efforts towards privatisation, public-sector spending cuts and new public management methods. In the Nordic countries (Denmark, Finland and Sweden), public-sector unionisation (90–95 per cent) is today somewhat higher than in the industrial sector (85–90 per cent) and appreciably higher than in the private service sector (around 70–75 per cent). The same relative lead holds also for Norway, though at lower overall membership levels. While the public–private gap is relatively small in the high-density countries (see Table 6.2), unionisation in the public sector is much higher than in the market sector, especially in private services, in the countries with overall lower union membership levels. A good example is Britain: unionisation is still three times higher in the public (60 per cent) than in the private sector (19 per cent). On the Continent, too, the public–private gap is significant, particularly where hostile private employers and more benevolent central and lower-level governments prevail. With the exception of Italy, Ireland and Portugal, all other Continental European unions in the public sector enjoy membership mobilisation at least twice the level of the market sector.

Many factors are conducive to better recruitment conditions (Keller 1991): public employers are more likely to recognise unions and accept union membership across all levels; collectively regulated advancement and pay schemes are more common; bureaucratisation is on average higher; and unions have more say in staff policies. In addition to the role as regulator of employment relations, the welfare state as employer has a major impact on national labour relations, often providing a model of 'good practice' and remaining a stronghold for union movements (Traxler 1999). Where overall unionisation is relatively low and declining, union movements thus become increasingly dependent on the better labour

Table 6.2 Net union density in Western Europe, 1996

	Net %	with U* %	Men %	Women %	W/M ratio	Age 35-54 %	Age -34 %	-34/35-54 ratio	Age 55+ %	55+/35-54 ratio
Sweden	88.5	87.0	86.9	89.9	1.03	92.1	80.6	0.88	89.9	0.98
Norway	63.4	60.4	60.8	66.6	1.10	69.0	52.7	0.76	71.3	1.03
Great Britain	34.8	32.6	34.4	35.1	1.02	36.4	35.1	0.96	25.3	0.70
Ireland	46.3	41.0	50.1	40.4	0.81	55.3	41.3	0.75	29.2	0.53
Germany (E.)	30.3	30.3	30.1	30.4	1.01	32.7	24.0	0.73	32.4	0.99
Germany (W.)	26.8	26.4	33.9	15.1	0.45	30.2	23.2	0.77	25.3	0.84
Switzerland	22.1	22.1	25.9	17.5	0.68	24.3	17.7	0.73	25.5	1.05
France	17.3	15.4	18.7	15.7	0.84	22.0	9.9	0.45	29.3	1.33
Italy	32.0	32.0	36.9	23.2	0.63	45.7	16.1	0.35	37.7	0.82
Spain	15.9	12.8	16.8	14.0	0.83	20.0	12.6	0.63	15.1	0.76

	Net %	Private %	State %	S/P %	P-Blue ratio	P-White %	W/B %	35+ hrs ratio	-35 hrs %	-35/35+ ratio
Sweden	88.5	81.9	94.5	1.15	–	–	–	88.3	88.9	1.01
Norway	63.4	47.7	82.8	1.74	59.3	39.8	0.67	64.5	53.7	0.83
Great Britain	34.8	22.6	66.6	2.95	–	–	–	37.1	27.4	0.74
Ireland	46.3	32.7	72.8	2.23	43.2	19.9	0.46	48.6	35.6	0.73
Germany (E.)	30.3	27.0	38.4	1.42	29.1	24.7	0.85	30.0	–	–
Germany (W.)	26.8	23.5	33.9	1.44	30.6	19.1	0.62	28.6	13.1	0.46
Switzerland	22.1	21.3	32.5	1.53	19.9	21.8	1.10	24.8	16.0	0.65
France	17.3	9.6	31.5	3.28	10.1	8.7	0.86	18.3	12.1	0.66
Italy	32.0	26.3	43.5	1.65	–	–	–	31.3	–	–
Spain	15.9	11.9	26.0	2.18	12.1	8.9	0.74	15.9	–	–

Source: ISSP (1996); author's calculations; GB, Italy, Sweden, France, and Switzerland: weighted.

Notes
Only dependent employed (V213 = 2, V206 = 1 + 2, more than 15 hrs); V222 (Membership); with U*: including unemployed; Private: private sector; State: public sector; P-Blue: private-sector blue-collar workers; P-W: private-sector white-collar workers.

relations in the public sector. The growth to limits of today's welfare states, as well as increased privatisation, decentralisation and public management, are increasingly undermining this traditional power base. Thus far, attempts at welfare retrenchment have had a mobilising effect in the public sector across Europe, at times leading to major strikes, while some governments have sought to negotiate public-sector reforms (Fajertag and Pochet 2000).

The blank spot: private white-collar employees

Having discussed the traditional union movement's core industrial workforce and the unions' remaining welfare state stronghold, we need to discuss the 'blank spot' of union organisation: the difficulty of organising the rising white-collar workforce in the private sector: technical and office employees in industry and sales as well as professional and other white-collar employees in the private service sector (Dølvik 2001a). Many of the white-collar occupations, particularly those of male employees and those that require professional or academic degrees, belong to privileged groups of employees with interests tied to old social risks that had been covered by paternalistic employer initiatives, by private voluntary insurance, and later by state schemes. The introduction of earnings-related pension insurance for white-collar employees in Germany and Austria before World War I are good examples, as is the extension of earnings-related occupational pensions from white-collar employees to all workers in Sweden in the 1960s (Esping-Andersen and Korpi 1984).

There are large differences across countries and across sectors in unionisation of white-collar workers in the private sector. The Nordic countries show particularly high levels of unionisation among private-sector white-collar workers (Table 6.2). Interestingly, male white-collar workers (particularly in higher-level grades) tend to be less organised than women in Sweden, and probably other Nordic countries. Except in Switzerland (where white-collar employees seem as little organised as blue-collar workers), white-collar employees in the private sector are 20–50 per cent less organised than blue-collar workers on average. Transport and the finance sector are often better organised than the average, while a lower degree of unionisation is common to the other private service sectors with high female employment in decentralised small workplaces, including retailing and catering. Case studies of service-sector unionisation

> show that the density levels in retail trade range from 60–80 per cent in Sweden, Denmark and Finland, around 25 per cent in Ireland and Norway, to 10–20 per cent in the UK, the Netherlands, Germany, Italy, and Austria, with France as an outlier with minimal unionisation. A similar pattern can be found in hotel and restaurants.
>
> (Dølvik 2001b, pp. 497–8)

This is largely due to the weakness of collective bargaining in these decentralised sectors and the difficulties of union access or works council representation in the small-scale private service sector. The finance sector is an exception to this rule.

Although the top end of the 'service class' has increased faster than the bottom-end servicing jobs, 'unskilled service jobs in the private sector tend, however, to be characterised by sometimes severe disadvantages: very low pay, no fringe benefits, precarious job rights and weak trade union representation' (Esping-Andersen 1993: 230). Efforts to privatise public service tasks, the increasingly flexible employment in private services, and freelance contracts in the professional services provide further challenges.

> Most European union movements, except in some of the Ghent-system countries, therefore face the dilemma whether to compete for attention and members among the growing numbers of highly-skilled professionals and white-collar service employees, or radically improving their organizing capacity among the less protected and (less) skilled groups in the lower end of the private service labour market.
>
> (Dølvik 2001b, p. 501)

Thus, the under-representation in private services poses major questions for the future of unionism in general and in the balance between OSR and NSR.

Ageing of union membership

Ageing has also had its impact on most trade unions' membership base and has shaped their interest politics. Most striking is the role of pensioners in the Italian union movement (Chiarini 1999; Wolf *et al.* 1994), where every second member has retired from the labour force (see Table 6.1). Over the past few years, unions have become major proponents in the debate on the restructuring of welfare states in Europe. At national and EU levels, reforms of the pay-as-you-go pension system and a reversal of early retirement are put forward as responses to current and future fiscal problems, to the demographic 'time-bomb', and to the low overall employment rates in most parts of Europe (Ebbinghaus 2006). Despite a lower membership level in France, pension politics has a high mobilising potential, especially among public-sector employees, as indicated by the 1995 strike wave against the Juppé government's cuts of public employee pensions, although this had been imposed on private employees two years earlier (Ebbinghaus and Hassel 2000). In Continental Europe, pensioners represent a substantial share of overall union membership, particularly in the public sector and mining (see Table 6.1). But in contrast to the more militant Southern trade unions, other Continental union movements rely on pressure group politics and their positions in the self-administered social insurance bodies to advance their interests (Reynaud 2000). In contrast, British, Irish and Nordic unions customarily have a workplace orientation focusing on active members, while allied interest groupings provide the main political and social organisation for pensioners. Whereas British and Irish unions have more limited involvement as a pressure group in public pension politics, and do not play much of a role in employer-provided occupational pensions, Nordic unions are regularly consulted on public policy, though the competing unions do not always agree on social policy issues.

Unions remain more ambivalent about the organisation and representation of pensioners' interests than is often assumed when looking merely at the number of pensioners. Except in Italy, most unions have not sought to organise pensioners to the same degree as those still active in the labour market. Indeed, the older working-age groups (45–64) – those that expect to retire soon – are the best-represented group among members, delegates and officials in most union movements. Thus, it is less the membership level of pensioners and more the high level of unionisation among workers with seniority rights that shifts the balance towards a defence of the status quo (Brugiavini *et al.* 2001).

Trade unions and NSR interests

The missing young

The ageing of union membership is not merely the result of demographic shifts; it also results from the failure to mobilise young people. Survey research shows that the likelihood of joining a union decreases with age, and recruitment conditions are unlikely to improve in the future (Klandermanns and Visser 1995). Today's low level of mobilisation will thus have consequences for decades to come, especially since the well-organised cohorts will soon retire. Certainly, the same structural and cyclical factors that affect the overall membership levels also explain some of the decline in youth membership. Compared to earlier periods and older age groups, today's youth have higher risks of joblessness (especially in Southern Europe), more difficulty in finding an apprenticeship, engage more frequently and longer in tertiary education, obtain more part-time and atypical contracts, and increasingly work in white-collar and service-sector jobs. In countries with low or declining membership trends, the age gap is particularly pronounced, while in the well-organised Nordic and Belgian union movements, which provide strong selective incentives and workplace representation, youth membership is relatively high, albeit still lower than the national average.

Membership density among young people is difficult to discover: few unions report this regularly and survey results are available for only a few

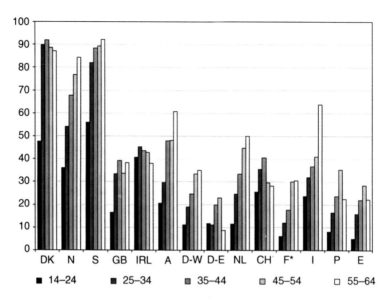

Figure 6.2 Net union density by age group, Western Europe (source: author's calculations based on ISSP 1998).

countries (see Figure 6.2). The low unionisation rate among young people is not merely a life course phenomenon, but a combined effect of age-related opportunities for union exposure and a secular change in 'decollec-tivisation' from cohort to cohort. The low density among young workers and subsequent under-representation of youth interests in West European union movements should be a major cause for concern about future membership developments. For many of these young people, unions seem to be rather old-fashioned movements and are certainly less attractive than 'new' social movements and 'fun' leisure activities. Moreover, the majority of union members, congress delegates and union officials seem to be older than '40-something'. Since current young cohorts are relatively small, union officials may not see the immediate effect of recruitment efforts, though this reinforces the problem of low representation. In countries where youth unemployment, atypical work and low levels of training are particular problems, young people will be less willing to commit them-selves to long-term membership. Thus, in Southern Europe, where seg-mented labour markets provide few opportunities to young people (Samek Lodovici 2000), the alienation from union policies favouring older workers may be highest. For instance, in order to win the consent of the trade unions (and the membership referendum), the Italian pension reform of 1995 included 'grandfather' rules to protect the interests of older workers, while the main effect of the reform affected the younger cohorts (Regini and Regalia 1997).

The unemployed

Since the mid-1970s, long-term mass unemployment has become a major problem of European welfare states; it has also aggravated the membership problems and taxed the bargaining power of unions. The negative impact of long-term unemployment on membership growth was already postulated by business cycle studies before the mass unemployment of the late 1970s (Bain and Elsheikh 1976), though the proposed relationship proved weak and with considerable lags in statistical models. Unemployed people are expected to be more likely to leave the union, while recruitment and retention of members will be more difficult, given the potential threat of dismissal by employers. Traditionally, some craft unions had even excluded the unemployed from their ranks, while those unions of less skilled workers that relied strongly on firm-level recruitment (if not closed shop arrangements) *de facto* excluded the jobless. The need to organise the unemployed became recognised only after the onset of mass unemployment in the late 1970s, though their representation remained very low.

Membership among unemployed persons is particularly high in Scandinavian countries and Belgium, which have union-led Ghent unemployment funds. In most other countries the unemployed are still hardly organised and represent a small proportion of all members. The unemployed were certainly under-represented in most non-Nordic unions, and their 'outsider' interests were seen as not present at the bargaining table at firm or higher levels. A non-representative survey of British workers found that half of the non-unionised unemployed think that 'unions are only for the employed' (Lewis 1989: 275). In some cases the jobless have organised their own protest groupings outside the labour movement, particularly in France, which has a social movement tradition of collective action. On the other hand, the German *Erwerbsloseninitiativen*, local groups of unemployed, have been relatively powerless, given the lack of the strike weapon and their need of support from union movements (Baumgarten 2003: 10).

The rise in mass unemployment since the mid-1970s only partly explains the decline in overall membership, and does not greatly help in explaining cross-national variation. Under some conditions, unemployment may help rather than hurt membership mobilisation. As several comparative studies have shown, union-led unemployment insurance, common in Denmark, Finland, Sweden (and to some extent Belgium), provides a selective incentive to join and stay in a union (Rothstein 1992; Scruggs and Lange 2001; Western 1997). Even though there is no legal obligation, potential members perceive such a link. But involvement by unions in social insurance is not always a union security. In France and the Netherlands, unemployment or early retirement schemes jointly run by social partners cannot provide a 'club good' since non-members are also covered under collective agreements. Indeed, union movements with 'Ghent' systems have achieved high union density levels, and continued to grow in the early 1990s (Ebbinghaus and Visser 1999; Golden *et al.* 1999); however, this 'union security' may not last for ever. The increased costs of union-run unemployment and early retirement schemes (as in Denmark) entail financial and political risks. These voluntary schemes are heavily subsidised by the state (or by mandatory employer contributions), while only the administrative costs are borne by membership dues. The Nordic governments, facing exceptionally high unemployment in the early 1990s, introduced cost-saving measures or attempted to undermine union-run unemployment schemes, as recently occurred in Denmark.

The low skilled

The low skilled are no 'new' social risk group; however, job opportunities for those with low skills have become less frequent through rationalised production methods and higher labour costs. Moreover, large-scale labour shedding of low-skill jobs since the mid-1970s has led to particularly high long-term unemployment and early retirement. In fact, older workers, who tend to be over-represented among the low skilled, have been pushed out of work with the help of early retirement provisions, particularly in Continental welfare states, and the tendency to leave work was the highest among the low skilled in all European countries (Ebbinghaus 2006). Because young people today have more education and occupational skills, given the expansion in general education and occupational training, being low skilled or having dropped out of school has become a stigma for those low-skilled persons entering and remaining in work (Solga 2002). In countries with dual vocational training, an apprenticeship is the pathway for young people to find subsequent employment. Those who fail to attain adequate credentials and occupational skills are clearly disadvantaged for the rest of their employment careers. While low skills were large-scale phenomena of the blue-collar industrial workforce in the past, today's low-skilled men and women are competing for low-paid service jobs at the 'bottom' of the service class (Esping-Andersen 1993).

Trade unions have traditionally sought to organise unskilled or semi-skilled blue-collar workers within general trade unions in Britain, Ireland and Denmark, or elsewhere in industrial unions that sought to be inclusive at all skill levels. Today, the shrinking number of low-skilled blue-collar workers has received less attention from union organisers, while unions face important obstacles in organising the new service 'proletariat'. Even in Nordic countries, unskilled workers, particularly men, tend to be less organised than skilled blue-collar workers, though lower-grade white-collar employees too are less likely to organise. In Britain and Ireland, unskilled men are organised to nearly the same degree as their more skilled colleagues, thanks to the dominance of general unions. However, among women there is a clear negative relationship between the level of education and unionisation, largely due to the higher rate of well-organised women with higher qualifications in the public sector. In Continental European countries, industrial unions have found it more difficult to organise unskilled workers, particularly those with unstable employment careers. Particularly when unions rely on vocational training as a strategy to increase the skilled workforce and thereby maintain high wages, unions are not very receptive to the interests of the low skilled. Moreover, the industrial unions, together with the main service-sector unions, have sought to maintain the high wage strategy in the service sector too. The high wage costs plus social contributions reduced job opportunities for the low skilled in the service sector (Scharpf 2000).

Female representation

A major long-term change – some have called it the 'most difficult revolution' (Cook *et al.* 1992) – has been the promotion of female participation in union movements. The proportion of female union membership increased in all countries in recent decades, but there are wide North–South differences in female labour force participation, union membership and union density. In Nordic welfare states, women not only are as likely to be working as men, but are even more prone to join a union today (see Tables 6.1 and 6.2). Because of high employment and membership rates, Nordic women have more or less achieved parity in overall membership with their male colleagues; they are in a majority position in many public-sector and private service-sector organisations. Similarly, given relatively high female participation and similar levels of union density in Britain and Ireland, women represent 45 per cent of union confederation membership.

On the other hand, female labour force participation, union density and membership remain much lower in Continental Europe (see Tables 6.1 and 6.2). In Germany, Austria, Belgium and the Netherlands, the likelihood of being organised is 20–40 per cent lower for women than for men. Only every fourth Belgian and Dutch union member and every third German and Austrian member is a woman. This gender gap is even wider in Southern Europe, though membership figures are difficult to obtain, which may be indicative of underdeveloped gender-specific policies. Even during the past decade, in comparison to their membership share women remained under-represented on the main executive committees of most union confederations, except in a few cases, such as the French CFDT and the Italian CGIL, which had applied quota representation (Curtin 1999; Garcia 2000). Besides the CFDT and its Belgian socialist sister organisation, two Nordic union confederations with strong blue-collar Social Democratic traditions have also elected female presidents.

At the European level, representation of women has been rather slow, given the large differences across the European Trade Union Confederation's

(ETUC) member organisations (Garcia 2000), but some progress was made at the ETUC Congress 1991, with *ex officio* representation of the advisory Women's Committee. In recent years, female interests have been directly affected by several EU-level social policy activities, in particular the framework agreements on parental leave (1995) and on part-time workers (1997), as well as EU policy initiatives and European Court of Justice decisions on equal opportunity. The Swedish EU presidency in early 2001 was an opportunity for the governing Swedish Social Democratic government to advance gender mainstreaming not only at the national level, but also at the European level.

Gender pay differences are still around 15–20 per cent in the Nordic countries, Ireland, France and Benelux, and even higher in the other Continental European countries and the United Kingdom, which cannot solely be attributed to gender-related differences in employment patterns. Indeed, governments have thus far focused less on equal pay issues than on formal anti-discrimination policies and promotion of female employment, while the collective bargaining partners were less willing to renegotiate the wage structure than to push for general pay increases. 'As a matter of fact, women are largely absent from the collective bargaining process, and the content of agreements at the national level remains male-oriented' (Bergamaschi 2000: 172). In countries with social concertation on income policies, as in Finland, Belgium or Ireland, gender equality issues are more likely to be discussed, while in countries with sectoral or decentralised bargaining, unions seem to leave gender equality issues to government policies.

Part-time and flexible employment

Part-time work is expanding in most countries.

> Although part-time employment is still a female phenomenon concentrated in lower functions within the service sector, recent developments point towards convergence of the rates between men and women and a spread of part-time employment towards the industrial sector and higher-level jobs.
>
> (Delsen 1998: 73)

Part-time employees are less likely to be organised by trade unions, largely because of recruitment problems, not least because they are more difficult for union officials to approach. Part-timers are concentrated in particular sectors that are difficult to organise and tend to be employed in smaller organisations. To the degree that part-timers, particularly those with few hours, are not sufficiently covered under collective bargaining arrangements, labour regulations or social insurance coverage, they may not see any advantage in becoming a union member. This then reinforces the under-representation dilemma.

The gap between full-time and part-time workers is considerable (see Table 6.2), with few significant exceptions. In Continental Europe, union density for part-time employees tends to be between half (e.g. Western Germany) and about two-thirds (e.g. France) of the overall rate, while the part-time rate is somewhat closer (three-quarters) to the rate of full-timers in Britain and Ireland, and equally high, or nearly so, in Nordic countries. In the 'first part-time economy of the world' (Visser 2002), the Netherlands, union density for full-time workers was above 30 per cent in the 1990s, around 23–25 per cent for those working more than half-time (20–34 hrs), and 13 per cent for those working less than half-time (12–19 hrs), and only 3 per cent for those working a few hours per week (under 11 hrs) (Ebbinghaus and Visser 2000: 452). In Britain, union density for part-time workers has remained at around 21 per cent since the early 1990s, while the rate of union membership receded significantly from 44 per cent in 1989 to 32 per cent in 2002 (Labour Force Survey, UK, 2002, cited in *Labour Market Trends*, July 2003, p. 338). In both countries the rate of unionisation among part-time workers remained stable throughout the 1990s, indicating that it is less a declining level of organisation among part-time workers, rather the overall increase in such employment that increasingly challenges union movements, in addition to the declining density of unionisation among full-time workers.

Even more difficult is the organisation of those on other atypical employment contracts (fixed-term contracts, posted workers, etc.). In the Netherlands, non-standard 'flexible' contracts have grown considerably, partially regulated through the 'flexicurity' arrangements via labour law and collective bargaining. Nevertheless, the unionisation rate of Dutch flexi-workers was only one-third (10 per cent) that of those with standard (permanent) work contracts (30 per cent) in the 1990s (Ebbinghaus and Visser 2000: 452). Similarly in the United Kingdom, temporary workers are less likely to be union members than those permanently employed (19 per cent versus 30 per cent), while the gap is nearly twice as high in the private sector (11 per cent versus 19 per cent) and public sector (32 per cent versus 62 per cent), which has a higher degree of temporary contracts and special working arrangements in a more union-friendly environment (Labour Force Survey, UK, 2001, cited in *Labour Market Trends*, July 2002, pp. 343–55). Similar obstacles to organising the 'new social risk' group with flexible employment contracts will be common in the other countries; however, not much information has thus far been gathered, and organisational strategies devised by the trade unions in Continental European countries are still insufficient.

Conclusion

The main findings concerning the OSR/NSR difference can be subsumed as particular organising patterns in the four 'families' of union movements across Western Europe. The Nordic union movements have adapted most to the changing labour force. All Nordic unions rely on strong workplace organisation, and they are capable of enforcing relatively encompassing bargaining coverage and can use political influence through corporatist arrangements. The Danish, Finnish and Swedish unions profit from the selective incentives of unemployment insurance, while Norwegian unions are somewhat less well organised, particularly in the white-collar private service sector. The high level of unionisation is common to most sectors and occupational groups, and female employees are even more likely to be unionised than their male colleagues. Given high female labour force participation, women represent a majority of workers in many union confederations and service worker unions.

Nordic unions have been largely successful in maintaining high wages for skilled workers, fostering a high level of employment and avoiding segmentation of labour markets through flexibilisation and deregulation. Yet there are also some areas of concern: today's younger people tend to organise at a lower level than earlier cohorts at the same age, and integration of low-skilled jobseekers requires particular activation policies. The unemployment crisis of the 1990s and the employer-driven push towards decentralisation have also provided a particular challenge to the Nordic union movements. In both pension reforms and activation policies, trade unions have taken a generally supporting, though partly critical, stance on particular issues.

Trade unions in Britain and to a lesser degree in Ireland have suffered from decreasing membership, labour market deregulation and bargaining decentralisation since the 1990s. Given rapid declines in the private sector, the public sector has become the remaining stronghold of British unionism. The degree of unionisation among the former core group of male blue-collar workers has declined considerably, while unionisation among women today even exceeds that of men, thanks to the larger concentration in the public sector. While unions traditionally have not been keen to organise the unemployed, the general unions cater for unskilled workers to the same degree as for others. The major challenge British unions face is to organise young workers and to overcome employer resistance to recruitment (Waddington and Kerr 2002). Only every third British worker is a trade union member, and not many more are covered under collective bargaining; thus, many low-skilled workers have to rely on the state-regulated minimum wage. Lacking bargaining power and widespread coverage in addition to their limited political influence, British unions are currently unable to advance the interests of the groups facing new social risks. The situation is somewhat better in Ireland, owing to the higher level of organisation, the recent economic boom and the national social pacts that have led to framework agreements. New efforts are now made to also bring in the 'outsider' interests into the tripartite bargaining process (O'Donnell and O'Reardon 2002).

Union movements in Continental Europe have spent much mobilisation effort and political capital to defend the old social groups, yet they lag behind in organising and taking on the interests of the new social groups. Corporatist institutionalisation in the bargaining and social policy arena (e.g. via self-administration) as well as statutory workplace representation rights have provided some 'buffer' against direct losses of power due to declining or low union membership (Ebbinghaus and Visser 1999). Continental European union movements tend to be more dominated by male blue-collar workers, public employees with secure employment and older workers with seniority rights than those in the Nordic countries. The status quo defence of early retirement rights is one example of the age bias of Continental union movements (Ebbinghaus 2006). Trade union membership is certainly ageing, while young people tend to be much less likely to join and are unlikely to become members at later ages. Although the share of female membership has expanded with increased labour force participation, the gender gap among members, works councillors and union officers is still considerable. Although some public-sector and white-collar unions are now clearly dominated by female-member majorities, gender mainstreaming has only slowly entered the bargaining realm and policy agenda of unions (Garcia 2000).

A major difference between Southern and Central Continental European union movements is the importance of labour market segmentation. In Southern Europe, youth unemployment is a more pressing problem and flexible employment contracts, largely outside the control of unions, have also become a more serious trend. The apprenticeship orientation of Austrian, Belgium, German, Dutch and Swiss union movements have helped ease the unemployment problems of young people. However, the low skilled remain a major risk group for the rest of their working-age lives, as the high wage policies and the heavy payroll contributions pose a considerable obstacle for employment opportunities to the poorly educated.

The current dilemma for trade unions, particularly in Continental Europe, is not only how to open up to these diverse new social groups, while holding on to the traditional core groups, but also how to square the circle of representing these diverse interests in collective bargaining and the public policy arena. Particularly in Continental Europe, the question union leaders face is how to protect the old social risk interests of the core membership against bargaining decentralisation, labour market deregulation and social policy retrenchment, while simultaneously advancing the new social risk agenda for reconciling work and family life, enhancing employability for low-skilled workers, and extending coverage for those who have been excluded thus far. The situation is somewhat different in Britain and Ireland, given the more inclusive membership patterns. But the interests of NSR have become more pressing in these two countries, given the 'working poor' problem of the Liberal welfare regimes and the more competitive wage formation. The Nordic unions seem in a better-placed position to take on NSR interests in both the bargaining realm and the public policy arena; nevertheless, they also face hard decisions in balancing these interests within their movement and the reduced institutionalised influence since the 1990s. With few significant exceptions, the NSR interests are thus still weakly organised – and unions find it difficult to advance their representation of them internally and externally.

7   Combating old and new social risks

Evelyne Huber and John D. Stephens

'Old' versus 'new' welfare states

For roughly two decades now, commentators from different political camps have pronounced the welfare state to be in crisis. Journalistic commentators, primarily those with a neo-liberal bent, claim that it is too expensive, no longer affordable under conditions of slower economic growth, and that it needs to be greatly cut back in order to stimulate economic growth. Political commentators on the left and academics worry that expenditures are misallocated and privilege some groups at the expense of others, and they argue that the welfare state needs to be thoroughly restructured (Esping-Andersen 1999, 2002; Pierson 2001c). The debate about restructuring is to a large extent framed in terms of the 'old' versus the 'new' welfare state, or welfare states designed to deal with old as against new social risks.

The 'old' welfare state is conceptualized as transfer-heavy, oriented toward covering risks from loss of earnings capacity due to old age, unemployment, sickness, and invalidity. The modal (and model) client of the old welfare state is seen as a male blue-collar production worker who is the breadwinner for the family. The family is protected through the entitlements of the main breadwinner. The 'new' welfare state is conceptualized as more service-heavy, oriented toward increasing the earnings capacity of individuals through support for continuing education, training and retraining, and socialization of care work to facilitate the combining of paid work with raising a family. There is no real modal client of the new welfare state, and it certainly is not the male family breadwinner. Individuals can be clients of the new welfare state at different stages of the life cycle, be it as children of working parents, as adolescents in training, as adults in retraining, as working parents with small children, or as elderly people in need of care.

This distinction between old and new welfare states is valid and captures the need for important adaptations of welfare state structures to changing economic, demographic and social structures. However, two caveats are in order. First, there is a danger of underestimating the continued importance of old social risks. People still become sick, disabled and unemployed and need income support in those cases. Moreover, not only do people still get old, but they are getting older and older, spending more time in retirement and thus needing income support for longer. Thus, welfare state adaptations have to include reforms of these income support systems to put them on a firm financial basis.

Second, the debate about old versus new welfare states overlooks important differences between welfare state regime types. The characterization of the old welfare state fits the Continental European welfare states, or the Christian Democratic regime type, best. It also fits the Anglo-Saxon welfare states, or the Liberal regime type, though at a much lower level of comprehensiveness and generosity. In contrast, the Nordic welfare states, or the Social Democratic regime type, have incorporated essential elements of the new welfare state for decades. They have been oriented toward supporting training and retraining since the early post-World War II period, and since the 1970s they have expanded the provision of social services, prominently in the area of care for children and the elderly, which has facilitated the entry of women into the labor force (Huber and Stephens 2000, 2001a). At the same time, they have maintained transfers to prevent people from falling into poverty due to sickness, unemployment, or old age.

The affinity between the Social Democratic welfare state regime type and the concept of the new welfare state, of course, does not mean that these welfare states have necessarily found the right balance in allocating welfare state resources among competing needs. Here as well as in Christian Democratic welfare states, the question is whether some risks and groups are privileged over others and whether – in the era of slow growth and highly limited possibilities for welfare state expansion – expenditures might need to be reallocated across programs. Essentially these are empirical questions, in part to be answered by comparing groups exposed to old and new risks. If we assume that a common goal of old and new welfare states is to minimize poverty, a comparison of poverty rates among various population groups can tell us how effective welfare states are in dealing with old and new risks.

Given that Social Democratic welfare state regimes have already acquired traits of the new welfare state, it seems reasonable to hypothesize that the causal dynamics behind the expansion and adaptation of the Social Democratic welfare state regimes are also operating to some extent in the transformation of old into new welfare states. However, regime legacies are clearly of crucial importance here. In many ways it was easier to incorporate programs to deal with what are now called new social risks during the phase of welfare state expansion, as the Nordic countries did. It is more difficult to do this in the phase of welfare state retrenchment, when new programs are hard to finance through higher extraction from an existing resource base, and rather require an expansion of the resource base and/or a reallocation of resources away from established programs.

We would expect that the Continental European countries with the most generous welfare states, of the Christian Democratic variety, would have the most difficulties in adapting (Scharpf and Schmidt 2000; Scharpf 2000). In the Anglo-Saxon countries, where the welfare state has not grown to limits in comparative perspective, there should be more room for man-euver. On the other hand, to the extent that the factors that kept the liberal welfare states from expanding remain unchanged, we would expect them to obstruct successful adaptation and reduction of poverty resulting from new social risks as well.

New versus old social risks

New social risks can be conceptualized in a variety of ways. Bonoli in his introductory chapter of this book takes a broad view and includes five kinds of difficult situations brought about by the transition to post-industrialism and the massive entry of women into the labor force. Here we take a narrower view and concentrate on poverty. We conceptualize new social risks as risks that occur more frequently today than, say, two or three decades ago because changes in the economic, demographic and social structure have increased the number of social groups at risk and/or increased the risk of a given social group to fall into poverty. Prominent among these changes are the reduction in stability of family patterns, which in turn is related to increasing divorce rates and greater female labor force participation. Accordingly, the proportion of households headed by single mothers has increased, and thus so has the proportion of households in danger of being poor (Kilkey and Bradshaw 1999). This in turn has increased the probability that children will live in poverty.

Other changes are the decrease in stability of career patterns, the demand for higher skill levels for most jobs in the information society, the trend towards greater wage inequality (at least in some countries) and the increase in overall levels of unemployment, which work together to increase the likelihood that individuals will experience unemployment and thus the risk of poverty during their working age (Gallie 2002). Whereas poverty due to unemployment is an old risk for lower-skilled blue-collar workers, it has intensified for them in the information society, and it has come to affect employees with higher skill levels and in white-collar jobs too. Moreover, during the 1950s and 1960s, unemployment was so low (1–3 percent) in many European countries that it was not a large risk factor even for blue-collar workers. This contrasts sharply with the experience of the past two decades, in which double-digit unemployment rates have not been unusual. Thus, poverty among the working-age popu-lation can be regarded as a new social risk, insofar as the risk group (unemployed of working age) has grown. The increase in poverty risk among the working-age population also contributes to a higher probability that children will live in poverty.[1]

The prototypical old social risk is poverty in old age. Other than accident insurance for workers, pensions were the first social programs to be introduced (Hicks 1999). Even here, though, one might argue that demographic changes, namely the increase in life expectancy on the one hand and the declining fertility rates on the other, have increased the size of the risk group as a percentage of the population and thus turned it partly into a new social risk. Nevertheless, we will go with convention and treat poverty among elderly people as an old social risk.

Our analysis, then, will focus on poverty among four groups: elderly people, the working-age population, single mothers, and children. The first we treat as an old social risk, the other three as new social risks. We will first look at overall trends in the occurrence of these risks and then at how well welfare states deal with new and old social risks by protecting these different groups from falling into poverty. In the case of the working-age population, single mothers, and children, we will analyze a two-step process. We will analyze the determinants of poverty among these groups before taxes and transfers, and we will then analyze the reduction of poverty among these groups effected by taxes and transfers. In the case of the elderly, we will analyze post-tax and transfer poverty only, because pre-tax and transfer poverty is greatly inflated in countries with generous public pension systems. Since the public pension systems in these countries guarantee almost all retirees an adequate retirement income, few pensioners have significant alternative sources of income and thus almost all elderly people fall below the poverty line when transfers are not counted. Thus, pre-tax and transfer poverty is an almost meaningless figure in such countries.

Welfare state regime types and new versus old social risks

Table 7.1 offers a summary overview of trends in pre-tax and transfer poverty among different social groups. We compare the average for the period up to 1987 and the period after 1987. We use data from the Luxembourg Income Study (LIS) data base, which are available in waves from the late 1970s to the late 1990s (http://www.lis.ceps.lu). We choose 1987 as the dividing year rather than an earlier date closer to what is generally considered the onset of the period of welfare state retrenchment, because we would lose Denmark and Finland if we chose an earlier point for comparison, as their first LIS surveys were carried out in that year. The pre-1987 period, then, covers roughly 13 years from the mid-1970s on (plus one survey in Canada in 1971 and one in Germany in 1973), and the post-1987 period roughly the following 13 years. We also have to exclude Austria, Ireland and Italy, because we have no data for pre-tax and transfer income for these countries for either the earlier or the entire period. The mean for all countries shows that pre-tax and transfer poverty increased for all of our new-risk groups. It also shows that the percentage

Table 7.1 Levels of risks and outcomes up to and after 1987

	Social Democratic welfare states		Christian Democratic welfare states		Liberal welfare states	
	Average up to 1987	*Average after 1987*	*Average up to 1987*	*Average after 1987*	*Average up to 1987*	*Average after 1987*
Risks						
Pre-tax and transfer poverty						
Working age	11.6	17.0	15.7	16.8	15.1	19.3
Children	13.8	18.1	12.7	15.9	22.1	28.1
Single mothers	45.4	50.0	50.0	54.4	65.1	67.9
Percentage of households headed by single mothers	12.5	17.2	7.7	10.0	12.2	17.2
Outcomes						
Post-tax and transfer poverty						
Aged	16.4	9.2	14.2	9.7	23.7	18.5
Working age	4.4	3.9	6.4	7.1	10.5	12.0
Children	3.9	3.8	4.9	7.8	14.8	18.1
Single mothers	11.1	10.8	19.9	22.5	44.5	44.2

of households headed by single mothers increased steeply. So, more women and children live in female-headed households, and a greater percentage of these households are poor.

Table 7.1 also shows, though, that there are some systematic differences among welfare state regime types as regards the risk of poverty for the different groups grouped by welfare state type. The size of the risk group of female-headed households is roughly similar in the Social Democratic and the Liberal welfare states, but female-headed households in Social Democratic welfare states have a significantly lower probability of being in poverty than their counterparts in Liberal welfare states, a difference of roughly 19 percentage points. For children living in the two welfare state regime types, the difference in the incidence of poverty is 8–10 percentage points. For both risk groups, poverty in Christian Democratic welfare state regimes is closer to the Social Democratic than the Liberal regime type; for single-mother households, poverty is some 5 percentage points higher than in Social Democratic welfare state regimes, for children 1–2 percentage points lower.

As we will explain more fully later in the chapter, these differences are partly due to non-transfer aspects of the welfare state, particularly social services that facilitate the pursuit of paid work for mothers with pre-school and school-age children (Meyers *et al.* 1999).[2] Thus, single mothers are more likely to be employed in Social Democratic welfare states (Kilkey and Bradshaw 1999). In part, these differences are also due to the production regimes in which the different welfare state regimes are embedded. In the coordinated production regimes of the Nordic countries (with Social Democratic welfare state regimes) and the Northern Continental countries (with Christian Democratic welfare state regimes), high union density, high contract coverage and high coordination in wage-setting produce lower wage dispersion and higher minimum incomes (Kenworthy 2001; Rueda and Pontusson 2000; Wallerstein 1999), so single mothers who do work are more likely to keep themselves and their children out of poverty than single mothers in the uncoordinated production regimes characteristic of the Anglo-Saxon countries (with Liberal welfare state regimes).

Among the working-age population, the incidence of pre-tax and transfer poverty is roughly similar across the three regime types, particularly for the later period. The countries with Social Democratic welfare state regimes had a lower incidence of poverty in the earlier period, by some 4 percentage points, but with the economic crisis of the early 1990s, unemployment and thus pre-tax and transfer poverty increased more rapidly than in the other countries and caught up with the level in countries with Christian Democratic welfare states. The countries with Liberal welfare state regimes remained some 2 percentage points higher in their level of pre-tax and transfer poverty.

As one would expect, it is in the incidence of post-tax and transfer poverty that big differences between welfare state regime types emerge.

Table 7.1 shows that Social Democratic welfare state regimes performed best in handling the new social risks for every one of the risk groups, and the Liberal welfare states worst, with the Christian Democratic welfare states somewhat closer to the former than the latter. Furthermore, the Social Democratic welfare states managed to lower poverty or at least keep it constant for the working-age population, single-mother households, and children, despite the fact that pre-tax and transfer poverty had increased in every one of these groups. In the Liberal and Christian Democratic regime types, poverty increased among all the risk groups, with the only exception being single-mother households in Liberal welfare states, where poverty was held constant, but at a level four times higher than in the Social Democratic welfare states (44 percent compared to 11 percent).

The picture for the old social risk group of the elderly looks very different. Their level of poverty was reduced in every single welfare state regime type, and the Social Democratic and Christian Democratic regime types achieved roughly similar results. The level of poverty among the elderly was 2 percentage points higher in the earlier period in the Social Democratic than in the Christian Democratic welfare state regimes, but brought down to the same level in the later period. Though the average level of poverty among the elderly was also reduced in Liberal welfare states from the earlier to the later period, it was twice as high as in the Social Democratic and Christian Democratic welfare states in the later period.

The figures in Table 7.1 underestimate the degree of change over the past few decades because they are averages for almost a decade, and even more in some cases. We can produce estimates of the change over the period 1980–2000 within the regime types with simple regression analysis. For each welfare state regime, we regressed our dependent variables on time, to obtain a measure for the average change of the dependent variable over a ten-year period in a given welfare state regime type. Then we took the intercept as an indicator of the level of the dependent variable in 1980 (because time was specified as 0 in 1980). Table 7.2 summarizes the results, which are entirely consistent with the results derived from our inspection of averages in Table 7.1. The size of the new risk group of single mothers increased in every welfare state regime, though the level in 1980 was only about half in the Christian Democratic welfare state regimes. Pre-tax and transfer poverty also increased in every new risk group (single mothers, children, working-age population) and every welfare state regime type. Pre-tax and transfer poverty among the working-age population increased most rapidly in Christian Democratic welfare states, but at the same time they kept the increase of poverty among single mothers comparatively low.

The figures from our regressions for post-tax and transfer poverty confirm the findings in Table 7.1 that the elderly are the only risk group

Table 7.2 Level and change in risks and outcomes

	Social Democratic welfare states		Christian Democratic welfare states		Liberal welfare states	
	Estimated 1980 level	Average % change per decade	Estimated 1980 level	Average % change per decade	Estimated 1980 level	Average % change per decade
Risks						
Pre-tax and transfer poverty						
Working age	12.0	2.9	14.5	4.4	15.3	3.0
Children	12.7	3.3	11.6	4.1	22.5	3.9
Single mothers	48.0	3.4	49.9	0.9	65.8	3.1
Percentage of households headed by single mothers	12.4	3.1	6.7	3.1	11.9	3.4
Outcomes						
Post-tax and transfer poverty						
Aged	12.9	−2.2	15.3	−3.9	23.3	−4.3
Working age	4.8	−0.8	6.1	1.7	10.6	1.4
Children	3.9	−0.2	4.8	2.4	14.6	2.1
Single mothers	14.3	−1.9	21.8	1.6	43.2	−0.4

whose poverty rate has been lowered in all three regime types, and that the Social Democratic regime type is the only one to have lowered the poverty rate of all four risk groups. Post-tax and transfer poverty increased for all three new risk groups in the Christian Democratic and Liberal welfare states, with the exception of single mothers in Liberal welfare states, whose comparatively very high poverty rate was reduced very marginally. However, post-tax and transfer poverty increased at a lower rate than pre-tax and transfer poverty in every risk group in Christian Democratic and Liberal welfare states alike, with the exception of single mothers in Christian Democratic welfare states. This indicates that all three welfare state regime types successfully dampen increases in poverty resulting from the increase in new social risks, but that they do so with different degrees of success. A comparison of levels in 1980 also shows that Social Democratic welfare state regimes had built up the most effective poverty prevention and poverty reduction programs among new risk groups by that point in time.

Characteristics of welfare state regimes and labour market regimes

The next step toward understanding what makes some welfare state regimes more effective than others in preventing and lowering poverty is an analysis of the key characteristics of the different regime types. Here we have to look both at the overall generosity of the welfare states and at their structure in terms of composition of welfare state programs. By the mid-1980s, government expenditure in both Social Democratic and Christian Democratic welfare states on average amounted to over half of their GDP. In countries with Liberal welfare states, total government expenditure was only, on average, 42 percent of GDP.

In line with overall significantly lower levels of revenue and expenditures in Liberal welfare states, these welfare states have the lowest levels of transfer and non-transfer expenditures, and of pension spending per elderly person, indicating a highly limited role in providing income support and social services. Christian Democratic and Social Democratic welfare state regimes both have high levels of expenditure, but a systematically different pattern of allocation. Essentially, Christian Democratic welfare state regimes emphasize transfer payments in their allocation of expenditure, whereas Social Democratic welfare state regimes emphasize social services. The most telling difference that illustrates the importance of social services is in civilian government employment, which accounts for 19.2 percent of working-age population in Social Democratic and only 8.8 percent – less than half – in Christian Democratic welfare state regimes.[3]

The two most common social services provided in welfare state regimes in advanced industrial countries for the entire population are education and healthcare. Other social services, such as labor market assistance (support in retraining, re-employment, relocation), care for children and elderly people, and assistance for the handicapped, are provided mainly in the Social Democratic and in some Christian Democratic welfare state regimes, in the former typically by public and in the latter by private providers.

Labor market and care services are of particular importance for new risk groups, as they facilitate integration into the labor market, the former for both genders and the latter primarily for women. Strong retraining and re-employment support reduces the probability of long-term unemployment and entrapment in low-skill/low-pay jobs and thus of poverty among the working-age population (Esping-Andersen *et al.* 2002). Higher women's labor force participation raises the proportion of dual-earner households and thus further reduces the risk of poverty among the working-age population resulting from career instability and unemployment. It also raises the probability that single mothers are in paid employment and can keep themselves out of poverty. Higher proportions of dual-earner households and working single mothers in turn reduce the incidence of poverty among children.

By now, we know a significant amount about intergenerational educational achievement and risks of poverty. We know how poverty impairs learning among children through an unsupportive environment. We also know that educational achievement of parents and children is highly correlated (e.g. OECD/HRDC 2000), and to the extent that low educational achievement is a high risk factor for poverty in the new economy, that means that children of poor parents with low skills are more likely to end up in poverty as adults themselves.

The best comparable data across countries on actual skills – as opposed to educational enrollment and completion rates – come from a study done by the OECD and Statistics Canada (OECD/HRDC 2000). Representative samples of the population in 20 countries (12 of them in our set of countries) were tested for their ability to understand documents, prose and quantitative problems in the years 1994–98.[4] The proportion of the population scoring at level 3 or more, considered by the authors of the study as necessary for functioning competently in the information economy, varied from a low of 49 percent in the United States to a high of 74 percent in Sweden. If we look at the scores at the bottom, the average scores for the bottom 5 percent of the population ranged from 133 in the United States to 216 in Sweden, with Britain, Canada and Australia at 145–6 the next lowest and Norway and Denmark at 207–13 the next highest. Thus, we see a systematic difference between countries with Liberal and with Social Democratic welfare state regimes, the former with the lowest and the latter with the highest skill at the bottom of their skill distributions.

We have argued that this is in large part a result of the fact that the

Social Democratic welfare states had built up effective poverty prevention and poverty reduction programs, including good education and training programs, over a long period of time, whereas the Liberal welfare states had not. Thus, fewer children over time grew up in poor families and were hampered by poverty in their educational achievements in Social Democratic welfare states. This hypothesis receives support from a simple correlation analysis. Skill levels at the bottom 5 percent and 25 percent are not related to educational expenditures, but strongly negatively correlated with poverty and inequality (Huber and Stephens 2001b). What is important to emphasize is that these poverty prevention and reduction programs from the beginning entailed not just transfers but a very strong emphasis on services to promote labor market integration, first for males and – beginning in the 1960s – increasingly also for females. Of course, just being in the labor force may not be enough to keep oneself and dependents out of poverty, if wages are low. Thus, it is important to look at the labor market regimes in which the welfare state regimes are embedded.

If we look again at the situation in the mid-1980s, union density was much higher in the Nordic countries (an average of 71 percent) than in the Continental European (32 percent) and the Anglo-Saxon countries (also 32 percent).[5] However, legislation or agreements between employers' federations and unions extended contract coverage to a much higher percentage of the workforce than union members in the Continental European countries (to 80 percent, bringing them to the level of the Nordic countries (81 percent), and creating a large gap between those two and the Anglo-Saxon countries (51 percent). In the degree of coordination of wage-setting, the Nordic countries again ranked highest and the Anglo-Saxon countries lowest, with the Continental European countries more or less in the middle. As noted previously, these differences in labor market institutions had an important effect on wage dispersion, measured as the ratio of average earnings at the 50th to the 10th percentile of income earners, which was lowest in the Nordic countries and highest in the Anglo-Saxon countries, with the Continental European ratio closer to the Nordic than to the Anglo-Saxon countries.

These differences give us a second set of parameters, in addition to the characteristics of welfare state regimes, with which to understand determinants of poverty among new social risk groups. So far, we have looked at factors that enable men and women to participate in the labor market, such as labor market and care services. Now we turn our focus to the jobs that are available. While manufacturing has declined, all of the job growth over the past two decades has occurred in the service sector (Scharpf and Schmidt 2000: 346–8). In all of our countries, services have grown, but there have been significant differences between countries in the growth of public and private social services. In the Anglo-Saxon countries, low contract coverage and high wage dispersion have facilitated the emergence of a large low-wage private service sector, including social services such as day care and care of the elderly, and personal services such as restaurants, laundries, cleaning, etc. In the Nordic and the Continental European countries, comparatively high contract coverage and low wage dispersion have prevented the emergence of such a low-wage private service sector. In the Nordic countries the public social service sector expanded considerably, offering jobs with social security coverage and adequate wages; in the Continental European countries it did not. Accordingly, overall job growth has been low and labor force participation rates are on average the lowest in the Continental European countries. Since women are more likely than men to work in private and public social and personal services, this is one of the reasons why female labor force participation rates are particularly low in the Continental European countries. Female labor force participation is highest in the Nordic countries, with 74 percent, lowest in the Continental European countries, with 49 percent, and intermediate in the Anglo-Saxon countries, with 62 percent.

Determinants of welfare state regimes

To understand the causal dynamics of the formation of these welfare state regime types, we need to turn to political power distributions. As we have argued extensively, power constellation, state-centric and logic of industrialism theoretical approaches to welfare state formation have important insights to offer, but the power constellation approach has most explanatory power (Huber and Stephens 2001a). Here we present an updated analysis of welfare state formation, covering the period from 1960 to 1989, 1994, and 1998 for different variables, depending on data availability (Table 7.3). The determinants that emerge most consistently in regressions of our various indicators of welfare state expenditure and structure are incumbency of political parties with different ideological orientations and strength of women's organization. Our measure of women's organization is a cumulative average of estimated women's membership in non-religious organizations.[6]

These regressions show that Social Democratic and Christian Democratic incumbency were statistically highly significant and substantively important positive determinants of total government revenue and expenditure, transfer and non-transfer expenditure, pension generosity, and social security benefit expenditure. The regressions further show that left-wing incumbency was less significant for transfer expenditure and Christian Democratic incumbency was actually significant and negative for civilian government employment. These regression results, then, are consistent with the differences between welfare state regimes discussed earlier regarding emphasis on transfers in Christian Democratic and on social services in Social Democratic regimes. The strength of women's organization is highly significant and substantively strong for most of our dependent variables except for the proportion of public-sector health spending, where

Table 7.3 Determinants of various measures of welfare state effort

	Total government revenue	Total government expenditure	Non-transfer expenditure	Civilian government employment	Social security transfer expenditure	Pension spending per aged person	Public % of total health spending	Social security benefit expenditure
Left cabinet	0.312***	0.270***	0.163***	0.194***	0.095**	0.064***	0.148	0.178**
Christian Democratic cabinet	0.250***	0.388***	0.129**	-0.077***	0.220***	0.129***	-0.173	0.251***
Constitutional structure	-0.043	-0.247	-0.501*	-0.095	0.040	0.149^	-3.334***	-0.082
Women's organization	0.326***	0.380***	0.246***	0.170***	0.128*	0.071**	-0.262	0.301***
Voter turnout	-0.042	-0.029	0.032	0.025	-0.038	-0.003	1.602	0.009
% aged	1.442***	1.687***	0.583**	0.659***	0.918***	0.137*	0.131**	1.415***
Authoritarian legacy	-0.456	-0.096	0.033	-0.503*	0.146	0.035	3.457**	0.432
GDP per capita (1,000s)	-0.045	-0.303*	-0.067	0.102***	-0.119	0.008	0.327*	0.085
Consumer price index	1.107***	1.425***	0.576*	0.466***	0.456***	0.145*	0.125	0.126
Unemployment	0.058	0.670***	0.399***	-0.004	0.361***	0.077***	0.009	0.460***
Military spending	0.272	1.116***	1.017***	0.081	0.094	-0.016	-0.606	-0.209
Foreign direct investment out	-0.018	-0.156*	-0.167**	-0.019	-0.018	-0.012	-0.271*	-0.021
Trade openness	0.024	0.017	0.032	-0.008	0.000	0.001	0.005	0.020
Constant	-1.135	-2.573	0.075*	-8.230**	-3.187	-1.717	45.745***	-16.33***
Common rho	0.91	0.90	0.86	0.96	0.88	0.90	0.90	0.85
OLS adjusted R-square	0.78	0.80	0.72	0.84	0.68	0.65	0.62	0.79*
N	663	663	663	595	663	510	663	510

Notes
Level of significance: *** = 0.001, ** = 0.01, * = 0.05 (one-tailed test, except for openness). ^ = significant in the wrong direction
Years: 1960–89 ($N = 510$); 1960–94 ($N = 595$); 1960–98 ($N = 663$).

constitutional structure is overwhelming. Power dispersion through the constitutional structure, measured as an additive index of presidentialism versus parliamentarism, strong/weak/no bicameralism, strong/weak/no federalism, and the use of popular referendums as a normal part of the political process, was a statistically significant obstacle to increases in total government expenditure and revenue and in transfer expenditure in the period up to 1985. In the period of retrenchment, its effect was the opposite, slowing down cutbacks. Thus, in the regressions here, where we cover the eras of expansion and retrenchment, it loses significance for most variables but remains a highly significant and substantively overwhelming deterrent to a large public role in healthcare. The only other variable that is as consistently significant is the percentage of the population over 65, and unemployment is consistently correctly signed but not as consistently significant. Both are indicators of need that drive up expenditures on transfers and services at any given level of welfare state entitlements.

We are now in a position to draw on our comparative historical research (Huber and Stephens 2001a: chs 4 and 5) to weave these statistical findings into a coherent story about the development of welfare state characteristics that have implications for poverty among new social risk groups. In the Nordic countries both labor movements and Social Democratic parties were strong, and in cooperation they pursued full employment and generous transfer policies. Full employment policies included macroeconomic components, wage coordination and labor market support services. In the 1960s, labor shortages occurred and more women entered the labor force, creating a demand for public childcare and elderly care services. The 1960s also saw the emergence of a women's movement with a gender egalitarian agenda, which worked both inside and outside of the political parties. By the 1970s (earlier or later, depending on the country) this movement had gained enough influence inside the Social Democratic parties to extend the traditional commitment of these parties to equality from class to gender (Sörensen 2004). Accordingly, policy responded to women's demands for an expansion of subsidized care services through the public sector, which in turn created jobs in public social services that were predominantly filled by women (Huber and Stephens 2000). Other policy changes followed, such as expansion of maternity and parental leave, a shift to individual taxation, and greater flexibility in work schedules, thus supporting a shift from the male breadwinner to the dual-wage earner household as the modal pattern, with Norway being a laggard among the Nordic countries (Sainsbury 1999b; Sörensen 2004). This pattern reduces the risk of poverty among the working-age population and among single mothers and children, because mothers, whether single or married, are more likely to be able to combine gainful employment with raising children.

In the Continental European countries, except for France, Christian Democratic parties were very influential and unions were of intermediate strength. Christian Democratic parties pursued a class conciliation project (van Kersbergen 1995), which entailed transfers to keep people out of poverty. In most of these countries, left-wing parties were serious competitors, and this competition tended to increase the generosity of these transfers. Legislation extended contract coverage to the great majority of the labor force, but Christian Democratic governments did not develop full employment policies with strong active labor market services. When labor shortages emerged in the 1960s, they were eased through immigration, not entry of women into the labor force. The Christian Democratic parties continued to defend the traditional male breadwinner model. Thus, women's movements with a feminist agenda had a much more difficult task in these countries. Support for mothers' employment through subsidized childcare facilities, maternity and parental leave, etc. lagged behind that offered by Social Democratic welfare state regimes in the Nordic countries, with the notable exception of France and to some extent Belgium (Meyers *et al.* 1999). Accordingly, the social service sector remained smaller and women's labor force participation lower. Thus, fewer households than in the Nordic countries had two income earners as a buffer against poverty in the event of unemployment, and the chances of single mothers being employed remained lower, which meant a higher risk of poverty.

In the Anglo-Saxon countries, Social Democratic parties were comparatively weak or absent, Christian Democratic parties were totally lacking, and labor was of intermediate strength, except in the United States, where it was extremely weak. Only in Australia did contract coverage extend to the levels of the Nordic and Continental European countries.[7] The secular centrist and right-wing parties that dominated in these countries failed to develop full employment policies and strong labor market services, as they failed to develop generous welfare states, and particularly social services.[8] Women's movements grew to an intermediate strength, closer to their counterparts in the Nordic than the Continental European countries, but they lacked allies in strong left-wing parties and in government. They were effective in achieving some legislation protecting women in the labor market, but not in extending social services to facilitate mothers' employment (O'Connor *et al.* 1999). Thus, as women began to enter the labor force in greater numbers, the demand for private services increased. The restricted contract coverage and high wage dispersion facilitated the emergence of a low-wage private service sector to meet this demand. As in the Nordic countries, jobs in this sector were predominantly filled by women, but unlike in the Nordic countries, these jobs were generally poorly paid and lacked social security protection. Therefore, though women's labor force participation has risen to an intermediate level and dual-earner households have become frequent, they provide less protection against poverty in the working-age population and among single mothers than dual-earner households and employment of single mothers in the Nordic countries. Single mothers who work in Liberal welfare state regimes are likely not only to work for lower wages than their counterparts in Social Democratic welfare state regimes, but also to have to pay for private day care, which makes them less able to keep themselves and their children out of poverty (O'Connor *et al.* 1999; Huber *et al.* 2001; Kilkey and Bradshaw 1999).

Determinants of pre-tax and transfer poverty

We now turn to a summary of our findings on the determinants of pre-tax and transfer poverty and poverty reduction among the working-age population (Moller *et al.* 2003), and among single mothers and children (Huber *et al.* 2001). These regressions are based on data from the Luxembourg Income Study for 14 advanced industrial countries from the 1970s to the 1990s, and we follow the convention of defining poverty as receiving less than 50 percent of the median income.[9] We use OLS estimation of the regression coefficients combined with a robust-cluster estimator of the standard errors (StataCorp 1999: 256–60) to deal with the problems of correlated errors in panel data. For pre-tax and transfer poverty we ran separate regressions on sets of variables relating to economic development (GDP per capita, agricultural employment, youth population, education, vocational education), the U-turn problematic (deindustrialization, LDC imports, capital mobility, immigration, unemployment, female labor force participation, single-mother households, frequency of part-time work), labor market institutions (union density, coordination of wage-setting), and politics and policies (left-wing cabinet, Christian Democratic cabinet, welfare generosity, unemployment replacement rates, means-tested benefits, child and family allowances, maternity allowances). We then carried forward all the variables with significance at $p < 0.10$ into a combined model, using an *F*-test for the joint significance of all variables with insignificant individual effects to ensure that they could be safely dropped from the model. We repeated this step with the combined model to arrive at a reduced model, which is what we are presenting in Table 7.4.

Pre-tax and transfer poverty among the working-age population has three statistically significant determinants. It is negatively related to industrial employment and to wage coordination, and positively related to unemployment. Thus, deindustrialization does increase poverty, because low-end jobs in the manufacturing sector generally are better paid than low-end jobs in the service sector. However, if coordination of wage-setting is practiced and raises wages at the bottom, as in the Nordic and the Northern Continental European countries, this reduces the probability that people with jobs remain poor. That unemployment increases pre-tax and transfer poverty is certainly no surprise.

Pre-tax and transfer poverty among single mothers shares one statistically significant determinant with poverty among the working-age

Table 7.4 Determinants for pre-tax and transfer poverty

	Working-age population		Children		Single mothers	
	b	β	b	β	b	β
Unemployment	0.48*	0.35	0.93***	0.50	–	–
Percentage of young	–	–	0.59**	0.25	–	–
Wage coordination	-1.16**	-0.36	-0.96**	-0.21	–	–
Percentage of families headed by single mother	–	–	0.85***	0.60	–	–
Percentage in industry	-39.97**	-0.37	–	–	-132.65***	-0.48
Percentage of women working part time	–	–	–	–	0.61***	0.47
Taxes and transfers	–	–	-0.92**	-0.25	–	–
Migration						
Child and family allowances	–	–	0.05	0.16	–	–
Left cabinet	0.06	0.14	–	–	–	–
Vocational education	0.04	0.13	–	–	-0.35***	-0.5
Constant	22.14***	–	-9.30	–	73.94	–
R-square	0.66	–	0.84	–	0.52	–
N	61	–	70	–	71	–

Notes
b, unstandardized coefficient; β, standardized coefficient.
Level of significance: *** = 0.001, ** = 0.01, * = 0.05.

population, industrial employment. The other statistically significant determinants are the proportion of working women who work part time and undergo vocational education. Vocational education strengthens skill levels at the bottom of the educational levels, enabling the least educated to obtain better-paying jobs. If the proportion of women who work only part time rather than full time is higher, the probability that single mothers work only part time and earn wages insufficient to lift themselves and their children out of poverty is higher also.

Pre-tax and transfer poverty among children has five statistically significant determinants: Not surprisingly, unemployment increases child poverty, as it increases poverty in the working-age population and among single mothers. A larger proportion of the population that is young also increases poverty among children, since it increases the likelihood of large families, and since family size tends to be negatively correlated with income levels, it increases the incidence of large families with low incomes. Wage coordination has a depressing effect on child poverty, just as it does on poverty among the working-age population. The proportion of female-headed households has a substantively large effect on poverty among children, which is easy to understand since poverty among single mothers is generally higher than among the working-age population at large. Finally, total taxes and transfers have a depressing effect on pre-tax and transfer child poverty, indicating that the tax side of this measure captures the provision of free or subsidized social services that make it possible for mothers, whether single or married, to engage in full-time employment and thus raise the household income.

It is also worth commenting on some of the variables that were not significant. Most importantly, we had included total taxes and transfers, unemployment replacement rates, means-tested benefits, child and family allowances, and maternity allowances to test the argument made by critics of the welfare state that generous transfers constitute a disincentive to work and thus raise pre-tax and transfer poverty levels. None of these variables emerged as significant, except for taxes and transfers in the case of child poverty, but there it was negatively signed, demonstrating that generous welfare states by no means increase but instead reduce pre-tax and transfer poverty among children.

Determinants of poverty reduction

For reduction in poverty among the working-age population and among single mothers and children, we ran separate regressions on the controls (economic, demographic and labor market institutional variables), on politics and on policies, and then proceeded as already described to arrive at the combined and reduced equations presented in Table 7.5. The regressions demonstrate the importance of taxes and transfers and of a left-wing cabinet for poverty reduction among all three of our new risk groups.

Those two variables are highly significant and substantively important determinants of poverty reduction. These results square with those of other studies showing that more generous welfare states have lower post-transfer poverty rates (Burtless *et al.* 2001; Kenworthy 1999; Kim 2000; Korpi and Palme 1998; McFate *et al.* 1995) and that they distribute more income and reduce poverty to a greater extent (Goodin *et al.* 1999; Kenworthy 1999; Kim 2000). Why higher taxes and transfers would reduce poverty more effectively is self-evident, unless one makes the unrealistic assumption that taxes are highly regressive and transfers go predominantly to non-poor groups.[10] The reason why a left-wing cabinet shows a direct effect independent of the generosity of the welfare state is that generosity does not capture the structure of taxes and transfers. If we had a perfect measure for the progressivity of taxes and the allocation of transfers, we would expect that measure to absorb the effect of having a left-wing cabinet. We did develop various measures for the structure of transfers, such as proportion of all benefits that are means tested, proportion going to family and child allowances, to maternity allowances, and generosity of unemployment replacement rates, but none of them individually was strong enough to make a difference, and the only one that was significant was the proportion of all transfers going to family and child allowances, which reduces poverty among the working-age population. Thus, left incumbency retains its effect as an indicator of a welfare state structure that is particularly effective in levying taxes and channeling transfers in a way that reduces poverty among the working-age population, single mothers, and children.

Power dispersion through the constitutional structure emerges as an obstacle to poverty reduction among the working-age population and children but not single mothers; the coefficient for single mothers is correctly signed but not significant. Power dispersion means that there are more opportunities for opponents of generous poverty-reducing policies to block passage and implementation of such policies.[11] As with a left-wing cabinet, we would expect the main effect of this variable to work through overall welfare state generosity, but the remaining effect indicates that poverty reduction policies for working-age households and children are particularly vulnerable to mobilization by opponents in systems with many veto points. Unemployment increases poverty reduction among the working-age population and children, which can be explained by the fact that, at any given level of entitlements, more unemployed people will be drawing on these entitlements and have their poverty reduced. Strangely, though, from the point of view of the logic of this argument, pre-tax and transfer poverty among children has a negative effect on poverty reduction in this group. We would expect that, again at any given level of entitlements, greater poverty would lead to more poverty reduction. It seems that high levels of poverty among children may put too many demands on the welfare system for special programs, so these programs may be

Table 7.5 Determinants of welfare state outcomes

| | Reduction in poverty | | | | Single mothers | | Post-tax and transfer poverty among the aged | |
| | Working age | | Children | | | | | |
	b	β	b	β	b	β	b	β
Taxes and transfers	4.41***	0.39	2.57***	0.25	6.11***	0.49	−1.62**	−0.37
Left cabinet	0.60***	0.31	0.60***	0.36	0.68**	0.34	–	–
Constitutional structure	−2.29***	−0.20	−2.94***	−0.17	−2.30	−0.18	–	–
Unemployment	1.60***	0.26	1.66**	0.31	–	–	–	–
Young	–	–	–	–	–	–	1.21**	0.41
Pre-tax and transfer poverty^	–	–	−1.01***	−0.35	–	–	–	–
Wage coordination	1.93*	0.14	–	–	–	–	–	–
Family transfer proportion	0.13**	0.15	–	–	–	–	–	–
Constant	23.43	–	56.08**	–	47.99**	–	−9.42	–
R-square	0.84	–	0.82	–	0.72	–	0.44	–
N	61	–	72	–	71	–	69	–

Notes
b, unstandardized coefficient; β, standardized coefficient; ^, poverty for the group in the analysis.
Level of significance: *** = 0.001, ** = 0.01, * = 0.05.

short-changed and less effective in lifting children out of poverty. Wage coordination emerges as a statistically significant but substantively not very important determinant of poverty reduction among the working-age population; indeed, it has the smallest substantive effect of all the significant variables. The explanation of this effect must be similar to that of a left-wing cabinet; in systems where solidarity in wage-setting is high, welfare states are likely to be structured in a way that is more favorable towards poverty reduction among the working-age population.

As noted above, an analysis of pre-tax and transfer poverty among the aged would be distorted by the rational calculations of people in welfare states with comprehensive earnings-related public pension systems. The average wage-earner in such welfare states pays higher taxes during his or her working life but accumulates less in private pensions and savings and thus has a lower or no pre-transfer income in old age than an average wage-earner in welfare states with less generous public pension systems and greater reliance on private pensions and savings. Instead, we analyze determinants of post-tax and transfer poverty among the aged, and we find that indeed overall generosity of the welfare state is a highly significant and substantively important predictor of poverty among the elderly. Large welfare states are effective in keeping people over 65 out of poverty. A large youth share of the population, in contrast, increases poverty among those over 65. The interpretation here is a straightforward competition for resources; with size of the welfare state held constant, a larger population of youngsters absorbs a greater share of these welfare state resources and leaves a smaller share for the elderly.

The fact that we do not find any direct effects of political variables on poverty among the elderly is consistent with our earlier finding that all welfare state regime types have reduced the level of post-tax and transfer poverty among the elderly over the past 40 years or so. It is worth noting that we are making a comparison of post-tax and transfer poverty over time here, not a statement about reduction from pre- to post-tax and transfer poverty. In part, this is due to the maturation of pension systems, and in part to the fact that among welfare state programs, pensions tend to be the most popular in all societies. They are generally the most universalistic, and everyone faces the risk of growing old. However, it is also important to remember here the strong and consistent effects of left-wing and Christian Democratic incumbency that we found on welfare state generosity and thus indirectly on poverty. Accordingly, levels of poverty among the elderly in the less generous Liberal welfare state regimes remain clearly above those in the more generous Christian Democratic and Social Democratic welfare state regimes; in the post-1987 period they were at roughly twice the average level (Table 7.1).

Explaining the effectiveness of welfare state regimes towards old and new social risks

Arguably the most central of the new social risk groups is single mothers, so we shall begin our analysis with them. Poverty among children is largely derivative, insofar as it is affected by the growth of the proportion of single-mother households and the higher incidence of poverty in these households than in the general working-age population, as well as by the growth of poverty among the working-age population at large. Single mothers in Social Democratic welfare states start out in the most favorable position with regard to pre-tax and transfer poverty, whereas single mothers in the Liberal welfare states start out in the most unfavorable position, with a roughly 20 percentage point difference between them (Table 7.1). Single mothers in Christian Democratic welfare states have a 5 percentage point higher pre-tax and transfer poverty rate than their counterparts in Social Democratic welfare states. As our analysis of the determinants of pre-tax and transfer poverty showed, the welfare state regime effect works mainly through employment levels of single mothers – that is, a greater proportion of working women working full time rather than half time (Table 7.4). These higher employment levels are facilitated by active labor market policies and policies supportive of mothers' employment.

From this already more favorable starting point, Social Democratic welfare states reduce poverty much more effectively through the tax and transfer system than Christian Democratic welfare states, and those in turn do so much more effectively than Liberal welfare states. The explanation of the comparatively poor job done by Liberal welfare states in reducing poverty among single mothers is that those welfare states are neither generous nor structured specifically to lift single-mother households out of poverty. Our regressions on poverty reduction of single-mother households showed that welfare state generosity (measured as total taxes and transfers) is the overwhelming determinant, and that long-term incumbency of left-wing parties results in a structure of the welfare state that is particularly effective in reducing poverty among this new risk group (Table 7.5).

If we now compare this pattern to the pattern of poverty in our old risk group, elderly people (Table 7.1), we see that post-tax and transfer levels of poverty among the aged are roughly comparable to those of single mothers in Social Democratic welfare states (somewhat higher in the pre-1987 period, somewhat lower later), but clearly lower in Christian Democratic welfare states (a difference of 6 percentage points pre-1987 and 13 points later), and much lower in the Liberal welfare states (a difference of 20 percentage points pre-1987 and 26 points later). Thus, though poverty levels among the aged overall are higher in the Liberal than in the other two types of welfare state regimes, the difference is not as great as it is for single mothers. The main reason for the higher poverty level among the aged in the Liberal welfare state regimes is the much lower generosity of the welfare states overall, as well as in pension spending per aged person. The regression presented in Table 7.5 confirms that welfare state generosity is a key determinant of poverty among the aged, but the fact that the difference between Liberal welfare states and the other two regime types is not as great for poverty among the aged as it is for poverty among single mothers suggests that Liberal welfare states seem to prioritize the aged over single mothers in their allocation of meager resources.

A similar argument can be made for this comparison between Social Democratic and Christian Democratic welfare state regimes. As noted, post-tax and transfer poverty among the aged and single mothers is roughly comparable in Social Democratic welfare states (5 percentage points higher pre-1987 and two points lower post-1987), but in Christian Democratic welfare states the post-tax and transfer poverty level among the aged is 6 to 13 percentage points lower than the poverty level among single mothers. Post-tax and transfer poverty levels among the aged are roughly the same in the two welfare state regime types, but among single mothers they are markedly higher in Christian Democratic welfare states (9 to 12 percentage points). As we know, Christian Democratic welfare state regimes are almost as generous overall as Social Democratic welfare state regimes, more generous overall in transfers, and almost identical in pension generosity. As was the case for Liberal welfare state regimes, this suggests that Christian Democratic welfare state regimes are more strongly oriented towards keeping the aged out of poverty than single mothers. Social Democratic welfare state regimes, in contrast, are equally effective in keeping these old and new risk groups out of poverty.

In other words, Christian Democratic and Liberal welfare state regimes perform worse in dealing with new than with old social risk groups, whereas Social Democratic welfare state regimes perform equally well toward both kinds of risks. Christian Democratic welfare state regimes do as well by their elderly as Social Democratic welfare state regimes, but not nearly as well by their single mothers. Liberal welfare state regimes do worse by their elderly than the other two regime types, and much worse by their single mothers.

A closer look at pre- and post-tax and transfer poverty among our other two new risk groups confirms the findings that welfare state regimes differ more in their ability to keep those in new risk groups out of poverty than those in old risk groups, that the Social Democratic welfare state regimes are the best equipped to deal with new social risk groups, and that the Liberal welfare state regimes do consistently worst among all risk groups. The pre-tax and transfer poverty levels among the working-age population do not show such large differences as those among single mothers across the welfare state regimes. However, when we look at post-tax and transfer poverty among the working-age population, the differences become very large again, albeit at a much lower average level than among single mothers. We see a consistent ordering of Social Democratic–Christian Democratic–Liberal welfare state regimes, but the Christian Democratic are closer to the Social Democratic than to the Liberal welfare state regimes. As in the case of single mothers, these differences are greater than the differences in poverty among the aged, confirming that welfare state regimes differ more in handling new than in handling old social risks.

If we look at pre-tax and transfer poverty among children, we see the usual differences between countries with Liberal welfare state regimes on the one hand and those with Social Democratic and Christian Democratic regimes on the other, but here the order of Social Democratic and Christian Democratic welfare state regimes is reversed, with the Christian Democratic regimes being the lowest, albeit by 2 percentage points only. When we come to post-tax and transfer poverty, though, the ordering is reversed again, with Social Democratic welfare state regimes having the lowest poverty rates, Christian Democratic welfare state regimes being some 1 to 4 percentage points higher, and Liberal welfare state regimes 10 to 14 percentage points higher, or $3\frac{1}{2}$ to $4\frac{1}{2}$ times higher than Social Democratic welfare state regimes – again a much bigger discrepancy than for poverty among the aged.

What are the implications of these findings for theories of the welfare state? All of our evidence confirms that one of the two most important factors for reducing poverty among new social risk groups and keeping the old social risk group of the elderly out of poverty is generosity of the welfare state. Thus, the theories that explain generosity of the welfare state explain this part of combating new and old social risks well. We have presented evidence in Table 7.3 that long-term incumbency of Christian Democratic and left-wing parties and strength of the women's movement are the most consistent determinants of overall welfare state generosity.

Our evidence also shows that long-term incumbency of Social Democratic parties retains a direct effect on poverty reduction among new social risk groups, but not on poverty among the elderly. Additional evidence confirms that the difference between the performance of the three welfare state regime types in keeping people out of poverty is less in regard to the elderly, the old risk group, than in regard to the three new risk groups. With generosity of the welfare state (total taxes and transfers) held constant, it is the structure of the welfare state that determines how well it deals with new risk groups. We found only one significant effect of the composition of transfers on poverty reduction, the proportion going to family transfers, which did reduce poverty among the working-age population. However, we measured different types of transfers separately and our measurements were not able to capture the complexity of the total composition of transfers, not to speak of the incidence of taxation. Thus, we conclude that left-wing parties shape the tax and transfer systems in ways that are more appropriate for reducing poverty among new risk groups than Christian Democratic or secular center or right-wing parties.

As noted, our measure of poverty is based on final disposable income and does not take into account the value of free or subsidized goods and services. No doubt if we could take their value into account, the differences between the welfare state regimes would be enhanced. Social Democratic welfare state regimes are more service oriented than the other two welfare state regime types. In particular, they stand out in their provision of labor market services and care services for children and the elderly. What we can do here is to trace an indirect effect on pre-tax and transfer poverty among our new risk groups. The level of unemployment significantly increased pre-tax and transfer poverty among the working-age population and children (Table 7.4). Thus, to the extent that labor market services are effective in lowering unemployment, they are effective in lowering pre-tax and transfer poverty in these groups. In addition, the proportion of all women in paid employment who work part time rather than full time significantly increased pre-tax and transfer poverty among single mothers (Table 7.4). Thus, to the extent that childcare services make it possible for single mothers to hold full-time jobs, they are effective in lowering pre-tax and transfer poverty among single-mother households.

With regard to theories of the welfare state, these findings support the arguments pioneered by Esping-Andersen (1990) and developed by many others since, that regime types are crucial variables. Theories that explain the formation of the different regime types also explain the degree of effectiveness of welfare states in confronting new social risks. Again, we go back to Table 7.3 and see that it is the effects of left-wing incumbency and the strength of women's organization that are overwhelmingly important as determinants of civilian government employment, our proxy for the size of public social services. In addition, we go back to our narrative about the interaction of Social Democratic government, strong unions and the growing strength of the women's movement in shaping the expansion of the public social service sector, the commitment to gender equity, and the emergence of the dual-earner household as the modal pattern. We also need to re-emphasize here that Social Democratic parties and unions had already built up strong labor market services, which meant that there was a policy legacy favorable for the construction of this gender-egalitarian, service-oriented welfare state regime. It is this interaction, then, between Social Democratic governments and strong women's movements, in the context of strong unions and favorable policy legacies, that accounts for the formation of the welfare state regime type that is more effective than the others in dealing with new social risks. So, the same theoretical perspectives, power constellations and state-centered factors explain success in dealing with old and new social risks, but the cast of characters assumes somewhat different importance, with alliances between women's movements and Social

Democratic parties and a legacy of service provision playing the key roles in the fight against poverty among new social risk groups.

Notes

1 One might add youth poverty, which has resulted from the high levels of youth unemployment, particularly in countries with strong employment protection of 'insiders', to our list of new risks. Unfortunately, the small numbers of observations for this group in the LIS data make the data too unreliable and thus prevent us from exploring this issue.

2 These differences also serve as a general reminder that the pre-tax and transfer income distribution is not the same as a pre-welfare state income distribution. People's behavior in the labor market and in financial matters is affected by many factors, including the availability of services and expected transfers.

3 Civilian government employment of course includes the entire state bureaucracy, not only social services. However, employment in basic administrative branches of the state does not vary nearly as much as employment in social services. There are some cross-sectional data for public employment in health, education and welfare (Cusack 1991; Cusack and Rein 1991) that follow the same pattern as overall civilian government employment (correlation of 0.95; see Huber and Stephens 2000: 51).

4 The other eight countries are not in our set and from our set there are no test data for Austria, France or Italy. Thus, the following figures refer only to the countries for which there are data, which includes all the countries in our set with Social Democratic and with Liberal welfare state regimes. Calculations were done by the authors on the basis of the OECD/Statistics Canada figures.

5 Since 1985, union density has been declining further in some countries, notably Germany and the United States, but the general pattern still holds.

6 The data on membership in non-religious organizations come from the World Values surveys (Inglehart 1997). We estimated missing data points using women's representation in parliament adjusted for proportional representation. See Moller *et al.* (2003: 35) for a precise explanation of our procedures.

7 In fact, the Australian welfare state and production regime up to 1980 was different enough from the other Liberal welfare state regimes that it merited a separate label, wage-earner welfare state, along with New Zealand (Castles 1985; Huber and Stephens 2001a). By the 1980s it was converging on the Liberal regime type, and for the purposes of analyzing new social risks can be treated as a member of this group.

8 Britain's health service is the exception here, but it is a legacy of the post-World War II Labour government.

9 Because we are using household income, we have to make adjustments for household size. We use equivalence scales to adjust the number of persons in a household to an equivalent number of adults. We choose the commonly used OECD scale that adjusts for household size and composition (OECD 1995).

10 This assumption is unrealistic for advanced industrial democracies, where all welfare states redistribute income downward (Bradley *et al.* 2003). It is not unrealistic for Latin American countries (Huber *et al.* 2004).

11 Immergut (1992) and Maioni (1998) have shown the same for health insurance.

Part II

Patterns of policy adaptation

8 New social risks and pension reform in Germany and Sweden

The politics of pension rights for childcare

Karen M. Anderson and Traute Meyer

Introduction and overview

Recent comparative welfare state research suggests that socio-demographic and economic changes in post-industrial societies lead to the emergence of new social risks (Esping-Andersen 1999; Bonoli and Armingeon 2003; Pierson 2001a). Where welfare state policies once focused on the male breadwinner with stable employment as the modal beneficiary and focal point of policy, governments across Europe now face pressure to update welfare state institutions to meet the needs of increasingly diverse clienteles. Those with family care obligations, especially women, are among the most prominent of these new welfare state clienteles. Women are particularly prone to caring as a new social risk, because nowadays mothers are more likely to be employed, households with children are increasingly likely to be headed by one parent, and wages in the female-dominated service sector are comparatively low. The welfare state, the argument goes, needs to take this risk into account in order to ensure social stability. Mothers without access to affordable childcare facilities will resort to income support and drive up welfare expenses, and couples who consider their environment family-hostile will decide not to have children at all, thus exacerbating already unfavourable demographic trends.

Welfare states differ in the extent to which the risks of childrearing are collective. Nearly all parts of the welfare state influence the degree to which caring for children results in costs that must be individually borne. Childcare facilities and parental insurance are the most obvious programmes that influence whether persons with caring responsibilities have access to an independent source of income, but social insurance programmes like pensions are also important. If no pension rights can be accrued during periods of caring for children, parents face higher social risks. The decommodifying potential of pension systems, in other words, is relevant for family-friendly social policies. However, expanding social policies to cover caring-related social risks is likely to be difficult because family-friendly policies are expensive and the current climate is one of fiscal austerity, not expansion.

Parenting: a new social risk

Child-caring is a long-standing social risk in market societies because it reduces the carer's capacity to be employed. It is nevertheless analytically helpful to distinguish between childcare as a 'new', or modern, social risk – in contrast to childcare as an 'old', or traditional social risk (Table 8.1). The distinction between 'modern' and 'traditional' indicates that the risk can occur under very different societal circumstances. The traditional social risk of parenting is mainly caused by the carer's dependence on personal ties, by the fact that the relationship with the breadwinner can become insecure – it may end, or the 'breadwinner's' income may decrease. Parenting is a modern social risk when market ties replace personal ties. Then the carer's main risk is that markets ties become insecure because of unemployment or the difficulty of combining work with family.

Why Sweden and Germany?

The risks associated with childrearing in Sweden and Germany are very different. In Sweden, parenting has been a modern social risk since the mid-1970s, and Swedish social policies actively promoted this shift. In contrast, in Western Germany parenting is still a traditional social risk for many, and social policies have contributed to this situation. Thus, the question of how pension reform addresses parenting as 'new' social risk takes on a different meaning for the two countries. For Sweden we ask whether and why a model sensitive to modern social risks is preserved under conditions of austerity; for Germany we ask whether and why a model sensitive to traditional social risks can be transformed – despite cost containment.

The chapter proceeds as follows. We first discuss why Germany and Sweden can be classified as societies with, respectively, a predominantly traditional and predominantly modern social risk profile. We ask whether carers are mainly supported by personal or by market ties, using trends in female employment participation and family structure since the 1960s as empirical indicators, and we discuss how the two welfare state regimes

Table 8.1 Parenting as traditional and modern social risk

	Traditional social risk	*Modern social risk*
Main carers	Mothers	Mothers and fathers
Main social practice	Mothers caring at home	Mothers/fathers reconciling work and care
Main source of financial support for carers	Personal ties	Market ties
Carers' main poverty risk	Insecurity or breakdown of personal ties	Insecurity or breakdown of market ties

contributed to different trends. Next we analyse how the risk is accounted for in recent pension reforms. Finally, we discuss the implications of our analysis for the study of the politics of new social risk coverage.

The chapter develops the following argument. In Germany and Sweden, expanding coverage for childcare as a new social risk has not been a major motivation for policy change in recent pension reforms. In Germany, high unemployment and the financial costs of unification – as well as the long-term spectre of an ageing society – provided the rationale for change. In Sweden the latest reforms were driven by the goal of ensuring long-term financial sustainability and correcting programme weaknesses. These results, however, do not mean that political actors were detached from the major transformations in their societies and the poverty risks these cause. Swedish reformers did not need to emphasize these issues because their society, their and their pension system have recognized childcare as a 'new social risk' since the 1970s. Since then, an aim of Swedish social policy has been to help wage-earners combine family responsibilities with paid employment. Nevertheless, the recent Swedish pension reforms include some repackaging of new social risk coverage, and these affect the risk of combining work and family responsibilities. In contrast, West German society and social policy addressed childcare as a traditional social risk by assuming children should be looked after by their mothers and by compensating mothers for looking after them. This policy was resilient to change, despite some signs of erosion. Since unification, childcare as a modern social risk has played a larger role because a more Sweden-like society, the former East Germany, was incorporated into the conservative Federal Republic. However, socialist influence was not strong enough to effect more fundamental change. In the face of a comparatively slow degree of social and economic transformation in the West, and the huge financial constraints caused by unification, political actors have not prioritized the expansion of pension rights associated with childcare in recent reforms.

Childcare as modern and traditional social risk: labour market and household change

In order to assess whether personal ties are less important for mothers as their main source of financial support, and to what extent childcare obligations have emerged as a new social risk, we will use the change in female employment participation rates since the 1960s as a broad indicator.

Between 1960 and the early 1990s, the labour market behaviour of Swedish and German women developed very differently. In 1960, about half of women in both countries did not work outside the home, but this similarity quickly disappeared. Between 1960 and 1988, female employment rates in Sweden shot up by 25 percentage points to about 79 per cent, compared with an increase of only 2.1 percentage points to 50 per cent in Germany in the same period (Table 8.2). Moreover, women

Table 8.2 Civilian employment/population ratio 15–64, women

| | 1960 | 1965 | 1970 | 1975 | 1980 | 1984 | 1988 | 1990 | 1994 | 1998 | 2000 | 2001 | Pace of change | | |
													1960–88	1988–2001	1960–2001
Ger	48.8	48.8	47.8	48.6	50.6	47.3	50.9	53.4	55.2	56.9	58.6	59.1	2.1	8.2	10.3
Sw	53.4	53.2	58.4	66.2	72.4	74.8	78.5	79.4	69.4	69.5	71.0	72.0	25.1	−6.5	18.6
Gap, G/S	4.6	4.4	10.6	17.6	21.8	27.5	27.6	26.0	14.2	12.6	12.4	12.9	–	–	–

Source: OECD (online) http://www1.oecd.org/scripts/cde/members/LFSINDICATORSAuthenticate.asp.

Note
1960 Sweden figures are from 1963. From 1991: reunified Germany, before: W. Germany.

consolidated their labour market ties beginning in the mid-1980s: the significance of full-time work increased and that of part-time work declined (Table 8.3). By 2001, 34 per cent of working women were part-timers, a decline of 12 percentage points since 1980. Thus, since the mid-1960s, Swedish women have strengthened their market ties, and this has led to changes in the practice of caring for children. In sum, childcare changed from being a traditional to being a modern social risk in the 1970s.

In West Germany, female employment has been low for a long time. It was not until the late 1980s, just before unification, that employment participation rates of women started to increase, from 51 per cent in 1988 to 53 per cent in 1990 (Table 8.2). This increase was accompanied by an increase in part-time work: in 1982, 30 per cent of all employed women worked part time; in 1990, the share was 34 per cent. Because two very different labour markets merged as part of unification in 1990, we examine East and West German trends in the 1990s separately (Table 8.4). Before 1989 the employment rate for women in East Germany was much higher than that in West Germany; however, the sudden adaptation of the East German economy to Western conditions meant that many lost their jobs. Between 1991 and 2001, female employment declined by about 11 percentage points. Full-time rates also decreased during this period, but full-time work remained the norm for East German working women. Compared to the rapid adjustments in the *Neue Länder*, West Germany changed little. During the 1990s, women's employment grew by only about 1 percentage point and the significance of part-time work increased by 9 percentage points. Thus, by the end of the decade, the figures suggest stability in the pattern of West German women's high degree of personal dependency; for them, childcare was still mainly a traditional social risk. In East Germany, many more women had to reconcile work and care, and when mothers' poverty risks increased, this was due to the collapse of the East German economy, not of personal ties (IAB 2000).

East German mothers continue to have a more pronounced labour market orientation than those in West Germany. They return to the labour market earlier, they are more likely to be employed when their children are small, and they are more likely to work full time after their children go to school (IAB 1997, 2001). High unemployment in the East means that many mothers cannot work even though they want to: the activity rate in the East is much higher than employment; in 1998 it comprised 73 per cent of all women (ANBA 2000). Thus, in the *Neue Länder* childcare obligations can be classified as new social risk; Eastern Germany resembles Sweden more than it does Western Germany. However, Western women's attitudes are ahead of the social structure. Surveys show that mothers have fewer employment opportunities than they want, that the majority reject the one-earner household and that they would prefer an expansion of part-time work and public childcare (IAB 2001). This

Table 8.3 Female part time as a percentage of total female employment

| | 1976 | 1980 | 1982 | 1984 | 1986 | 1988 | 1990 | 1992 | 1996 | 1998 | 2000 | 2001 | Pace of change | |
													1980–2001	1982–2000
Sw	42.2	46.2	46.5	45.2	42.8	43.3	40.4	40.9	39.0	37.3	34.9	34.2	−12.0	−11.6
Ger	n/a	n/a	30.0	28.6	29.8	30.6	33.8	30.7	35.6	39.9	41.0	n/a	n/a	11.0

Source: OECD (online) http://www1.oecd.org/scripts/cde/members/LFSINDICATORSAuthenticate.asp.

Note
1982 figures for Germany are from 1983; 2000 figures for Germany are from 1999.

Table 8.4 Female employment in East and West Germany

	Employment/population ratio, 15–65			Female part time, % of total female employment		
	1991	1998	2001	1991	1998	2001
East Germany	66.7	56.4	55.6	17.5	21.7	24.2
West Germany	54.6	55.3	56.0	34.3	40.0	43.0

Source: ANBA (2000).

Note
Figures for 2001: *German Statistical Yearbook 2002*, own calculations.

means that a substantial part of the West German public now expects the state to enact reforms based on the definition of childcare as new social risk.

In sum, we see a much earlier and more profound labour market transformation in Sweden and in Eastern Germany, where carers became dependent on the market and the state instead of on a husband, and the reconciliation of employment and care became their main social practice. This contrasts with the more recent and less dramatic changes in Western Germany, where personal ties are still an important protection against social risks.

Welfare regimes and parenting as social risk

The welfare state helped to shape differences in the extent and the character of parenting as social risk. The entry of Swedish women into the labour market in the 1970s was part of a deliberate Social Democratic project – advocated by Social Democratic women's groups and other feminist organizations – to promote the emancipation of women by getting them into the paid labour market and strengthening their financial independence. Feminist demands for equality coincided with labour market shortages that provided the rationale for the trade unions, Social Democrats and employers to support women's demands. The result is well known and made Sweden the epitome of the Social Democratic welfare state: over the past three decades, Swedish governments created welfare state institutions that maximize employment and thereby provide access to paid work for women; they greatly expanded the public service sector; they implemented individual taxation; and they adopted generous parental benefits.[1]

The pension system also facilitated female employment and the reconciliation of work and caring responsibilities. In contrast to pension schemes in other West European states, the Swedish system included a relatively generous set of eligibility rules designed to enable wage-earners to withdraw from full-time participation in the labour market for education, care of children, or part-time employment without significantly reducing their public pension benefits. In addition, the Swedish pension system had fewer risks to cover, because almost all wage-earners, including women, had independent employment.

The cornerstones of public pensions were laid in 1914, 1946 and 1957. The basic pension and the supplementary pension (ATP) provided generous coverage for parents with childcare responsibilities. For retirees with insufficient ATP pension rights, the basic pension system provided a flat-rate pension and means-tested supplements, while the ATP system provided income-related pensions calculated according to 'defined benefit' principles. A full ATP pension paid 60 per cent of average income for the best 15 years of at least 30 years of labour market participation, up to the benefit ceiling. Combined with the basic pension, the replacement rate was 65 per cent of average wages (of the best 15 years). Parental insurance has been pension-carrying income since its introduction in 1974, and years spent at home to care for children were made eligible for pension credits in 1982. Thus, by the 1980s the Swedish pension system included specific *pension-related* institutions that allowed wage-earners to combine work with family responsibilities without risking poverty during retirement. These programme rules and the high rate of female labour market participation mean that most women, including mothers, are eligible for a decent pension on the basis of employment. In other words, these are 'old' institutions that protect against what are often seen today as 'new' social risks.

The West and East German welfare states defined the risk of childcare differently. The West German policy regime addressed childcare as a traditional risk. For decades, West Germany was the exemplar of the male breadwinner model (Daly 2000a). Its tax system rewarded the one-earner marriage: there were generous transfers for mothers of young children to stay at home, and a very low number of publicly provided childcare places, as well as no afternoon schooling. Individuals' social insurance contributions for healthcare, unemployment protection and pensions automatically included derived rights for spouses. Several factors contributed to the entrenchment of the breadwinner model. As Moeller shows, the male breadwinner model met the demands of several important groups: the organized working class, who wanted a 'family wage'; conservative pronatalists; and, probably most important, those who wanted to come to terms with National Socialism by creating a depoliticized family stability (Moeller 1993: 5). The creation, restoration and protection of the patriarchal family thus became a crucial element of the post-war West German political identity (Moeller 1993: 7, 213). At the time when the egalitarian project was launched in Sweden in the 1970s, the German women's movement challenged many of the conservative assumptions and the first left-Liberal government since the war abolished some patriarchal elements of marriage legislation in 1976 and 1977. However, in contrast to their Swedish counterparts the Social Democrats were ambivalent about women's position in society; they expressed their worries about the desta-bilizing effect of mothers' employment on children and in 1979 introduced six months of paid maternal leave for mothers of newborns (Opielka 2002). Another contrast to Sweden was that the left was in office for a much shorter time, and in 1982 the Conservatives took office again for another long spell of government.

In the former East Germany the state adopted a mode of intervention similar to Sweden's. The goal of economic and family policy was to enable women – not men – to combine childbearing with full-time employment, and there were a range of measures to achieve this aim (Opielka 2002). After unification, most of these family and economic policies were abol-ished; for example, mothers' workplace-related rights vanished with the disappearance of the *volkseigene Betriebe* (businesses owned by the people). However, in one very important respect carers did not lose their protection: many public childcare facilities remained open (Statistisches Bundesamt Deutschland 2004). East German social policy therefore con-tinued to acknowledge the existence of childcare as new social risk.

For decades the West German pension system's provisions for respond-ing to childcare as social risk followed the same logic as West German labour market and family policies. Public pensions are income related and until recently offered those with a full employment biography a high replacement rate of about 70 per cent of average net wages. Carers and anyone else without a full employment biography received pensions related to their contributions, so mothers' independent pensions were much lower than their partners' (Langelüddeke and Rabe 2001). Despite this pension gap, old age poverty has not been an issue in recent debates. The system protected spouses by providing a survivor's pension equal to 60 per cent of their partner's pension. These entitlements could largely be added to their independent pensions. Only retirees with an incomplete employment biography and no entitlement to derived rights had to rely on means-tested income support in old age. The pension system therefore suggested to carers that the safest way to be protected against childcare as traditional social risk was to be married.

The previous paragraphs support our initial claim that in Sweden, par-enting has been defined since the 1970s as modern social risk, protected by the welfare state. For Germany, however, the situation is more complex than described at the start. In the West, parenting is still a traditional social risk for many, although women increasingly reject its prevalence. For the East, the 'traditional' label does not stick. Instead, in Eastern Germany parenting is a modern social risk. We can therefore conclude that Germany's welfare state settlement is more out of sync with carers' lives and aspirations than Sweden's. This brings us back to our main ques-tion: to what extent and why has the Swedish 'modern' system been pre-served, and to what extent and why has the German one been transformed?

Childcare as social risk in the Swedish pension system

When pension reform reached the top of the political agenda in the early 1990s, political actors did not need to focus on childcare-related pension rights since the existing system provided generous coverage for them.[2] Reformers' main concerns centred on improving the financial sustainability of the system so that its essential features (such as childcare-related pension rights) could be maintained.

The 1994/98 pension reform is a radical overhaul of the existing system supported by five of the seven parties represented in Parliament. The original deal was struck by the ruling non-socialist minority coalition and the opposition Social Democrats in 1994, and subsequent Social Democratic minority governments have implemented the remaining details.[3] The following discussion of pension coverage for periods of parenting will focus on the new, reformed pension system with references to the old system where appropriate.

The reformed pension system includes several important changes. A new pension-tested 'guarantee pension' replaces the old flat-rate basic pension (*folkpension*), and two defined contribution (DC) schemes replace the old earnings-related ATP pension. The new public pension is called the 'income pension' and is a 'notional defined contribution' (NDC) system that provides the bulk of retirement income, while the new 'premium pension' is a funded individual account administered by a state agency. Besides these fundamental changes, the new system includes several other important features. First, earnings-related benefits are based on lifetime earnings rather than the best 15 years of 30. Second, pension contributions are divided between employers and employees. Previously, employers paid the entire contribution. Third, benefits are linked to the rate of real economic growth, whereas the old system indexed pensions to inflation. Fourth, pension rights may be shared by spouses, and pension points are earned for military service, the care of small children, and higher education. This was intended to compensate women and white-collar workers adversely affected by the switch to the lifetime earnings principle. As in the old system, sickness and unemployment compensation earn pension points, but now the state pays the contributions for these benefits. The new pension rules apply to those born after 1954.

How well does the revamped pension system cover the risk of childcare? For those exposed to different types of new social risks, access to a decent level of income is the single most important consideration. In this sense the Swedish system provides an adequate level of protection in the form of the new guarantee pension and other means-tested forms of income support. As noted, the guarantee pension replaces the old universal flat-rate pension that was available to all citizens, and the pension supplement. The level of the new guarantee pension is slightly higher than the combined effect of the basic pension and pension supplement, but it is *income tested.* This means that retirees can only draw the guarantee pension if they have inadequate pension rights in the earnings-related system. The guarantee pension is not means-tested, however. Like the old basic pension, the guarantee pension requires 40 years of residence between the ages of 25 and 64. For retirees who do not meet this requirement, means-tested social assistance is available. In 1999 about 12 per cent of pensioners received only the basic pension and pension supplements, and the number is likely to be about the same for the new guarantee pension. Thus, the reformed Swedish pension system provides a basic minimum level of income support in old age. However, it is important to note that the financing structure of minimum support has changed. Earmarked payroll taxes paid by employers financed about 70 per cent of the costs of the old basic pension, while general revenues financed the rest. In contrast, general revenues pay all of the costs of the new guarantee pension.

How do the rules for *earnings-related* pensions affect pension rights for periods of childcare? The switch from the best 15 of 30 years to the lifetime earnings principle represents a deterioration of protection for those who do not have a complete employment biography. The old formula gave carers (mainly women) ample opportunity to combine employment with childrearing, although this was not the original motivation for the benefit formula.[4] Any change that strengthens the actuarial fairness of the benefit formula will mean decreased protection for carers, unless these cuts are compensated for with pension credits for childrearing. The new Swedish system provides pension rights for periods of parental leave (12 months; the national insurance administration pays the contribution out of general revenues) and the first four years of a child's life. This pension credit is awarded in addition to pension rights earned from income and/or parental insurance.[5] However, this probably does not compensate for the generous protection built into the old system via the 15/30 rule. In sum, the lifetime earnings formula (even with credits for childrearing) is likely to mean a deterioration for most carers relative to what the old system provided (Statens Offentliga Utredningar 1994: 21).

The essential point here is that the old system probably provided somewhat better protection for parents with childcare responsibilities, but also had significant disadvantages (financial unsustainability; declining real value of pensions; and redistribution from blue-collar women to white-collar women; see Anderson and Meyer 2003). The price for correcting these weaknesses is that wage-earners face a very different set of rules regarding their pension coverage. The overall effect is mild recommodification, which will always disadvantage those who do not work full time, including those with childcare responsibilities.

Explaining the low profile of childcare as social risk on the Swedish reform agenda

Expanding protection for parents with childcare responsibilities played very little role in the recent Swedish reform. Instead, ensuring financial sustainability was the overarching goal of the political parties behind the agreement. In order to achieve this, the reform introduced several changes in the administration/organization of pension provision that affect how the pension system manages childcare as a social risk. These changes are the result of the introduction of a clear set of principles not present in the old system. One of the central objectives of the pension reform is to separate 'social insurance' (collective provision for risk) from 'social policy' (objectives not based on shared risk), in terms of both programme structure and financing. In the new system, the government budget finances contributions to the pension system for periods when wage-earners draw unemployment benefits, parental insurance and sickness insurance. The same is true for pension credits earned by periods spent in higher education and 'child years'. In the old system, these pension credits were unfunded. In other words, the main consideration regarding new social risks in the pension reform debate was how to *repackage* them. In the new system, provision for new social risks, including child years and parental insurance, is transparent and is funded from general revenues.

As noted, the switch to the lifetime earnings benefit formula is a major departure from the previous system and inevitably means a decrease in coverage for anyone with an incomplete earnings profile, and this is likely to disproportionately affect those with childcare responsibilities. This deterioration in coverage is somewhat compensated by the introduction of pension credits for periods of non-employment. However, other features of the new system have the potential to enhance the coverage of new social risks, most notably rules for flexible retirement starting at age 61 and the introduction of the option to work past the regular retirement age of 65. To the extent that employment for older workers is available, these provisions make it possible for persons near retirement age who do not have a complete employment biography to continue to earn pension rights or to combine work with a part-time pension.

During the reform process there was no discussion of rolling back the coverage of childcare periods in the pension system. Simply put, the strength of the pro-welfare coalition in Sweden remained intact, but it was increasingly on the defensive because of concerns about how to ensure the financial sustainability of the welfare state. As with other aspects of the pension system, the political parties behind the reform wanted to 'rationalize redistribution' (see Myles and Pierson 2001) by changing the way the pension system covered periods of childcare. The overriding goal of the reform was to improve financial sustainability, so the reform's negotiators closely examined all of the redistributive aspects of existing policy, including the manner in which childrearing earned pension rights.[6] The idea was that the pension system should continue to cover periods spent caring for small children, but that these entitlements had to be quantified and financed. And once political actors put an actuarial price tag on pension entitlements, the benefit level is liable to decrease for some groups. This is precisely what happened with the switch from the best 15 of 30 years benefit formula to lifetime earnings as the basis for entitlement.

To summarize, the recent Swedish reforms represent a mild rollback in coverage for periods of childcare. Considering the magnitude of the economic crisis that hit Sweden in the early 1990s and the cuts sustained in other parts of the welfare state, it is surprising that coverage for periods of childcare was not reduced even more.[7] We attribute this stability to path dependence (Esping-Andersen 1999; Pierson 1994) and policy legacies specific to Sweden. As we argue elsewhere (Anderson and Meyer 2003), capital accumulated in the national Swedish pension funds (AP funds; more than 30 per cent of GDP) was used to finance the transition to the new system, most importantly the funding of non-employment related pension rights (including periods of childcare).

Childcare as social risk in the German pension system

Since the mid-1980s, care-related pension rights have been gradually extended in German public pensions. Until 1996 this was done by improving independent protection for carers who give up employment for care – that is, it was in line with the traditional logic of German social policy that defined childcare as traditional social risk. In 1986 the Christian Democratic–Liberal government introduced pension entitlements for childcare for the first time; government contributions to the pension fund granted per child were equivalent to the yearly contributions made by someone with an income 25 per cent below average. In 1989 two additional years were added, also under the CDU–Liberal government and with the support of the SPD opposition. In 1996 the conservative logic changed for the first time, when the CDU–Liberal coalition made it possible to combine care-related pension rights with employment-related rights. They thus stipulated that someone combining work and care would get a better pension than the full-time carer. At the same time, care-related pension entitlements were raised from 75 per cent to 100 per cent of average wages.

In addition to these changes, in 1989 the protection for employees with low lifetime incomes (mainly part-time workers) was improved retroactively for the time between 1972 and 1992, and women's pensionable age was raised to 65 (Meyer 1998b: 822). In sum, the changes enacted until the 2001 pension reform gave carers more independent rights and increased incentives for employment, thus weakening carers' dependence on the breadwinner and showing the first signs of the recognition of childcare as a modern social risk, though without making the breadwinner obsolete.

The pension reform adopted under the Social Democratic–Green coalition in 2001 weakens the principle of childcare as a traditional social risk, but this was an unintended side effect of benefit cuts. The reform is widely seen as a significant departure from existing policy, because the statutory pension is no longer intended to maintain wage-earners' standard of living in retirement. Instead, the law makes it clear that a combination of both statutory and private pension benefits is necessary (for overviews, see Heller 2001; Langen 2001). The main goal of the 2001 reform is financial stability: to keep current contribution levels below 22 per cent until 2030 – despite population ageing. This goal could only be achieved by spending cuts, so the system was overhauled in two respects: first, benefits were cut across the board; and second, to compensate for lower statutory pensions, the law promotes private pension provision through tax incentives or subsidies. The highest possible level of public pensions will gradually decrease from 70 per cent to 64 per cent of average net earnings for those with full employment careers. In addition, the widow's pension was cut again for those without children. The aim of this measure is to increase incentives for both partners to work if they do not have children.

Obviously, the general levelling down of pension entitlements affects everyone, but those on low incomes before the reform were at greatest risk of falling into poverty after retirement because of the effects of the reform. The Red–Green coalition addressed this risk by special measures aimed at families and carers. These measures do not encourage full-time employment for mothers, but see as a norm the part-time working mother of one child and the full-time housewife with two children. Carers with one child are encouraged to go back to work part time when their child is three years old. As long as their income is below average wages, earnings-related pension rights will be doubled (up to average wages) until their child is ten years old, provided they have an employment biography of at least 25 years. A parent with at least two children does not need to be employed in order to receive the maximum support the parent of one receives.

Tax incentives encourage participation in voluntary private pension schemes. Because of progressive tax rates, low-wage earners receive flat-rate support, whereas higher-income earners are better off with tax deductions. In addition, to acknowledge child-raising, either the mother or the father is entitled to a flat-rate sum per child.

Those who fail to earn a pension sufficient to lift them out of poverty under this new system will be entitled to income support. The old system also provided means-tested support, but the new rules make it easier to claim this benefit. Means testing remains the condition for receiving income support, and people owning property or with savings will not be eligible. Thus, the minimum pension is combined with social control and penalizes saving.

How well does this revamped pension system protect against the consequences of childcare responsibilities? To what degree is the protection granted based on the recognition of caring as traditional or modern social risk? The 2001 reform continues the legacy of earlier reforms in that it further extends independent public pension entitlements for carers; however, as we have shown, the Red–Green coalition did not intend to use pensions to push modernization. The governing coalition still views caring as a traditional social risk for many, and the modernizing steps it undertook do not aim to make the dual-earner family the norm. With these measures the governing coalition was responsive to risks generated by West German women's typical employment biographies (Langelüddeke and Rabe 2001), and it was not prepared to give extra support to carers with a more pronounced labour market orientation, ignoring the preferences of East German mothers in particular. The statutory part of the reform can therefore be classified as slow, path-dependent adaptation of the strong breadwinner model to changing West German circumstances.

However, the inadequacy of the protection granted may mean that regardless of political intentions, childcare will become a modern social risk. Simulations show that the improved recognition of caring within the statutory system does not compensate carers with incomplete employment biographies for the losses they face because of public pension cuts (Langelüddeke and Rabe 2001). At the same time, it is unlikely that carers will be able to compensate for these cuts by contributing to private schemes, because groups bearing 'bad risks' are disadvantaged by these schemes. Given their lower average incomes, many women will find it difficult to save at all. In addition, lower-income households receive less state support for private pensions (Ebert 2001). The tax exemptions granted to households with middle to higher incomes are more generous in comparison to the flat-rate subsidies lower-income households receive (Fehr and Jess 2001: 11). Some analysts predicted that low-income households would probably not contribute to private pension schemes (Ebert 2001: 183), and three years later these apprehensions seem to be borne out: take-up rates for state-approved private pension schemes are very low, not just among low-income earners (*Der Spiegel*, 20 August 2003). This means that after the reform, more citizens with incomplete employment biographies risk becoming recipients of means-tested income support after retirement. The redistributive measures in the statutory part of the pension system therefore do not adequately protect against the traditional social risk of childcare any more, especially for lower-income couples. Stronger economic incentives for mothers to be employed may result, causing a further push towards the modernization of caring as social risk.

Explaining the low profile of childcare as social risk on the German reform agenda

The 2001 pension reform is a paradigm shift because it increases carers' social risks. Why did this likely consequence matter so little in the policy-making process? The simple answer is that government was driven by other motives and that in this particular reform, carers' most powerful non-parliamentary representative in the past, the Constitutional Court, did not have as much leverage.

In the German power structure the political parties and the Constitutional Court (Schmidt 2003: 45; Clasen 2002: 72), are the most influential actors likely to promote the issue of carers' improved protection (cf. Kreckel 1992: 269–84; Seeleib-Kaiser 2002: 39). Employers have little interest in this issue, because they want to externalize the costs of caring responsibilities. Trade unions campaign for the interests of their members; in Germany these are predominantly male and their average age is fairly high (Anderson and Meyer 2003), and the interests of women trade unionists have been marginalized (Koch-Baumgarten 1997). The associations that do promote carers' interests – charities, the churches, women's organizations – are at the margins of the political system (von Winter 1997). The improving of carers' social rights is likely to be pushed mainly by political parties and government, and through litigation.

As we have discussed, governments of both left and right have maintained and slowly modernized the conservative pension system in recent years. Changes in political party ideology have been an important part of this process. Both Bleses and Seeleib-Kaiser argue that a 'dual transformation' of the German welfare state towards a more family-friendly system has been under way for some time, driven by changing belief systems among the political elite (Seeleib-Kaiser 2002; Bleses 2003). This seems to be true for pensions: in all reform debates since the mid-1980s, politicians have acknowledged that independent pension rights for mothers and carers needed to be increased in order to compensate mothers for their unpaid work. However, can we therefore say that the family ideology of parties has driven change?

We believe there are good reasons to doubt whether ideological positions account for the changes described above; rather, it is the systemic constraints posed by the rulings of the Constitutional Court that are responsible. In fact, no matter how family-friendly parties sounded before reforms, all extensions of independent care-related rights since the mid-1980s have originated in rulings of that court (Bundesverfassungsgericht 1975, 1993, 1997).

For example, in 1992 two women in their seventies made an appeal to the court. One woman had raised five children, who contributed to the pension system as employees. The woman's pension was only about DM 390 – a small percentage of the DM 3,250 her children paid in contributions. The woman argued that other pensioners benefited from these mandatory contributions, whereas she could not expect her children to contribute to her support when they were already paying large amounts to the public pension system (Bundesverfassungsgericht 1993: 13–15). The Constitutional Court agreed, a clear loss to the ruling CDU–Liberal coalition, which had argued against the plaintiff. In its decision the court criticized the shortcomings of the pension system: 'Raising children is still considered to be a private matter, while security in old age is recognized as a societal responsibility.' The legislature was therefore required to 'reduce this discrimination gradually to a greater extent than hitherto' (Bundesverfassungsgericht 1993: 38–9). The legislature had to comply; there was no choice for the Conservative government but to include a gradual improvement of carers' entitlement in its reforms.

This was not the first time the court had influenced pension legislation in favour of carers. The first extension of care-related rights, in 1986, was also a response to a court decision made in 1975; the same is true of a court decision in 1996, when the court obliged the legislature to make entitlements additive to a certain limit (Bundesverfassungsgericht 1975: 194–5; 1997: 243). While the CDU–Liberal government publicly acknowledged the important role of the court (e.g. *Frankfurter Allgemeine Zeitung*, 28 January 1997; Bundestagsdrucksache 13/8011), it presented these changes to the electorate as its own family-friendly policies. It was only logical for government to rely on such legitimization, given the potential popularity of the step. The crucial point here is that the CDU–Liberal governments that adopted care-related pension entitlements did so only when the Constitutional Court forced them to, and this evidence does not support Seeleib-Kaiser's and Bleses' 'elite beliefs' thesis.

It is impossible to know what the reforms of the 1980s and 1990s would have looked like without the court, but it is clear that these policy changes were not voluntary, ideologically driven decisions alone. We want to make a different point, however: the most obvious discrimination of carers by the pension system had been dealt with by 2001, and the government had met the court's main requirements. This meant that by 2001 the court had less leverage than in the previous reforms. The latest reform is therefore a good case by which to assess the strength of government's determination to support the family. Although the government did pay attention to childcare issues in its changes to both the first and the second tiers, these steps were small, and they still leave those with childcare responsibilities more vulnerable.

Financial considerations rather than family-friendly party ideology were the main rationale for the 2001 reform. As noted, a Red–Green coalition took power in 1998, and one of its central goals was pension reform. The government faced very strong pressure to ensure the financial sustainability of the pension system. After the early 1990s, with the costs of unification soaring and unemployment figures increasing, cost containment became a central issue. The reserves of the pay-as-you-go system fell below required levels on repeated occasions, despite earlier reforms. When the Social Democrats and Greens won the election in 1998 they had to act immediately. In this context a reduction of benefits was almost inevitable, and the Minister of Social Affairs soon released a draft for a reform designed to achieve this aim. In this situation the modernizing family ideology displayed by both the SPD and the Green Party on earlier occasions did not disappear completely, but it had less relevance for policy.

Conclusion

The task of this chapter has been to investigate the politics of managing a specific 'new social risk', caring for children, in recent pension reform processes in Germany and Sweden. Our analysis shows that in both countries, the expanding of pension-related coverage for periods of childcare played very little role in the reform processes. Instead, concerns about the financial sustainability of the pension system dominated reform processes in both Germany and Sweden. Both reforms strengthen the link between contributions and benefits, at the same time as they compensate parents by awarding them pension credits for 'child years' (Sweden and Germany), periods of parental insurance (Sweden), or subsidies for private pension coverage (Germany). For both pension systems, this represents a reorganization and/or expansion of existing provisions for those responsible for bringing up children.

The Swedish reform is notable for its repackaging of care-related pension rights. In the old system, carers earned pension rights for parental insurance and care of small children, but these were unfunded liabilities. Moreover, the generous benefit formula (the best 15 of 30 years) in the old ATP system gave employed parents the opportunity to withdraw from employment for significant periods of time without experiencing a significant decrease in pension entitlements. Relatively widespread access to inexpensive publicly provided childcare, individual taxation, and full employment policies provided strong incentives for parents to undertake employment. Indeed, the interaction of all of these parts of the welfare state provided relatively good coverage against childcare as a new social risk, because paid employment means that carers earn pension rights that will result in adequate income in retirement. This employment logic also applied not just to partnered mothers, but also to single mothers, the majority of whom are employed.

We argue that the Swedish case is one of maintaining coverage of childcare as a new social risk in the face of strong financial pressures. Incentives for carers to be employed are as strong as they were in the old system, if not stronger. As long as carers have access to paid work, they will earn pension-carrying income. As noted, however, any increase in the actuarial fairness of a pension system will disadvantage those without full-time, uninterrupted employment, unless compensating mechanisms are introduced. The Swedish reform significantly changes the way that periods of non-employment are administered. The repackaging of care-related pension rights (and other types of non-employment) is likely to result in some deterioration of pension rights relative to the old system. Thus, we characterize Sweden as a case of mild rollback of coverage for childcare as a new social risk.

As in Sweden, German pension reformers were primarily concerned with improving the financial stability of the pension system. Despite these financial constraints, the reform included a modest improvement in care-related pension rights. These changes only moderately modernized the conservative model, while preserving some embedded assumptions about childcare as a traditional social risk. However, the fairly substantial cuts introduced by the reform hollow out the conservative structure. They increase carers' poverty risks and thus increase work incentives. The reform therefore helps to transform caring into a modern social risk in West Germany – without protecting against it sufficiently.

The welfare state and path dependence literatures tell us that welfare regimes adapt to changing political and social conditions in predictable, path-dependent ways. Given that governments make pension promises decades in advance, the notion of a 'path' is inherent, even overwhelming, in pension development, and actors adapt their behaviour to the prevailing structure and incentives provided by pension schemes. Our analyses of the German and Swedish reform trajectories of the past decade provide much support for these broad claims. However, both pension regimes demonstrate that some path departure is possible, for reasons not well documented by the path dependence and welfare regime literatures. In Germany the Constitutional Court played a major role in pushing German pension policy along a more childcare-friendly path, but the process unfolded in a manner constrained by past choices. So, German adaptation was predictable (i.e. it was consistent with previous policy choices), but the impetus for change was unpredictable (i.e. it came not from political parties or interest groups, but from individuals who put their case to the Constitutional Court).

Swedish reforms were also heavily constrained by past policy choices. There was little discussion of rolling back coverage for parents with childcare responsibilities; indeed, public support for female participation in the labour market and the socialization of the costs of raising children (including pension rights for periods spent caring for children) remains high. However, the switch to the lifetime earnings formula can be seen as 'rationalizing redistribution', because it reduces the pay-off to those with incomplete earnings biographies.

To summarize, Swedish and German pension reforms show a healthy dose of path dependence. However, the long-term effects of reforms in both countries are likely to weaken the salient features of the Swedish and German pension regimes, whether political actors intended this or not. The weight of past choices in Sweden and Germany was heavily constraining, but the long-term effects of reforms in both countries are likely to result in even more substantial weakening of Social Democratic principles in the Swedish regime and conservative/corporatist principles in the

German pension system. The long-term effects of the German cuts consti-tute a dramatic deterioration of the principle that public pensions should guarantee an income commensurate with a wage-earner's standard of living during employment, and this is a radical shift from existing prin-ciples. This recommodification, moreover, will disproportionately affect women. In other words, women (on average) will receive lower pensions if they combine employment with childcare responsibilities or if they rely on pension entitlements based on their role as spouse. This is a modernization of (West German) women's status in the sense that to ensure adequate retirement income women will have to be less dependent on personal ties and rely more on market ties. Thus, in Germany the commodification of carers in the pension system coexists with the fact that other parts of the welfare state still provide strong incentives for them not to combine work and family but to view caring as traditional social practice. The joint taxa-tion and tax-splitting rules that penalize spousal employment, health insur-ance financing that is based on derived rights, and inadequate access to inexpensive childcare in the West all still create powerful incentives for mothers of young children to stay at home. If the modernization of the 'strong German breadwinner model' is not extended to these areas quickly, there is a danger that many will realize too late the commodifying force of the pension reform.

A dynamic weakening of previous core principles is likely to emerge in Sweden, too. Recent reforms mean that the Swedish pension system now has more 'liberal' and 'conservative' elements than the previous regime. The Swedish system still provides coverage for parents with childcare responsibilities, but this redistribution has been repackaged, made trans-parent and scaled back.

Expanding coverage for periods of childcare in mature, pay-as-you-go pension schemes like those in Germany and Sweden is expensive. More-over, expanding this type of protection is difficult in the current period of fiscal austerity and demographic ageing. While the Swedish pension reform appears to have largely achieved its goal of financial stability, at least in the short term, Germany is still beset by pressures for additional pension reform measures. Substantial pension reform appeared on the political agenda again only a few years after the passage of the last reform, and additional cuts appear likely. Given the dismal nature of the current economic climate and the low political salience of expanding care-related pension rights, it does not appear likely that the next reform will do much to respond to the increase of childcare as social risk.

Notes

1 See Mahon (2001b), Winkler (2002), Sainsbury (1996), Hirdman (1989) and Morgan and Zippel (2003). Note that all of these authors argue that the emanci-pation of Swedish women is far from complete, despite the introduction of these 'women-friendly' policies.

2 Women's pensions are, on average, about 35 per cent lower than men's, largely because of differences in income during employment.

3 For details, see Anderson (2003).

4 The original purpose of the best 15/30 benefit formula was to gain the support of white-collar workers for the ATP reform. See Heclo (1974).

5 The pension credit is calculated according to the most favourable of three methods and goes to the mother unless the parents decide otherwise. One of the calculation methods is to award the pension credit for income equivalent to one 'base amount', or about 4,400 euro. Sixty per cent of women are eligible for a higher credit. See RFV redovisar (1999: 12).

6 For all insured periods outside formal employment (unemployment, sickness, higher education, military service), the reform negotiators devised specific rules for calculating and *paying for* pension entitlement. The general rule is that each social insurance sector should pay actual contributions to the pension system for an insured person's entitlement, while general revenues finance the contributions for those in military service and those caring for children who are not covered by parental insurance.

7 See Huber and Stephens (1998, 2001a) and Pontusson (1992) on the economic crisis in Sweden and welfare state restructuring.

9 New labour market risks and the revision of unemployment protection systems in Europe

Jochen Clasen and Daniel Clegg

Introduction

Employment patterns have undergone fundamental changes across the developed world in the past two to three decades. As advanced economies have become more service based, the profile of risks generated by the operation of their labour markets has gradually evolved. Long-term unemployment and skill shortages, which were only marginal problems in the golden age of industrial capitalism, have become far more prevalent. Contributory unemployment insurance, the fundamental institution for the regulation of labour market risks in most of the post-war welfare states in Europe, appears to offer an inadequate response to such problems, and is occasionally even accused of compounding them.

Even those with very different ideological opinions could probably agree that the emergent profile of labour market risks calls for a considerable reconsideration of traditional systems of unemployment protection, although they would certainly clash over what exactly this reconsideration should entail. Accordingly, we might reasonably expect the underlying 'logic' of contemporary policy adaptation to be broadly similar cross-nationally, albeit with the exact content and structure of policies in different states reflecting the nationally specific balance of political forces. This chapter argues instead that two quite distinct logics underlie current trajectories of labour market policy reform in Europe. This is explained, we argue, by the impact of cross-national variations in pre-existing institutional frameworks. Although unemployment insurance systems were superficially similar cross-nationally in the golden years of welfare state development, they were actually embedded in broader social and industrial relations in quite different ways. The nature of these inherited frameworks, we suggest, has a crucial influence on the extent to which a fundamental overhaul of existing institutions is even conceivable.

Our contribution is deliberately focused on reforms which seek to directly alter the principles and operation of mainstream unemployment protection. By analogy with Hacker's recent work (2004) on retrenchment, we can characterise this type of 'formal' adaptation of labour market policy to the new risk context as the 'revision' of unemployment protection. Such revision is important because it is a necessary, if not sufficient, element in any 'smooth' adaptation of public policy to labour market change. It should, however, be noted at the outset that the absence of revisions that are in step with the new risk context – and even the adoption of revisions that are manifestly out of step with it – in two of our cases is not sufficient evidence to conclude that in these cases policy-makers have simply failed to adapt public policies to new labour market risks. Just as there are varying modes of retrenchment (Hacker 2004: 248), so too, it can be argued, there are different modes of adaptation to new labour market risks, and the formal immovability of the logic of mainstream labour market policy may conceal – and perhaps accelerate – forms of 'rough' adaptation at the margins. We shall return to this issue in the conclusion.

The chapter begins by more extensively analysing the limits of established systems of insurance-based unemployment compensation in the face of the challenges of post-industrial labour markets, before a second section proceeds to isolate three policy strategies – the *de-differentiation* of benefit rights, the *activation* of the unemployed and the *coordination* of social and labour market policy institutions – that are together put forward as means of adjusting unemployment insurance to the emergent risk profile of contemporary labour markets. Using evidence from labour market policy reforms enacted in four European countries since the early 1980s, it will then be demonstrated that while this policy logic has indeed been largely followed – albeit in markedly different ways – in countries as different as Denmark and the United Kingdom, it has been much more tentatively embraced in states like France and Germany. As the fourth section shows, explaining these outcomes requires sensitivity to the differing mechanisms through which golden-age unemployment insurance systems were institutionalised in industrial labour markets. It is where such mechanisms partially detached traditional unemployment insurance from the sphere of electoral conflict and competition, we conclude, that labour market policy has to date proved – for better or worse – least susceptible to being swept up in an overarching 'new politics' of post-industrial labour market regulation.

Post-industrial labour markets and the limits of unemployment insurance

Changes in the labour markets of developed countries were long seen through the prism of the oil crises of the 1970s, which in the majority of these nations were followed by a dramatic increase in unemployment. In part disguised by these exogenous shocks, though, were more endogenous and structural changes, notably the quickening transition from a primarily industrial to an increasingly service-based economic model, resulting in pressures for a less routinised organisation of production within firms and at the level of the economy. These developments are sometimes presented in terms of 'long waves' of capitalist development, with current trends marking an evolutionary shift from 'industrialism' to 'post-industrialism', or from 'Fordism' to 'post-Fordism' (e.g. Jessop 2002). Such interpretations can no doubt be criticised as overly functionalist. Just as the industrial labour market could only fully 'emerge' with the help of political intervention (cf. Polanyi 1944), so transitions to flexible, service-based economies have also been a highly political process everywhere. The causal relationship between economic transformations and policy decisions works in both directions (Wood 2001). Accordingly, there remain important differences across developed countries in the scope and nature of the labour market re-regulation projects that have been pursued, especially since the early 1980s. Nonetheless, even if it has differed in intensity in different national contexts, a universal trend towards a purposeful recasualisation of employment relationships can be identified. Accordingly, though unemployment has remained a most salient issue in public and political debate, the actual nature of the risk of employment absence has, arguably, changed considerably.

Joblessness in the post-industrial labour market has a number of novel dimensions. For example, with increasing labour market volatility and selectivity, transitions into and out of employment have become rather more frequent and, at certain stages of the life cycle in particular, more protracted (cf. Schmid 2002). The demise of industrial production has also resulted in the permanent disappearance of the principal repository of unskilled manual jobs, with the result that labour market integration has become more heavily dependent than in the past on individual skills and experience (Berman *et al.* 1998; McIntosh 2004). Finally, given the more limited scope for productivity gains in services, capital accumulation depends on increasing levels of flexibility, often implying – especially in 'low-end' task-intensive sectors – the downward adjustment of wages and employment conditions (e.g. security of tenure) for workers.

The unemployment insurance schemes that are still the core institutions of labour market policy in most European countries were born into – and also helped to consolidate (cf. Salais *et al.* 1986; Topalov 1994; Walters 2000) – a quite different labour market model. Their underlying assumption was that periods of unemployment would essentially result from cyclical, and short-lived, downturns in economic activity – an assumption that was largely proved accurate in the immediate post-war decades of rapid growth and full (male) employment. While providing an income to the unemployed ensured that consumption did not slump during the bad times, providing it on a contributory basis encouraged workers to adopt regular 'productive habits' during the good. Thus, unemployment insurance always combined a social and an economic rationale, a fact that is perhaps too quickly forgotten in contemporary debates (Clasen 1999). The real difficulty today is thus not that unemployment insurance is too much of a 'burden' in the new economy, but rather that unemployment insurance, in its conventional form, is increasingly ill suited to performing the same synthesis between social and economic objectives under radically changed labour market conditions. Essentially there are three main reasons for this.

The first concerns the ability of contributory unemployment insurance to adequately cover those in need because of involuntary absence from work in the new labour market context. With the expansion of atypical forms of work and the increased 'churning' at the bottom end of the labour market, it is often difficult for workers to establish (full) eligibility to social protection for future periods of joblessness. This applies particularly to women, who tend to be over-represented in atypical employment and to have more irregular employment trajectories than men (Grimshaw and Rubery 1997). Coverage is also a problem with respect to young 'primo-demanders' in the labour market, who, owing to the difficulties of initial labour market integration, often have a protracted period of unemployment at the start of their working life. A contributory unemployment insurance system inherently provides no help to those who have never worked. Finally, having been designed to essentially cover the risk of short-term cyclical or frictional unemployment, time-limited unemployment insurance benefits are also often ill adapted to the problem of long-term unemployment, which is considerably more prevalent than at any time before the 1970s, particularly among those with low or no professional qualifications.

A second distinctive problem relates to the role of labour market policy in helping people to move back into the labour market after a period out of work. In the golden age of welfare state expansion the active management of the economy relied on the use of macroeconomic, demand-side stimuli, leaving labour market policy to play an essentially supportive and stabilising role. As Keynesian regulation has fallen into discredit, however, an increasing emphasis has once again been placed on the supply side of the economy. In this context it is contended that labour market policies must themselves become stimuli for economic adjustment and growth, notably by intervening more actively in the labour market reintegration of those without work. A more interventionist, proactive labour market policy strategy is perceived to be particularly important with respect to young people and those at risk from long-term unemployment, for whom a protracted period of labour market detachment can itself prove a handicap to future labour market integration (Esping-Andersen 2002; Ferrera *et al.* 2000). According to hysteresis theory, actively maintaining the 'employability' of the unemployed also prevents the build-up of inflationary pressures in the economy (Layard 2000). Because its traditional economic role was on the contrary mainly 'passive', in the new labour market environment unemployment insurance thus finds itself accused of contributing to unemployment at both an individual and a collective level.

A final problem, partially overlapping with the previous one, stems from the 'collision' of old unemployment insurance systems with the increasingly flexible new labour market. Owing to downward flexibility of wages and/or employment conditions at the bottom end of the labour market, as well as the increasing number of part-time positions and fixed-term contracts, the incentives for returning to work from unemployment benefit receipt are probably less sharp than in the past for large sections of the unemployed population. Work does not always 'pay' as obviously as it did in the past, whether in narrow financial terms or more broadly in terms of the levels of personal gratification and status it procures. Though long-term receipt of unemployment insurance benefits may in a growing number of situations therefore be individually rational, such rational choices are seen as a brake on economic growth and as an unproductive use of public resources at a time of 'permanent austerity' (Pierson 2001b). High levels of 'dependency' on public benefits may also, from a more social perspective, be seen as troubling by those concerned with social cohesion.

These policy problems overlap in significant ways. For example, if the coverage of unemployment benefit is inadequate, then it is likely that more of the unemployed will be reliant on means-tested social assistance benefits that, because of high effective tax rates on return to work, are particularly associated with financial incentive problems. Similarly, the availability of reasonable unemployment protection at the end of a fixed-term contract will most likely help to counteract the disincentive to take such work, even at marginal tax rates of over 100 per cent. It is thus far from clear that the evolution of labour markets sounds the death knell of unemployment insurance *per se*; today, as in the past, it can be a useful instrument for the reconciliation of social cohesion and economic performance. What is clear, though, is that there are good arguments for making significant adaptations to its traditional structure, and embedding it within a broader proactive labour market strategy that sees an increasing emphasis on 'active' relative to 'passive' policies. In contexts where public budgets are tight, this is likely to involve some reallocation of resources, from generous benefit provision for 'insiders' towards both more active policies and greater recognition of the needs of social protection 'outsiders'. It is also likely, because of the incentive problems mentioned above, to involve a more directive treatment of the unemployed than was common in most unemployment insurance schemes.

A 'three-pronged adaptation formula' for labour market policy: de-differentiation, activation and coordination

Though the different dimensions of a reform agenda for unemployment insurance in the post-industrial labour market are necessarily linked, for analytical purposes they can be separated into three main orientations, two programmatic and a third more institutional. The first of the programmatic orientations relates to eligibility and entitlement criteria. In industrial-era unemployment insurance, access to benefits and their generosity was often differentiated according to seniority and/or prior contribution conditions, with among other motivations the intention of rewarding the stable employment relationships that were crucial to the functioning of industrial capitalism, and of ensuring that skill and status differentiations, as well as normal consumption patterns, were reproduced and maintained during temporary economic downturns. The economic functionality of such arrangements is contested in post-industrial labour markets, where employment relationships are far less stable, and where workers are exhorted to be more adaptable in matching their skills to available jobs. In a rapidly changing labour market, an unemployment insurance scheme granting rewards in accordance with traditional status and skill differentials, i.e. status confirming, seems poorly equipped to provide protection and incentives that are congruent with a flexible post-industrial economy. For example, generous entitlements to benefit (in amount or duration) for workers with longer contribution histories are sometimes considered an impediment to necessary labour market adjustment.

The programme orientation that emerges from such considerations can be called the *de-differentiation* of benefit rights. In principle, unemployment benefit systems should be redesigned to ensure that access to basic support during periods of joblessness reflects the realities of how post-industrial labour markets operate, where necessary financing corrections to the 'undershoot' of inherited systems by removing any manifestations of 'overreach' that may exist in the benefit status quo. In practice, of course, public policy understandings of notions such as 'undershoot' and 'overreach' may be heavily biased by ideological considerations, just as ideological predispositions often intruded into assessments of the 'appropriate' generosity of golden-age unemployment insurance systems. In other words, the homogenisation or standardisation of benefit rights can in principle take a variety of forms, between the extremes of downward alignment of transfers on those traditionally poorly protected, and something closer to the generalisation to all groups of conditions once available only to workers in stable employment. But although the substantive implications of these extreme policy options are obviously very different, in both cases there is a decisive break with a model of unemployment insurance calibrated to the needs of a disappearing industrial economy.

A second programme orientation is towards the *activation* of benefits, whereby unemployment insurance is reformed to make it an instrument apt to increase the 'proximity' of the unemployed to the labour market. Active labour market policies such as labour exchange services and training programmes of course have very long histories of their own, and were already a complementary feature of most states' labour market policy repertoires during the golden age of industrial capitalism.[1] Contemporary proponents of activation highlight the positive role that such measures can play in a labour market context where it is seen to be desirable to use periods of unemployment to 'work on' the qualifications and aspirations of the unemployed, and argue that they should be far more closely articulated with conventional provision of income maintenance to the unemployed. This would imply, for example, directly financing training and employment measures out of unemployment insurance receipts, or tightening the links between benefit administration and individualised support with job search. It is also increasingly argued that participation in active measures should become a formal condition for the continued receipt of benefit, thereby using the latter to counteract perceived disincentive problems posed by the flexible re-regulation of the labour market.

Again, it is possible to identify a continuum between 'high-road' and 'low-road' variants of activation, each corresponding to rather different political and ideological predispositions (e.g. Barbier and Ludwig-Meyerhofer 2004; Torfing 1999; Lødemel 2004). At the high-road end, using unemployment benefit to finance periods of training or retraining helps to better equip the unemployed for competition for jobs matching their aspirations and expectations. At the low-road end, tightening the various conditions for the continued receipt of benefit – for example, the definition of suitable employment or the criteria of active job search – serves to force those unemployed people with few or obsolete skills to adjust their aspirations and expectations to match opportunities and salaries available at the 'low end' of the post-industrial labour market. In both cases, however, the provision of temporary support to the unemployed is explicitly used as a lever to modify labour market transitions.

Each of these programme orientations in unemployment insurance is often articulated with calls for more institutional reforms in the position and functions of unemployment insurance institutions within the broader landscape of social and labour market policy, and specifically for the increased *coordination* of unemployment insurance with other pre-existing policy streams and institutions (e.g. OECD 1997). The de-differentiation of benefit rights suggests breaking down the conventional distinctions between the unemployment insurance, unemployment assistance and social assistance schemes that usually combined to provide for different groups of working-age claimants in need of social support. For its part, the activation of benefit spells is argued to call for closer cooperation between administrations traditionally concentrated on the provision of income support, on the one hand, and the provision of placement services and training programmes, on the other (Clasen *et al.* 2001). Programme reorientation and institutional reform in labour market policy are thus perceived as complementary and mutually reinforcing.

These three policy orientations can be used as indicators to track the extent to which unemployment insurance schemes have been reformed to reflect the changing profile of post-industrial labour market structures. Their apparent limit as indicators is that they are in themselves incapable of capturing the precise content and nature of such reforms, between the extremes of 'upward' and 'downward' generalisation of benefit rights, or 'high-road' and 'low-road' activation strategies, which might be seen as the most crucial questions with respect to the adaptation of unemployment insurance to the changing profile of labour market risks. Their utility, however, is that they help to demonstrate that in some countries there has in fact been virtually no explicit adaptation of this kind at all in recent reform efforts, and sometimes quite the opposite.

The three-pronged adaptation formula in unemployment policy reform: evidence from four European countries

In Denmark, France, Germany and the United Kingdom, unemployment insurance was the core institution of post-war labour market policy. Their respective systems of unemployment insurance differed quite considerably in terms of generosity and distributive profile. For example, Danish unemployment benefit entitlement has been one of the most generous in Europe for the past two decades (although not necessarily for short-term unemployed persons on average or above average earnings; see below), while the United Kingdom grants one of the lowest levels of unemployment support. Average replacement rates in France and Germany are closer to the EU average (OECD 2004b). As we shall show, however, it is only in the distributively 'polar' cases of Denmark and the United Kingdom that the legislative record provides much evidence that these reforms have really taken on board the three-pronged adaptation strategy that is suggested by the changing profile of labour market risks.[2]

In *Denmark*, the system of unemployment insurance has always been one of the least differentiated in Europe. Benefit thresholds and ceilings make transfers resemble a flat-rate system for a large section of unemployed persons. Though the level of employment protection has indeed declined further since the 1980s (Nickell 2003: 23), Denmark has also long had one of the most flexible labour markets in Europe, particularly with respect to the hiring and firing of employees. An accessible and relatively generous – particularly for lower-paid workers, owing to a low cap on benefits – unemployment insurance system has traditionally been perceived as supportive of, rather than a hindrance to, the operation of this flexible and proto post-industrial labour market (Goul Andersen 2002). In a way, it could thus be said that golden-age Danish labour market policy was *already* adapted to the post-industrial labour market, at least as regards eligibility and entitlement to unemployment benefit.

Under the twin pressures of tight public budgets and high unemployment, some reforms to unemployment insurance in the early to mid-1980s actually seemed to push tentatively away from this model, through the embrace of greater selectivity and differentiation in unemployment benefit. In most cases, however, such moves have been rapidly reversed.

For example, eligibility conditions for unemployment insurance were tightened in 1985, and a lower-rate benefit was introduced for those who no longer had access to full benefits. But this reform was overturned in 1988, when full-rate benefit was reinstated. Similarly, the more generous entitlements for older workers implemented between 1992 and 1994 – which allowed effective retirement from the labour market on full unemployment benefit for those as young as 50 – have been progressively scaled back in counter-reforms since 1996.

In the second half of the 1990s, Danish governments made considerable cuts to unemployment benefits rights. The bulk of these cuts, however, came not through selective reductions in benefit levels, but instead through across-the-board changes in the maximum duration of benefit entitlement, which was reduced in successive stages from seven to four years between 1993 and 1998 (Goul Andersen 2002). Though eligibility conditions were also considerably tightened in a reform of the mid-1990s (Kvist 2002), they remain relatively loose in comparative perspective (52 weeks of paid work in the previous three years, instead of 26 in three previously). The Danish unemployment insurance system thus continues to provide relatively *undifferentiated* access to social rights, and in the late 1990s had a coverage rate of around 80 per cent, making it one of the most encompassing systems in Europe (Samek 2000: 61).

If encompassing and relatively undifferentiated unemployment benefit is nothing new to Denmark, the remarkable embrace of *activation* in the 1990s represents on the contrary a considerable novelty. Since 1993 there has been a vast expansion of activation measures, with a particular emphasis on training programmes, which are both a 'right and a duty' for the unemployed (for details, see Torfing 1999; Goul Andersen 2002). The length of time that it is necessary to be unemployed before being subject to this 'right and duty' has been reduced in successive reforms, and since 1998 has been one year for the adult unemployed and six months for the young. Parallel reforms in social assistance have furthermore generalised this principle to the small number of jobless who fall outside the unemployment insurance scheme. By 2000, OECD data show that expenditure on active measures in Denmark had overtaken that on unemployment benefits, despite the latter themselves representing over 1.3 per cent of GDP. Over 70 per cent of active expenditures were directed towards training programmes.

The new labour market policy orientation has been accompanied, finally, by an increased effort towards institutional *coordination*. The pre-existing institutional actors in labour market policy – the trade union-run unemployment insurance system, local authorities that are in control of social assistance, and the state-run public employment service – have retained their institutional identity, but their activities and interventions are increasingly channelled through, and coordinated by, tripartite labour market authorities which operate at the regional level (Dahl *et al.* 2002b; Ebbinghaus 2002b: 17).

FRA

The recent labour market reform trajectory in *France* contrasts starkly with the Danish experience. The contribution-financed French unemployment insurance system has in the main coped with a context of consistently high unemployment since the early 1980s by tightening eligibility conditions rather than reducing benefit rates. Important reforms in 1982–84 tied benefit eligibility and entitlement more closely to prior contributions, and created a separate tax-financed system (the 'solidarity system') alongside unemployment insurance for some of those with inadequate contributory records. Further reforms in 1992 tightened the contributory requirements for unemployment insurance once again, and deepened the dualism of the unemployment protection system. Although some of these cuts have been partially 'repaired' by other reforms, enacted in periods of stronger economic growth (in 1997 and 2001, notably), the dualism has not been challenged. Indeed, spare resources have as often been devoted to improving benefits for certain groups of insured claimants, for example with the creation of a special measure in 1997 granting rights to full benefit up to the age of 60 for workers with long contribution records. Meanwhile, coverage of unemployment insurance fell by around 10 percentage points in the 1990s. In sum, the overall story of French unemployment benefit reform in recent decades is more one of increasing *differentiation* than of de-differentiation of benefit rights (cf. Daniel 2001).

Attempts to introduce the principle of *activation* into the unemployment insurance system have also been comparatively limited. Though the unemployment insurance system did finance some active measures in the 1990s, these were never systematically or automatically linked to benefit, and places were limited in number; these measures covered a little over 250,000 beneficiaries by 1997 (Daniel and Bassot 1999: 22–3). Furthermore, some were active in name only.[3] Only in 2000 was a bolder proposal for the systematic activation of the unemployment insurance system brought forward. But although as a result, recipients of unemployment insurance have since 2001 had to sign a plan for help with return to work (the so-called *Plan d'Aide au Retour à l'Emploi* (PARE)), the actual ability of the unemployment insurance system administration to oblige participation in training or job search activities remained for some time uncertain and contested (cf. Supiot 2004).

The effectiveness of the already limited activation initiatives has been further undermined by the marginal impact of efforts to improve institutional *coordination*. Different aspects of French labour market policy – unemployment insurance, unemployment assistance and social assistance on the one hand, benefit policies and active labour market policies on the other – are still made largely in isolation from one another, by separate and autonomous institutions. Levels of trust and cooperation between these different institutions are often low, as conflicts between the public employment service (ANPE) and the unemployment insurance system over the implementation of the PARE highlighted (Tuchszirer 2002).

Though the present government has recently passed a law to try to encourage the development of 'single gateways' to different services for the jobless through multi-partner *maisons d'emploi* at the delivery level, the potential of this formula depends heavily on the as yet uncertain outcome of delicate negotiations still (at time of writing) to take place between the principal stakeholders (such as the state-run ANPE and the unemployment insurance scheme, managed by the social partners) at the national, policy level.

The reform trajectory in *Germany* has, at least until very recently, been somewhat similar to the French, marked by increasing differentiation of rights for the unemployed, little emphasis on activation at federal level, and limited institutional reforms. Incremental legislative change during the 1980s and 1990s made benefit eligibility more difficult and reduced the generosity of unemployment protection at the margins of the labour market, e.g. for job starters and those with repeated spells of joblessness. By contrast, benefit levels remained largely untouched for claimants in receipt of unemployment insurance, and particularly those with dependent children. In fact, the position of core workers, i.e. those with longer contribution records (above a certain age), actually improved as a result of repeated rounds of extending entitlement periods to unemployment insurance in the 1980s (to a maximum of two and a half years). This trend was reversed only recently when unemployment assistance was merged with social assistance in 2005, thereby creating a much larger pool of unemployed people who no longer rely on wage replacement-based support. Far from abolishing the differentiation of unemployment protection, however, the recent legislation has widened the gap between a smaller core of claimants in receipt of insurance-based support which reflects previous labour market status and a larger periphery of recipients of means-tested unemployment assistance (Clasen 2005).

Moreover, activation-type policies were introduced with much less vigour than in Denmark or the United Kingdom (Reissert 2006). While local authorities have had the right to 'activate' long-term unemployed persons for some time, and some have made extensive use of this, not least out of financial considerations (Buhr 2003), claimants of unemployment insurance have not been subjected to a routine form of 'work testing'. Despite recent legislation which introduced tighter job suitability criteria for continuous benefit entitlement and a stronger emphasis on individual cooperation with job search activities, an automatic mandatory 'activation' period equivalent to the British New Deal (see later in the chapter), or Danish legislation, has been implemented only for under-25 year old unemployed persons. At the same time, access to training and other forms of up-skilling has structurally favoured claimants of unemployment insurance.

The difficulty of creating a more standard form of unemployment benefit support or activation regime across all jobseekers has to be linked to the fragmented governance structure of active and passive labour market policy in Germany (Clasen 2005). The recent creation of the new unemployment assistance (ALG II) scheme in 2005, for example, is by no means a new idea. However, its introduction has always been hampered by the joint funding of active and passive labour market policy and a multilevel policy structure involving the federal government, the Federal Labour Office (BA), local authorities and separate social insurance, notably public pension or health insurance schemes, all of which are affected by legislative changes of unemployment insurance. Hence, cost shifting has been a perennial problem, and coordination deficits can be assumed to remain even after the creation of ALG II.

The *United Kingdom*, finally, is a case where reforms have broken radically with the established pattern of labour market policy. Unlike in Germany or France, the 1980s and 1990s saw a gradual *de-differentiation* of benefit rights for the unemployed. Unlike in Denmark, however, this was pursued – as part and parcel of the Thatcherite attack on the welfare state – via an alignment of rights to social support on the traditional situation of the *least* protected. The modest earnings-related supplement (ERS) paid to the unemployed with the longest contribution records was scrapped in 1982. Reforms in 1988 then tightened the contribution requirements for access to insurance-based unemployment benefit (UB). More importantly, however, the duration of entitlement of these was reduced from one year to a mere six months with the introduction of the Jobseeker's Allowance (JSA) in 1996, and their monetary value aligned with means-tested benefits for the jobless (so-called income-related JSA). New Labour did not reverse these reforms, enacted by the last of four successive Conservative governments, on its return to office in 1997. As a result, while around half of the unemployed received insurance-based benefits in 1980, this figure was around 16 per cent by 2001 (DWP 2003). Insurance-based benefits have been made so exclusive and modest that they are becoming increasingly irrelevant to the social protection of the jobless in Britain.

Activation has also been a major feature of recent British labour market policy. Successive reforms under the Conservatives in the 1980s and 1990s moved towards a 'stricter benefit regime', by tightening the conditions of active job search for the receipt of unemployment benefits, relaxing the definition of appropriate employment, and toughening sanctions for non-compliance (Finn 1997). After the running down of employment and training programmes from the late 1980s onwards, more 'positive' forms of activation were essentially limited to providing increased help with job search, through initiatives such as 'Restart' interviews. As well as making compulsion in labour market policy more explicit, New Labour's New Deal initiative since 1997 has built on the Restart concept with respect to its 'gateway period' of intensive counselling and employment guidance for the unemployed, but has also reintroduced some more investment-intensive training and job subsidy programmes. Despite a significant and growing emphasis on activation, not merely for the unemployed but also for other working-age beneficiaries of social support (disabled people, lone parents, jobless partners of the registered unemployed), actual expenditure on active labour market policies in the United Kingdom nonetheless remains one of the lowest in Europe.

These reforms, finally, have been accompanied by significant institutional reforms in labour market policy. First, social assistance for the jobless and UB were merged and harmonised with the creation of the JSA in 1996. Second, since Restart there has been an ever closer *coordination* between the administration in charge of employment policy (the Employment Service) and that in charge of benefit policy administration (the Benefits Agency), culminating in their recent merger to create a 'Working Age Agency'.[4] At the delivery level, finally, benefit and job search services are increasingly brought together in the so-called Jobcentre Plus, which is now the point of contact not only for the registered unemployed, but also for all working-age benefit claimants, facilitating the transition of UK labour market policy from an emphasis on unemployment to an increasing emphasis on 'worklessness' (Clasen 2005).

Summarising the development of labour market policies from the early 1980s in these four European countries, with a specific emphasis on the different ingredients of the 'three-pronged adaptation formula', gives rise to quite contrasting results. Table 9.1 shows while in Denmark and the United Kingdom, revisions to mainstream labour market policies involved virtually all of the programmatic and institutional reform options outlined above, this has been much less true in Germany and France. Notwithstanding the quickening pace of labour market change, in France and Germany benefit rights are as, or even more, differentiated than in the past, activation has been embraced belatedly and tentatively, and efforts at institutional reconfiguration and coordination have been hesitant until very recently. Although very different political programmes have been pursued within them, labour market policy in Denmark and in the United Kingdom have seemingly, and in contrast, long been set on a policy path that is more sensitive to the novel problems posed by new labour market change. The question arises how these bifurcating trends can be explained. The subsequent section argues that an appreciation of contemporary

Table 9.1 Adaptation to new labour market risks in revisions to unemployment protection

	Denmark	France	Germany	UK
De-differentiation of benefit rights	+	−	−	+
Activation of benefits	+	−/+	−/+	+
Coordination of policy institutions	+/−	−	−	+
	High	Low	Low	High

cross-national variations requires a look back into the golden age of welfare state development.

Institutional frameworks for unemployment insurance and patterns of adaptation to labour market change

Conventionally, structural comparisons of unemployment protection systems have focused on distributive policy outputs, for example through consideration of the coverage and level of benefits offered. On such variables, three or four ideal-typical 'models' of unemployment protection can thus be identified in Europe (e.g. Esping-Andersen 1990; Gallie and Paugam 2000b). But such models fail to capture other crucial dimensions of underlying variation, such as the managerial and financial framework of unemployment insurance and its relations to the sphere of industrial relations. Our claim here is that it is such institutional mechanisms that have made labour market policies in some countries amenable to political intervention and wholesale reorientation, while in other countries they have rendered explicit revision of labour market policy in the face of new risks far more problematic.

The French case provides evidence for the impact that the *devolved management of unemployment insurance* can have on patterns of policy adjustment. In many countries, some managerial and governance responsibilities for public unemployment insurance (and other social policies) have traditionally been devolved to non-statutory organisations, such as trade unions, acting alone or in partnership with the state and/or with employers' associations (Crouch 1999; Ebbinghaus 2002b). The French unemployment insurance system is an extreme example of such devolution. The national unemployment *caisse*, UNEDIC, is a formally private institution governed jointly by the social partners, with decisions regarding adjustments to benefits and contributions being made through collective agreements, and then validated by the state so they can be generalised across all firms. Rarely needing to come before Parliament, reforms are often enacted with minimal political debate and limited media attention. The 'industrial bias' that is evident in recent French labour market policies stems partly from this decision-making and governance structure. In contrast, in a traditionally entirely state-controlled system like the British one, political actors have both the obligation and the opportunity to design policies more suited to (competing interpretations of) the 'general interest'.

It is of course the case that the union-controlled 'Ghent system' of unemployment insurance in Denmark is also, in formal terms, a non-state institution. Here, however, the importance of the interaction between devolved governance and the *financing structure of unemployment insurance* becomes clear. The Danish system of unemployment insurance is financed by around 80 per cent from general tax revenues, which gives the state considerable leverage over reforms in unemployment insurance. Though Danish governments usually consult with the unions (Ebbinghaus 2002b: 16), it is they who take the lead in unemployment insurance reforms, which are a prerogative of Parliament (Ploug 2006). By contrast, since 1984 French unemployment insurance has been financed entirely out of contributions by workers and employers, an arrangement the social partners are attached to because of the legitimacy it affords to their managerial role in unemployment insurance, which also acts as a powerful argument against political 'interference' in this domain.

Looking in a little more detail at the debates surrounding some recent French reforms, we can see how this institutional configuration has effectively ruled out certain adaptation strategies. When, for example, in 1992–93 negotiations between the social partners were blocked over the reform of unemployment insurance – the employers refusing further increases in contribution rates, the unions any reduction in benefit levels – a possible solution to avoid increasing the exclusivity of the unemployment protection system would have been for the state to take on a permanent role in the financing of UNEDIC, as it had in a brief period between 1979 and 1984. This, however, was impossible for the government to envisage without increasing its governance role in the system.[5] As the latter was something the social partners in unison refused to countenance, the only remaining option was a more *de facto* transfer of financial responsibility to the state, by increasing the differentiation of rights for the unemployed according to contribution conditions.

Activation and coordination initiatives have also run into the difficulty posed by the established division of financial and managerial responsibilities for unemployment protection. Most obviously, the French state lacks the authority to legitimately impose decisions regarding the utilisation of UNEDIC funds on the social partners. UNEDIC, meanwhile, has a natural incentive to target any of its own activation initiatives on those best covered by unemployment insurance, who are not necessarily those most at risk of long-term unemployment and labour market detachment. If these initiatives are large scale, they will further risk crowding out government-sponsored policies to reintegrate those outside the unemployment insurance system into the labour market, the issue which underpinned the Jospin government's hostility to – and refusal to agree, except in a much watered-down form (see Freyssinet 2002) – the PARE initiative put forward by the social partners in 1999–2000. Activation of whatever kind in fact requires policy coordination if it is to be efficient. It is because the latter has to date been effectively ruled out by a 'pre-political' agreement to maintain the established division of responsibilities that the former has been kept largely off the policy agenda in France.

Though the social partners also play a role in the German system of unemployment insurance, the leverage of the state in the system is – contrary to conventional wisdom – considerably greater than in France (Clegg and Clasen 2004). For example, while unemployment insurance is entirely funded by employers and employees, annual deficits are met out of general taxation. In addition, the secondary unemployment assistance (ALH, abolished in 2005) was entirely tax funded. Thus, the particular funding mechanism has made a wholesale institutional adaptation to new labour market risks difficult in the German unemployment insurance system too, but less so than in France. Of more and wider relevance is the 'tight coupling' (see Hemerijck *et al.* 2000) between unemployment insurance and the wage bargaining system. Though a two-way relationship between social policies (and especially unemployment insurance policies) and models of labour market regulation exists everywhere, in few countries has this relationship been as close and explicit as in Germany.

The historical development of Germany's social insurance system generally cannot be understood without reference to its role in collective bargaining and industrial relations (Manow 1997). In unemployment insurance, for example, the rule that no unemployed person must accept a job offer below the wage set in collective bargaining, which is a constitutionally protected prerogative of the social partners, has allowed the German model of wage coordination to function effectively on an industry-wide level (Manow 2002). Despite recent reforms which have put considerable pressure on the model, the notion of unemployment insurance providing 'deferred' or 'social' wages (see Rhodes 2000) to a declining number of core workers continues to be a constitutive element for the smooth functioning of the industrial relations system, particularly within the more export-oriented high skill sector of German industry. This principle was recently reiterated by the government when it considered proposals for a uniform decrease of unemployment previous Red–Green benefit insurance (ALG) generosity as economically and socially unjustified, unlikely to improve work incentives and as potentially undermining a 'clearly discernible' distance between contributory-based benefits and means-tested support (Bundesregierung 2004: 38). The influence of such notions and their linkages to the collective bargaining system have guided any retrenchment efforts of the 1980s and 1990s away from core workers and towards more peripheral groups in the labour market (Clasen 2005).

In France and Germany the protection of short-term core workers (sometimes referred to as labour market insiders) has more generally remained central to, and limited debates about, welfare reform. This is no surprise, given that German and French core workers have traditionally enjoyed very high levels of social security in a European comparative perspective, in relation to both levels of employment protection (see OECD 2004a) and levels of income maintenance. Net replacement rates of unemployment insurance benefits for short-term unemployed people with average and above-average previous earnings are considerably higher in the two Continental European countries than in the otherwise generous Danish system (OECD 2004b). The level of employment protection is also much higher in France and Germany than in Denmark or the United Kingdom. This does not, however, mean that the likelihood for far-reaching reform is merely a function of national variations in levels of employment protection. The extent of protection of regular workers against individual dismissal is much lower, for example, in either France or Germany than in the Netherlands, and yet the Dutch system of unemployment insurance was, like the Danish one, significantly reformed during the 1990s, with activation initiatives playing a major role (Green-Pedersen 2002; Green-Pedersen *et al.* 2001) and the nexus between work and welfare being far more thoroughly reworked than was the case in France or Germany (Clasen *et al.* 2001).

In addition to a strong level of employment protection, it is, in short, the different institutional frameworks and relationships in which respective unemployment insurance policies have traditionally been embedded that have served to make wholesale reform in France and Germany difficult and amenable only to a low degree of adaptation to new labour market risks (see Table 9.2). It could be said that in both cases the institutional 'attachment' of unemployment insurance to the industrial labour market, and the resulting focus on core workers and short-term unemployed people, has ensured that the conventional notion of the unemployment risk – the temporary absence of stable employment – has retained a disproportionately central place in labour market policy, even as the reality of contemporary labour markets has slowly changed.

Conclusion

While Denmark and the United Kingdom have in recent decades made significant revisions to their systems of unemployment protection to align them, in different ways, with the emergent profile of new labour market risks, this has been far from the case in France and Germany. This should not, however, be taken to imply that these risks have simply been ignored in the latter two cases. Apparently paradoxically, indeed, such risks have

Table 9.2 Institutional parameters of unemployment protection and adaptation to new labour market risks

	Strength of employment protection	Devolved governance of UI	Auto-financing of UI	'Tight coupling' of UI and IR	Adaptation
Denmark	−	+	−	−	High
France	+	+	+	−	Low
Germany	+	+	+/−	+	Low
UK	−	−	−	−	High

Note
UI, unemployment insurance; IR, industrial relations.

often been higher-profile rhetorical concerns in these countries than in either Denmark or the United Kingdom. In Germany the concept of the '*Neue Soziale Frage*' (New Social Question) was used by sections of the then conservative opposition in the 1970s to demand a 'reorientation' of social policy, away from industrial workers (who arguably had been successfully integrated in society) towards the newly underprivileged and insufficiently protected – that is, immigrants, older people, single parents and other groups which had arguably been neglected because they lacked organisational support and interest representation (Geissler 1976). In France, most spectacularly, the themes of the 'new poverty' and then 'social exclusion' became staples of public debate in the mid-1980s, being used particularly with reference to those who, because of inadequate labour market attachment, fell through the net of conventional insurance-based social protection (Paugam 1993).

Nor, furthermore, has there been no policy adaptation with respect to the situation of bearers of these risks. But instead of adapting unemployment protection to new problems such as long-term unemployment, these problems have been repackaged and treated in quasi-isolation. To continue with the French example, the growing exclusivity of the system of unemployment protection thus combined with new policies for the (thereby) 'excluded' to produce a significant activation of the French social protection system (cf. Clasen and Clegg 2003). This, then, can be seen as a gradual and piecemeal form of adaptation to new labour market risks, not captured by indicators centred on revisions to mainstream labour market policies of the type used above. Just as a full account of retrenchment requires not only analysis of policy revisions but also attention to less spectacular and more incremental changes in form (Hacker 2004), so this is probably also true for fully understanding the full range of patterns of policy adaptation to new labour market (and other social) risks.

If there is, as we have however demonstrated above, no single mode or logic of adaptation to new labour market risks at work everywhere in contemporary Europe, it is also because there is no one single 'politics of labour market risks'. The promise of a 'modernised Social Democracy', articulating a new equilibrium between economic competitiveness and social justice, has received much attention in comparative social policy analysis in recent years (e.g. Bonoli and Powell 2003; Lewis and Surender 2004). This 'third way' agenda has informed recent reforms in Danish labour market policy (Green-Pedersen *et al.* 2001), as well as, of course, many initiatives of the Blair governments in the United Kingdom. In the latter case, though, labour market policies still bear more of an imprint of an alternative 'top-down' political revolution, articulating a quite different vision of the appropriate balance between the economic and the social, namely Thatcherite neo-liberalism. Far more than the specific problems faced by bearers of new labour market risks, it is these competing variants of an overarching 'new politics' of social protection that have driven recent policy development forward in Denmark and the United Kingdom. Relatively 'roped off' from mainstream political conflict by the institutional mechanisms demonstrated above, unemployment protection in France and Germany has until now found itself largely insulated from each of these ideological projects. Political conflict around French and German labour market policy, at least normally, is far more institutionally bounded and constrained. Depending on which alternative ideological 'clean sweep' one has in mind, this may of course be considered as either a penalty or a blessing for French and German bearers of new labour market risks.

More analytically, it is, in conclusion, important to be aware that the possibility of making general statements about the 'politics of labour market risks' may be limited by the existence of important contextual differences that impact on the very way the same objective facts are interpreted in different national contexts. Problems of generalisation can be overcome by the identification of broad patterns on important variables. With respect to 'new' social risks, these should include not only the structure of cleavages between the bearers of different kinds of risk (Bonoli 2004b) but also, it has been argued here, the varying institutional frameworks in which conventional forms of protection against social risks have been embedded. While such variables cannot explain the precise form and content of adaptation to new risks, they do help to illuminate the very different modes and logics underpinning contemporary reform efforts.

Notes

1 In some rare cases, active labour market policies were actually the main instrument of labour market regulation in the golden age of the welfare state, where they formed part of an interventionist supply-side strategy that accompanied and supported the macroeconomic management of the economy. Sweden is the most notable example.

2 The following section draws in part on legislative data gathered for a broader study of changes in European social security systems since the early 1980s which was funded by the British Economic and Social Research Council (ESRC; grant reference 000223983).

3 Through the *Allocation de remplacement pour un premier emploi* (ARPE) scheme, the unemployment insurance system thus contributed to financing early retirement packages for older workers who would in principle be replaced by a first-time jobseeker.

4 This was paralleled at ministerial level by the merger of the Department of Social Security (DSS) and the employment functions of the Department for Education and Employment (DfEE) to create a new Department for Work and Pensions (DWP).

5 The *paritaire* management of the partially tax-financed *régime unique* between 1979 and 1982 had resulted in almost permanent dispute and 'buck-passing' between the social partners and the government, which was one of the considerations underlying the clarification of financial responsibilities effected by the distinction between 'insurance' and 'solidarity' adopted in 1984.

10 Childcare policies in diverse European welfare states

Switzerland, Sweden, France and Britain

Anne Daguerre

Introduction

The issue of childcare has received greater attention at the European Union level since the mid-1980s. On the one hand, childcare is crucial to female participation in the labour market, which is increasingly seen as one of the necessary conditions for European economic prosperity. On the other hand, it is hoped that by reducing the trade-off between employment and motherhood, childcare provision may actually help reverse the decline in fertility rates and thus improve future demographic prospects (Esping-Andersen 2002). However, progress in the development of comprehensive childcare systems remains uneven across the European Union with strikingly different levels of provision, especially for children aged under three (the focus of this chapter). Conventional wisdom assumes that childcare provision reflects the nature of the gender contract – that is, the extent to which welfare settlements developed along the lines of female paid work or women's care in the private sphere. Lewis and Ostner (1995) rate modern welfare states according to the degree of women's independence from a male breadwinner model on a scale of weak, moderate or strong breadwinner models. In a strong breadwinner model, women and children are dependent on the husband's income while the mother looks after the children. The Netherlands, Germany, Britain and Switzerland are typical strong breadwinner regimes, whereas France and Sweden are weak male breadwinner regimes, where both parents are expected to be wage-earners (see also Naumann 2001).

The traditional pattern of childcare policy in most West European countries appears to corroborate the key hypotheses of the feminist literature on the welfare state. In more recent years, however, we have seen significant advances in some welfare states that have traditionally been seen characterised by a strong male breadwinner orientation, such as Britain and Switzerland. While these countries are still lagging behind the most advanced countries in this field, the measures adopted are not negligible and need to be accounted for. Our view is that childcare policy can develop also in countries which have traditionally been used to a male breadwinner welfare model. For this to happen, however, an overall convergence of the interests of several actors in the political arena is required. Of crucial importance is the position of employers. If these are part of the pro-childcare coalition, then policy change is more likely to occur.

In this chapter I analyse recent childcare policy developments in four welfare states, selected to include two countries with a long-standing tradition in the provision of childcare (France and Sweden), and two countries which have got to grips with this issue only very recently (Britain and Switzerland). My general hypothesis is that the type of coalition that develops around the childcare issue is crucial to the shape that childcare policy will take. In order to study the process of coalition formation and its result, we use the Advocacy Coalition Framework (ACF), an analytical tool which focuses on how likeminded political actors can join forces and produce policy change. As I shall show, childcare is a potentially divisive issue, with several very different interests involved. As a result, we will not always see the emergence of long-lasting, stable policy communities with a consistent orientation, as is the case in many other policy fields. Coalitions are more likely to be short-lived, contingent upon labour market developments and characterised by shifts in actors' positions. When these alliances are volatile, I use the term 'issue networks'. When they are long-lasting and characterised by strong shared beliefs, I refer to them as policy coalitions. I assume that strong policy communities or advocacy coalitions reflect the institutionalisation of childcare within the state and civic society. Such coalitions are more likely to be found in progressive welfare regimes, while volatile issue networks are more likely to be observed in traditionally strong male breadwinner regimes where the family is seen as a private matter (Hantrais and Letablier 1996).

The chapter starts by briefly discussing the mostly feminist literature on childcare; it then moves on to present the ACF and illustrates how this model can be usefully applied to childcare policy. The following sections provide narrative accounts of recent childcare policy developments in our four countries. Finally, in the conclusion, I examine the implications of my findings for the future of childcare policy in Europe.

Childcare: a women's issue?

Women's interest group mobilisation exerted relatively little influence on early childcare and education (ECE) policies when compared to civil or reproductive rights. This relative lack of feminist activism can be partially explained by the nature of the issue: unlike reproductive rights, childcare cannot be labelled as uniquely a woman's problem. Women are much less likely to be divided among themselves about the right to vote or to abort than about ECE policies. Indeed, there is an ontological ambiguity in the definition of childcare since it involves women's conflicting roles as mothers and workers. As reconciliation of work and family life raises complex questions about gender roles, childcare has been defined as a labour movement or an educational issue rather than a purely feminist issue (Charles 2000: 197; Bertone 2003: 246). The difficulty of achieving consensus in relation to childcare affects feminist movements' ability to develop any form of strong group consciousness. It also limits their capacity to form stable advocacy coalitions, either directly or indirectly. Thus, women advocating childcare need to find powerful allies in order to promote their policies. These allies can be business interests, Social Democratic parties, trade unions, family lobbies, or the state. Cultural, ethnic and class cleavages play a strong role in the agenda-setting process, as the childcare issue may be perceived in many different ways by women belonging to different ethnic groups or social strata. This quality of childcare reinforces the need for alliances between feminist movements and other forces such as labour movements or business interests.

That the mainstream of welfare literature has for too long ignored the 'gender question' is now well established and has been corrected in the last few years. Gender studies and mainstream welfare state literature have started a fruitful dialogue over the past ten years (Mahon 2001a). The extent to which women are freed from family obligations (de-familialisation) is now being examined in full by Esping-Andersen (1996, 1999). This author argues that generous childcare programmes, by enabling female participation in the labour market, are key to an European anti-poverty strategy based on the provision of services in kind rather than benefits redistribution (Esping-Andersen 2002). Various explanations of welfare state restructuring have been offered by feminist theorists. The mainstream of the literature explores at length the move towards a dual-income household in the 1990s and the ways in which welfare regimes adapt the original household contract to changing labour market conditions (Lewis 1992, 2001; Mahon 2002; Daly and Rake 2003). Some authors stress the importance of macro-sociological factors rather than micro-level explanations concerning the role of political actors for understanding the dynamics of policy change. This is most obvious in one of Jane Lewis's contributions, which, owing to its emphasis on the gender dimension of unpaid care-work, tend to portray women as a homogeneous entity with similar agendas and interests (Lewis 2002). Lewis argues that in Britain there has been a move towards an adult worker model since New Labour returned to power in 1997. She identifies similar trends in Conservative male breadwinner regimes such as the Netherlands. The problem with this approach is that it seldom focuses on the actors of policy change, and does not generally investigate the impact of contemporary feminist activism and childcare organisations on childcare policies. However, more recently a variety of research has analysed the influence of childcare lobbies and feminist groups on childcare policies (Daune-Richard and Mahon 2001; Bertone 2003; Bergman 2004). The Advocacy Coalition Framework (ACF) and/or the policy network models provide useful heuristic tools for understanding the role of various policy actors in the dynamics of policy change. Thus, the ACF can complement recent strands of feminist research which investigate the dynamics of coalition building and its impact on public policy.

The Advocacy Coalition Framework and childcare policy

The main objective of the ACF model is to understand policy change (Jenkins-Smith and Sabatier 1994, 1999; Kübler 2001). It observes the policy-making process by actor coalitions that advocate given measures in a given policy field 'i.e. those actors from a variety of public and private organizations who are actively concerned with a policy problem or issue' (Jenkins-Smith and Sabatier 1994: 179). A policy coalition is composed of various actors who share similar values and beliefs. This belief system is composed of a deep core (ontological norms), a policy core (the coalition's normative assumptions about the policy issue) and narrower values. The deep core is the most resilient to change (Jenkins-Smith and Sabatier 1994: 180). In these authors' words,

> The basic argument of the ACF is that while policy-oriented learning is an important aspect of policy change, and can often alter secondary aspects of a coalition's belief system, changes in the policy core aspects of governmental programmes are usually the results of perturbations in the non-cognitive factors external to the sub-system, such as macro-economic conditions or the rise of a new systemic governing coalition.
>
> (Jenkins-Smith and Sabatier 1994: 183)

These policy coalitions can be more or less stable over time. The most unstable coalitions are known as 'issue networks' (see also Marsh and Rhodes 1992, 1998), which are characterised by an opportunistic aggregation of a wide variety of actors who share temporarily coinciding objectives. At the opposite end of the spectrum, policy communities are composed of actors who share similar core beliefs, meet frequently and have a more permanent nature. Thus, issue networks are more likely to be associated with policy change and can be more easily disturbed by exogenous events than policy communities, which typically foster policy continuity or incremental change. The core beliefs of the dominant coalition are very resistant to change and can thus go unchallenged for a decade or more. The dominant policy community adapts its secondary values for strategic purposes. However, as long as the coalition which instituted that policy remains in power, the policy core attributes will not change (Jenkins-Smith and Sabatier 1994: 183). The authors identify two conditions for radical policy change: (1) exogenous shocks to the subsystem; and (2) the emergence of a window of opportunity for a previously minority policy coalition.

The ACF model is particularly useful to account for processes of coalition-building and policy-making in the field of childcare. Policy coalitions relevant to childcare can develop around two rather different issues: family values, and in particular normative views concerning the appropriate role of women in society; and labour supply, where childcare is seen as a means to enable women to participate in the labour market and thus be available for a country's economy.

These two issues elicit the involvement of different actors. In relation to family values, we find moral authorities such as the churches, women's organisations (both partisan and non-partisan) as well as general political actors such as parties and the social partners. With regard to labour supply, the key actors are employers, but also the unions and non-governmental organisations (NGOs). As women's employment acquires relevance in the national political arena, we are likely to see the emergence of policy coalitions with contrasting views on childcare. In relation to family values, it is possible to have a coalition based on the belief that the welfare of the child is paramount and that a child should be looked after by its own mother instead of strangers, or, alternatively, one that supports the externalisation of unpaid caring work through formal childcare. In relation to labour supply, it is possible to have a coalition based on the view that in order to contain (male) unemployment, women's market employment should not be encouraged; alternatively, it is possible to see a coalition emerging around the belief that more women's employment is good for the economy. The kind of dominant coalition that will emerge in relation to each of these two issues will be crucial in determining the scope for developing childcare services in a country. Childcare services are more likely to be developed if both issues simultaneously generate pro-childcare dominant coalitions.

This convergence of interests between two normally distinct policy communities can result in the emergence of an 'issue network'. This seems to be a necessary condition for the development of childcare polices in countries where social policy has been characterised by a strong male breadwinner orientation (Britain and Switzerland, in our sample). In contrast, in countries characterised by a weak male breadwinner orientation, further developments in the childcare domain are less dependent on the emergence of issue networks, as they can rely on more stable policy communities with shared views and objectives. In the remainder of the chapter I test this hypothesis on the basis of recent developments in childcare policy observed in our four country sample.

Childcare policy in France, Sweden, Britain (England and Wales) and Switzerland

This section looks at the development of childcare policy in the four-country sample selected for this study. For each country, I begin by providing the historical background to childcare policy. I then summarise the most important developments that have occurred in recent years, paying particular attention to the shape of the coalitions behind policy-making.

Sweden: the childcare alliance and the model of the working mother

Sweden is portrayed as a pioneer in terms of family-friendly policies and gender equality. However, until the 1960s, family policy was dominated by notions of women's primary roles as mothers and housewives (Ginsburg 2001: 213). This ideology was very strong, especially in the trade union movement, thus allowing the perpetuation of the traditional 'household contract' in 1930–60 (Hirdman 1998: 38). As Sweden's birth rate was the lowest in Europe before the Second World War, family policies had a strong natalist component. The main concern was the declining population; most of the measures introduced in the 1930s were designed to support poor families. In 1948 a universal child benefit was introduced. In the 1950s a statutory provision of birth control and family planning by the health service was created, but abortion remained illegal. In the 1950s and 1960s the 'household contract' survived in a rational, modern form, owing to the introduction of some provision for working mothers (Hirdman 1998).

In the 1960s the economic boom created a need for female employment, which coincided with the emergence of second-wave feminism. Trade unions, especially the Labour Organisation, the blue-collar workers' movement, began to lobby for public childcare 'because of the need for female labour' (Bergman 2004: 223). Women's federations advocated for institutionalised day care within the Social Democratic Party. In 1972, during the Social Democratic Party congress, Olof Palme argued that equality between the sexes had to be grounded in the labour market. He advocated the expansion of social services and day care facilities as well as the introduction of the right to a six-hour working day (Hirdman 1998: 41). Thus, a relatively stable advocacy coalition was formed as a result of ideological and economic pressures which opened a policy window for gender equality measures in order to increase female participation in the workforce. This resulted in a series of measures: the implementation of mandatory individual taxation for married couples; universal provision of pre-school services for young children; and the right to work part time for six hours a day without loss of status for parents with pre-school children. In 1974 a statutory parental leave insurance was introduced (Ginsburg 2001). Parents received 90 per cent of their usual income for the first 12 months after childbirth. Parents caring for a child during this period were statistically counted as being in paid employment. These policies represented the basis of the famous dual breadwinner model, whereby women as well as men were encouraged to form autonomous households. This policy led to a sharp increase in the proportion of women participating in the labour market – from 53 per cent in 1963 to 86 per cent in 1990 (Hirdman 1998).

Generous day care provision continues to represent the pillar of Swedish family policies. For instance, a statutory right to public day care was introduced in 1985. It was expanded further in the 1990s despite the implementation of budget cuts due to the economic slowdown, through the introduction of a cap on fees that can be requested from parents. However, the center-Conservative government introduced a home care allowance in 1994. This measure was criticised by left-wing and feminist movements, for it marked a break with the dual-income earner. The home care allowance was abolished as soon as the Social Democrats regained power (Bergman 2004: 228).

In Sweden the alliance between the feminist and the labour movements supportive of childcare policy enabled the issue to reach agenda status. This change was partly due to the internal mobilisation of feminists within the Social Democratic Party. The cooperation between labour and feminism is closer to the advocacy coalition model defined by Sabatier or the policy community described by Marsh and Rhodes. This alliance is strong and long-lasting, characterised by shared values which act as a policy glue. Individual rights to work and care for children have represented the core values of this advocacy coalition since the late 1970s. Female participation has never been seriously questioned even at times of economic crisis and rising unemployment in the 1990s. This helps to explain the pattern of continuity in Swedish childcare policies in the late 1990s.

France: from pragmatic natalism to the working mother model?

French familialism goes hand in hand with a pragmatic attitude towards female employment, which is seen as a necessary condition for the preservation of high fertility rates. The model of the working mother has been given priority in French family policies since 1945. It received increased political impetus in the 1970s. Public day care became part of the modernising programme initiated by the right-wing President Valéry Giscard d'Estaing. The social administration followed this pragmatic move. The National Family Allowance Fund (*Caisse nationale des allocations familiales*, CNAF) implemented a programme of massive investment in public early education and childcare such as day nurseries and primary schools, the *écoles maternelles*. When President François Mitterrand came into office in 1981, his government increased investment in public day care in order to accommodate women's aspirations to financial autonomy as well as to promote the well-being of the child and the family (Jenson and Sineau 1995). The implementation of family-friendly policies enabled mothers' paid employment to be supported. In 2000, 80 per cent of French mothers with a young child worked (OECD 2002b).

In the late 1980s the need to create jobs at times of strong pressures in the labour market as well as the need for greater flexibility in childcare arrangements became the driving force of childcare policies. The development of childrearing allowances enabled to increase the number of child minders to the detriment of public day care such as nurseries (Jenson and Sineau 1995). The creation of a new childrearing allowance, the *Allocation de garde d'enfants à domicile* (AGED) in 1987 marked a turning point in childcare policies. AGED made it possible to hire a personal employee to look after children within their own homes until they reach the age of six. In 1990 the government created a private childcare allowance, *l'aide à la famille pour l'emploi d'une assistante maternelle agrée* (AFEAMA). The Family Allowance Fund (CAF) covered the child minder social security contributions in order to help a household recruit a registered child minder. New generous measures were targeted at better-off families who employed a carer in the home, and, to a lesser extent, at average-income dual-earner households using the services of registered child minders. A normative assumption, i.e. the right for parents to make a free choice between state-provided and private childcare, was used to justify this policy (Martin *et al.* 1998). This policy led to increased diversification and individualisation in existing childcare arrangements for the under-threes.

When the Socialist Party returned to power in 1997, it decided to place more emphasis on public day care, owing to the lack of places for the under-threes. In June 2000, Ségolène Royal, Minister for the Family, created a special investment fund (*Fonds d'investissement pour l'enfance*) in favour of public care for young children. The government also announced that day care facilities would stay open longer in order to help parents working atypical hours to reconcile care duties and paid employment. Investment should have created about 30,000–40,000 additional places (Kassai-Kocademir 2002: 18). The Socialists did not abandon the notion of free choice, but became aware of the need to enable low-paid families to have access to day care. Overall childcare policies showed a pattern of continuity since the mid-1980s. Party politics or ideological orientations exerted little influence on a relatively consensual policy.

Jacques Chirac, the Gaullist president re-elected with an exceptional share of the vote in 2002, usually takes a Conservative stance on the family, which regards extended parental leave and maternal wages as the best policy for women with children below school age. In his 2002 election leaflet, 'My commitment to France' (*Mon engagement pour la France*), President Chirac recommended that 'a single childrearing allowance should be granted whether or not the mother is working, which would be used as a maternal income or help with childcare costs' (*Le Monde*, 16 March 2002).

The presidential proposal came dangerously close to the notion of a maternal wage (*salaire maternel*). The prime minister, Jean-Pierre Raffarin, appointed Christian Jacob, a former agricultural policy activist, as

Minister for the Family (2002–04). This choice was slightly surprising, since Christian Jacob's area of expertise was agricultural policy, not the family. His mission was to transform the presidential proposal into a political reality. However, the predominance of the model of the working mother in French family policies made this project politically unfeasible. The adjunct Director of the Cabinet, Jean-François Verdier, warmly certified that the Minister did not want to send mothers back home. On the contrary, the Ministry was proud of the French specificity, which combines high birth rates (the second in Europe after Ireland) and high female employment rates (80 per cent for women aged 25–39):

> These are particularities which make our neighbours like Germany or Spain quite jealous. Our policy is to reinforce this strength. We are equally adamant that we do not want women to retire from the labour market. On the contrary, we want them to stay in paid employment because this is good for birth rates. Our objective is to advance the age of the first birth from 30 years old to 25 so that women will have three children instead of two.[1]

Christian Jacob thus developed much more consensual policies than could have been expected at first. The creation of the Young Children Benefit (*Prestation d'accueil du jeune enfant*, PAJE) represents the best example of this policy. The Ministry had to translate the presidential promise concerning a unique childrearing allowance into a concrete measure. In October 2002 the Minister set up three working groups composed of experts, social partners and MPs in order to make concrete proposals for a Family Conference scheduled for June 2003. During the policy-making process the notion of the mothers' wage disappeared from official discourse. The PAJE was part of the Social Security Spending Act and was passed by Parliament in October–December 2003 (*Loi de Finances pour le Financement de la Sécurité Sociale*, Assemblée Nationale 2003). The PAJE, which came into force in January 2004, unifies previously diverse childcare allowances. Parents are encouraged to work at least part time since they can cumulate the supplementary benefit for the free choice of activity, '*le complément de libre choix d'activité*'.

The only bone of contention was the decision to help enterprises create their own nurseries through a tax credit largely financed by the budget of the family benefit fund (CNAF). During the meetings of the fund's administrative council, the Confédération Générale du Travail (CGT) and Force Ouvrière (FO) always opposed this measure. The Confédération Française Démocratique des travailleurs (CFDT) abstained. Big companies like Hachette, Macdonald and BSN welcomed this initiative. They decided to set up day nurseries for their employees. Their commitment was motivated by economic interests since they acknowledge that the crèches should enable to keep their employees at times of labour shortages. Likewise, the business association, the Mouvement des Entreprises de France (MEDEF), has become less indifferent to the issue of work–life balance since 2002–03 because it was becoming increasingly concerned by repeated predictions of future labour shortage. The organisation became more interested in childcare policies which could improve the attractiveness of enterprises as well as employees' productivity. Ernest-Antoine Seillère, the MEDEF president, attended the 2003 Conference on the Family, which represented a symbolic break with past practices.

The PAJE illustrates the impossibility of questioning the long-lasting consensus regarding the model of the working mother, despite the current government's ideological preferences. The role of the CNAF ensures a relative continuity in French childcare policies, which are less prone to ideological U-turns than other sectors of social policy. Another mitigating influence in the French childcare debate is the family lobby. In contrast to the British case, where family organisations were never given special status and exert very little influence on government thinking, family associations are very powerful in France. The French social administration has a relatively weak role in the formation of childcare policies and must gain the support of strong players such as the CNAF. These policy communities are institutionalised within the management of the family branch of the social security system. Thus, policy change is the product of policy learning and is essentially adaptive and incremental.

Britain: the emergence of a modernising childcare alliance

Classified as a Liberal welfare regime in Esping-Andersen's typology, Britain is certainly not neutral vis-à-vis women's roles (Lewis 1992). The British post-war settlement rests on the mother and housewife model and the absence of public day care. Britain has been characterised as a country without explicit family policy, unlike France or Scandinavia (Hantrais and Letablier 1996). The lack of an explicit family policy is linked with the fact that the family was considered a private affair. Despite the increase of female participation in the labour force post-Second World War, both the Beveridge Report and the post-1945 benefit system viewed women's employment as secondary. The average male worker was at the heart of the Beveridge Report. By contrast, the need to reconcile work and family life was seldom mentioned. Women could work temporarily before marriage or childbirth, but their main role was to care for their husbands, their children and older parents (Beveridge 1942). In exchange, under normal conditions they had a share of their husband's earnings. At times of unemployment, sickness or old age, their access to benefits was derived from their husbands. Women were treated as dependants in the benefit and social insurance system.

This male breadwinner model was reinforced by the ideology of motherhood, also referred to as 'maternalism'. This ideology was especially strong in 1950s Britain. For instance, the work of John Bowlby (1951, 1953) based on the notion of *maternal deprivation* proved especially influential in child protection work. Bowlby showed that a young child would suffer a variety of mental disorders ranging from mere anxiety to severe depression and antisocial behaviour when separated from its mother. Social workers and teachers believed for generations that a child would always be better off with its mother, especially at a very young age, except in acute cases of abuse or neglect. As the welfare of the child was the paramount consideration in professional practice, the sanctity of the bond between the natural mother and the child enabled chronic underinvestment in childcare facilities to be justified. As noted by Daguerre and Taylor-Gooby,

> Of the 634 thousand child-care places officially registered in 2000, 55 per cent were provided through private registered childminders and 41 per cent through private nurseries. A large number of additional places of varying quality is provided informally. Payment for private child-care is thus a major issue which bears most heavily on lower-paid workers.
>
> (2003: 635)

Not surprisingly, mothers tend to work part time to compensate for the lack of affordable, publicly funded childcare. In 2000, 40 per cent of mothers with one young child worked part-time; the proportion rises to 60 per cent if the mother has two children (OECD 2002b).

In the mid-1990s a new consensus emerged regarding the need to implement a national childcare strategy. This consensus was based on a temporary agreement between employers, the trade unions and left-wing think tanks. All the major children's organisations as well as the Equal Opportunities Commission, the Trades Union Congress (TUC) and the Confederation of British Industry (CBI) supported this idea. Since the early 1990s the CBI has supported the launch of a national childcare strategy. The CBI claimed that the best way to close the gender pay gap was to remove the barriers to equality of opportunity between men and women in the workplace. All organisations campaigned for a better coordination of childcare services for young children. The focus on children in need provided by the Children Act 1989 was criticised by employers, since private childcare could not meet the childcare costs of most working parents, thus effectively creating employment disincentive for the second wage earner – that is, the mother (EU 1998).

The Labour Party became increasingly interested in the issue, and set up the Commission on Social Justice in 1992. The Commission supported the case for requiring lone and (other) mothers of older children to be available for at least part-time paid work as a condition for receiving benefits. The Commission's proposal was predicated on the availability of adequate childcare facilities (Commission on Social Justice 1994). A comprehensive package of in-work benefits and help with childcare costs was needed in order to make work pay for parents, especially lone mothers. Aware of this problem, the Conservative government took some cautious steps to improve the situation. In 1994 it announced an initiative to provide a pre-school place for all four-year-olds (which left the question of children under three unresolved). Although the need for a national childcare strategy featured prominently in the policy debate in the 1990s, it was not tackled seriously before 1997, when New Labour came to power.

Labour's return to power opened a window of opportunity for the childcare alliance which emerged in the mid-1990s. The radical change in relation to the family brought about by the New Labour administration is now well documented (Lewis 2001; Driver and Martell 2002). To tackle the gender gap in terms of female participation in the labour force became the number one priority. The move towards an active society required increased participation rates of the potential labour force whose talents and skills were being wasted. The rationale for reform was both normative – all able-bodied people should work – and cognitive – female participation in the labour force was the key to national competitiveness. There was thus a radical pendulum shift when New Labour came into office. Whereas in the past the social security system was built upon the notion of a male breadwinner model, even though it never existed in the stricter sense of the word, 'there is now a pendulum shift towards what might be termed an adult worker family, whereby it is assumed that all adults are in the labour market' (Lewis 2001: 154–5). The National Childcare Strategy, launched in 1997, intends to carry out this strategy.

The Strategy aimed to develop more high-quality childcare services which parents with small children could afford. The programme includes provision in the form of nurseries, after-school childcare and Sure Start, which is aimed at children in disadvantaged areas. In 2000–01 over 168,000 new childcare places were created. Although the Labour administration prefers to rely on private mechanisms through the expansion of childcare tax credits rather than the development of public childcare facilities, it can no longer ignore the negative impact of the lack of public childcare on female participation in the labour force. Only just over 10 per cent of single mothers with a child under one year are in work, and this figure rises to just 48 per cent for those with older children (Paull *et al.* 2002). In the light of these hard facts, there is a change in the governmental discourse since the publication of the Green Paper *Meeting the Childcare Challenge* (Department of Education and Employment 1998).

Despite the preference for tax credits as a way to subsidise childcare costs, there is now a wider consensus regarding the need to expand publicly provided childcare, since it is both more affordable and reliable, and therefore offers greater security to parents. The government has taken cautious steps towards a pattern of decommodification of childcare in the face of these strong normative and cognitive arguments. The current consensus among employers and employees' associations regarding the need for improving public childcare does account strongly for this paradigm shift.

One of the main driving forces behind the inscription of childcare on the institutional agenda in the 1990s was the need for highly qualified female workers in a context of labour shortage. This need prompted a radical change in traditional policy values and the adoption of the model of one and a half breadwinner household. Party politics equally played a crucial role in the formation of childcare policies. Labour's return to power provided a window of opportunity for childcare policy advocates. However, the modernising alliance between the New Labour government and social partners can hardly be defined as a new policy coalition. The childcare policy coalition is a wide alliance where social partners, especially business interests and, to a lesser extent, the TUC, play a dominant role. Feminist groups are consulted by the government on a regular basis and are relatively well represented in the current Labour government. Until recently the heterogeneity of the childcare coalition has not been a major obstacle to the formation of childcare policy. However, the CBI has recently opposed Labour's proposal to extend maternity leave from six months to one year on the grounds of costs, in particular for small businesses. Opposing interests could potentially lead to a fragmentation of this fragile childcare alliance in the near future.

Switzerland: policy change in a strong male breadwinner regime

Although Switzerland is sometimes considered a Liberal welfare state (e.g. by Esping-Andersen 1990), in so far as policy for women and families is concerned, its orientation is clearly Conservative. Switzerland was the last West European country to grant women voting rights, in 1971, and social policy has traditionally considered women as mothers confined to the family sphere. As in Britain, childcare has always been considered a private affair and the federal government has never been involved in the provision of day care, the organisation of which was left to families and to local authorities (Ballestri and Bonoli 2003). The state's role was subsidiary, with the expectation that marriage-based patriarchal families would look after their children, the home and the maintenance of the family unit. Family lobbies such as Pro Familia and Pro Juventute are powerful actors who have traditionally supported Conservative family policies. Unions and business interests, especially the Union of Swiss Business (Union du Patronat Suisse, UPS), which by instinct oppose all new social policies, shared a non-interventionist stance. Like their British counterparts, Swiss mothers were more likely to abstain from work, or not to work because of the lack of childcare facilities. But this was hardly a choice: in the mid-1990s, 50 per cent of mothers who were not in paid employment would have preferred to work if their children could have been placed in day care (Enquête suisse sur la population active 1995).

In Switzerland, childcare did not achieve agenda status until the late 1990s and early 2000s. The development of work–life balance policies was due to an alliance between feminist movements and business interests at times of labour shortage, as well as in the context of a lack of flexible and highly qualified labour force. The Conservative familialist consensus became open to criticism in the mid-1990s. Indeed, the pattern of underinvestment in childcare facilities became less sustainable at times of high female participation in the labour market. Between 1990 and 1999, the female participation rate in the labour market rose from 70.6 to 74.5 per cent (Enquête suisse sur la population active 2000). This led to increased demand for childcare places: over the past ten years, the proportion of families using this type of services more than doubled: it rose from 14 per cent in 1991 to 30 per cent in 2001 (Enquête suisse sur la population active 2001).

However, family needs alone cannot account for the inscription of childcare on the official agenda in the late 1990s. The crucial factor was labour shortage in the service sector, especially skilled labour. The UPS wanted to keep skilled mothers in paid work. This prompted business interests to develop a new policy discourse according to which female participation in the labour market was the key to macroeconomic development. Moreover, the UPS acknowledged that work–life balance measures would have a positive impact on employees' working conditions, thus improving productivity. The UPS forged an alliance with family lobbies. Pro Familia insisted on the need to develop childcare for the sake of the family, while Pro Juventute focused on the welfare of the child. Trade unions were more reluctant to support childcare policies, as they feared that a massive entry of mothers into paid employment would reduce wages. Lastly, the Social Democratic party, the Parti Socialiste Suisse (PSS), supported these policies for ideological and, possibly, electoral reasons. The value system of the PSS made it receptive to gender and social equality arguments, which are crucial to justify the expansion of day care. Moreover, as women constituted an important fraction of the PSS electorate, the party was more sympathetic to women's needs than its right-wing counterparts. It is thus no coincidence that in 2002 the parliamentary initiative in favour of childcare expansion came from Jacqueline Fehr, a PSS member.

By 2002 the UPS, pro-family lobbies and Social Democratic forces formed a wide modernising coalition in favour of childcare policies, which resulted in the adoption of a new programme for subsidies to newly created childcare places. The programme is to run for a four-year period initially and can count on a budget of approximately 30 million euros per annum. This is a very modest effort in comparison to existing policies in countries such as France or Sweden, but in the Swiss context it represents a significant step. First, because of the country's peculiar set of political institutions, which generate an extreme level of power fragmentation, it is very difficult for the federal government to adopt a new policy. Second, as was pointed out earlier, the country lacks a tradition of childcare policy, and the subsidiarity principle has so far prevented the federal government from intervening in this area of policy (Ballestri and Bonoli 2003).

The ACF model helps explain changes in childcare policies since the late 1990s. Indeed, shifting macroeconomic and demographic conditions, such as risks of labour shortages, have created a rather short-lived window of opportunity which has been exploited by women's organisations and women's groups within political parties (in particular the PSS) by forging an alliance with employers in the late 1990s. Successful policy change was possible only thanks to the coincidence of a series of favourable factors, most notably the perception by employers that the country faces the risk of labour shortage in the years to come. Such favourable conditions played a crucial role in the construction of a modernising childcare coalition. However, as in Britain, this alliance remains fragile, since it is composed of an array of temporarily coinciding interests. It can be labelled an issue network. This alliance can hardly be described as a new policy coalition, owing to its volatility. What remains clear is that in Switzerland, as in Britain, a radical recasting of traditional familialist policy discourses enabled childcare to reach the political agenda.

Conclusion

The comparative analysis of childcare policy in four countries illustrates the points made at the beginning of this chapter. First, the pro-childcare coalition is much stronger and more entrenched in countries which have a long-standing tradition of supporting women's (and mother's) employment, such as France and Sweden. Attempts by Conservative political forces to radically reorient family policy in a more traditional direction, for example by diverting subsidies away from formal childcare towards full-time carers, have systematically failed. On the contrary, these countries have further reinforced their commitment to childcare policy over the last few years. Policy continuity is thus strong in Sweden and France, which can be accounted for by the presence of highly developed policy communities within the state itself and the strong level of public support for the model of the working mother.

By contrast, policy change in Britain and Switzerland is more sudden and radical. Macroeconomic changes, especially the need for female labour in the context of a booming service economy, opened a policy window for British and Swiss childcare of advocates. The support of business interests appears to have played a crucial role in those two countries, especially in Switzerland. Whether the coalitions which have played a role in recent advances in childcare policy are stable and capable of withstanding possible future backlashes, however, remains doubtful. In these two countries, childcare alliances can be portrayed as loose issue networks rather than strong and stable policy coalitions. Their achievements are thus more likely to be vulnerable to exogenous changes than those in France and Sweden.

These findings suggest that the recent divergence in childcare policy trajectories in Western Europe is unlikely to be corrected in the next few years. Countries with a strong childcare policy tradition are likely to continue along this path, and possibly further improve the level and the quality of provision. In contrast, countries lacking such a tradition may develop a system of childcare provision only if a sufficiently strong coalition develops. Crucial to its chances of success seems to be the presence of employers among the coalition's members. Employers are likely to mobilise in defence of childcare only if they perceive a risk of labour shortage, and this is more likely in countries with low and falling unemployment rates, as was the case in Switzerland and Britain in the late 1990s and early 2000. Things may be different in other West European countries which lack childcare provision. Countries like Germany or Italy, which are currently struggling with high unemployment rates, may have to wait longer before seeing a strong pro-childcare coalition emerge. The strong male breadwinner tradition in social policy is combined with concerns that an increase in labour supply may further increase (male) unemployment.

Acknowledgement

The author would like to warmly thank Professor Giuliano Bonoli, whose works on the Swiss case as well as suggestions about the theoretical framework and more general remarks were essential for the writing of this chapter.

Note

1 Interview with Jean-François Verdier, Adjunct Director of the Cabinet of the Minister of the Family, Paris, 13 February 2004.

11 Providing coverage against new social risks in Bismarckian welfare states

The case of long-term care

Nathalie Morel

Introduction

Ageing populations, changing family models, women's increasing participation in the labour market, and changing values and attitudes towards informal caregiving are new variables which are increasingly challenging the adequacy of present welfare systems by raising, among other things, the question of whose responsibility it is to care for dependent elderly people. Up until fairly recently, the care needs of the elderly have, in most countries, been considered a private family matter and have therefore not been a focus of attention for social policy-makers. However, the present situation, characterised by a dwindling proportion of available carers coupled with an increasing proportion of people in need of care, has turned the private issue of care into a public concern in many countries. Long-term care for the elderly has thus come to be defined as a 'new social risk'.

The mid-1990s witnessed the creation of new policies for dealing with the long-term care needs of the dependent elderly in several countries. In 1994, Germany created a fifth social insurance scheme to deal with dependency. In 1997, France set up a new social assistance benefit for the dependent elderly, and this was expanded in 2002. Austria also opted for assistance benefits in 1993, while Luxembourg (1998) and Japan (voted in 1997 but implemented in 2000) followed the social insurance line.

The creation of these new policies is somewhat puzzling, since the 1990s have generally been described as a period of retrenchment, or at least of 'permanent austerity' for welfare states (Pierson 2001b). Indeed, faced with a global economic crisis, high unemployment, increasing pressure to keep budgets in check, but also adverse demographic trends, governments have attempted to reform the main insurance programmes, not least retirement pensions and health insurance, in order to reduce or contain spending. Even more puzzling is the fact that all the above-mentioned countries are Bismarckian, Conservative welfare states, generally perceived as the most 'frozen' welfare states (Esping-Andersen 1996). These countries are thought to face considerable difficulties in adapting to the new challenges posed to the welfare state (Scharpf and Schmidt 2000, especially vol. 1, ch. 1).

These policy developments therefore raise a series of questions. First of all, how can one account for these cases of policy expansion in times of austerity? Can traditional explanations of welfare state growth account for policy expansion in this field? Second, how and to what extent were these 'frozen' Conservative welfare states able to respond to the new challenge of the long-term care needs of the elderly? And why did some of these countries, all of Bismarckian inspiration and based on the social insurance principle, opt for a social insurance scheme while others chose social assistance as a policy response?

In dealing with these questions I shall focus on France and Germany only, each representing one of the two policy responses outlined above. As we will see, the very fact that these two countries did not choose the same policy option for responding to long-term care needs points to the social construction of the problem and to the importance of institutional and political factors in determining the options available. The comparison between these two countries thus allows us to gain a better understanding of the nature and dynamics of this process of expansion.

We argue that if ageing populations are indeed an objective fact and can be considered as a new social risk, this alone did not prompt governments to act. As we shall see, in both the French and the German case the problem for policy-makers was less the societal demand than the rising cost of programmes that had been diverted from their initial purpose. However, the programmes that suffered from rising costs were not the same in both countries, thus calling for different policy responses.

In order to understand the policy process leading to the creation of new benefits for long-term care, we shall start by looking at how the dependent elderly were taken care of previously and at what was identified as the main problem(s). Second, we shall look at how the policy reform came about: what debates took place; what were the political, economic and institutional contexts; and who were the actors instrumental in bringing this issue onto the agenda. In this respect, timing also emerges as an important variable. By looking at these different variables we are able to test the different approaches which have been used for explaining welfare state development in the past and current literature, namely the functionalist approach, the power resources approach and neo-institutional explanations, and see whether these also apply to policy-making with regard to new social risks, or whether other determinants need to be considered.

A new social risk

Ageing populations

In the European Union the number of people over the age of 65 will have more than doubled between 1960 to 2010, climbing from 34 to 69 million, a growth about ten times greater than for the total population, which will only have increased by about 22 per cent during the same period. The ageing of the population is also characterised by an increase in the category of people over 80, from 1.6 per cent in 1960 to 4.1 per cent in 2003 (Assous and Ralle 2000; Eurostat 2004). Figures for France and Germany correspond to the EU average.

These figures are significant on many accounts. For instance, though it is by no means automatic, there is evidence that the risk of losing one's autonomy increases with age, 80 being somewhat of a turning point (DREES 1999b). An ageing population therefore means a growing proportion of dependent people in need of care.

Who cares?

The dependent elderly have traditionally been taken care of by the family, especially in Conservative welfare states, where the principle of subsidiarity has long prevailed. Thus, in Germany in the early 1990s, as much as 90 per cent of the care services for disabled and frail elderly people living at home were provided informally by family members and, to a lesser extent, by other relatives, friends and neighbours (Götting *et al.* 1994). Figures were similar for France: about 80 per cent of the frail elderly received care from family and other relatives. Of this group, 50 per cent received informal help exclusively. About a third of the dependent elderly received both formal and informal help (Breuil-Genier 1999).

While this informal aid provided by the family has long been taken for granted, ageing populations are creating new pressures on the caring capacity of countries. Indeed, population ageing also entails a shrinking proportion of the population of caring age and therefore of potential carers. Since care work has traditionally been provided essentially by women – mostly old people's daughters and daughters-in-law – Alber (1995) suggests that the caring capacity of a country can roughly be indicated by the ratio of women aged 45 to 69 to the number of people above that age. In Europe this ratio was 30 percentage points lower in 1990 than in 1960.

Population ageing is not, however, the only factor which has an impact on the supply of informal care. Another factor is the increasing participation of women in the labour market. This has reduced the number of women who are able or willing to take care of dependent elderly relatives.

New social risk bearers

It is this combination of scarce resources (in terms of potential carers) and of a new and rapidly growing demand that has led to what is increasingly being referred to as a 'new social risk'. In this respect, it is important to note that while long-term care is generally thought of as a new risk for the frail elderly, it is also an important issue for caregivers, whose employment patterns and career opportunities as well as access to social rights are affected by their caring responsibilities. Thus, when discussing long-term care needs as a new social risk it is important to distinguish between these two groups of 'new risk bearers', not least as they may have conflicting interests.

This has important ramifications in terms of their capacity to mobilise around a unified goal, and therefore their capacity to bring the issue of long-term care needs onto the political agenda. Indeed, what we can observe is that neither the elderly nor informal carers have been particularly active, at least in France and Germany, in bringing about policy changes. There are several reasons for that.

With respect to the elderly, it appears that those who are still healthy have some difficulty in projecting themselves into a situation of dependency – it is something they would rather not think about. In fact, this appears to be the case in the population at large, irrespective of age. This is as true of France (Frinault 2003), as it is of Germany or the United States (Campbell and Morgan 2003). The frail elderly, for their part, have not mobilised either, and one can reasonably assume that this has to do with their very condition. In the case of informal caregivers, possible explanations are that caring for a dependent elderly parent is experienced as a moral duty and that it is a solitary activity which offers little potential for collective mobilisation.

The creation in 1994 of a social insurance scheme for long-term care needs in Germany (the *Pflegeversicherung*) and of a social assistance benefit in France in 1997 (the *Prestation spécifique dépendance*) cannot therefore be understood simply as governments responding to a strong societal demand. As we will see, changes in family patterns and female preferences have not been the key drivers of change.

The problem is not the problem

Indeed, the family has not been the only actor providing for the frail elderly. Even before the *Prestation spécifique dépendance* and the *Pflegeversicherung* came about, the frail elderly were already receiving various forms of social help in both countries. In France, the frail elderly could claim the *Allocation compensatoire pour tierce personne* (ACTP), which is a cash benefit created in 1975 for disabled people. This benefit is means-tested and open to people who have permanent incapacities estimated at a minimum of 80 per cent and who need help from someone in order to perform daily tasks. By the early 1990s, over 70 per cent of ACTP beneficiaries were dependent elderly people (Huteau and Le Bont 2001). Following the decentralisation laws of 1983, this social assistance benefit has been managed by the *départements*, which also bear the cost of the programme.

In Germany the high cost of professional care led many elderly people to poverty and also meant that many could not afford to receive the care they needed. Those most in need could claim social assistance benefits (*Sozialhilfe*). Benefits were means-tested and provided as a last resort, when no other income sources (including the income of the family) were available. The municipalities and the *Länder* were financially responsible for this programme. The increase in the number of dependent elderly people during the 1970s and 1980s led to a dramatic increase in social assistance expenditure. Outlay on care nearly trebled between 1970 and 1976, and more than doubled during the subsequent decade (Götting *et al.* 1994). By 1992, out of the DM42 billion (€21.5 billion) spent on social assistance, 14.7 billion (€7.52 billion) were spent on the dependent elderly (Götting *et al.* 1994).

As the number of dependent elderly increased in both countries, both the ACTP and the *Sozialhilfe* came under pressure. The French *départements* and the German municipalities and *Länder* sought to draw attention to the fact that these programmes had not been designed to deal with long-term care for the elderly, and complained about their high cost. It is from this point forward that the long-term care needs of the elderly became a social problem.

This appears quite clearly when one looks at the actors who mobilised to bring about policy change and at the arguments used and the options put forward for dealing with long-term care. In the following section we will look at the process leading to the *Pflegeversicherung* in Germany in 1994 and then at the process in France that led to the *Prestation Spécifique Dépendance* in 1997 and subsequently to the *Allocation Personnalisée d'Autonomie* in 2002.

Germany: from informal care to long-term care insurance

Defining the problem

As mentioned above, the cost of social assistance in Germany began to increase rapidly, especially in the early 1970s, owing to the rising number of elderly people in need of long-term care. As a result, from the mid-1970s onwards there was rising discontent on the part of the municipalities and *Länder*, whose budgets were considerably strained.

The high cost of institutional care meant that more than two-thirds of people living in nursing homes were dependent on social assistance. Some voices were raised against the fact that elderly people, having worked all their lives, could become stigmatised welfare claimants in old age, left with mere 'pocket money'. There was also growing concern that the supply of care would not be sufficient to meet the increasing demand. Indeed, policy-makers worried that fewer women might be willing to continue to care if the working conditions of informal carers did not improve. And finally, there were some doubts as to whether the supply and quality of professional services would be adequate to meet the increasing demand for care (Götting *et al.* 1994).

Solutions put forward and position of the various actors

Debates and a series of reports by experts ensued, but without leading to any immediate action. Indeed, while there was broad consensus on the definition of the problem, there was less agreement on the type of answer to offer: while some favoured the creation of a separate insurance scheme for long-term care, others argued for private insurance or even the status quo. Other options included the introduction of a universal tax-financed benefit with a shift of financial responsibility to the federal government or an expanded health insurance system.

The Kohl-led Christian Democratic government (CDU) was initially opposed to any wide-ranging reform. The Christian Democrats, along with their Liberal allies (the FDP), argued that an increase in public intervention in the field of care for elderly people might undermine families' readiness to provide informal care and might also lead to an increase in institutional care. For the CDU, budget consolidation was to take precedence over social policy expansion. Thus, little happened until 1988, when it was decided to make the statutory health insurance responsible for the support of home care in order to offer some relief to municipalities. This did not come into force, however, until 1991.

The next important step came shortly before the 1990 general election when Norbert Blüm, the CDU Minister of Labour and Social Affairs, announced that a new social insurance scheme for long-term care would be introduced during the following parliamentary term. Though members of his own party were divided on this issue, Blüm successfully argued that the CDU, as a 'people's party', could not afford to ignore the older generation, emphasising the decisive electoral weight of the elderly.

Blüm's proposal for this long-term care insurance involved new social contributions paid in equal parts by employees and employers, as for the other social insurance schemes. This greatly displeased employers, who argued that the risk of requiring long-term care was an individual life-risk, not a work-related risk. Thus, they saw no reason why employers should be made to contribute (Hinrichs 1996). They argued their case by pointing to the negative effects on competitiveness of a rise in non-wage labour costs. However, in their role as 'social partners' they refrained from opposing the reform entirely, but they did seek to be exempted from the cost of it.

The more radical faction of the CDU, along with their Liberal allies, were also very much against the idea and favoured instead the development of private insurance. However, this was discarded as unlikely to solve the problem. While private insurance schemes did already exist, they had not been particularly successful in a field where people tend to greatly underestimate the risk.[1] Furthermore, such an option would not be able solve the needs of the present elderly, as they would not be able to take out insurance.

Blüm's proposal had the advantage over the private insurance option that it would benefit not just the elderly but also younger people in need of long-term care, and it could be effective immediately. A further advantage of his proposal was that it built upon the existing German social insurance tradition. In 1990 the social insurance system had not yet been called into question (this was clearly demonstrated by the way the West German social insurance model was completely transposed to East Germany following reunification in 1989) and continued to enjoy popular support. The social insurance option was considered an effective way to address social problems and was something policy-makers knew how to put into effect.

The Social Democrats (SPD), for their part, supported the creation of a new social insurance scheme, partly because they believed it to be the best solution given the circumstances (a universal tax-financed benefit was not seen as politically feasible following the cost of German reunification) and partly because they saw it as a political strategy to undermine the CDU/CSU and FDP coalition. In fact, the SPD presented its own social insurance proposal in the summer of 1991.

Finally, the trade unions rather favoured a reform which would take away the stigma of means-testing, but they did not mobilise as much on this issue as they did on other 'work-related' risks. They were also somewhat reluctant towards an increase in social contributions.[2]

The idea of expanding the health insurance scheme in order to deal with long-term care needs was discarded almost as fast as the private insurance option. Indeed, there were already struggles over healthcare reform, and the government was keen to keep the issue of long-term care separate. Furthermore, sickness funds and physicians' associations opposed this proposal because of their interest in keeping the sickness insurance contribution rates low, to avoid creating more competition over scarce resources. It was also thought that a distinct scheme would give more salience to the reform and that the population would be more tolerant of additional social security payments if the money was clearly earmarked for long-term care (Götting *et al.* 1994).

Making the issue of long-term care one of the cornerstones of the election campaign was somewhat of a gamble. First of all, as was mentioned earlier, the people most affected by this risk – that is, frail elderly people and the informal caregivers – had not mobilised and pressed for change. Thus, it was not known whether long-term care for the elderly would be a significant issue for the electorate: would there be any political benefits to implementing such a reform? Second, by making such an announcement Blüm brought the issue of long-term care into focus, thus drawing voters' attention to it. This done, it became politically hazardous for him and his party not to act.

It thus became important to get the reform through in time for the following elections that were to be held in 1994. Extra pressure came in the form of the SPD presenting its own social insurance proposal in 1991. With both parties seeking to persuade the same potential electorate (pensioners and their children), getting the reform through became even more pressing for the CDU.

The main task was to convince the Liberals, employers and those inside the CDU who opposed this reform. Their concern was to keep employers from having to contribute to the cost of the reform. A compromise solution was finally reached whereby social contributions would be paid in equal shares by employers and employees, but in order to compensate employers for this extra cost, one paid holiday would be abolished. The reform was finally passed just before the 1994 general election.

It should be mentioned at this point that despite their disagreement on the type of scheme that should be implemented, all parties and actors had agreed on a few important points from the beginning. The first point was that home care should take precedence over care in nursing homes. Second, the scheme was not to cover the cost of room and board in nursing homes. In fact, the scheme should not cover the whole cost of care either. Third, time spent in formal care work deserved credit within the pension scheme. The idea was to make caring more attractive so that caregivers, especially women of working age, would continue to care rather than enter the labour market. Indeed, the reform was by no means intended to reduce the quantity of care provided informally; in fact, it provides measures aimed at *encouraging* informal care. These elements come out clearly both in the design of the *Soziale Pflegeversicherung* and in its outcomes.

The German statutory long-term care insurance scheme (Soziale Pflegeversicherung)

The law on long-term care insurance in Germany was passed in 1994 and implemented in two stages: in 1995 for domiciliary care cash benefits, and in 1996 for care in an institutional context. Long-term care insurance was set up as a fifth branch of the social insurance scheme, and membership conditions are the same as for statutory healthcare. Insurance is compulsory for the entire population. Depending on employment status and income levels, citizens either are covered by the statutory scheme or must take out private insurance. In the latter case, the level of coverage must be at least equal to that offered by the statutory scheme.

The statutory scheme covers about 90 per cent of the population and insures family members with no or limited income free of charge. Altogether, about 80 million people are insured (BMGS 2003). It is a universal benefit, open to people of all ages rather than restricted to the elderly (in fact, 17.8 per cent of recipients were under 60 years of age in 2002 (BMGS 2003)). It is neither means-tested nor income related.

The amount depends on the level of dependency (assessed by doctors affiliated with the health insurance funds) and on whether the person receives institutional or domiciliary care. In the case of domiciliary care, recipients can choose between cash benefits (*Pflegegeld*), in-kind benefits or a combination of both. Benefits are not intended to cover the whole cost of care. In 2003 the maximum benefit for the highest level of dependency was €665 per month for domiciliary care and €1,432 for in-kind benefits. For the lowest level of dependency, these figures were respectively €205 and €384 (BMGS 2003).

The scheme is financed through social contributions levied on earnings up to a certain ceiling. These contributions (1.7 per cent of gross income) are split evenly between employees and employers. In 2001 there were 1.84 million people in receipt of benefits (Statistisches Bundesamt Deutschland 2003).

France: more responsibilities for the *départements*

Defining the problem

In France the problem of the long-term care needs of the elderly emerged in the 1970s, but the term 'dependent elderly' did not appear until 1979 (Arreckx 1979). A number of reports on the topic were produced in the 1980s and 1990s (Braun and Stourm 1988; Boulard 1991; Schopflin 1991; IGAS 1993), all of them highlighting the threat posed by the demographic situation as well as the inadequacy of existing services. The problems induced by the lack of coordination between the various medical and social institutions and the often poor quality of services were consistently pinpointed. The problem of financing was the other big concern. Despite this consensus on the diagnosis of the problem, these numerous reports did not lead to any political action for a long time.

It was in the early 1990s that the long-term care needs of the dependent elderly became a more serious issue for policy-makers. Indeed, the number of elderly people claiming disability benefits (ACTP) had increased dramatically, to the extent that they represented 70 per cent of beneficiaries. This cash benefit had been created for disabled people to partially cover the cost of hiring someone to help with daily tasks. Being a social aid benefit, it is financed and managed locally by the *départements*. An increase in the number of beneficiaries obviously entailed an increase in costs, much to the *départements*' displeasure.

The plight of the dependent elderly suddenly became a more pressing issue. Different arguments were put forward for creating a separate scheme. First, it was argued that the ACTP was ill adapted to the specific needs of the elderly, not least because the criteria of eligibility were poorly defined, the procedure too slow and the amount insufficient to cover the cost of long-term care in institutions (pointed out in the reports by Braun and Stourm 1988; Boulard 1991; Schopflin 1991; see also Kessler 1995).

Second, there was some concern that with the ACTP being a cash benefit, some people were misusing the money or even just saving it, and thus not receiving the care they needed (cf. Terrasse Report 2001).

This growing concern about the rising cost and misuse of the ACTP comes out clearly in a 1995 statement by the Senate regarding a legislative proposal for an autonomy benefit for the dependent elderly:

> The Law Commission has considered that while the proposed benefit does respond to a legitimate social preoccupation, its implementation should be realised within a coherent framework which should make it possible, *first and foremost*, to put a stop to the deficiencies of the present scheme, characterised in particular by the financial drift of the ACTP.
>
> (Sénat, 1995; my translation, emphasis added)

Another issue was the decline in the ratio between potential informal caregivers and the number of frail elderly. Here, as in Germany, the issue became one of providing incentives to families to keep on caring, the rationale behind this being, of course, that informal care is much less costly than care in institutions, but also that too much state intervention is harmful to society, as it makes families feel less responsible for their kin (a view, as we will see later on, shared by the right and the left alike).

Finally, all the reports linked 'dependency' to old age. This determined to a large extent the way the problem was subsequently treated in the political arena (Lafore 2003). Indeed, what these reports identified were the specific *needs* of the dependent elderly (especially in terms of financial resources and in terms of getting access to better-coordinated medical and social services), rather than loss of autonomy as a lifelong *risk*. This in turn largely predefined the choice of response: in a Bismarckian context, the notion of risk calls for a social insurance response whereas that of need is linked to social assistance.

Solutions put forward and position of the various actors

Thus, it comes as no surprise that there was very little debate on the choice of solutions. Although a few experts had mentioned in rather vague terms the possibility of creating a new social insurance scheme (mainly the 1988 Braun and Stourm report and the 1993 IGAS report), this idea was never seriously considered by policy-makers. This general consensus around a new assistance benefit managed by the *départements* has several explanations.

The first explanation has to do with the uncertainty that prevailed around the number of people concerned. Not only were there different predictions about the number of dependent elderly people in the future, but there was also a lack of information about the number of dependent people at the time of these debates. The concern was therefore that the cost of the benefit would be very high and that a new benefit would also create more demand.

Second, the early 1990s in France was characterised by a bad economic situation with high unemployment (already 9.5 per cent in 1991 and up to 12.3 per cent in 1994[3]). The big deficit in the social security funds regularly made headlines, and the system itself was increasingly called into question. There was a fairly strong feeling that social contributions were too high and were therefore damaging the competitiveness of French industries. As such, the idea of creating a new insurance scheme and therefore adding new social contributions did not have much appeal.

Finally, one has to consider the position of the various actors involved. It should be noted from the start that, as in Germany, neither the frail elderly nor the informal caregivers were mobilised.

Unsurprisingly, the employers' association (MEDEF) was clearly against the creation of a new form of social insurance, especially for the reasons just mentioned. The trade unions, for their part, were generally favourable to such a reform, as can be gathered from the consultations carried out by Brin (1995) in relation with the government's proposal in 1995 to create a new autonomy benefit. However, trade unions did not actively press for a new insurance scheme, as they did not consider the plight of the frail elderly to be one of their main prerogatives, their attention being more focused on pensions and other work-related risks, and on preventing further increases in social contributions.

Unlike Germany, medical associations did not get involved much in the debate. More involved were the home help associations and the directors of old people's homes: both these groups called for a new social insurance scheme, as such an option would allow for more stability in the profession and for greater professionalisation (Frinault 2003).

The social security institutions in charge of health insurance (CNAM) or old-age insurance (CNAV) would have been likely candidates for managing a new long-term care insurance scheme; however, neither showed much interest at the time (Frinault 2003).

Politicians, for their part, were all concerned with limiting the cost of a new benefit and were all generally agreed that raising social contributions was not an option. They also rejected the idea of a new social insurance scheme, as they wanted to avoid the risk of a policy lock-in effect (Frinault 2003). Indeed, as attempts to reform the pension insurance in 1993 had already demonstrated, there is a high political cost attached to attempting to cut back insurance schemes. Tinkering with social aid benefits, on the other hand, does not usually meet with as much resistance. Political parties did differ on one point, which was that while those on the right favoured a means-tested social aid benefit, the left argued for a universal benefit. What the left did not contest, however, was that the benefit would continue to be managed locally by the *départements* as a social assistance benefit.

Part of the explanation for this consensus is that following the decentralisation laws of 1983, the responsibility for social assistance was transferred to the *départements*. The law specifies that if a new form of legal social aid is created, it will automatically be the responsibility of the *département* unless the law states otherwise.

Furthermore, it was felt that the *départements* had already gained some experience with the dependent elderly while administering the ACTP and that it would therefore be more efficient to take advantage of this experience rather than have some other institution manage the new benefit (the 1995 Senate report already quoted emphasised 'the long experience acquired by the *départements* in the field of social assistance' (Sénat 1995)). This point was also made by the *départements* themselves, which, as new actors, were keen to demonstrate their competency and legitimacy in the field of social intervention.

The *départements* also had some financial reasons for wishing to stay in charge of the dependent elderly. First of all, had the responsibility for this new benefit been transferred to the state or to a social security institution, the *départements* would have lost part of the subsidies they received for dealing with the elderly. Second, a proposal for a new autonomy benefit drawn up in 1995 by Mrs Codaccioni, the Minister for Solidarity between Generations, had led the *départements* to believe that they would receive new monies from the state. Indeed, this proposal suggested doubling the amount of money spent on the elderly through new state subsidies (Long 1997). Even though in the end the proposal was not passed and no such increase in state subsidies materialised, the *départements* still considered it vital to be able to manage and control benefits for the dependent elderly as they themselves deemed fit, in order to avoid the kind of economic difficulties linked to the ACTP (Frinault 2003).

The 1995 presidential election

After years of debate, what finally prompted politicians to act was the presidential elections of 1995. Both the left and the right sought to appeal to pensioners, who had become an important part of the electorate, and to demonstrate their capacity to act. During the political campaign, Jacques Chirac (candidate for the right) claimed that old-age dependency was a new social risk which, in the name of national solidarity, called for a collective response. He further suggested that the time had come to take a step forward by quickly implementing a 'dependency benefit'.[4] On the political left, Lionel Jospin announced that

> solidarity will have to be shown towards the dependent elderly, whose number will increase and whom it will be essential to provide with the necessary care and attention they deserve. A complete scheme will be drawn up by the government: it will include a 'dependency benefit'.[5]

After Chirac's election, Prime Minister Juppé also promised the creation of a new benefit for the dependent elderly in his inaugural speech. The new government immediately proceeded to prepare legislation (the above-mentioned Codaccioni bill), but its proposal was heavily criticised, not least by deputies on the left, who went so far as to appeal to the Constitutional Council on the grounds that the benefit proposed would lead to unequal treatment among citizens. A report by the Economic and Social Council (Brin 1995) was also very critical of this proposal. The government brought some modifications to its project, and the law on the *Prestation spécifique dépendance* (specific benefit for dependency) was passed on 24 January 1997.

However, this law was, from the beginning, a very unsatisfactory and transitory law, as its title suggests: 'Law no. 97-60, tending, while awaiting the vote on the law establishing an autonomy benefit for dependent elderly people, to better respond to the needs of the elderly by instituting a specific benefit for dependency' (Journal Officiel, 1997: 1280; my translation).

Thus was the lofty goal of promoting autonomy replaced by a more modest attempt at 'better responding' to the problem of dependency.

The Prestation spécifique dépendance

The *Prestation spécifique dépendance* (PSD) came into force in January 1997. It is a means-tested benefit for people over the age of 60, based on their level of dependency. It is a social assistance benefit, open to anyone residing in France. The benefit can be used for care received either in institutions or at home. The resources criteria are the same as for the ACTP. The allowance is not subject to tests regarding family obligations to maintain, but the state can reclaim some of the cost via the elderly person's legacy or by mortgaging the person's estate.

The amount of the benefit is based on the person's resources as well as those of his or her spouse or partner, and on the level of dependency of the person, which is assessed by a socio-medical team according to a national grid (AGGIR grid) that distinguishes between six levels of dependency. Only those who fall into groups 1, 2 and 3 are entitled to the benefit.

The maximum amount of the benefit was €897 per month in 2001. Only people whose total resources were below €9,528 a year could receive the maximum benefit (€17,318 for a couple). For people at or above that ceiling, the maximum benefit was €717 per month (DREES 2001a). When personal resources and the benefit are added up, the total cannot exceed €10,976 a year for a single person, or €18,294 per year for a couple. Here, as in Germany, the idea was not to cover the whole cost of care but rather to supplement and encourage the informal care provided by families (in both France and Germany the benefit can be used to pay an unemployed relative, *other than a spouse*, who provides care).

Though the maximum amount of the benefit was specified, no such guidelines were provided regarding minimum levels. This has meant that there were wide territorial disparities between the *départements*.

There were 86,000 beneficiaries of the PSD in 1998 (DREES 1999a). By 2001 the figure was only up to 139,000 beneficiaries (DREES 2001a), which means that only about 15 per cent of people who needed some form of care were covered by this scheme, according to INSEE estimates (Martin 2003).

Criticisms of the PSD

This poor coverage of the population in need, along with the fact that there were wide territorial inequalities in terms of the amount paid to beneficiaries, led to increasing criticism which culminated in 1998 in the production of a 'Black book of the PSD' (*Le Livre noir de la PSD*), produced by the National Committee for Retired and Elderly People (CNRPA), along with over 20 different organisations of home-help services, elderly-care institutions and NGOs. This 'Black Book' (CNRPA *et al.* 1998) argued for abolishing means-testing and for nationwide regulations concerning the amount of the benefit, and opposed the fact that the state could reclaim some of the cost through the elderly person's legacy or through mortgaging the person's estate. Indeed, this had been shown to effectively discourage elderly people from applying for the PSD. What the authors of this report wanted was a new social insurance scheme for dealing with long-term care, a position they further developed in their 'White Book for an Autonomy Benefit' (*Livre blanc pour une prestation autonomie*, CNRPA *et al.* 1999).

Basically, the PSD presented the same problems as the ACTP (variations between local authorities in terms of the amount paid and limited coverage of the population), which was hardly surprising as the PSD had been copied directly from the ACTP. The PSD therefore appeared largely as a cosmetic change to the way the dependent elderly were taken care of. The main change was for the *départements*, which could better control the way benefits were provided.

However, even the *départements* were dissatisfied with this new benefit, essentially because they did not receive the extra subsidies they had anticipated. Many *départements* also began to press for change. After the 1997 legislative elections, which propelled the left into government, there was hope for change, as those on the left had shown a clearer preference for a collective solution to the care needs of the elderly and had been very critical towards the types of inequalities engendered by the PSD. They had even voted against the PSD.

Despite all this, the socialist-led government did not do anything for four years. There were several reasons for this, as pointed out by Frinault (2003). First of all, the dependent elderly were not a top priority for the then Minister of Employment and Solidarity, Martine Aubry. Indeed, the legislation on the 35-hour week, the creation of the CMU (a universal health coverage scheme) and the development of the *emplois-jeunes* (a youth employment scheme) were more pressing issues for the government. Second, the EU context represented a constraining environment for developing new and expensive social insurance schemes.

These were not the only reasons, however. There were also more ideological and institutional reasons for this lack of enthusiasm for the creation of a new insurance scheme, as Aubry's speech before the national Committee for Geriatric Coordination in April 1999 illustrates. Her three main points were, first, that a social insurance benefit would still have to be means-tested as, whatever the mode of financing, the community could not ignore the resources of a person in determining how much help that person should receive. Second,

> unlike a health service, which requires input from professionals, *help to a dependent elderly person relies in actual fact first and foremost on relatives* (spouse, children or other) and *only secondarily on the intervention of professionals*. To reverse this order by making the community finance a substitutive rather than a subsidiary benefit would lead to the destruction of natural family solidarity, which would have a very high cost for society.
>
> (Martine Aubry, April 1999, my translation; emphasis in the original)

Finally,

> The PSD should remain something managed locally in order to be as close to the needs as possible. A benefit granted automatically on the basis of a national needs scale would not be well adapted. Help should be calibrated within a framework of a personalised aid plan which takes into account the help provided by relatives and which is inserted within the framework of a real local geriatric coordination that relies on local actors.
>
> (Martine Aubry, April 1999, my translation)

Since it was clear that the PSD had to be reformed nonetheless, Aubry commissioned Jean-Pierre Sueur in December 1999 to write a report on a new autonomy benefit that would be more equal across the country and would cover a much larger proportion of the elderly in need of care. However, his mission statement clearly indicated that an insurance scheme involving new social contributions was out of the question. The report came out in May 2000 and was followed by a law on a new personalised autonomy benefit (*Allocation personnalisée d'autonomie*).

The **Allocation personnalisée d'autonomie**

Voted on in 2001, the *Allocation personnalisée d'autonomie* (APA) came to replace the PSD in January 2002 and sought to remedy some of the main problems identified with the PSD. First and foremost, although it remains a social assistance scheme, managed at the regional level, it guarantees the same access to benefits everywhere in France. The state redistributes resources across all the *départements* to compensate for the differing levels of resources.

The benefit has been extended to people who fall into level 4 (GIR 4) according to the AGGIR grid, which has considerably increased the number of people eligible for this benefit. Levels of dependency continue to be assessed by a socio-medical team, and benefits can be claimed for either institutional or domiciliary care.

The benefit is no longer means-tested, but the amount is reduced progressively (from 0 per cent to 80 per cent) for beneficiaries who have resources in excess of €949 a month. This is referred to as the *ticket modérateur*, a term borrowed from the social insurance vocabulary. In January 2002 the maximum benefit for domiciliary care for people in GIR 1 was €1,090 per month; it was €935 for GIR 2, €701 for GIR 3 and €467 for GIR 4 (DREES 2003). The state can no longer reclaim some of the cost on the person's legacy.

By December 2002 there were 605,000 APA recipients (DREES 2003). This figure was expected to increase to 800,000 by 2005 (Sueur 2000). In the Sueur Report that paved the way to the reform, the cost of the APA was estimated at €2.5 billion. As it turns out, the cost has risen to €3.7 billion, which has prompted the right-wing Raffarin-led government to introduce new reforms in 2003 to reduce the cost of this benefit.

This reform lengthens the delay before the benefit can be received; it introduces control mechanisms on the way the benefit has been spent by the beneficiary; and, most controversial of all, it dramatically reduces the income ceiling below which one is entitled to full benefits (from €949 down to €623).

What impact on new social risk bearers?

In Germany the introduction of the long-term care insurance scheme has considerably improved the financial situation of frail elderly people and reduced the risks associated with dependency. However, because the benefits do not cover the whole cost of care, many continue to be dependent on social assistance. As a result, the *Pflegeversicherung* is increasingly being contested.

In France the situation was a lot less favourable to the elderly following the PSD than it was in Germany, but the introduction of the APA in 2002 marked a clear improvement. Indeed, the APA was so successful that the number of beneficiaries – and with it the cost of the benefit – increased more rapidly than had been expected. Only a year after it was implemented, the new right-wing government started cutting back on it. This was made possible by the very nature of the scheme, which – although universal – remains a means-tested social aid benefit (Palier 2002a).

While there have been some positive outcomes for the frail elderly, it is nonetheless important to emphasise that the plight of the dependent elderly was not the main concern in either country. As several authors have pointed out, the debates that led to the introduction of the long-term care insurance scheme in Germany focused essentially on the rising number of frail elderly people dependent on social assistance, and on rising municipal expenses. Issues such as the situation of informal care-givers or the quality of care played only a subordinate role (Götting *et al.* 1994; Schneider 1999). Very much the same can be said about France: it was the rising number of dependent elderly people claiming the ACTP – a social benefit originally designed for the disabled – that fuelled the debate and prompted policy-makers to act.

Of even less concern was the situation of informal caregivers. In both countries, the main objective was to find ways of getting the families, and not least women, to keep on caring. In fact, despite the introduction of long-term care schemes in both France and Germany, figures for informal care have remained virtually the same as a decade ago. Thus, in France, of the 3.2 million frail elderly people who receive some form of help, about half of them receive only help from family and friends or neighbours, while 29 per cent receive both professional and informal help. Only 21 per cent receive only formal help (DREES 2001b). In Germany, 70.3 per cent of beneficiaries received domiciliary care in 2001, and of those, 72.6 per cent had opted for cash benefits (BMGS 2003). These figures indicate that the introduction of long-term care insurance has not eroded the provision of informal care; the main difference as compared with the early 1990s is that informal carers now receive some form of payment and social security rights.

Discussion and conclusion

We started off with two main questions: how did it happen that France and Germany, both 'frozen' Conservative welfare states, each introduced new policies for dealing with the long-term care needs of the frail elderly at a time generally described as a period of retrenchment, or at least of 'permanent austerity'? Put differently, how can one account for these cases of policy expansion, and are traditional explanations of welfare state growth able to account for this expansion? Second, why did Germany opt for a social insurance scheme while France, breaking with its social insurance model, implemented a social assistance benefit?

Traditional theories of welfare state growth

A functionalist approach would suggest that these new policies were created to deal with what appeared to be an increasingly important new social risk, that of requiring long-term care in old age. The argument would be that the process of modernisation of societies, characterised among other things by family break-ups and new family forms, changing values, women's participation in the labour market, etc., has weakened the traditional modes of social protection, thus requiring the state to step in as a substitute. However, as the case studies of France and Germany illustrate, the problem for policy-makers was less the societal demand than the rising cost of programmes that had been diverted from their initial purpose. Furthermore, it was clear in both countries that the state should *not* step in as a substitute, but should rather encourage and reinforce informal care structures. Finally, the choice of different policy responses in Germany and in France demonstrates that 'needs' do not automatically dictate appropriate 'solutions'; that is, political solutions are not selected or designed only according to functional requirements (cf. Götting *et al.*'s discussion of the German *Pflegeversicherung*, 1994). One therefore cannot assume some kind of direct causality between problems and policy.

Theories of welfare state growth based on the power resources approach – that is, explanations based on the relative strength of the labour movement and/or of left-wing parties in the government – are also unsatisfactory. The power resources approach does help to account for the conservative and weakly decommodifying nature of the policies (in that they encourage informal caregiving), since both the *Pflegeversicherung* and the PSD were introduced by right-wing governments. However, it does not help to understand why these policies were created in the first place. Indeed, there was neither any class mobilisation nor even any mobilisation on the part of new social groups – in this case the new social risk bearers. Even trade unions, which should have been a strong component of a group-based mobilisation, failed to mobilise in both countries owing to the nature of this new 'risk', which was not perceived to be work related.

Neo-institutionalist accounts prove more fruitful. Indeed, as we have argued, it was not the ageing of the population *per se* that was the problem. This had been going on for 20 years already and had been highlighted in several reports without policy-makers doing anything about it. It is only once certain institutions were affected by these demographic trends (in terms of rising costs and in terms of programmes being diverted from their initial purpose) that the problem became an issue for policy-makers. What the latter were responding to was the growing discontent not of the elderly and the caregivers but of the institutions that were thus put under pressure. In fact, because it highlights certain mechanisms of path dependency, historical neo-institutionalism also helps to account for the different responses offered in France and Germany.

Explaining differences in France and Germany

As we have seen, gaining support for the creation of a new social insurance scheme was not a straightforward task in either country. This difficulty was linked to the nature of the risk in question. Indeed, long-term care of the elderly was not perceived as a work-related risk. As such, it was difficult for Bismarckian welfare systems to agree to finance this 'risk' through social contributions paid by employees and employers. In Germany, the fact that needing long-term care was defined as a *risk*, independently of age and cause, made it easier to justify the provision that employers should contribute too (not least because loss of autonomy linked to work injuries is covered by this scheme). In France, on the other hand, long-term care was defined as a *need* linked to old age. Needs, in a Bismarckian welfare state, are associated with social assistance.

However, the choice of vocabulary for defining this 'new' problem in each country was not made randomly or innocently. In Germany, faith in the social insurance model was still strong at the time of the debates, and the economy was still quite healthy. Even though raising social contributions was no longer a straightforward choice (policy-makers were trying to make the country a profitable place of investment and production once more (Götting *et al.* 1994)), neither was raising taxes, owing to the increase that had already taken place following the reunification of East and West Germany. The municipalities and *Länder* had clearly stated their wish to be rid of the financial burden of providing for the needs of the frail elderly and were in a sufficiently strong political position to push for a shift of financial responsibility. Thus, it was necessary to find new actors to put in charge of the needs of the frail elderly. Getting the social partners (employers and employees) to manage a new insurance scheme was made possible by effectively relieving employers of the cost of the new insurance by compensating them through the abolition of a paid holiday. This way, the cost of labour did not increase for employers and allowed Germany to remain competitive. So, in developing long-term care insurance, Germany stuck to the well-trodden path of social insurance.[6]

In France the debate was about 'old-age dependency' rather than long-term care. There was no discussion about dependency or loss of autonomy as a risk that could befall people at any age, nor was there any discussion about adopting a more global approach to disability and lack of autonomy. This is rather surprising, seeing that the elderly had for some years been taking advantage of the disability benefit (ACTP). Expanding this benefit so that it could respond to the needs of both the elderly and the disabled would have made good sense.[7] Instead, in line with the French tradition of putting people into discrete categories of intervention (a tradition inherited from the social assistance model of the Third Republic), a new category of 'dependent elderly' was identified. This choice was also linked to the fact that the *départements*, which were managing the ACTP and which had therefore found themselves in charge of the dependent elderly, were the ones who effectively mobilised not only to create a new benefit, but also to be put in charge of this new benefit. This was both because they were hoping for fresh subsidies and because they wanted to gain more legitimacy as social actors. Furthermore, the decentralisation laws of 1983 specified that any new form of legal social aid should be the responsibility of the *départements*. There were therefore strong institutional reasons to continue along the same path.

However, another important factor in the French decision to quickly discard the idea of a new form of insurance was the economic and employment situation at the time. As a result, it was felt that raising social contributions was simply not an option. Indeed, since the late 1980s, governments of different political orientations have adopted contribution exemptions for employers in order to encourage job creation, most prominently through the creation of the CSG (the generalised social contribution) in 1990 (Palier 2002b). Finally, as compared with Germany, there was less faith in the insurance model, owing to the important budgetary difficulties experienced by the social security system.

New political determinants for new social risk policies?

There was nonetheless one common factor in the development of long-term care policies in France and Germany that needs to be emphasised: in both countries the policy reforms were part of a promise made during general election campaigns. Politicians seized upon this issue of long-term care in the hope of attracting voters, not least as the elderly represent an increasingly important part of the electorate. This credit-claiming opportunity is most likely an important determinant in accounting for why parties on both the right and the left vied with each other to introduce new policies, even in times of 'austerity'.

Less evident is whether the shape taken by these reforms is explicable with reference to this context of general 'austerity' (preventing policy-makers from launching costly, large-scale programmes) or whether it is due to deeply entrenched values in these Bismarckian countries regarding the proper equilibrium between state and family in the provision of care. Indeed, the new policies did not bring any fundamental change to the care structure (care continues to be provided essentially informally – even if caregivers now receive some form of payment), what has changed is the mode of financing and of management. The main trigger for the development of these policies was the appearance of structural or institutional problems: some programmes were being 'misused' and therefore saw their cost rising drastically. It was to deal with that, rather than merely with a newly recognised social 'risk', that policy-makers sought to develop new schemes. Thus, without dismissing the fact that these reforms marked a clear improvement for citizens in both countries, one could argue that these new policies aimed first and foremost at restructuring the existing welfare state, rather than at recasting and expanding it.

Notes

1 Campbell and Morgan (2003) show that this was the case not just in Germany but even in the United States, where private insurance policies against the risk of long-term care have not been very successful.
2 For a more detailed account of the position of the different political parties and actors, see Götting *et al.* (1994).
3 Compared to 5.6 per cent in Germany in 1991 and 8.4 per cent in 1994 (Commission Européenne, 1999).
4 In 'Extrait des réponses des candidats à l'élection présidentielle', Le Lien, ADMR, April 1995, quoted in CNRPA (1998).
5 In 'Propositions pour la France', programme de Lionel Jospin à l'élection présidentielle, quoted in CNRPA *et al.* (1998).
6 Though it should be pointed out that, unlike for the other four traditional insurance schemes, benefits are flat-rate rather than income related.
7 That this was not done has in fact raised some new problems. Indeed, disabled people find that they lose their right to disability benefits when they turn 60 and have to rely on the less well-adapted dependency benefit thereafter. Yet as some commentators have pointed out, disability does not 'retire' at the age of 60!

12 The European Union and new social risks

The need for a differentiated evaluation

Oliver Treib and Gerda Falkner

This chapter looks at the European Union's role in designing viable policy solutions that may help modern welfare states to cope with the challenge posed by the emergence of 'new social risks'. As an important example we analyse the impact of one specific European policy, the Parental Leave Directive. We focus on both the European decision-making and the domestic implementation process in all 15 (pre-2004) member states, revealing that the Directive induced significant policy reforms in the majority of member states and thus facilitated the reconciliation of work and family life for many working parents. Drawing on the experience of a number of other EU Directives from the field of new social risk policies, however, we conclude by arguing that not all of the factors identified in this case apply to the area of regulating new social risks in general. Instead, we argue that the European Union does not treat new social risks in a systematically different way from other social policy issues covering 'old' social risks, and we make the case for a differentiated approach to studying the European Union's role in the political regulation of new social risks.

Introduction: the European Union and new social risks over time

In recent decades, European welfare states have been confronted with 'new social risks' whose emergence was 'the result of multiple social transformations in the labour market, in family structures and gender roles as well as of changing general cultural orientations like secularisation and the decline of the work ethos of industrial society' (Armingeon and Bonoli 2003). At the heart of traditional welfare states was the typical 'male breadwinner' working on a full-time basis and with an open-ended contract. Hence, the main function of traditional welfare programmes was to protect male workers from 'old' social risks like invalidity, sickness, unemployment or ageing. In contrast, employees nowadays are increasingly faced with new problems such as reconciling work and family life, single parenthood, providing care for elderly, disabled or sick relatives, unemployment as a result of low or obsolete skills, and insufficient social security coverage as a result of child-related career interruptions or 'atypical' forms of employment such as part-time, fixed-term and temporary agency work (Bonoli 2003a: 3–5).

In the light of these new socio-economic challenges, governments have reacted by introducing policies specifically aimed at supporting people negatively affected by these new social risks. Political responses to these new socio-economic challenges, however, have not been confined to the national level. The European Union has also been active in this area. Although there is no specific and encompassing policy with regard to new social risks, some of the recent social policy measures have targeted this area.

One of the earliest manifestations of EU interest in what are now called new social risks could be found in the context of measures to combat *gender discrimination*. The Treaty of Rome, adopted in 1957, laid down the general principle of equal pay between women and men (Article 119 ECT, now Article 141). This was one of a small number of concessions for the more 'interventionist' delegations in the Treaty negotiations, among which there were different schools of thought on social policy. While some member states (notably Germany) insisted on the neo-liberal concept of market-making, and even wanted to unleash market forces in the realm of labour and social security costs, others opted for at least a limited degree of harmonisation with a view to social and labour costs (Beutler *et al.* 1987: 437). In the end a compromise was found which did not provide for social policy harmonisation at the European level. The dominant philosophy of the Treaty was that welfare would be provided by the economic growth stemming from the economics of a liberalised market and not from the regulatory and distributive capacity of public policy (Kohler-Koch 1997: 76). The concession on equal pay was to accommodate the French, who by 1957 already had provisions on equal pay for both sexes and therefore feared competitive disadvantages after opening up their market to the European partners.

However, it took a long time before any practical follow-up ensued, as governments did not bother to fulfil their obligation to pay women workers equally. Starting in the 1970s, this non-discrimination principle was reinforced and considerably extended by the European Court of Justice in extensive case law (Warner 1984; Mazey 1995; Ostner and Lewis 1995; Hoskyns 1996). A number of Directives that outlawed discriminatory practices against women with regard to pay, working conditions and statutory social security systems followed. In terms of addressing new social risks, these measures in general enhanced the social situation of the growing number of women participating in the labour market. More specifically, the European Union's gender equality policies also improved the position of part-time workers. After the European Court of Justice had invented the concept of 'indirect discrimination', arguing that most part-time workers were women and that therefore discrimination against part-timers also constituted an indirect form of sex discrimination, this principle was used to fight some of the most obvious disadvantages faced by this part of the workforce, such as the widespread exclusion from occupational and statutory social security schemes.

In the 1990s the European Union strengthened its policies to improve the *employment conditions of 'atypical' workers*. A package of draft Directives was issued in 1990, targeting discrimination against part-time, fixed-term and temporary agency workers (Falkner 1998). The European Commission, as the main promoter of this legislative project, suggested that such atypical work should only be used in exceptional cases. The general thrust of the Commission's approach was to restrict atypical work as much as possible and to protect those actually working under such conditions by providing that their social protection should be equal to that of permanently employed persons.

Only one of these Directives was adopted shortly afterwards. It guaranteed fixed-term and temporary agency workers the same occupational health and safety protection as 'normal' workers employed on a permanent basis. The debates surrounding the other proposals were much more protracted. Finally it became possible for two Directives on non-discrimination against part-time and fixed-term workers concerning their employment conditions to be passed, in 1997 and 1999.[1] It is crucial to highlight that the restrictive approach was largely dropped, the new strategy in vogue in many EU countries being employment promotion via flexible labour markets. The Directives finally adopted combine the two goals of liberalisation/flexibilisation and of worker protection. At the moment, the last part of this 'atypical workers' package, a proposal on equal pay and equal employment conditions for temporary agency staff, is still being debated in the Council of Ministers.

Another focus of EU social policy related to new social risks is the area of *reconciling work and family life*. In this context a Directive on maternity leave and health and safety protection for pregnant workers was adopted in 1992. Among other things, this Directive guaranteed every working mother the right to at least 14 weeks of paid maternity leave and a right to return to her job afterwards. It is part of a large number of Directives in the field of 'health and safety at the workplace'. That the EEC institutions 'have permanently expanded their competence in the field of industrial safety' (Schnorr and Egger 1990: 82) relates, however, less to social concerns in a narrow sense than to the free movement of goods: the effective functioning of the Common Market was perceived to necessitate action with a view to common minimum provisions for worker protection. The issues regulated under various action programmes on worker health and safety include protection of workers exposed to emissions and loads as well as protection against risks of chemical, physical and biological agents at work (e.g. lead or asbestos). The requirements of the Common Market reportedly made Community action necessary in the perception of relevant policy-makers (see, for example, Schulz 1996: 18). Nevertheless, the rights conferred on pregnant mothers in this Directive are significant if compared to the *status quo ante* in a number of EU countries.

A wider perspective on reconciling work and family life was finally offered by the Parental Leave Directive, enacted in 1996. This Directive applied not only to women but also to men, and it covered provisions not only for parents to look after their babies, but also for employees to take care of sick or otherwise needy family members. This Directive will be the focus of the first part of this chapter. More specifically, we aim to assess the policy effect of this particular measure in the member states to give one in-depth example of the effects of an EU measure in the field of new social risks. We can draw on the results of a collaborative project carried out at the Max Planck Institute for the Study of Societies entitled *New Governance and Social Europe: Theory and Practice of Minimum Harmonisation and Soft Law in the European Multilevel System.*[2] This project studied the negotiation and implementation of the main EU Directives of the 1990s concerning labour law (on the subjects of written employment contracts, working time, protection of young workers, protection of pregnant workers, part-time work, and also on parental leave) from a comparative perspective in all 15 (pre-2004) EU member states. When the Parental Leave Directive was adopted, experts (for example, see Keller and Sörries 1997, 1999; Streeck 1998) and specialist journals such as the *European Industrial Relations Review* (EIRR) had the impression that policy changes would only be required in a very small number of countries and that these changes would have only an altogether limited impact. We shall show that in actual fact the impact is more profound and certainly more extensive than expected.

The chapter is structured as follows. In the next section we will sketch the process that led to the adoption of the Parental Leave Directive at the European level and provide an overview of its provisions and effects. Next, we will discuss the framework conditions that facilitated the adoption of this specific policy in the field of new social risks, outlining also how they were absent in other cases. We will conclude by discussing the lessons to be drawn from our findings with a view to the European Union's role in the transformation of the welfare state to cover new social risks.

The European Union's success in regulating new social risks: the Parental Leave Directive in practice

The first Commission proposal for a Directive on parental leave, and leave for family reasons, dates back as far as 1983 (COM [83] 686 final). On the basis of the argument that the quite diverse national provisions were thought to hamper the harmonious development of the Common Market, an approximation on the basis of Article 100 EEC Treaty was suggested. The minimum standards suggested were three months of parental leave for either parent (to be taken up to the third birthday of the child), and an unspecified number of days off for family reasons, to be decided by the individual member state. With regard to social insurance and pay, leave for *family reasons* was to be treated as time off with pay. In contrast, pay or indemnity for parental leave was only an option, to be met by public funds. The Commission advocated an unequivocal non-transferability of these rights.

As a result of opposition by the United Kingdom and a number of other member states, however, unanimous agreement on the draft was impossible. While the Conservative UK government was opposed to the Directive for ideological reasons, the Belgian and German governments were reluctant to accept the proposal because it would have interfered with ongoing domestic reforms. However, party politics also played a role in triggering resistance by these countries. In Germany, debates on the establishment of a parental leave scheme were under way when the Commission tabled its draft. The envisaged scheme was relatively generous, but provided for parental leave to be a family entitlement which could be transferred between mothers and fathers. The draft Directive, in contrast, included the principle of non-transferability, which meant that fathers would have stronger incentives to go on leave. This was not acceptable for the centre-right German government, and therefore Germany was among the opponents of the Commission's parental leave proposal (Buchholz-Will 1990).[3] In Belgium, in the early 1980s the Ministry for Social Affairs had tabled plans to introduce a national parental leave scheme, but this motion encountered opposition within the centre-right government coalition. As a compromise, a more moderate (and more employer-friendly) scheme of career breaks was created which offered the possibility of up to one year off work, but depended on the employer's agreement and required replacement by an unemployed person. The draft Directive would have called for a significant upgrading of that compromise and was thus refused by the Belgian government in 1985 (Malderie 1997, interview B6: 30–7). Hence, the proposal was set aside for almost a decade.

Surprisingly, it was the Belgian Social Council presidency that brought the Directive back to the agenda in 1993. This policy shift was caused by a domestic change of government. The Liberals had switched place with the Socialists, who now formed a grand coalition with the Christian Democrats. Hence, the political climate for parental leave in Belgium was much friendlier than eight years earlier. Therefore, the Belgian presidency presented a new compromise proposal on parental leave. The new text did not provide for non-transferability any more, which made the proposal acceptable to Germany. British resistance continued, however. During the

Social Council's November session, the United Kingdom reportedly tried in vain to obtain derogation from the Directive, and then restated its opposition.[4] Fruitless negotiations continued until autumn 1994. Despite consensus among 11 delegations in the last relevant Council debate on 22 September 1994, adoption of the proposal was still not possible, owing to a British veto (Ministerrat 1994; Hornung-Draus 1995).

This was the ideal situation for an application of the Maastricht Social Agreement, which by then had already been in force for almost a year. It excluded the United Kingdom from the social policy measures adopted by the other (then) 11 member states and allowed for the adoption of Euro-collective agreements between the major interest groups on social issues that could be implemented by the EC Council Directives (for details on the Social Agreement, see Falkner 1998). Hence, consultation of labour and management on the issue of 'reconciliation of professional and family life' was instigated by the Commission on 22 February 1995, and an agreement between the major interest groups was signed soon thereafter (see the next section).

The *general aim* of this so-called framework agreement (and hence the ensuing Council Directive) is, according to the preamble preceding the main text, 'to set out minimum requirements on parental leave and time off from work on grounds of *force majeure*, as an important means of rec-onciling work and family life and promoting equal opportunities and treat-ment between men and women'. The purpose of the agreement is therefore to enable working parents to take a certain amount of time off from work to take care of their children. In this context, particular emphasis is put on enabling and encouraging men to take on a greater share of childcare responsibilities.

The *compulsory minimum standards* of the Directive thus encompass seven provisions: (1) workers must be granted the right to at least three months' parental leave; (2) this entitlement is to be an individual right of both male and female workers; (3) parental leave has to be provided not only for parents with children by birth, but also to those who have adopted a child; (4) workers may not be dismissed on the grounds of exercising their right to parental leave; (5) after the leave, workers must be able to return to the same or, if that is not possible, to an equivalent or similar job; (6) rights acquired by workers before the beginning of parental leave are to be maintained as they stand until the end of the leave period and have to apply again thereafter; and, finally (7), workers have to be granted the right to 'force majeure leave', i.e. a certain amount of time off from work for unforeseeable reasons arising from a family emergency making their immediate presence indispensable.[5]

These binding provisions notwithstanding, establishing the access con-ditions and modalities for applying the right to parental leave and leave for urgent family reasons is left to the national governments and social partners. Hence, the Directive includes a number of *exemptions and derogations* from the above-mentioned standards. First, the entitlement to parental leave may be made subject to workers having completed a certain period of work or length of service, which, however, may not exceed one year. Furthermore, a worker planning to take parental leave may be required to notify his or her employer of the dates at which the period of leave is to start and finish. It is up to the member states to decide upon the length of the notice period. Moreover, employers may be allowed to postpone the grant-ing of parental leave for 'justifiable reasons related to the operation of the undertaking'. In addition, member states can establish special parental leave arrangements for small undertakings. Finally, the conditions of access and detailed rules for applying parental leave may be adjusted to the special cir-cumstances of adoption.[6]

What was the difference between the binding standards of the Directive and the existing policies at the national level? Given the largely sceptical assessment of the Directive after its adoption, it might come as a surprise that our in-depth analysis of the Directive's compulsory reform implica-tions reveals that some sort of *pressure for adaptation was created in all 15 member states*. However, the amount of 'hard' policy misfit differs widely among different countries. *Four countries did not have any generally binding legal provisions on parental leave when the Directive was adopted.* For *Ireland*, *Luxembourg* and the *United Kingdom*, the Directive really meant a complete policy innovation in the sense that employees for the first time were given the right to take parental leave. *Belgium* also had no statutory parental leave scheme covering all employees, but the practical relevance of this considerable legal misfit was somewhat softened by the fact that parental leave was already established in the public sector and that, additionally, a scheme of career breaks was in operation.

The remaining member states had parental leave systems in place. At first sight these systems were all more generous than required by the Directive, e.g. concerning longer leave periods than the Directive's three months and/or some sort of payment during parental leave. However, an exclusive perspective on the length of, and payment during, parental leave overlooks crucial issues. In a considerable number of countries parental leave was not an *individual right* of male and female workers alike. In these countries the Directive hence demanded the introduction of qualitative improvements to the existing schemes. In *Austria* and *Italy*, the parental leave regulations were mainly focused on women, whereas fathers were entitled to take the leave only if the mother refrained from using her right. In contrast, the Directive required the entitlement to parental leave to apply equally to women and men. Less significantly, the *Austrian*, *German*, *Greek* and *Portuguese* systems excluded single-income families; that is, the typical male breadwinner could not take parental leave if his partner was not employed but, for example, worked at home as a housewife, or was studying. Meanwhile, almost all of these shortcomings have been removed as a reaction to the Directive.[7]

Moreover, two countries completely debarred further important categories of the workforce from being covered by the scheme. In *Greece*, all workers in small and medium-sized enterprises with fewer than 50 employees had no entitlement to parental leave. As a reaction to the Directive, this exclusion was repealed. In *the Netherlands*, the pre-existing parental leave scheme excluded part-time employees whose weekly working time was below 20 hours from the right to take parental leave (Interview NL4: 60–76). However, when the Directive was adopted, a national review process of the existing legislation was already under way, and the reform proposals issued by the government as a result of that review already provided for an extension of the parental leave scheme to all employees (Clauwaert and Harger 2000: 68). As a result of this parallel domestic reform process, the incorporation of the Directive into domestic law did not pose any major problems.

Furthermore, the majority of member states needed to change their legislation in regard to *force majeure* leave. While Denmark, Ireland, Luxembourg and the United Kingdom did not have generally binding legal rules on time off from work due to urgent family reasons, Finland, France, Greece, Spain and Sweden had to adapt their existing regulations, mostly by including emergencies relating to family members other than children in the scope of the leave.[8] Hence, certain improvements were also brought about in this area. In sum, there is *not one country whose rules and regulations were already completely in line* with the Directive.

In order to categorise the observed domestic policy effects of the Parental Leave Directive, we use a fourfold typology.[9] The first category is *no or only negligible effect*, which means that there was no impact at all or that the effect was only very small. Four countries may be included under this heading. Denmark, Finland, France and Sweden only had to adapt parts of their existing policies on leave for urgent family reasons and did not enact any further voluntary reforms in the context of implementing the Directive. The lack of reactions to the soft-law provisions in these countries may be explained by the fact that, especially in Finland and Sweden, many of the recommendations had already been fulfilled (e.g. the possibility to take part-time leave). The second category is *reinforced policy*, denoting cases where the existing policies were neither transformed fundamentally nor supplemented with qualitatively new elements. Instead, the old policy remained in place and similar elements were added. This applies only to Spain, where the Directive brought about a more explicit protection of leave-takers from dismissal as well as a small (voluntary) adaptation of the rules on *force majeure* leave.

The third category is *patchwork addition*. Here, the fundamentals of the existing system remained unchanged, but qualitatively new elements were added. This pattern could be observed in Austria, Germany, Greece, Italy, the Netherlands and Portugal. The final category is *paradigmatic change*, including both the complete reversal of an existing policy and the creation of an entirely new policy from scratch. In this group, we have Belgium, Ireland, Luxembourg and the United Kingdom. Ireland and the United Kingdom were forced to create completely new parental leave systems, but did not enact any significant voluntary reforms. Belgium already had to qualitatively transform its existing system of career breaks. However, the government supplemented this step by considerable voluntary reforms (higher payment during parental leave, right to work part time), thereby again creating something qualitatively new. Luxembourg, finally, complemented the creation of a completely new system of parental leave with significant voluntary steps, especially by offering six instead of three months' leave and by providing for generous payment during the leave.

To conclude, the example of the Parental Leave Directive highlights that the European Union actually has the *potential* to be a powerful and effective player in the regulation of new social risks. It follows that we need to discuss, in the next section, why these potentials were not exploited to a similar extent in the field of other new social risks.

An exception rather than the rule? Putting the Parental Leave Directive in context

In the previous sections of this chapter we have looked at the European Union's role in designing viable policy solutions that may help modern welfare states to cope with the challenge posed by the emergence of new social risks. The Union has so far enacted several measures that relate to this area of social policy. Many other possible measures have not even been discussed at the EU level, have never been adopted, or have been accepted by the Council of Ministers only in seriously diluted versions. In fact, the industrial relations context was of primary importance when the Parental Leave Directive was adopted. This section will discuss the favourable framework conditions underpinning this particular case, which did not exist to the same extent when similar issues came onto the agenda.

Most crucially, some recent EU social policy Directives have been negotiated by the EU-level social partner federations. The Council of Ministers only accepted the details agreed by UNICE, CEEP and ETUC.[10] Within these collective negotiations, general industrial relations considerations have played as important a role as concrete policy preferences (for a detailed account, see Falkner 2000). The 1992 Maastricht Treaty set up the corporatist patterns which have since characterised EU social policy. The Amsterdam Treaty introduced into the EC Treaty (which is binding for all) what had previously been rules pertaining to the member states with the exception of the United Kingdom. The Treaty provisions effectively give primacy to agreements between management and labour. Euro-level interest groups may, on the occasion of obligatory consultation by the Commission on any envisaged social policy measure, inform the Commission of their wish to initiate negotiations in order to reach a collective agreement on the matter under discussion. This brings traditional supra-national decision-making (which involves the Commission as initiator, the Council and its working groups as most relevant decision-maker, and the European Parliament as an increasingly important co-actor) to a standstill for at least nine months (Article 137 TEC).[11] If a collective agreement is signed, it may, at the joint request of the signatories, be incorporated in a 'Council decision', on a proposal from the Commission (Article 138 TEC).[12] The issue of introducing works councils at the European level was the first to be discussed using the Social Protocol as a legal basis. Since industry had until recently vigilantly opposed European works councils, the ETUC was sceptical regarding this (presumably tactical) new approach and suggested *preliminary talks* on the possibility of entering into formal negotiations. After two exploratory meetings between the three cross-sectoral peak federations, during the spring of 1994, the poten-tial 'social partners' indeed failed to conclude an agreement (for details, see again, for example, Falkner 2000).

Therefore, great expectations rested on the next potential Euro-social partner agreement, on parental leave. Only a year after the failure of the talks on works councils, the Commission started the extensive consultation process again in early 1995. This time the three major cross-sectoral feder-ations UNICE, CEEP and ETUC were very keen to show that the Euro-corporatist procedures of the Maastricht Treaty could actually be put into practice. Reportedly, the issue was perceived as a suitable 'guinea pig' (interview with Commission official). The industrial relations aspect was by then a central concern of both sides of industry, since the impending Intergovernmental Conference preceding the Amsterdam Treaty could have changed the corporatist patterns if they were not perceived to be workable.

The collective negotiations had been well prepared behind the scenes and indeed were successfully concluded after only five months, on 6 November 1995 (Agence Europe 8 November 1995: 15). Soon after the formal signature of the agreement on 14 December 1995, the Commission proposed a corresponding Directive to the Council. Reportedly, the draft was a matter of controversy in the Social Affairs Council (Agence Europe 29 March 1996: 8).[13] Nevertheless, a political consensus was reached on 29 March,[14] and the Directive was formally adopted without debate on 3 June 1996.[15] In the case of negotiating the Parental Leave Agreement and Directive, general considerations concerning the development of an indus-trial relations culture at the EU level have been as important as material interests in the negotiations between UNICE, CEEP and ETUC. They also mattered to several of the delegations in the Council of Ministers. In such a situation, the common interest of all 'EU social partners' tends to be upgraded and each of the negotiators is rather more ready for compro-mise in the policy dimension, which may give rise to more far-reaching material outcomes than would otherwise possibly have resulted.

A similar effect, albeit to a probably somewhat lesser extent, was at work in the two ensuing collective negotiations under the Maastricht Social Agreement, on atypical work. Euro-collective negotiations on part-time and fixed-term work confirmed the corporatist patterns we have outlined. However, the chances for further collective agreements seemed poor at the outset, considering that the issue of atypical work is at the heart of the contemporary debates on deregulation versus worker protection (and hence: on new social risks); that UNICE had always been opposed to regulative action at the Euro level; and that various drafts had been discussed controversially in the Social Affairs Council since the beginning of the 1980s. However, political developments put pressure on the negotiators. An Intergovernmental Conference on EU Treaty Reform made the social partners want to prove that the corporatist patterns were operational more than once only. Additionally, the Renault affair[16] brought to the attention of the wider public the question of whether European economic integration was sufficiently counterbalanced by social policy rules.

The consultations on 'atypical work' under the Social Agreement started in September 1995. Under the heading 'flexibility in working time and security for employees', the Commission tried to reconcile employers' needs for greater flexibility with part-time and temporary workers' needs for job security. In October 1996, UNICE, CEEP and ETUC formally launched negotiations on an agreement concerning 'flexibility of working time and security for workers'. Very antagonistic starting positions meant that the three federations were 'stumbling over the content of the negotiation' (Agence Europe 28 January 1997: no. 35) for several months. UNICE argued that its negotiating mandate from the member organisations was (at least for the moment) restricted to 'permanent part-time' work only, thus excluding the huge number of part-timers on atypical contracts (notably fixed-term workers). The ETUC wanted to cover all forms of atypical work, i.e. part-time, temporary, casual and agency work, homework and telework (although not necessarily all in the framework of these negotiations). Following the ETUC's demand, the part-time agreement's preamble included the statement that the signatories intended to 'consider the need for similar agreements relating to other forms of flexible work'. With a view to content, the Part-Time Work Agreement aims to 'provide for the removal of discrimination against part-time workers and to improve the quality of part-time work', while on the other hand it seeks to 'facilitate the development of part-time work on a voluntary basis and to contribute to the flexible organization of working time' (Clause 1). More specifically, it lays down (only) one broad compulsory minimum standard: with regard to working conditions, part-time workers may not be treated less favourably than comparable full-time workers unless such unequal treatment is objectively justified.

Separate negotiations on fixed-term workers were initiated in March 1998. This issue proved even more politically sensitive and technically difficult than the part-time one (EIRR 304: 15). Towards the end of the official nine-month deadline in late 1998, the positions still seemed irreconcilable. UNICE stressed that fixed-term contracts were a vital means of enabling employers to respond to fluctuating market demands and wanted to secure a significant degree of flexibility and autonomy for companies. The ETUC, by contrast, fought for more security for workers on such contracts and against potential abuse of fixed-term work. Nevertheless, a compromise was hammered out in January 1999 and an agreement formally signed by UNICE, CEEP and ETUC on 18 March 1999. This was made possible by the very strong framework character of the final text and by acceptance on the part of the ETUC that initial recourse to fixed-term contracts was not regulated. By contrast, the employers accepted measures against the potential abuse of successive fixed-term contracts.

When they were adopted, it seemed that in both cases *low substantive standards*[17] were accepted by labour *in exchange for industrial relations interests*.[18] Particularly in the part-time case, this may be considered a trading of women's interests (according to Eurostat data, 32 per cent of female but only 5 per cent of male employees were part-timers when the agreement was negotiated; see Agence Europe 20 September 1997: no. 30) against the organisational self-interests of the ETUC and its member organisations. The ETUC's Women's Committee's rejection of the deal did, however, not affect the result of the vote in the ETUC's executive committee, because a simple majority of votes in favour was sufficient.

While on part-time and fixed-term work, compromises could finally be reached, the ensuing negotiations on temporary agency work failed entirely.[19] Euro-collective negotiations have been conducted on *temporary work* but collapsed in spring 2001 (see Agence Europe 23 and 28 May 2001, EIROnline 28 June 2001). At least procedurally, the European-level management and labour organisations could easily have made temporary agency work the subject of a Euro-collective agreement, since this issue represents the final part of the atypical work package as suggested by the Commission in the early 1980s and as incorporated in the second and third agreements under the 'negotiated legislation' track.

However, these talks had been intricate from the very beginning, with several issues being very controversial. The crucial stumbling block was, in the end, the notion of a 'comparable worker' when determining the conditions of non-discrimination of temporary workers.[20] In March 2002 the Commission presented a draft Directive to the Council and the European Parliament that has not been adopted to date (see EIRR 23 April 2002 and, on the most recent failure to come to an agreement, EIROnline 24 June 2003).

It must be mentioned that a further issue in the field of new social risk regulation (in the wider sense) has been on the European Union's agenda, albeit in a different perspective. A legally non-binding agreement on *telework* has been agreed between UNICE, CEEP and ETUC on 16 July

2002. From the outset, the goal of these negotiations was only a document of voluntary character, since UNICE considered telework as a form of working (and not a legal status) and argued that it was inappropriate for a statutory instrument. This agreement will serve as the crucial test case for the potentials of a purely voluntaristic approach to EU-level industrial relations, and to the 'regulation' of new social risks (on the concept of neo-voluntarism in EU social policy, see Streeck 1995).[21]

Conclusions

The European Union has at times co-shaped the regulation of new social risks to an extent that had not been foreseen even by experts. This has been underlined here with one particular policy, namely the Directive on parental leave and leave for urgent family reasons. However, there is no consistent or even predefined EU policy on new social risks in general. There are also no stable actor coalitions (the United Kingdom has traditionally been very reluctant to regulate in this field, but even this has changed since Labour assumed power and since EU regulation shifted more towards liberalisation and flexibilisation).

Rather, changing circumstances have decided on the fate of the various proposals that were elaborated by the Commission over time. The most important factors included two crucial issues. The first (and predominantly of relevance before the Maastricht Treaty) was whether a proposal could be subsumed under the area of 'health and safety at the workplace' with a distinctive and facilitating Treaty basis (not demanding unanimity in the Council of Ministers, but only qualified majority). In the cases of the Pregnant Workers Directive and the Health and Safety of Atypical Workers Directive, this was the case. Second (but of relevance only since the Maastricht Treaty), the industrial relations interests of the major Euro-federations also help decide the fate of proposed EU regulation on new social risks. This helped push through the Parental Leave Directive, with its significant adaptation pressures for the member states and two further Directives in the field of atypical work, but did not suffice to reach agreements in other cases.

To conclude, EU citizens actually have at times benefited from supra-national rules concerning one or the other new social risk. Most import-antly, atypical workers and working parents have gained more rights through EU Directives. At the same time, there is still a very long way to go towards a fully fledged EU policy *vis-à-vis* new social risks, in a larger sense. Recent EU policy-making in this area suggests that new social risks are not treated in a systematically different way from social policy issues covering old social risks. There is no specific EU policy on new social risks, and there is no particular actor coalition which would support these kind of policies more than other social policy initiatives. Just as in relation to EU social policy in general, therefore, a differentiated approach in evaluating the existing EU measures on new social risks (and in pondering the prospects of pending proposals) is indispensable.

Notes

1 As has already been noted, many forms of discrimination against part-time workers at the workplace had already been outlawed on gender equality grounds. Nevertheless, the Part-Time Work Directive brought about an improvement, since it defined very specific criteria for establishing discriminatory practices, and it extended non-discrimination to those part-time employees who had hitherto been unable to prove that they were being discriminated against, since they lacked a comparable full-time worker belonging to the opposite sex.

2 Parts of the empirical data presented in this chapter were gathered by our two collaborators Simone Leiber and Miriam Hartlapp. For further details on Germany, the Netherlands, Ireland and the United Kingdom, see the dissertation by Oliver Treib (2004); on Greece, Spain, Portugal, France and Belgium, see the dissertation by Miriam Hartlapp (2005); and on Denmark, Sweden, Finland, Austria, Luxembourg and Italy, see the dissertation by Simone Leiber (2005). For a comprehensive comparison across all 15 countries and all six Directives studied, see our book (Falkner *et al.* 2005). More details on the project group as well as information on publications resulting from this research are available on our project website at http://www.mpi-fg-koeln.mpg.de/socialeurope.

3 In September 1985 the German Social Democrats tabled an alternative proposal (BT-Drucksache 10/3806). Although not including non-transferability, it provided for a prolongation of the leave period if both parents shared the leave. The government, however, refused this idea and went ahead with its own transferable scheme, which was finally adopted in December 1985.

4 At one point, a lowest common denominator solution seems to have emerged: the United Kingdom wished parental leave to be only granted to mothers, not to fathers. Reportedly, only the Irish delegation and the Commission were immediately against this 'awful' change (as one Commission official described it in an interview), which made the Commission threaten to bring in the European Court of Justice against this discrimination on grounds of sex.

5 The Directive does not define the term 'family'. This is explicitly left to the member states (Ministerrat 1996). It is crucial to note, however, that by using this term, *force majeure* leave cannot be restricted solely to sickness or accidents of children, but must at least cover unforeseeable emergencies of spouses, too (for a similar interpretation, see Schmidt 1997: 122).

6 In addition to these binding standards and derogation possibilities, the Directive contains no fewer than nine *non-binding soft law provisions*. The large number of non-binding recommendations relating to important features of the envisaged leave schemes (such as social security coverage during parental leave, flexible forms of making use of the leave, or the time up to which the leave can be taken) seems to be due to the fact that trade unions and employers in the collective negotiations at the European level could not agree on definite standards on these issues.

7 At the time of writing, the Greek legislation still excludes single-income couples, while the Austrian scheme still includes a small advantage for the mother.

8 In Denmark, *force majeure* leave was granted to many employees on the basis of collective agreements, which considerably reduces the policy impact of this

lack of generally binding legislation. However, adaptation to the Directive met with specific difficulties, since the adoption of generally binding legislation in this area clashed with the Danish tradition of autonomous social partnership. As the focus of this chapter lies on the policy impact of the Directive, we will not discuss this very interesting effect here. For more details, see Falkner and Leiber (2004).

9 This typology is a modified version of a number of other categorisations suggested in the literature (Héritier 2001: 54; Radaelli 2001: 119–20; Börzel 2005). Note that in principle the typology includes five categories. But the fifth category, weakened policy, did not play a role in the present cases. Theoretically, however, it is perfectly possible for a European policy to undermine the existing domestic system without completely replacing it and without adding qualitatively new elements.

10 The Union of Industrial and Employers' Confederations of Europe, the European Centre of Enterprises with Public Participation and the European Trade Union Confederation.

11 The Commission and the social partners may jointly decide to extend this period.

12 The Council acts by qualified majority, except where the agreement in question contains one or more provisions relating to one of the areas which need unanimous decision-taking. The alternative to implementation of Euro-level collective agreements via EU law is through 'the procedures and practices specific to management and labour and the Member States' (Article 138 TEC). For background information on the new decision patterns, see, for example, Gorges (1996), Keller and Sörries (1997, 1999), Leibfried and Pierson (1995) and Platzer (1997).

13 For some delegations, the content of the framework agreement left too much room for interpretation, making proper application in the member states a difficult task. Others thought that the social partners had neglected powers of the EU institutions by introducing a non-regression clause and a time limit for implementation.

14 There was unanimous agreement. Adoption was, however, postponed with a view to gaining parliamentary approval in Germany (Agence Europe 30 March 1996: 7).

15 Directive 96/34/EC of 3 June 1996 on the framework agreement on parental leave concluded by UNICE, CEEP and ETUC, Official Journal L 145, 19 June 1996: 4–9. Since the British Conservative government had secured an opt-out from the European Treaty's social chapter at the Maastricht summit, the United Kingdom was initially not covered by the Directive. Tony Blair's Labour government, which had assumed power in May 1997, signed up to the social chapter and declared its willingness to implement the Directives that had been enacted during the United Kingdom's opt-out (EIRR 282: 2; EIRR 284: 2). As a consequence, the United Kingdom also had to implement the Directive, the only difference being that its transposition deadline was later than the one applying to the other member states.

16 A plant in Vilvoorde (Belgium) was shut down in order to profit from cheaper labour and higher subsidies in Spain (see, for example, Agence Europe 3 March 1997: no. 34). This provoked renewed controversies on the role of labour costs (and subsidies) in the internal market, and prompted ETUC support for simultaneous protest actions and strikes in Belgium, France and Spain. This may be considered a new quality of European trade union activism.

17 There was, at least initially, much criticism of the standards agreed (see, for example, references in Hartenberger 2001; Keller and Sörries 1999: 122). To date, there is no profound implementation study on the effect of these

Directives in the member states. The Part-Time Work Directive, at least, is covered in a forthcoming study (Falkner *et al.* 2005). Note that the crucial binding standard set by the Fixed-Term Directive is again on non-discrimination, similarly to the above-quoted standard of the Part-Time Work Directive.

18 And for greater involvement of the 'social partners' at all layers of the European multilevel system. Note that a multifaceted role for the national social partners is foreseen in both the Part-Time and the Fixed Term Agreements, e.g. in the specification of details during the implementation of the agreement and in the periodical review of certain aspects.

19 For sure, a number of other Commission proposals outside the field of new social risks were also not negotiated by the social partners, e.g. the burden of proof in sex discrimination cases, an instrument on sexual harassment and a Directive on worker information and consultation in national enterprises.

20 For the purposes of equal treatment, the ETUC was not ready to accept that the member states should be allowed to determine the comparator (from the level of either the respective user company or the agency). Instead, the unions wanted to establish the principle of the user firm as comparator and, at most, were prepared to allow derogations from this principle if endorsed in domestic collective agreements. UNICE, by contrast, was not prepared to allow for the agreement to stipulate that a comparison had to be made with the company using temporary work (except for a few defined areas).

21 It is not possible here to conduct a survey on the follow-up in the member states.

Bibliography

Adema, W. (2001) *Net Social Expenditure*, 2nd edn, Labour Market and Social Policy – Occasional Papers 52, Paris: OECD.

Adserà, A. and Boix, C. (2002) 'The Political Economy of Trade and Economic Integration: A Review Essay', unpublished manuscript, University of Chicago.

Alber, J. (1995) 'A Framework for the Comparative Study of Social Services', *Journal of European Social Policy*, 5 (2): 131–49.

Allan, J.P. and Scruggs, L. (2004) 'Political Partisanship and Welfare State Reform in Advanced Industrial Societies', *American Journal of Political Science*, 48 (3): 496–512.

ANBA (Amtliche Nachrichten der Bundesanstalt für Arbeit) (2000) *Arbeitsmarkt für Frauen*, 4. Available http://www.arbeitsamt.de.

Anderson, K. (2003) 'Sweden: Radical Reform in a Mature Pension System', paper presented at the workshop 'Social Policy Responses to Population Ageing in the Globalization Era Shinkawa', Sapporo, February.

Anderson, K. and Meyer, T. (2003) 'Social Democracy, Unions, and Pension Politics in Germany and Sweden', *Journal of Public Policy*, 23: 23–54.

Armingeon, K. (1983) *Neo-Korporatistische Einkommenspolitik: Eine vergleichende Untersuchung von Einkommenspolitiken in Westeuropäischen Ländern*, Frankfurt am Main: Haag & Herchen.

—— (2004) 'Reconciling Competing Claims of the Welfare State Clientele: The Politics of Old and New Social Policies in Comparative Perspective', paper prepared for the 14th Conference of the Council of European Studies, Chicago, March.

—— (2005) 'OECD, EU, and Active Labor Market Policy', paper prepared for the ISA Conference, Honolulu, March.

Armingeon, K. and Bonoli, G. (2003) *The Political Regulation of New Social Risks: Conference Outline*, Bern: University of Bern.

Armingeon, K., Beyeler, M. and Menegale, S. (2002) *Comparative Political Data Set, 1960–2000*. Online. Available http://www.ipw.unibe.ch/armingeon/cpds-korrigiert.zip.

Armingeon, K., Leimgruber, P., Beyeler, M. and Menegale, S. (2005) *Comparative Political Data Set, 1960–2003*, Bern: Institute of Political Science. Online. Available http://www.ipw.unibe.ch/mitarbeiter/ru_armingeon/CPD_Set_en.asp#cpdsI.

Arreckx, M. (1979) *L'Amélioration de la qualité de vie des personnes âgées dépendantes*, Paris: Assemblée Nationale.

Assemblée Nationale (2003) *Rapport sur le projet de loi de financement de la Sécurité Sociale*, vol. 3, Paris: Assemblée Nationale.

Assous, L. and Ralle, P. (2000) 'La Prise en charge de la dépendance des personnes âgées: une mise en perspective internationale', DREES, Collection 'Etudes' 1.

Aubry, M. (1999) 'Discours de Martine Aubry, Ministre de l'emploi et de la solidarité, au Comité National Gérontologique', 29 April.

Aust, A. and Bönker, F. (2004) 'New Social Risks in a Conservative Welfare State: The Case of Germany', in P. Taylor-Gooby (ed.) *New Risks, New Welfare*, Oxford: Oxford University Press.

Bain, G.S. and Elsheikh, F. (1976) *Union Growth and the Business Cycle*, Oxford: Basil Blackwell.

Baldwin, P. (1990) *The Politics of Social Solidarity: Class Bases of the European Welfare State, 1875–1975*, Cambridge: Cambridge University Press.

Ballestri, Y. and Bonoli, G. (2003) 'L'Etat social suisse face aux nouveaux risques sociaux: genèse et déterminants de l'adoption du programme d'impulsion pour les structures de garde pour enfants en bas âge', *Swiss Political Science Review*, 9 (3): 35–58.

Barbier, J.-C. and Ludwig-Mayerhofer, W. (2004) 'Introduction: The Many Worlds of Activation', *European Societies*, 6 (4): 423–36.

Baumgarten, B. 'The German Unions and the Unions' Organisations of the Unemployed', paper presented at the ECPR Conference, Marburg, September 2003.

Beattie, R. and McGillivray, R. (1995) 'On Averting the Old Age Crisis', *International Social Security Review*, 48 (3/4): 13–22.

Bélanger, A. and Ouellet, G. (2001) 'A Comparative Study of Recent Trends in Canadian and American Fertility', Ottawa: Statistics Canada.

Benner, M. and Vad, T. (2000) 'Sweden and Denmark: Defending the Welfare State', in F.W. Scharpf and V. Schmid (eds) *Welfare and Work in the Open Economy*, Oxford: Oxford University Press.

Bergamaschi, M. (2000) 'The Gender Perspective in the Policies of European Trade Unions', in M. Rossilli (ed.) *Gender Policies in the European Union*, New York: Peter Lang.

Bergman, S. (2004) 'Collective Organizing and Claim Making on Child Care in Norden: Blurring the Boundaries between the Inside and the Outside', *Social Politics*, 11 (2): 217–46.

Berman, E., Bound, J. and Machin, S. (1998) 'Implications of Skill-Biased Technological Change: International Evidence', *Quarterly Journal of Economics*, 113: 1245–79.

Bertone, C. (2003) 'Claims for Child Care as Struggles over Need: Comparing Italian and Danish Women's Organizations', *Social Politics*, 10 (2): 229–55.

Beutler, B., Bieber, R., Pipkorn, J. and Streil, J. (1987) *Die Europäische Gemeinschaft: Rechtsordnung und Politik*, Baden-Baden: Nomos.

Beveridge, W. (1942) *Social Insurance and Allied Services*, Cmnd 6404, London: HMSO.

Blekesaune, M. and Quadagno, J. (2003) 'Public Attitudes toward Welfare State Policies: A Comparative Analysis of 24 Nations', *European Sociological Review*, 19 (5): 415–27.

Bleses, P. (2003) 'Der Umbau geht weiter: Lohnarbeit und Familie in der rot–grünen Sozialpolitik', *Zeitschrift für Sozialreform*, 49 (4): 557–82.

BMA (Bundesministerium für Arbeit/Federal Ministry for Work) (2000) *Statistisches Taschenbuch*.

BMGS (Bundesministerium für Gesundheit und Soziale Sicherung/Federal Ministry of Health and Social Security Schemes) (2003) 'Soziale Pflegeversicherung: Leistungsempfänger nach Altersgruppen und Pflegestufen am 31.12.2002'. Online. Available http://www.bmgs.bund.de.

—— (2003) 'Zahlen und Fakten zur Pflegeversicherung'. Online. Available http://www.bmgs.bund.de.

Bönker, F., Aust, A. and Wollmann, H. (2003) 'Labour Market Policy, Social Assistance and Women's Employment', *WRAMSOC Working Paper*. Online. Available http://www.kent.ac.uk/wramsoc/workingpapers/index.htm.

Bonoli, G. (2003a) 'The Politics of New Social Policies: Providing Coverage against New Social Risks in Mature Welfare States', paper presented at the workshop 'The Politics of New Social Risks', Lugano, September.

—— (2003b) 'Social Policy through Labour Markets: Understanding National Differences in the Provision of Economic Security to Wage Earners', *Comparative Political Studies*, 36: 983–1006.

—— (2004) 'Modernising Post-war Welfare States: Explaining Diversity in Patterns of Adaptation to New Social Risks', paper presented at Wramsoc Berlin Conference, Berlin, April.

—— (2005) 'The Politics of the New Social Policies: Providing Coverage against New Social Risks in Mature Welfare States', *Policy and Politics*, 33: 431–49.

Bonoli, G. and Armingeon, K. (2003) 'Introductory Paper for New Social Risks Workshop', paper presented at the workshop 'New Social Risk', Lugano, October.

Bonoli, G. and Powell, M. (eds) (2003) *Social Democratic Policies in Contemporary Europe*, London: Routledge.

Bonoli, G., George, V. and Taylor-Gooby, P. (eds) (2000) *European Welfare Futures: Toward a Theory of Retrenchment*, Cambridge: Polity Press.

Börzel, Tanja A. (2005) 'Europeanization: How the European Union Interacts with Its Member States', in S. Bulmer and C. Lequesne (eds) *The Member States of the European Union*, Oxford: Oxford University Press.

Boulard, J.C. (1991) *Vivre ensemble*, Rapport d'information déposé par la Commission des Affaires culturelles, familiales et sociales sur les personnes âgées dépendantes, Paris: Assemblée Nationale 2135, juin.

Bourdieu, P. (1977) *Outline of a Theory of Practice*, Cambridge: Cambridge University Press.

Bowlby, J. (1951) *Maternal Care and Mental Health*, Geneva: World Health Organization; London: HMSO; New York: Columbia University Press.

—— (1953) 'Some Pathological Processes Set in Train by Early Mother–Child Separation', *Journal of Mental Science*, 99: 265–72.

Bradley, D., Huber, E., Moller, S., Nielsen, F. and Stephens, J. (2003) 'Distribution and Redistribution in Post-industrial Democracies', *World Politics*, 55 (2): 193–228.

Braun, T. and Stourm, M. (1988) *Les Personnes âgées dépendantes*, Rapport d'étude de la commission nationale sur les personnes âgées dépendantes, Paris: La Documentation française.

Breuil-Genier, P. (1999) 'Aides aux personnes âgées dépendantes: une très grande hétérogénéité des pratiques', *MIRE, Comparer les systèmes de protection sociale en Europe du Nord et en France*, 4 (1), Paris: MIRE-DREES.

Briggs, A. (2000/1969) 'The Welfare State in Historical Perspective', in C. Pierson and F.G. Castles (eds) *The Welfare State Reader*, Oxford: Polity Press.

Brin, H. (1995) *Projet de création d'une 'prestation autonomie' destinée aux person-nes âgées dépendantes*, Avis présenté au nom du Conseil économique et social, séances des 12 et 13 septembre, *Journal Officiel, Avis et Rapports du CES*, 4, 15 September.

Brugiavini, A., Ebbinghaus, B., Freeman, R., Garibaldi, P., Holmund, B., Schludi, M. and Verdier, T. (2001) 'Part II: What Do Unions Do to the Welfare States?' in T. Boeri, A. Brugiavini and L. Calmfors (eds) *The Role of Unions in the Twenty-first Century: A Report to the Fondazione Rodolfo Debenedetti*, Oxford: Oxford University Press.

Buchholz-Will, W. (1990) 'Kinder erziehen bleibt Privatsache: Elternurlaub in der EG', in S. Schunter-Kleemann (ed.) *EG-Binnenmarkt: EuroPatriarchat oder Aufbruch der Frauen*, Bremen: WE FF Verlag.

Budge, I., Klingemann, H.D., Volkens, A., Bara, J. and Tanenbaum, E. (2001) *Mapping Policy Preferences: Estimates for Parties, Electors, and Governments 1945–1998*, Oxford: Oxford University Press.

Buhr, P. (2003) 'Wege aus der Armut durch Wege in eine neue Armutspolitik?', in A. Gohr and M. Seeleib-Kaiser (eds) *Sozial- und Wirtschaftspolitik unter Rot–Grün*, Wiesbaden: Westdeutscher.

Bundesregierung (2004) 'Jahreswirtschaftsbericht 2004', Berlin: Bundesminis-terium der Finanzen.

Bundesverfassungsgericht (ed.) (1975) Urteil vom 12. März 1975 (1 BvL 15, 19/71 und 32/73; 1 BvR 297, 315/71, 407/72 und 37/73), 'Erschwerende Voraussetzung der Witwerrente gegenüber der Witwenren in der Rentenversicherung der Angestellten und Arbeiter', *Entscheidungen des Bundesverfassungsgerichtes*, 39, Tübingen: J.C.B. Mohr.

—— (ed.) (1993) Urteil vom 7. Juli 1992 (1 BvL 51/86, 50/87 und 1 BvR 873/90, 761/91), 'Berücksichtigung von Kindererziehungszeiten in der gesetzlichen Rentenversicherung der Arbeiter und Angestellten ("Trümmerfrauen")', *Entscheidungen des Bundesverfassungsgerichtes*, 87, Tübingen: J.C.B. Mohr.

—— (ed.) (1997) Urteil vom 12. März 1996 (1 BvR 609, 692/90) Zur Auswirkung des Gleichheitssatzes (Art. 3, Abs. 1 GG) auf die Bewertung von Kinder-erziehungszeiten beim Zusammentreffen mit breitragsbelegten Zeiten in der gesetzlichen Rentenversicherung, *Entscheidungen des Bundesverfassungs-gerichtes*, 94, Tübingen: J.C.B. Mohr.

Burtless, G., Rainwater, L. and Smeeding, T.M. (2001) 'United States Poverty in a Cross-national Context', in S.H. Danziger and R.H. Havemann (eds) *Under-standing Poverty*, New York: Russell Sage Foundation.

Campbell, A. and Morgan, K. (2003) 'Federalism, Risk-Pooling, and Social Policy: The Politics of Long-Term Care in Germany and the United States', paper pre-sented at the RC19 Conference, Toronto, August.

Castles, F.G. (1978) *The Social Democratic Image of Society: A Study of the Achievements and Origins of Scandinavian Social Democracy in Comparative Perspective*, London: Routledge & Kegan Paul.

—— (ed.) (1982) *The Impact of Parties. Politics and Policies in Democratic Capital-ist States*, London and Beverly Hills, CA: Sage.

—— (1985) *The Working Class and Welfare: Reflections on the Political Develop-ment of the Welfare State in Australia and New Zealand, 1890–1980*, Sydney: Allen & Unwin.

—— (2002) 'The World Turned Upside Down: Below Replacement Fertility,

Changing Preferences and Family-Friendly Public Policy in 21 OECD Countries', *Journal of European Social Policy*, 13 (3): 209–27.

—— (2004) *The Future of the Welfare State: Crisis Myths and Crisis Realities*, Oxford: Oxford University Press.

Charles, N. (2000) *Feminism, the State and Social Policy*, London: Macmillan.

Chiarini, B. (1999) 'The Composition of Union Membership: The Role of Pensioners in Italy', *British Journal of Industrial Relations*, 37 (4): 577–600.

Clark, T. (2002) *Rewarding Saving and Alleviating Poverty*, IFS Briefing Note 22.

Clark, T. and Emmerson, C. (2002) 'The Tax and Benefit System and the Incentive to Invest in a Stake-Holder Pension', *IFS Bulletin* 28.

Clark, T.N. and Seymour, M.L. (2001) *The Breakdown of Class Politics*, Baltimore and London: Johns Hopkins University Press.

Clasen, J. (1999) 'Beyond Social Security: The Economic Value of Giving Money to Unemployed People', *European Journal of Social Security*, 1 (2): 151–80.

—— (2002) 'Modern Social Democracy and European Welfare State Reform', *Social Policy and Society*, 1: 67–76.

—— (2005) *Reforming European Welfare States: Germany and the United Kingdom Compared*, Oxford: Oxford University Press.

Clasen, J. and Clegg, D. (2003) 'Unemployment Protection and Labour Market Reform in France and Great Britain in the 1990s: Solidarity Versus Activation?', *Journal of Social Policy*, 32 (2): 361–81.

Clasen, J., Duncan, G., Eardley, T., Evans, M., Ughetto, P., van Oorschot, W. and Wright, S. (2001) 'Towards "Single Gateways"? A Cross-national Review of the Changing Roles of Employment Offices in Seven Countries', *Zeitschrift für ausländisches und internationales Sozialrecht*, 15 (1): 43–63.

Clauwaert, S. and Harger, S. (2000) *Analysis of the Implementation of the Parental Leave Directive in the EU Member States*, Brussels: European Trade Union Institute.

Clayton, R. and Pontusson, J. (1998) 'Welfare State Retrenchment Revisited: Entitlement Cuts, Public Sector Restructuring, and Inegalitarian Trends in Advanced Capitalist Societies', *World Politics*, 51 (1): 67–98.

Clegg, D. and Clasen, J. (2004) 'State "Strength", Social Governance and the Reform of Labour Market Policy in France and Germany', paper presented at ESPAnet conference, Oxford, September 2004.

CNRPA *et al.* (1998) *Le Livre noir de la PSD*, Paris: La Documentation française.

—— (1999) *Livre blanc pour une prestation autonome*, Paris: La Documentation française.

Commission Européenne (1999) *L'Emploi en Europe 1998*, Luxembourg: OPOCE.

Commission on Social Justice (1994) *Social Justice: Strategies for National Renewal*, London: Vintage.

Cook, A.H., Lorwin, V.R. and Daniels, A.K. (1992) *The Most Difficult Revolution: Women and Trade Unions*, Ithaca, NY: Cornell University.

Crouch, C. (1999) 'Employment, Industrial Relations and Social Policy: New Life in an Old Connection', *Social Policy and Administration*, 33 (4): 437–57.

Curtin, J. (1999) *Women and Trade Unions: A Comparative Perspective*, Aldershot, UK: Ashgate.

Cusack, T.R. (1991) 'The Changing Contours of Government', PIB Paper 91-304, Wissenschaftszentrum Berlin.

Cusack, T.R. and Rein, M. (1991) 'Social Policy and Service Employment', unpublished paper, Wissenschaftszentrum Berlin.

Daguerre, A. and Taylor-Gooby, P. (2003) 'Adaptation to Labour Market Change in France and the UK: Convergent or Parallel Tracks?', *Social Policy and Administration*, 37 (6): 625–38.

Dahl, K., Boesby, D. and Ploug, N. (2002) 'Welfare Systems and the Management of the Economic Risk of Unemployment: Denmark', SFI Research Paper 8.

Dahrendorf, R. (1959) *Class and Class Conflict in Industrial Society*, Stanford, CA: Stanford University Press.

Dalton, R.J. and Wattenberg, M.P. (eds) (2000) *Parties without Parties: Political Change in Advanced Industrial Democracies*, Oxford: Oxford University Press.

Daly, M. (2000a) *The Gender Division of Welfare: The Impact of the British and German Welfare States*, Cambridge: Cambridge University Press.

—— (2000b) 'A Fine Balance: Women's Labor Market Participation in International Comparison', in F.W. Scharpf and V.A. Schmidt (eds) *Welfare and Work in the Open Economy*, vol. 2, Oxford: Oxford University Press.

Daly, M. and Rake, K. (2003) *Gender and the Welfare State: Care Work and Welfare in Europe and the USA*, Oxford: Polity Press.

Daniel, C. (2001) 'Les Politiques sociales françaises face au chômage', in C. Daniel and B. Palier (eds) *La Protection sociale en Europe: le temps des reformes*, Paris: La Documentation française.

Daniel, C. and Bassot, J. (1999) 'L'Indemnisation du chômage depuis 1979: un analyse par cas-types', IRES Working Paper, March, Noisy le Grand: IRES.

Daune-Richard, A.-M. and Mahon, R. (2001) 'Sweden: Model in Crisis', in J. Jenson and M. Sineau (eds) *Who Cares?*, Toronto: University of Toronto Press.

DEE (Department of Education and Employment) (1998) *Meeting the Childcare Challenge*, Green Paper, London: HMSO.

Delsen, L. (1998) 'When Do Men Work Part-Time?', in J. O'Reilly and C. Fagan (eds) *Part-Time Prospects: An International Comparison of Part-Time Work in Europe, North America and the Pacific Rim*, London: Routledge.

Detzel, P. and Rubery, J. (2002) 'Employment Systems and Transitional Labour Markets: A Comparison of Youth Labour Markets in Germany, France and the UK', in G. Schmid and B. Gazier (eds) *The Dynamics of Full Employment: Social Integration through Transitional Labour Markets*, Cheltenham, UK: Edward Elgar.

Dølvik, J.E. (ed.) (2001a) *At Your Service? Comparative Perspectives on Employment and Labour Relations in the European Private Sector Services*, Brussels: PIE–Peter Lang.

—— (2001b) 'The Impact of Post-industrialisation on Employment and Labour Relations: A Comparative Review', in J.E. Dølvik (ed.) *At Your Service? Comparative Perspectives on Employment and Labour Relations in the European Private Sector Services*, Brussels: PIE–Peter Lang.

DREES (1999a) 'La Prestation spécifique dépendance: premier bilan au 31 décembre 1998', *Etudes et Résultats*, 13.

—— (1999b) 'Les Personnes âgées dans les années 90 perspectives démographiques, santé et modes d'accueil', *Etudes et Résultats*, 40.

—— (2001a) 'La Prestation spécifique dépendance au 30 juin 2001', *Etudes et Résultats*, 143.

—— (2001) 'Les Aides et les aidants des personnes âgées', *Etudes et Résultats*, 142.

—— (2003) 'L'Allocation personnalisée d'autonomie au 31 décembre 2002', *Etudes et Résultats*, 226.

Driver, S. and Martell, L. (2002) 'New Labour, Work and the Family', *Social Policy and Administration*, 36 (1): 46–61.

DSS (Department of Social Security) (1998) *A New Contract for Welfare*, Cm 3805, London: HMSO.

DWP (Department for Work and Pensions) (2002) *Simplicity, Security and Choice*, Cmnd 5677, London: HMSO.

—— (2003) *Benefit Expenditure Tables*, table C1, DWP Statistics and Research, London: DWP.

Ebbinghaus, B. (2000) 'Any Way Out of "Exit from Work"? Reversing the Entrenched Pathways of Early Retirement', in F.W. Scharpf and V.A. Schmidt (eds) *Welfare and Work in the Open Economy: Country and Special Studies*, vol. 2, Oxford: Oxford University Press.

—— (2001) 'The Political Economy of Early Retirement in Europe, Japan and the USA', in B. Ebbinghaus and P. Manow (eds) *Comparing Welfare Capitalism: Social Policy and Political Economy in Europe, Japan and the USA*, London: Routledge.

—— (2002a) *Varieties of Social Governance: Comparing the Social Partners' Involvement in Pension and Employment Policies*, Cologne: Max Planck Institute for the Study of Societies.

—— (2002b) 'Trade Unions' Changing Role: Membership Erosion, Organisational Reform, and Social Partnership in Europe', *Industrial Relations Journal*, 33 (5): 465–83.

—— (2004) 'The Changing Union and Bargaining Trends', *Industrial Relations Journal*, 35 (6): 574–87.

—— (2006) *Reforming Early Retirement in Europe, Japan and the USA*, Oxford: Oxford University Press.

Ebbinghaus, B. and Hassel, A. (2000) 'Striking Deals: Concertation in the Reform of Continental European Welfare States', *Journal of European Public Policy*, 7 (1): 44–62.

Ebbinghaus, B. and Visser, J. (1999) 'When Institutions Matter: Union Growth and Decline in Western Europe, 1950–1995', *European Sociological Review*, 15 (2): 1–24.

—— (2000) *Trade Unions in Western Europe since 1945* (Handbook and CD-ROM), London: Palgrave/Macmillan.

Ebert, T. (2001) 'Rentenreform 2001: Sozialverträgliche Modernisierung?', *Sozialer Fortschritt*, 8: 182–7.

Enquête suisse sur la population active (ESPA) (1995) Office fédéral de la Statistique.

—— (2000) Office fédéral de la Statistique.

—— (2001) Office fédéral de la Statistique.

Erikson, R. and Goldthorpe, J.H. (1992) *The Constant Flux: A Study of Class Mobility in Industrial Societies*, Oxford: Oxford University Press.

Erikson, R., Goldthorpe, J.H. and Portocarero, L. (1979) 'Intergenerational Class Mobility in Three Western European Societies: England, France and Sweden', *British Journal of Sociology*, 30 (4): 425–41.

Erikson, R., Mackuen, M.B. and Stimson, J.A. (1998) 'What Moves Macropartisanship? A Response to Green, Palmquist, and Schickler', *American Political Science Review*, 92 (4): 901–12.

—— (2002) *The Macro Polity*, Cambridge: Cambridge University Press.

Esping-Andersen, G. (1985) *Politics against Markets: The Social Democratic Road to Power*, Princeton, NJ: Princeton University Press.

—— (1990) *The Three Worlds of Welfare Capitalism*, Princeton, NJ: Princeton University Press.

—— (1992) 'The Emerging Realignment between Labour Movements and Welfare States', in M. Regini (ed.) *The Future of Labour Movements*, London: Sage.

—— (1993) 'Mobility Regimes and Class Formation', in G. Esping-Andersen (ed.) *Changing Classes: Stratification and Mobility in Post-Industrial Societies*, London: Sage.

—— (1996) *Welfare States in Transition: National Adaptations in Global Economies*, London: Sage.

—— (1999) *Social Foundations of Postindustrial Economies*, Oxford: Oxford University Press.

—— (2000) 'Who Is Harmed by Labour Market Regulations? Quantitative Evidence', in G. Esping-Andersen and M. Regini (eds) *Why Deregulate Labour Markets?*, Oxford: Oxford University Press.

—— (2002) *Why We Need a New Welfare State*, Oxford: Oxford University Press.

Esping-Andersen, G. and Korpi, W. (1984) 'Social Policy as Class Politics in Post-War Capitalism: Scandinavia, Austria and Germany', in J.H. Goldthorpe (ed.) *Order and Conflict in Contemporary Capitalism*, Oxford: Clarendon Press.

Esping-Andersen, G., Gallie, D., Hemerijck, A. and Myles, J. (2002) *Why We Need a New Welfare State*, New York: Oxford University Press.

EU (2003) *Adequate and Sustainable Pensions*, Brussels: DGESA.

—— (1998) *A Review of Services for Young Children in the European Union, 1990–1995*, Brussels: European Commission on Network for Childcare.

European Commission (ed.) (2000) *Report on Social Protection in Europe 1999*. COM 163 final, Brussels.

Eurostat (1999) *Demographic Statistics*. Luxembourg: Eurostat.

—— (2004) 'EU population: People by age classes'. Online. Available http://europa.eu.int/comm/eurostat/.

Faggio, G. and Nickel, S. (2003) 'The Rise of Inactivity among Adult Men', in R. Dickens, P. Gregg and J. Wadsworth (eds) *The Labour Market under New Labour*, Basingstoke, UK: Palgrave.

Fajertag, G. and Pochet, P. (2000) 'A New Era for Social Pacts in Europe', in G. Fajertag and P. Pochet (eds) *Social Pacts in Europe: New Dynamics*, Brussels: ETUI.

Falkner, G. (1998) *EU Social Policy in the 1990s: Towards a Corporatist Policy Community*, London: Routledge.

—— (2000) 'The Council or the Social Partners? EC Social Policy between Diplomacy and Collective Bargaining', *Journal of European Public Policy*, 7/5: 705–24.

Falkner, G. and Leiber, S. (2004) 'Europeanisation of Social Partnership in Smaller European Democracies?', *European Journal of Industrial Relations*, 10 (3): 239–60.

Falkner, G., Treib, O., Hartlapp, M. and Leiber, S. (2005) *Complying with Europe:*

EU Harmonisation and Soft Law in the Member States, Cambridge: Cambridge University Press.

Fargion, V. (2000) 'Timing and the Development of Social Care Services in Europe', *West European Politics*, 23: 59–88.

Fehr, H. and Jess, H. (2001) 'Gewinner und Verlierer der aktuellen Rentenreform', *Die Angestelltenversicherung*, 5/6: 1–12.

Ferrera, M. (1996) 'The "Southern Model" of Welfare in Social Europe', *Journal of European Social Policy*, 6: 17–37.

—— (1998) 'The Four "Social Europes": Between Universalism and Selectivity', in M. Rhodes and Y. Mény (eds) *The Future of European Welfare: A New Social Contract?*, London: Macmillan.

Ferrera, M., Hemerijck, A. and Rhodes, M. (2000) 'Recasting European Welfare States for the 21st Century', *European Review*, 8 (3): 151–70.

Finn, D. (1997) 'The Stricter Benefit Regime and the New Deal for the Unemployed', in E. Brunsdon, H. Dean and R. Woods (eds) *Social Policy Review 10*, London: Social Policy Association.

Flora, P. (ed.) (1986) *Growth to Limits: The Western European Welfare States since World War I*, Berlin: Walter de Gruyter.

—— (1993) 'Europa als Sozialstaat?', in B. Schäfers (ed.) *Lebensverhältnisse und soziale Konflikte im neuen Europa*, Frankfurt am Main and New York: Campus.

Franklin, M.N., Lyons, P. and Marsh, M. (2004) 'Generational Basis of Turnout Decline in Established Democracies', *Acta Politica*, 2 (39): 115–50.

Freysinnet, J. (2002) 'La Réforme de l'indemnisation du chômage en France (mars 2000–juillet 2001)', IRES Working Paper 02.02, Noisy le Grand: IRES.

Frinault, Thomas (2003) 'L'Hypothèse du 5ᵉ risque', in C. Martin (ed.) *La dépendance des personnes âgées: quelles politiques en Europe?*, Rennes: PUR.

GAD (2002) *Occupational Pension Schemes 2000*, London: HMSO.

Gallagher, M., Laver, M. and Mair, P. (2005) *Representative Government in Western Europe*, 4th edn, New York: McGraw-Hill.

Gallie, D. (2002) 'The Quality of Working Life in Welfare Strategy', in G. Esping-Andersen, D. Gallie, A. Hemerijck and J. Myles (eds) *Why We Need a New Welfare State*, New York: Oxford University Press.

Gallie, D. and Paugam, S. (2000a) 'The Experience of Unemployment in Europe: The Debate', in D. Gallie and S. Paugam (eds) *Welfare Regimes and the Experience of Unemployment in Europe*, Oxford: Oxford University Press.

—— (eds) (2000b) *Welfare Regimes and the Experience of Unemployment in Europe*, Oxford: Oxford University Press.

—— (2002) *Social Precarity and Social Integration*, Brussels: Directorate General Press and Communication, European Commission.

Ganzeboom, H. and Treiman, D.J. (1994) 'International Stratification and Mobility. File: Conversion Tools'. Online. Available http://www.fss.uu.nl/soc/hg/ismf.

—— (1996) 'International Comparable Measures of Occupational Status for the 1988 International Standard Classification of Occupations', *Social Science Research*, 25 (3): 201–39.

Garcia, A. (2000) 'The "Second Sex" of European Trade Unionism', in E. Gabaglio and R. Hoffmann (eds) *European Trade Union Yearbook 1999*, Brussels: European Trade Union Institute.

Geissler, H. (1976) *Die neue soziale Frage*, Freiburg in Breisgau: Herder.

Ginsburg, A. (2001) 'Sweden: The Social Democratic Case', in A. Cochrane, J. Clarke and S. Gewirtz (eds) *Comparing Welfare States*, London: Sage.

Golden, M.A., Wallerstein, M. and Lange, P. (1999) 'Post-war Trade-Union Organization and Industrial Relations in Twelve Countries', in H. Kitschelt, P. Lange, G. Marks and J. Stephens (eds) *Continuity and Change in Contemporary Capitalism*, New York: Cambridge University Press.

Goldthorpe, J.H. (1982) 'On the Service Class: Its Formation and Future', in A. Giddens and G. Mackenzie (eds) *Social Class and the Division of Labour*, Cambridge: Cambridge University Press.

—— (1983) 'Woman and Class Analysis: In Defence of the Conventional View', *Sociology*, 17 (4): 465–88.

Goode Committee (1994) *Pensions Law Reform*, Cmnd 2342-1, London: HMSO.

Goodin, R.E., Headey, B., Muffels, R. and Dirven, H.-J. (1999) *The Real Worlds of Welfare Capitalism*, New York: Cambridge University Press.

Goodman, A. and McGranahan, L. (2003) 'Access to Education', in R. Dickens, P. Gregg and J. Wadsworth (eds) *The Labour Market under New Labour*, Basingstoke, UK: Palgrave Macmillan.

Gorges, M.J. (1996) *Euro-corporatism? Interest Intermediation in the European Community*, Lanham, MD: University Press of America.

Gornick, J. (1999) 'Gender Equality in the Labour Market', in D. Sainsbury (ed.) *Gender and Welfare State Regimes*, Oxford: Oxford University Press.

Gornick, J., Meyers, M.K. and Ross, K.E. (1997) 'Supporting the Employment of Mothers: Policy Variation across Fourteen Welfare States', *Journal of European Social Policy*, 7: 45–70.

Götting, U., Haug, K. and Hinrichs, K. (1994) 'The Long Road to Long-Term Care Insurance in Germany', *Journal of Public Policy*, 14 (3): 285–309.

Gough, I. (1996) 'Social Welfare and Competitive', *New Political Economy*, 1 (2): 209–32.

Goul Andersen, J. (2002) 'Work and Citizenship: Unemployment Policies in Denmark, 1980–2000', in J. Goul Andersen and P. Jensen (eds) *Changing Labour Markets, Welfare Policies and Citizenship*, Bristol: Policy Press.

Green-Pedersen, C. (2002) *The Politics of Justification: Party Competition and Welfare State Retrenchment in Denmark and the Netherlands from 1982 to 1998*, Amsterdam: Amsterdam University Press.

Green-Pedersen, C., Hemerijck, A. and van Keesbergen, K. (2001) 'Neoliberalism, Third Way or What?', *Journal of European Public Policy*, 8 (2): 307–25.

Grimshaw, D. and Rubery, J. (1997) 'Workforce Heterogeneity and Unemployment Benefits: The Need for Policy Reassessment in the European Union', *Journal of European Social Policy*, 7 (4): 291–318.

Habermas, J. (1982) *Theorie des kommunikativen Handelns*, Frankfurt am Main: Suhrkamp.

Hacker, J. (2004) 'Privatizing Risk without Privatizing the Welfare State: The Hidden Politics of Social Policy Retrenchment in the United States', *American Political Science Review*, 98 (2): 243–60.

Hancké, B. (1993) 'Trade Union Membership in Europe, 1960–1990: Rediscovering Local Unions', *British Journal of Industrial Relations*, 31 (4): 593–613.

Hantrais, L. (1999) 'Socio-demographic Change, Policy Impacts and Outcomes in Social Europe', *Journal of European Social Policy*, 9 (4): 291–309.

Hantrais, L. and Letablier, M.T. (1996) *Families and Family Policies in Europe*, London: Longman.

Hartenberger, U. (2001) *Europäischer sozialer Dialog nach Maastricht: EU-Sozialpartnerverhandlungen auf dem Prüfstand*, Baden-Baden: Nomos.

Hartlapp, M. (2005) *Die Kontrolle der nationalen Rechtsdurchsetzung durch die Europäische Kommission*, Politik, Verbände, Recht: Die Umsetzung europäischer Sozialpolitik, Bd. 3, Frankfurt am Main: Campus.

Heclo, H. (1974) *Modern Social Politics in Britain and Sweden: From Relief to Income Maintenance*, New Haven, CT: Yale University Press.

Heller, B. (2001) 'Die Neuregelungen des Altersvermögensgesetzes', *DangVers* 7 (10): 1–8. Online. Available http://www.bfaberlin.de/ger/ger_nachschlagewerke.6/ger_dangvers.61/ger_ausgaben2001.613/ger_613_index.html.

Hemerijck, A. (2002) 'The Self-Transformation of the European Social Model(s)', in G. Esping-Andersen, D. Gallie, A. Hemerijck and J. Myles (eds) *Why We Need a New Welfare State*, New York: Oxford University Press.

Hemerijck, A., Manow, P. and van Kersbergen, K. (2000) 'Welfare without Work? Divergent Experiences of Reform in Germany and the Netherlands', in S. Kuhnle (ed.) *Survival of the European Welfare State*, London: Routledge.

Héritier, A. (2001) 'Differential Europe: National Administrative Responses to Community Policy', in M. Green Cowles, J. Caporaso and T. Risse (eds) *Transforming Europe: Europeanization and Domestic Change*, Ithaca, NY: Cornell University Press.

Hicks, A. (1999) *Social Democracy and Welfare Capitalism: A Century of Income Security Policies*, Ithaca, NY: Cornell University Press.

Hinrichs, K. (1996) 'L'Assurance soins de longue durée: une innovation institutionnelle de la politique sociale allemande', in *MIRE, Comparer les systèmes de protection sociale en Europe*, 2, Paris.

—— (2001) 'Elephants on the Move: Patterns of Public Pension Reform in OECD Countries', in S. Leibfried (ed.) *Welfare State Futures*, Cambridge: Cambridge University Press.

Hirdman, V. (1998) 'State Policy and Gender Contracts: Sweden', in E. Drew, R. Emerek and E. Mahon (eds) *Women, Work and the Family*, London: Routledge.

Hirdman, Y. (1989) *Att lägga livet till rätta: studier i svensk folkhemspolitik*, Stockholm: Carlssons.

Hornung-Draus, R. (1995) 'Elternurlaub: Erste Sozialpartner-Verhandlung auf der Grundlage des Sozialabkommens', *EuroAS*, 3 (9): 147–8.

Hoskyns, C. (1996) *Integrating Gender: Women, Law and Politics in the European Union*, London: Verso.

Huber, E. and Stephens, J.D. (1998) 'Internationalization and the Social Democratic Model: Crisis and Future Prospects', *Comparative Political Studies*, 31: 353–97.

—— (2000) 'Partisan Governance, Women's Employment and the Social Democratic Service State', *American Sociological Review*, 65: 323–42.

—— (2001a) *Development and Crisis of the Welfare State: Parties and Policies in Global Markets*, Chicago: University of Chicago Press.

—— (2001b) 'Globalization, Competitiveness, and the Social Democratic Model', *Social Policy and Society*, 1 (1): 47–57.

Huber, E., Ragin, C. and Stephens, J.D. (1993) 'Social Democracy, Christian Democracy, Constitutional Structure, and the Welfare State', *American Journal of Sociology*, 99 (3): 711–49.

—— (1997) Comparative Welfare States Data Set, Northwestern University and University of North Carolina. Online. Available http://www.lisproject.org/publications/welfaredata/welfareaccess.htm.

Huber, E., Stephens, J.D., Bradley, D., Moller, S. and Nielsen, F. (2001) 'The Welfare State and Gender Equality', Luxembourg Income Study Working Paper 279.

Huber, E., Nielsen, F., Pribble, J. and Stephens, J.D. (2004) 'Social Spending and Inequality in Latin America and the Caribbean', paper presented at the Meetings of the Society for the Advancement of Socio-Economics, Washington, DC, July.

Hult, C. and Svallfors, S. (2002) 'Production Regimes and Work Orientations: A Comparison of Six Western Countries', *European Sociological Review*, 18 (3): 315–31.

Huteau, G. and Le Bont, E. (2001) *Sécurité sociale et politiques sociales*, Paris: Armand Colin.

IAB (1997) 'Erziehungsurlaub – und was dann? Die Situation von Frauen bei ihrer Rückkehr auf den Arbeitsmarkt – Ein Ost/West-Vergleich', *Kurzbericht*, no. 8, 5 September.

—— (2000) 'Arbeitsmarktperspektiven bis 2010. Auch im Osten werden Frauen im Strukturwandel gewinnen', *Kurzbericht*, no. 11, 28 August.

—— (2001) 'Erwerbsbeteiligung von Frauen. Wie bringt man Beruf und Kinder unter einen Hut?', *Kurzbericht*, no. 7, 12 April.

IGAS (1993) *Rapport sur la dépendance des personnes âgées*.

ILO (1999) 'International Statistical Comparisons of Occupational and Social Structures: Problems, Possibilities and the Role of ISCO-88', ILO background paper. Online. Available http://www.ilo.org/public/english/stat/download/iscopres.pdf.

Immergut, E. (1992) *The Political Construction of Interests: National Health Insurance Politics in Switzerland, France and Sweden, 1930–1970*, New York: Cambridge University Press.

Inglehart, R. (1997) *Modernization and Postmodernization: Cultural, Economic, and Political Change in 43 Societies*, Princeton, NJ: Princeton University Press.

Inglehart, R. and Norris, P. (2000) 'The Developmental Theory of the Gender Gap: Women's and Men's Voting Behavior in Global Perspective', *International Political Science Review*, 21 (4): 441–63.

ISSP (1996) *International Social Survey Program: The Role of Government III*, Cologne: ZA 2900.

—— (1998) *International Social Survey Program: Religion*, Cologne: ZA 3190.

—— (1999) *International Social Survey Program: Role of Government III, 1996*, ICPSR computer file, Cologne, Germany, and Ann Arbor, MI: Zentralarchiv für Empirische Sozialforschung and Inter-university Consortium for Political and Social Research.

Iversen, T. (2001) 'The Dynamics of Welfare State Expansion: Trade Openness, De-industrialization, and Partisan Politics', in P. Pierson (ed.) *The New Politics of the Welfare State*, Oxford: Oxford University Press.

Iversen, T. and Cusack, T.R. (2000) 'The Causes of Welfare State Expansion: Deindustrialization or Globalization?', *World Politics*, 52: 313–49.

Iversen, T. and Soskice, D. (2001) 'An Asset Theory of Social Policy Preferences', *American Political Science Review*, 95: 875–93.

Iversen, T. and Wren, A. (1998) 'Equality, Employment and Budgetary Restraint: The Trilemma of the Service Economy', *World Politics*, 50: 507–46.

James, E. (1996) 'Social Security around the World', in P.A. Diamond (ed.) *Social Security: What Role for the Future?*, Washington, DC: Brookings Institution Press.

Jenkins-Smith, H. and Sabatier, P.A. (1994) 'Evaluating the Advocacy Coalition Framework', *Journal of Public Policy*, 14 (2): 175–203.

—— (1999) 'The Advocacy Coalition Framework: An Assessment', in P.A. Sabatier (ed.) *Theories of the Policy Process*, Boulder, CO: Westview Press.

Jenson, J. (2002) 'From Ford to Lego: Redesigning Welfare Regimes', paper presented at the Annual Meeting of the American Political Science Association, Boston, August/September 2002.

Jenson, J. and Sineau, M. (1995) 'Family Policy and Women's Citizenship in Mitterrand's France', *Social Politics*, 2 (3): 244–69.

Jessop, B. (2002) *The Future of the Capitalist State*, Cambridge: Polity.

Journal Officiel (1997) *Loi n° 97–60 tendant, dans l'attente du vote de la loi instituant une prestation d'autonomie pour les personnes âgées dépendantes, à mieux répondre aux besoins des personnes âgées par l'institution d'une prestation spécifique dépendance*, JO, 25 January.

Kangas, E.O. (1997) 'Self-Interest and the Common Good: The Impact of Norms, Selfishness and Context in Social Policy Opinions', *Journal of Socio-Economics*, 26 (5): 475–94.

Kassai-Kocademir, V. (2002) 'Encore trop de disparités', *Informations Sociales*, special issue on *Modes de garde, modes d'accueil*, 103: 14–20.

Katzenstein, P.J. (1985) *Small States in World Markets: Industrial Policy in Europe*, Ithaca, NY: Cornell University Press.

Keller, B. (1991) 'The Role of the State as a Corporate Actor in Industrial Relations Systems', in R.J. Adams (ed.) *Comparative Industrial Relations. Contemporary Research and Theory*, London: HarperCollins.

Keller, B. and Sörries, B. (1997) 'The New Social Dialogue: Procedural Structuring, First Results and Perspectives', *Industrial Relations Journal, European Annual Review*: 77–98.

—— (1999) 'The New European Social Dialogue: Old Wine in New Bottles?', *Journal of European Social Policy*, 9 (2): 111–25.

Keman, H. (2002) 'Policy-Making Capacities of European Party Government', in K.R. Luther and F. Müller-Rommel (eds) *Political Parties in the New Europe*, Oxford: Oxford University Press.

—— (2003) 'Explaining Miracles: Third Ways and Work and Welfare', *West European Politics*, 26 (2): 115–35.

Keman, H. and Pennings, P. (1995) 'Managing Political and Societal Conflict in Democracies: Do Consensus and Corporatism Matter?', *British Journal of Political Science*, 25 (2): 271–81.

—— (2004) 'The Development of Christian and Social Democracy across Europe: Changing Positions and Political Consequences', in D.Th. Tsatsos, E.V. Venizelos and X.I. Contiades (eds) *Political Parties in the 21st Century*, Berlin: Wissenschafts Verlag; Brussels: Emile Bruylant.

Kenworthy, L. (1999) 'Do Social-Welfare Policies Reduce Poverty? A Cross-National Assessment', *Social Forces*, 77: 1119–39.

—— (2001) 'Wage-Setting Measures: A Survey and Assessment', *World Politics*, 54: 57–98.

Kessler, F. (1995) 'Quelles prestations pour les personnes âgées dépendantes? Panorama des propositions de réforme', *Droit Social*, 1: 85–94.

Kilkey, M. and Bradshaw, J. (1999) 'Lone Mothers, Economic Well-Being, and Policies', in D. Sainsbury (ed.) *Gender and Welfare State Regimes*, Oxford: Oxford University Press.

Kim, H. (2000) 'Anti-poverty Effectiveness of Taxes and Income Transfers in Welfare States', *International Social Security Review*, 53: 105–29.

King, D. and Wood, S. (1999) 'The Political Economy of Neoliberalism: Britain and the United States in the 1980s', in H. Kitschelt, P. Lange, G. Marks and J.D. Stephens (eds) *Continuity and Change in Contemporary Capitalism*, Cambridge: Cambridge University Press.

Kitschelt, H. (1999) 'European Social Democracy between Political Economy and Electoral Competition', in H. Kitschelt, P. Lange, G. Marks and J.D. Stephens (eds) *Continuity and Change in Contemporary Capitalism*, Cambridge: Cambridge University Press.

—— (2001) 'Partisan Competition and Welfare State Retrenchment: When Do Politicians Choose Unpopular Policies?', in P. Pierson (ed.) *The New Politics of the Welfare State*, Oxford: Oxford University Press.

Kitschelt, H. and Rehm, P. (2004) 'Political Groups Alignments in Party Systems', paper presented at the 14th Conference of the Council of European Studies, Chicago, March.

Kitschelt, H., Lange, P., Marks, G. and Stephens, J.D. (eds) (1999) *Continuity and Change in Contemporary Capitalism*, Cambridge: Cambridge University Press.

Kjellberg, A. (1998) 'Sweden: Restoring the Model?', in A. Ferner and R. Hyman (eds) *Changing Industrial Relations in Europe*, Oxford: Blackwell.

Klandermanns, B. and Visser, J. (eds) (1995) *De vakbeweging na de welvaartsstaat*, Assen: Van Gorcum.

Koch-Baumgarten, S. (1997) 'Die selbstverständliche Dominanz der Männer in der (Gewerkschafts-)Öffentlichkeit. Überlegungen zur geschlechtsspezifischen Selektion von Interessen im politischen System', in B. Kerchner and G. Wilde (eds) *Staat und Privatheit*, Berlin: Leske & Budrich.

Kohler-Koch, B. (1997) 'Organized Interests in European Integration: The Evolution of a New Type of Governance?', in H. Wallace and A. Young (eds) *Participation and Policy-Making in the European Union*, Oxford: Oxford University Press.

Korpi, W. (1983) *The Democratic Class Struggle*, London: Routledge & Kegan Paul.

Korpi, W. and Palme, J. (1998) 'The Paradox of Redistribution and Strategies of Equality: Welfare State Institutions, Inequality, and Poverty in Western Countries', *American Sociological Review*, 63: 661–87.

—— (2003) 'New Politics and Class Politics in the Context of Austerity and Globalization: Welfare State Regress in 18 Countries – 1975–1995', *American Political Science Review*, 97 (3): 425–46.

Kreckel, R. (1992) *Politische Soziologie der Sozialen Ungleichheit*, Frankfurt am Main: Campus.

Krouwel, A. (1999) 'The Catch-all Party in Western Europe 1945–1990: A Study in Arrested Development', PhD dissertation, Vrije Universiteit Amsterdam.

Kübler, D. (2001) 'Understanding Policy Change with the ACF', *Journal of European Public Policy*, 8 (4): 624–41.

Kuhnle, S. (ed.) (2000) *Survival of the European Welfare State*, London: Routledge.

Kvist, J. (2002) 'Activating Welfare States: How Social Policies Can Promote Employment', in J. Clasen (ed.) *What Future for Social Security? Debates and Reforms in National and Cross-National Perspectives*, Bristol: Policy Press.

—— (2003) 'Scandinavian Activation Strategies in the 1990s: Recasting Social Citizenship and the Scandinavian Welfare Model', in R. Sigg and C. Behrendt (eds) *Social Security in the Global Village*, New Brunswick, NJ: Transaction Books.

Lafore, R. (2003) 'La Prestation spécifique dépendance et la construction de l'action publique', in C. Martin (ed.) *La Dépendance des personnes âgées: quelles politiques en Europe?*, Rennes: PUR.

Lange, P. and Garrett, G. (1996) 'Internationalization, Institutions, and Political Change', in R. Keohane and V.H. Milner (eds) *Internationalization and Domestic Politics*, Cambridge: Cambridge University Press.

Langelüddeke, A. and Rabe, B. (2001) 'Rentenreform 2000: Verbesserung der eigenständigen Alterssicherung von Frauen?', *Sozialer Fortschritt*, 1: 6–12.

Langen, H.-G. (2001) 'Die neue Rentenanpassung ab 1.7.2001', *DAngVers*, 7 (10): 1–5. Available http://www.bfaerlin.de/ger/ger_nachschlagewerke.6/ger_dangvers.61/ger_ausgaben2001.613/ger_613_index.html.

Layard, R. (2000) 'Welfare-to-Work and the New Deal', *World Economics*, 1 (2): 29–39.

Leiber, S. (2005) *Europäische Sozialpolitik und nationale Sozialpartnerschaft. Politik, Verbände, Recht: Die Umsetzung europäischer Sozialpolitik*, Bd. 2, Frankfurt am Main: Campus.

Leibfried, S. and Pierson, P. (eds) (1995) *European Social Policy: Between Fragmentation and Integration*, Washington, DC: Brookings Institution.

Levy, J. (1999) 'Vice into Virtue? Progressive Politics of Welfare Reform in Continental Europe', *Politics and Society*, 27: 587–8.

Lewis, J. (1992) 'Gender and the Development of Welfare Regimes', *Journal of European Social Policy*, 2 (3): 159–73.

—— (2001) 'The Decline of the Male Breadwinner Model: Implications for Work and Care', *Social Politics*, 8 (2): 153–9.

—— (2002) 'Gender and Welfare State Change', *European Societies*, 4: 331–57.

Lewis, J. and Ostner, I. (1995) 'Gender and the Evolution of European Social Policies', in S. Liebfried and P. Pierson (eds) *European Social Policies*, Washington, DC: Brookings Institution.

Lewis, J. and Surender, R. (eds) (2004) *Welfare State Change: Towards a Third Way?*, Oxford: Oxford University Press.

Lewis, P. (1989) 'The Unemployed and Trade Union Membership', *Industrial Relations Journal*, 20: 271–9.

Lijphart, A. and Crépaz, M.L. (1991) 'Corporatism and Consensus Democracy in Eighteen Countries: Conceptual and Empirical Linkages', *British Journal of Political Science*, 21: 235–56.

Lødemel, I. (2004) 'The Development of Workfare within Social Activation Policies', in D. Gallie (ed.) *Resisting Marginalization: Unemployment Experience and Social Policy in the European Union*, Oxford: Oxford University Press.

Long, M. (1997) 'La Prestation d'autonomie, une nécessité reportée', *Revue française des affaires sociales*, hors série: 247–61.

McFate, K., Smeeding, T. and Rainwater, L. (1995) 'Markets and States: Poverty Trends and Transfer System Effectiveness in the 1980s', in K. McFate, R. Lawson and W.H. Wilson (eds) *Poverty, Inequality, and the Future of Social Policy*, New York: Russell Sage Foundation.

McIntosh, S. (2004) 'Skills and Unemployment', in D. Gallie (ed.) *Resisting*

Marginalization: Unemployment Experience and Social Policy in the European Union, Oxford: Oxford University Press.

Mahon, R. (2001a) 'Theorizing Welfare Regimes: Toward a Dialogue?', *Social Politics*, 8 (1): 24–35.

—— (2001b) 'Welfare State Restructuring and Changing Gender Relations: The Politics of Family Policy in Sweden and Canada', in B. Fox (ed.) *Family Patterns and Gender Relations*, Oxford: Oxford University Press.

—— (2002) 'Child Care: Towards What Kind of "Social Europe"?', *Social Politics*, 9 (3): 343–9.

Maioni, A. (1998) *Explaining Differences in Welfare State Development: A Comparative Study of Health Insurance in Canada and the United States*, Princeton, NJ: Princeton University Press.

Mair, P. (2002) 'In the Aggregate: Mass Electoral Behaviour in Western Europe, 1950–2000', in H. Keman (ed.) *Comparative Democratic Politics: A Guide to Contemporary Theory and Research*, London: Sage.

Malderie, M. (1997) 'L'Union Européenne et le congé parental', *Revue du Travail*, January/February/March: 43–5.

Manow, P. (1997) 'Social Insurance and the German Political Economy', Discussion Paper 97/2, Cologne: Max-Planck-Institut für Gesellschaftsforschung.

—— (2002) 'Consociational Roots of German Corporatism: The Bismarckian Welfare State and the German Political Economy', *Acta Politica*, 37 (1/2): 195–212.

March, J. and Olsen, J. (1989) *Rediscovering Institutions: The Organizational Basis of Politics*, New York: Free Press.

Marsh, D. and Rhodes, R.A.W. (1992) 'Policy Communities and Issue Networks: Beyond Typology', in D. Marsh and R.A.W. Rhodes (eds) *Policy Networks in British Government*, Oxford: Clarendon Press.

—— (1998) 'The Development of the Policy Network Approach', in D. Marsh and R.A.W. Rhodes (eds) *Comparing Policy Network*, Buckingham, UK: Open University Press.

Marshall, T.H. (1950) *Citizenship and Social Class: The Marshall Lectures*, Cambridge: Cambridge University Press.

Martin, C. (ed.) (2003) *La Dépendance des personnes âgées: quelles politiques en Europe?*, Rennes: PUR.

Martin, C., Math, C. and Renaudat, E. (1998) 'Caring for Very Young Children and Dependent Elderly People in France', in J. Lewis (ed.) *Lone Mothers in European Welfare Regimes*, London: Jessica Kingsley.

Mayda, A.M. and Rodrik, D. (2005) 'Why Are Some People (and Countries) More Protectionist than Others?', *European Economic Review*, 49: 1393–430.

Mazey, S. (1995) 'The Development of EU Equality Policies: Bureaucratic Expansion on Behalf of Women?', *Public Administration*, 73 (4): 591–609.

Meyer, T. (1998a) 'Retrenchment, Reproduction, Modernisation: Pension Politics and the Decline of the German Breadwinner Model', *European Journal of Social Policy*, 8 (3): 212–27.

—— (1998b) 'Die Erosion des starken deutschen Brotverdienermodells. Sozioökonomische und institutionelle Faktoren', *Zeitschrift für Sozialreform*, 11 (12): 818–38.

Meyers, M.K., Gornick, J. and Ross, K.E. (1999) 'Public Childcare, Parental Leave, and Employment', in D. Sainsbury (ed.) *Gender and Welfare State Regimes*, Oxford: Oxford University Press.

Ministerrat (1994) 'Vermerk des Vorsitzes für den Rat (Arbeit und Sozialfragen) (Tagung am 22. September 1994). Betr.: Geänderter Vorschlag für eine Richtlinie über Elternurlaub', Brussels: Rat der Europäischen Gemeinschaften.

—— (1996) 'Entwurf eines Protokolls über die 1914. Tagung des Rates (Arbeit und Sozialfragen) am 29. März 1996 in Brüssel', Brussels: Rat der Europäischen Union.

Moeller, R.G. (1993) *Protecting Motherhood: Women and the Family in the Politics of Postwar West Germany*, Berkeley: University of California Press.

Moller, S., Bradley, D., Huber, E., Nielsen, F. and Stephens, J.D. (2003) 'Determinants of Relative Poverty in Advanced Capitalist Democracies', *American Sociological Review*, 68 (1): 22–51.

Le Monde (2002a) 'Sécurité, emploi, retraites, familles: les propositions du président-candidat', 16 March.

Le Monde (2002b) 'Une allocation unique devrait remplacer en 2003 toutes les gardes d'enfant', 24 August.

Morgan, K. (2001) 'Conservative Parties and Working Women in France', paper presented at the Annual Meeting of APSA, San Francisco, August/September 2001.

Morgan, K. and Zippel, K. (2003) 'Paid to Care: The Origins of Effects of Care Leave Policies in Western Europe', *Social Politics*, Spring: 49–85.

Müller, W. and Strom, K. (eds) (2000) *Coalition Governments in Western Europe*, Oxford: Oxford University Press.

Myles, J. and Pierson, P. (2001) 'The Comparative Political Economy of Pension Reform', in P. Pierson (ed.) *The New Politics of the Welfare State*, Oxford: Oxford University Press.

NAPF (2002) *Survey of Occupational Pension Funds*, London: National Association of Pension Funds.

Naumann, I.K. (2001) 'The Politics of Child Care: Swedish Women's Mobilization for Public Child Care in the 1960s and 1970s', Stockholm: paper presented at the ECSR Summer School.

Nickell, S. (2003) *Labour Market Institutions and Unemployment in OECD Countries*, CESifo DICE Report 2, Munich: Centre for Economic Studies and Institute for Economic Research.

Norris, P. (2002) *Democratic Phoenix: Reinventing Political Activism*, Cambridge: Cambridge University Press.

Norris, P. and Lovenduski, J. (1989) 'Women Candidates for Parliament: Transforming the Agenda?', *British Journal of Political Science*, 19: 106–15.

—— (2003) 'Westminster Women: The Politics of Presence', *Political Studies*, 51: 84–102.

O'Connor, J.S., Orloff, A.S. and Shaver, S. (1999) *States, Markets, Families: Gender, Liberalism and Social Policy in Australia, Canada, Great Britain and the United States*, Cambridge: Cambridge University Press.

O'Donnell, R. and O'Reardon, C. (2002) 'Ireland: Recasting Social Partnership in a New Context', in P. Pochet (ed.) *Wage Policy in the Eurozone*, Brussels: PIE-Peter Lang.

OECD (1993) *Education at a Glance: OECD Indicators*, Paris: OECD.

—— (1995) 'Income Distribution in OECD Countries: Evidence from the Luxembourg Income Study', *Social Policy Studies*, 18.

—— (1996) *Employment Outlook*, Paris: OECD.

—— (1997) *Enhancing the Effectiveness of Active Labour Market Policies: A Streamlined Public Employment Service*, Report (OECD/GD(97)161) of the meeting of the Employment, Labour and Social Affairs Committee, 15 October 1997, Paris: OECD.

—— (1999) *Employment Outlook*, Paris: OECD.

—— (2001a) *Employment Outlook*, Paris: OECD.

—— (2001b) *Social Expenditure Database* (SOCX).

—— (2002a) *Employment Outlook*, Paris: OECD.

—— (2002b) *Labour Force Statistics*, Paris: OECD.

—— (2003a) *Employment Outlook*, Paris: OECD.

—— (2003b) *Expenditures of Public Education*. Online. Available http://www.oecd.org/linklist/0,2678,en_2825_495609_2735794_1_1_1_1,00.html#3178636.

—— (2003c) *Social Expenditure Database*. Online. Available http://www.oecd.org/dataoecd/43/14/2087083.xls; http://www.oecd.org/dataoecd/3/63/2084281.pdf.

—— (2004a) *Employment Outlook*, Paris: OECD.

—— (2004b) *Benefit and Wages, OECD Indicators*, Paris: OECD.

—— (n.d.) *Tables and Figures on Ageing*.

OECD/HRDC, Organisation for Economic Co-operation and Development/Human Resource Development Canada (2000) *Literacy in the Information Age: Final Report of the International Adult Literacy Survey,* Paris: OECD, HRDC.

Oesch, D. (2003) 'Analyzing Labour Market Stratification with a Modified Class Schema: A Study for Britain, Germany, Sweden and Switzerland', unpublished manuscript, University of Zurich.

—— (forthcoming) 'Coming to Grips with a Changing Class Structure: An Analysis of Employment Stratification in Britain, Germany, Sweden and Switzerland', *International Sociology*.

Opielka, M. (2002) 'Familie und Beruf Eine deutsche Geschichte', *Aus Politik und Zeitgeschichte*, B: 22–3.

O'Reilly, J. and Fagan, C. (eds) (1998) *Part-Time Prospects: An International Comparison of Part-Time Work in Europe, North America and the Pacific Rim*, London: Routledge.

Ostner, I. and Lewis, J. (1995) 'Gender and the Evolution of European Social Policies', in S. Leibfried and P. Pierson (eds) *European Social Policy: Between Fragmentation and Integration*, Washington, DC: Brookings Institution.

Palier, B. (2002a) *Gouverner la Sécurité sociale*, Paris: PUF.

—— (2002b) 'Tracing the Political Processes of Path-Breaking Changes in French Social Policy', paper presented at the APSA Meeting, Boston.

Papadakis, E. and Bean, C. (1993) 'Popular Support for the Welfare State', *Journal of Public Policy*, 13 (3): 227–54.

Paugam, S. (1993) *La Société française et ses pauvres: l'expérience du revenu minimum d'insertion*, Paris: Presses Universitaires de France.

Paull, G., Taylor, J. and Duncan, A. (2002) *Mothers' Employment and Childcare in Britain*, IFS Report, London: Institute for Fiscal Studies.

Pennings, P. and Keman, H. (2002) 'Towards a New Methodology of Estimating Party Policy Positions', *Quality and Quantity*, 38: 55–79.

—— (2003) 'The Dutch Parliamentary Elections in 2002 and 2003: The Rise and Decline of the Fortuyn Movement', *Acta Politica*, 38 (1): 51–68.

Pettersen, P.A. (1995) 'The Welfare State: The Security Dimension', in O. Borre and E. Scarbrough (eds) *The Scope of Government: Beliefs in Government*, vol. 3. Oxford: Oxford University Press.

Pickering, A. (2002) *A Simpler Way to Better Pensions*, Department for Work and Pensions, London: HMSO.

Pierson, P. (1993) 'When Effect Becomes Cause: Policy Feedback and Political Change', *World Politics*, 45 (4): 595–628.

—— (1994) *Dismantling the Welfare State? Reagan, Thatcher, and the Politics of Retrenchment*, Cambridge: Cambridge University Press.

—— (1996) 'The New Politics of the Welfare State', *World Politics*, 48 (2): 143–79.

—— (1998) 'Irresistible Forces, Immovable Objects: Post-industrial Welfare States Confront Permanent Austerity', *Journal of European Public Policy*, 5: 539–60.

—— (ed.) (2001a) *The New Politics of the Welfare State*, Oxford: Oxford University Press.

—— (2001b) 'Coping with Permanent Austerity: Welfare State Restructuring in Affluent Democracies', in P. Pierson (ed.) *The New Politics of the Welfare State*, Oxford: Oxford University Press.

—— (2001c) 'Post-industrial Pressures on the Mature Welfare States', in P. Pierson (ed.) *The New Politics of the Welfare State*, Oxford: Oxford University Press.

Platzer, H.-W. (1997) 'Industrial Relations and European Integration: Patterns, Dynamics and Limits of Transnationalisation', in W. Lecher and H.-W. Platzer (eds) *European Union – European Industrial Relations? Global Challenges, National Developments and Transnational Dynamics*, London: Routledge.

Ploug, N. (2006) 'The Danish Employment Miracle: Contents and Impact of Institutional Reform of Labour Market Policies in Denmark in the 1990s', in J. Clasen, M. Ferrera and M. Rhodes (eds) *Welfare States and the Challenge of Unemployment: Reform Policies and Institutions in the European Union*, London: Routledge (forthcoming).

Polanyi, K. (1944) *The Great Transformation*, New York: Rinehart.

Pontusson, J. (1992) 'At the End of the Third Road: Swedish Social Democracy in Crisis', *Politics and Society*, 20: 305–32.

Powell, M. (2004) 'Social Democracy in Europe: Renewal or Retreat?', in G. Bonoli and M. Powell (eds) *Social Democratic Party Policies in Contemporary Europe*, London: Routledge.

Radaelli, C.M. (2001) 'The Domestic Impact of European Union Public Policy: Notes on Concepts, Methods, and the Challenge of Empirical Research', *Politique Europeénne*, 5: 107–42.

Regini, M. and Regalia, I. (1997) 'Employers, Unions and the State: The Resurgence of Concertation in Italy?', *West European Politics*, 20 (1): 210–30.

Rehm, P. (2004) 'On the Formation of Individual Preferences', Theme Paper, Duke University.

Reissert, B. (2006) 'Germany: A Late Reformer', in J. Clasen, M. Ferrera and M. Rhodes (eds) *Welfare States and the Challenge of Unemployment: Reform Policies and Institutions in the European Union*, London: Routledge (forthcoming).

Reynaud, E. (ed.) (2000) *Social Dialogue and Pension Reform: United Kingdom, United States, Germany, Japan, Sweden, Italy, Spain*, Geneva: International Labour Office.

RFV redovisar (1999) *Den nya allmänna pensionen*, 12.

Rhodes, M. (2000) 'Restructuring the British Welfare State: Between Domestic Constraints and Global Imperatives', in F.W. Scharpf and V.A. Schmidt (eds) *Welfare and Work in the Open Economy*, vol. 2, Oxford: Oxford University Press.

—— (2001) 'The Political Economy of Social Pacts: "Competitive Corporatism" and European Welfare Reforms', in P. Pierson (ed.) *The New Politics of the Welfare State*, Oxford: Oxford University Press.

Robinson, P. (2000) 'Employment and Social Inclusion', in P. Askonas and A. Steward (eds) *Social Inclusion, Possibilities and Tensions*, Basingstoke, UK: Macmillan.

Rogowski, R. (1987) 'Political Cleavages and Changing Exposure to Trade', *American Political Science Review*, 81 (4): 1121–37.

Roller, E. (1995) 'The Welfare State: The Equality Dimension', in O. Borre and E. Scarbrough (eds) *The Scope of Government: Beliefs in Government*, vol. 3, Oxford: Oxford University Press.

—— (2002) 'Erosion des sozialstaatlichen Konsenses und die Entstehung einer neuen Konfliktlinien in Deutschland?', in *Aus Politik und Zeitgeschichte*, B29-30/2002/B29-30/2002.

Room, G. (1999) 'Social Exclusion, Solidarity and the Challenge of Globalization', *International Journal of Social Welfare*, 8: 166–74.

Rothstein, B. (1992) 'Labor-Market Institutions and Working-Class Strength', in S. Steinmo, K. Thelen and F. Longstreth (eds) *Structuring Politics: Historical Institutionalism in Comparative Analysis*, New York: Cambridge University Press.

Rueda, D. (2005) 'Insider–Outsider Politics in Industrialized Democracies: The Challenge to Social Democratic Parties', *American Political Science Review*, 99 (1): 61–74.

Rueda, D. and Pontusson, J. (2000) 'Wage Inequality and Varieties of Capitalism', *World Politics*, 52: 350–83.

Sainsbury, D. (1996) *Gender, Equality and Welfare States*, Cambridge: Cambridge University Press.

—— (ed.) (1999a) *Gender and Welfare State Regimes*, Oxford: Oxford University Press.

—— (1999b) 'Gender and Social Democratic Welfare States', in D. Sainsbury (ed.) *Gender and Welfare State Regimes*, Oxford: Oxford University Press.

Salais, R., Bavarez, N. and Reynaud, B. (1986) *L'Invention du chômage*, Paris: Presses Universitaires de France.

Samek Lodovici, M. (2000) 'The Dynamics of Labour Market Reform in European Countries', in G. Esping-Andersen and M. Regini (eds) *Why Deregulate Labour Markets?*, Oxford: Oxford University Press.

Sandler, J. (2002) *Medium and Long-Term Retail Savings in the UK*, Treasury, London: HMSO.

Sarfati, H. and Bonoli, G. (2002) *Labour Market and Social Protection Reforms in International Perspective*, Aldershot, UK: Ashgate.

Sawer, M. (2000) 'Parliamentary Representation of Women: From Discourses of Justice to Strategies of Accountability', *International Political Science Review*, 21: 361–80.

Scarbrough, E. (2000) 'West European welfare states: the old politics of retrenchment', *European Journal of Political Research*, 38: 225–59.

Scharpf, F.W. (1992) *Crisis and Choice in European Social Democracy*, Ithaca, NY: Cornell University Press.

—— (1996) 'Negative Integration: States and the Loss of Boundary Control', in

G. Marks, F.W. Scharpf and Ph. Schmitter (eds) *Governance in the European Union*, London: Sage.

—— (2000) 'Economic Changes, Vulnerabilities, and Institutional Capabilities', in F.W. Scharpf and V. Schmidt (eds) *Welfare and Work in the Open Economy*, vol. 1, Oxford: Oxford University Press.

Scharpf, F.W. and Schmidt, V.A. (eds) (2000) *Welfare and Work in the Open Economy*, 2 vols, Oxford: Oxford University Press.

Scherer, P. (2001) *Age of Withdrawal from the Labour Force in OECD Countries*, Paris: OECD.

Schmid, G. (2002) 'Towards a Theory of Transitional Labour Markets', in G. Schmid and B. Gazier (eds) *The Dynamics of Full Employment: Social Integration through Transitional Labour Markets*, Cheltenham, UK: Edward Elgar.

Schmidt, M.G. (1982) *Wohlfahrtsstaatliche Politik unter bürgerlichen und sozialdemokratischen Regierungen: Ein internationaler Vergleich*, Frankfurt am Main and New York: Campus.

—— (1988) 'The Politics of Labour Market Policy: Structural and Political Determinants of Rates of Unemployment in Industrial Nations', in F.G. Castles, F. Lehner and M.G. Schmidt (eds) *The Future of Party Government*, vol. 3, *Managing Mixed Economies*, Berlin and New York: de Gruyter.

—— (1993) 'Gendered Labour Force Participation', in F.G. Castles (ed.) *Families of Nations*, Aldershot, UK: Dartmouth.

—— (1996) 'When Parties Matter', *European Journal of Political Research*, 30: 155–83.

—— (1997) 'Parental Leave: Contested Procedure, Creditable Results', *International Journal of Comparative Labour Law and Industrial Relations*, 13 (2): 113–26.

—— (2003) *Political Institutions in the Federal Republic of Germany*, Oxford: Oxford University Press.

Schneider, U. (1999) 'Germany's Social Long-Term Care Insurance: Design, Implementation and Evaluation', *International Social Security Review*, 52: 31–74.

Schnorr, G. and Egger, J. (1990) *European Communities*, International Encyclopaedia for Labour Law and Industrial Relations, Supplement 108, Deventer, the Netherlands: Kluwer.

Schopflin, P. (1991) *Dépendances et solidarités: mieux aider les personnes âgées*, rapport au Commissariat général du Plan, Paris: La Documentation française.

Schulz, O. (1996) *Maastricht und die Grundlagen einer Europäischen Sozialpolitik*, Cologne: Heymans.

Schwartz, H. (2001) 'Round Up the Usual Suspects! Globalization, Domestic Politics and Welfare State Change', in P. Pierson (ed.) *The New Politics of the Welfare State*, Oxford: Oxford University Press.

Scruggs, L. (2004) *Welfare State Entitlement Data Set: A Comparative Institutional Analysis of Eighteen Welfare States*, version 1. Online. Available http://sp.uconn.edu/~scruggs/wp.htm.

Scruggs, L. and Lange, P. (2001) 'Unemployment and Union Density', in N. Bermeo (ed.) *Unemployment in the New Europe*, New York: Cambridge University Press.

—— (2002) 'Where Have All the Members Gone? Globalization, Institutions, and Union Density', *Journal of Politics*, 64 (1): 126–53.

Seeleib-Kaiser, M. (2002) 'A Dual Transformation of the German Welfare State?', *West European Politics*, 25 (4): 25–48.

Sénat (1995) *Avis présenté au nom de la commission des lois constitutionnelles, de législation, du suffrage universel, du règlement et d'administration générale sur le projet de loi instituant une prestation d'autonomie pour les personnes âgées dépendantes* (Rapporteur: Girod, Paul). Publications du Sénat, 31 October, 55: 1–47.

Siaroff, A. (2000a) *Comparative European Party Systems: An Analysis of Parliamentary Elections since 1945*, New York: Taylor & Francis.

—— (2000b) 'Women's Representation in Legislatures and Cabinets in Industrial Democracies', *International Political Science Review*, 21: 361–80.

Siegel, N.A. (2000) 'Jenseits der Expansion? Sozialpolitik in westlichen Demokratien 1975–95', in M.G. Schmidt (ed.) *Wohlfahrtsstaatliche Politik: Institutionen, politischer Prozesse und Leistungsprofil*, Opladen: Leske & Budrich.

Smith, M., Fagan, C. and Rubery, J. (1998) 'Where and Why is Part-time Work Growing in Europe?', in J. O'Reilly and C. Fagan (eds) *Part-Time Prospects: An International Comparison of Part-Time Work in Europe, North America and the Pacific Rim*, London: Routledge.

Solga, H. (2002) ' "Ausbildungslosigkeit" als soziales Stigma in Bildungsgesellschaften: ein soziologischer Erklärungsbeitrag für die wachsenden Arbeitsmarktprobleme von gering qualifizierten Personen', *Kölner Zeitschrift für Soziologie und Sozialpsychologie*, 54 (3): 476–505.

Sörernsen, K. (2004) 'State Policy, Labor Market, and Gender Ideology in Norway and Sweden', Ph.D. dissertation, University of North Carolina, Chapel Hill.

Spiegel-Online (2002) 20 August 2003: SPD will Rente zur Pflicht machen'. Online. Available http://www.spiegel.de.

StataCorp (1999) *Stata Statistical Software: Release 6.0. User's Guide*, College Station, TX: Stata Corporation.

Statens Offentliga Utredningar (1994) *Reformerat pensionssystem: kostnader och individeffekter.*

Statistisches Bundesamt Deutschland (Federal Statistical Office Germany) (2003). Online. Available http://www.destatis.de.

—— (ed.) (2004) *Kindertagesbetreuung in Deutschland*, Wiesbaden.

Statistiska Centralbyrå (2002) *Statistisk årsbok för Sverige.*

Stephens, J., Huber, E. and Ray, L. (1999) 'The Welfare State in Hard Times', in H. Kitschelt, P. Lange, G. Marks and J.D. Stephens (eds) *Continuity and Change in Contemporary Capitalism*, Cambridge: Cambridge University Press.

Streeck, W. (1995) 'Neo-voluntarism: A New European Social Policy Regime?', *European Law Journal*, 1 (1): 31–59.

—— (1998) 'The Internationalization of Industrial Relations in Europe: Prospects and Problems', *Politics and Society*, 26 (4): 429–59.

Sueur, J.-P. (2000) *L'Aide personnalisée à l'autonomie: un nouveau droit fondé sur le principe d'égalité*, rapport remis à Martine Aubry Ministre de l'emploi et de la solidarité, Paris: La Documentation française.

Supiot, A. (2004) 'La Valeur de la parole donnée (à propos des chômeurs "recalculés")', *Droit Social*, 5: 541–7.

Svallfors, S. (1997) 'Worlds of Welfare and Attitudes to Redistribution: A Comparison of Eight Western Nations', *European Sociological Review*, 13: 283–304.

—— (2004) 'Class, Attitudes and the Welfare State', *Social Policy and Administration*, 38 (2): 119–38.

Svallfors, S. and Taylor-Gooby, P. (eds) (1999) *The End of the Welfare State?*, London: Routledge.

Taylor, A.J. (1989) *Trade Unions and Politics: A Comparative Introduction*, London: Macmillan.

Taylor-Gooby, P. (2001) 'Sustaining State Welfare in Hard Times: Who Will Foot the Bill?', *Journal of European Social Policy*, 11 (2): 133–48.

—— (2002) 'The Silver Age of the Welfare State: Perspectives on Resilience', *Journal of Social Policy*, 31 (4): 597–621.

—— (ed.) (2004) *New Risks, New Welfare: The Transformation of the European Welfare State*, Oxford: Oxford University Press.

—— (forthcoming) 'New Risks and social change', in P. Taylor-Gooby (ed.) *New Risks and New Welfare in Europe*, Oxford: Oxford University Press.

Taylor-Gooby, P. and Larsen, T. (2004) 'The UK: A Test-Case for the Liberal Welfare State', in P. Taylor-Gooby (ed.) *New Risks, New Welfare*, Oxford: Oxford University Press.

Terrasse, P. (2001) *Rapport fait au nom de la Commission des Affaires Culturelles, Familiales et Sociales sur le projet de loi (n° 2936) relatif à la prise en charge de la perte d'autonomie des personnes âgées et à l'allocation personnalisée d'autonomie.*

Therborn, G. (1986) *Why Some People Are More Unemployed Than Others*, London: Verso.

Timonen, V. (2001) 'Earning Welfare Citizenship: Welfare State Reform in Finland and Sweden', in P. Taylor-Gooby (ed.) *Welfare States under Pressure*, London: Sage.

—— (2003) 'Policy Maps, Finland and Sweden', *WRAMSOC Working Paper*. Online. Available http://www.kent.ac.uk/wramsoc/workingpapers/index.htm.

Tomz, M., Wittenberg, J. and King, G. (2003) *Clarify: Software for Interpreting and Presenting Statistical Results*, Statistical Software.

Topalov, C. (1994) *La Naissance du chômeur 1880–1910*, Paris: Albin Michel.

Torfing, J. (1999) 'Workfare with Welfare: Recent Reforms of the Danish Welfare State', *Journal of European Social Policy*, 9 (1): 6–28.

Tramblay, M. (1998) 'Do Women MPs Substantively Represent Women? A Study of Legislative Behaviour in Canada's 35th Parliament', *Canadian Journal of Political Science*, 31: 435–65.

Traxler, F. (1999) 'The State in Industrial Relations: A Cross-National Analysis of Developments and Socioeconomic Effects', *European Journal of Political Research*, 36: 55–85.

Traxler, F., Blaschke, S. and Kittel, B. (2001) *National Labour Relations in Internationalized Markets: A Comparative Study of Institutions, Change, and Performance*, Oxford: Oxford University Press.

Treib, O. (2004) *Die Bedeutung der nationalen Parteipolitik für die Umsetzung europäischer Sozialrichtlinien*, Politik, Verbände, Recht: Die Umsetzung europäischer Sozialpolitik, Bd. 1, Frankfurt am Main: Campus.

Tuchszirer, C. (2002) 'Réforme de l'assurance chômage du PAP au PAP/ND: le Programme d'Action Personalisée pour un Nouveau Départ', *La Revue de l'IRES*, 38: 51–77.

Ullrich, C.G. (2000) 'Die soziale Akzeptanz des Wohlfahrtsstaates: Anmerkungen zum Forschungsstand', Mannheimer Zentrum für europäische Sozialforschung. Arbeitspapiere 22.

UNICEF (2002) 'A League Table of Child Poverty in Rich Nations', *Innocenti Report Card*, Issue 1, Florence: Innocenti Research Centre.

van der Werfhorst, H. (2002) 'Conversion of Occupational Classifications'. Online. Available http://users.fmg.uva.nl/hvandewerfhorst/occrecode.htm.

Van Deth, J. and Scarbrough, E. (eds) (1995) *The Impact of Values*, Oxford: Oxford University Press.

van Kersbergen, K. (1995) *Social Capitalism: A Study of Christian Democracy and the Welfare State*, London: Routledge.

—— (1997) 'Between Collectivism and Individualism: The Politics of the Centre', in H. Keman (ed.) *The Politics of Problem-Solving in Post-war Democracies*, Basingstoke, UK: Macmillan.

—— (1999) 'Contemporary Christian Democracy and the Demise of the Politics of Mediation', in H. Kitschelt, P. Lange, G. Marks and J.D. Stephens (eds) *Continuity and Change in Contemporary Capitalism*, Cambridge: Cambridge University Press.

—— (2000) 'The Declining Resistance of National Welfare States to Change?', in S. Kuhnle (ed.) *Survival of the European Welfare State*, London: Routledge.

van Kersbergen, K. and Becker, U. (2002) 'Comparative Politics and the Welfare State', in H. Keman (ed.) *Comparative Democratic Politics: A Guide to Contemporary Theory and Research*, London: Sage.

van Waarden, F. (1995) 'Government Intervention in Industrial Relations', in J. van Ruysseveldt, R. Huiskamp and J. van Hoof (eds) *Comparative Industrial and Employment Relations*, London: Sage.

Visser, J. (2002) 'The First Part-Time Economy in the World: A Model to Be Followed?', *Journal of European Social Policy*, 12 (1): 23–42.

Visser, J. and Hemerijck, A. (1997) *'A Dutch Miracle': Job Growth, Welfare Reform and Corporatism in the Netherlands*, Amsterdam: Amsterdam University Press.

Waddington, J. and Kerr, A. (2002) 'Unions Fit for Young Workers', *Industrial Relations Journal*, 33 (4): 298–315.

Waine, B. (1995) 'A Disaster Foretold?', *Social Policy and Administration*, 29: 317–34.

Wallerstein, M. (1999) 'Wage Setting Institutions and Pay Inequality in Advanced Industrial Societies', *American Journal of Political Science*, 43: 649–80.

Wallerstein, M. and Western, B. (2000) 'Unions in Decline? What Has Changed and Why', *Annual Review of Political Science*, 3: 355–77.

Walters, W. (2000) *Unemployment and Government: Genealogies of the Social*, Cambridge: Cambridge University Press.

Warner, H. (1984) 'EC Social Policy in Practice: Community Action on Behalf of Women and Its Impact in the Member States', *Journal of Common Market Studies*, 23 (2): 141–67.

Weaver, K. (1986) 'The Politics of Blame Avoidance', *Journal of Public Policy*, 6: 371–98.

Western, B. (1997) *Between Class and Market: Post-war Unionization in the Capitalist Democracies*, Princeton, NJ: Princeton University Press.

Whiteside, N. and Salais, R. (1998) 'Comparing Welfare States: Social Protection and Industrial Politics in Britain and France', *Journal of European Social Policy*, 8: 139–54.

Wilensky, H.L. (1975) *The Welfare State and Equality: Structural and Ideological*

Roots of Public Expenditures, Berkeley and Los Angeles: University of California Press.

—— (1981) 'Leftism, Catholicism, and Democratic Corporatism: The Role of Political Parties in Recent Welfare State', in P. Flora and A.J. Heidenheimer (eds) *Growth to Limits: The Western European Welfare States since World War II*, Berlin: Walter de Gruyter.

Winkler, C. (2002) *Single Mothers and the State: The Politics of Care in Sweden and the United States*, Lanham, MD: Rowman & Littlefield.

Winter, T. von (1995) *Sozialpolitische Interessen: Konstituierung, politische Repräsentation und Beteilung an Entscheidungsprozessen*, Baden-Baden: Nomos.

Woldendorp, J. (1997) 'Neo-corporatism and Macroeconomic Performance in Eight Small West European Countries (1970–1990)', *Acta Politica*, 32 (1): 49–79.

Woldendorp, J., Keman, H. and Budge, I. (2000) *Party Government in 48 Democracies (1945–1998): Composition, Duration, Personnel*, Dordrecht: Kluwer Academic Publishers.

Wolf, J., Kohli, M. and Künemund, H. (eds) (1994) *Alter und gewerkschaftliche Politik: Auf dem Weg zur Rentnergewerkschaft?*, Cologne: Bund Verlag.

Wood, S. (2001) 'Labour Market Regimes under Threat? Sources of Continuity in Britain, Germany and Sweden', in P. Pierson (ed.) *The New Politics of the Welfare State*, Oxford: Oxford University Press.

Wright, E.O. (1985) *Classes*, London: Verso.

Zentralarchiv für Empirische Sozialforschung (2000) *Codebook. ZA Study 2900. ISSP 1996. Role of Government III*, Cologne: Zentralarchiv für Empirische Sozialforschung.

Index

eBooks – at www.eBookstore.tandf.co.uk

A library at your fingertips!

eBooks are electronic versions of printed books. You can store them on your PC/laptop or browse them online.

They have advantages for anyone needing rapid access to a wide variety of published, copyright information.

eBooks can help your research by enabling you to bookmark chapters, annotate text and use instant searches to find specific words or phrases. Several eBook files would fit on even a small laptop or PDA.

NEW: Save money by eSubscribing: cheap, online access to any eBook for as long as you need it.

Annual subscription packages

We now offer special low-cost bulk subscriptions to packages of eBooks in certain subject areas. These are available to libraries or to individuals.

For more information please contact webmaster.ebooks@tandf.co.uk

We're continually developing the eBook concept, so keep up to date by visiting the website.

www.eBookstore.tandf.co.uk